This collection of specially commissioned essays by experts in the field explores key dimensions of Robert Frost's poetry and life. Frost remains one of the most memorable and beguiling of modern poets. Writing in the tradition of Virgil, Milton, and Wordsworth, he transformed pastoral and georgic poetry both in subject matter and form. Mastering the rhythms of ordinary speech, Frost made country life the point from which to view the world and the complexities of human psychology. The essays in this volume enable readers to explore Frost's art and thought, from the controversies of his biography to his subtle reinvention of poetic and metric traditions, and the conflicts in his thought about politics, gender, science, and religion. This volume will bring fresh perspectives to the lyric, narrative, and dramatic poetry of an American master, and its chronology and guide to further reading will prove valuable to scholars and students alike.

CAMBRIDGE COMPANIONS TO LITERATURE

CAMBRIDGE COMPANIONS TO CULTURE

THE CAMBRIDGE
COMPANION TO

ROBERT FROST

EDITED BY
ROBERT FAGGEN

CAMBRIDGE
UNIVERSITY PRESS

PUBLISHED BY THE PRESS SYNDICATE OF THE UNIVERSITY OF CAMBRIDGE
The Pitt Building, Trumpington Street, Cambridge, United Kingdom

CAMBRIDGE UNIVERSITY PRESS
The Edinburgh Building, Cambridge CB2 2RU, UK
40 West 20th Street, New York, NY 10011–4211, USA
10 Stamford Road, Oakleigh, VIC 3166, Australia
Ruiz de Alarcón 13, 28014 Madrid, Spain
Dock House, The Waterfront, Cape Town 8001, South Africa

http://www.cambridge.org

First published 2001

Printed in the United Kingdom at the University Press, Cambridge

Typeface Adobe Sabon 10/13pt   *System* QuarkXPress®   [SE]

A catalogue record for this book is available from the British Library

Library of Congress Cataloguing in Publication data

The Cambridge Companion to Robert Frost / edited by Robert Faggen.
p.   cm. – (Cambridge companions to literature)
Includes bibliographical references and index.
ISBN 0 521 63248 X (hardback) – ISBN 0 521 63494 6 (paperback)
1. Frost, Robert, 1874–1963 – Criticism and interpretation.   2. Frost, Robert,
1874–1963 – Handbooks, manuals, etc.   I. Faggen, Robert.   II. Series.

PS3511.R94 Z559 2001   811'.52–dc21   00-052917

ISBN 0 521 63248 X hardback
ISBN 0 521 63494 6 paperback

CONTENTS

CONTRIBUTORS

Helen Bacon, Smith College, *emerita*
Lawrence Buell, Harvard University
John Cunningham, Hollins University
Robert Faggen, Claremont McKenna College
George Monteiro, Brown University
Judith Oster, Case Western Reserve University
Blanford Parker, City University of New York
William Pritchard, Amherst College
Mark Richardson, Eastern Michigan State University
Guy Rotella, Northeastern University
Donald G. Sheehy, Edinboro State University of Pennsylvania
Timothy Steele, California State University, Los Angeles

ACKNOWLEDGMENTS

The Cambridge Companion to Robert Frost represents the work and devotion of the contributors as well as the support and suggestions of other Frost scholars, especially Jonathan Barron, Lesley Lee Francis, Frank Lentricchia, and Lisa Seale.

In preparing the manuscript, Linda Tuthill, Adrienne Lilley, Karen Aguilar-Alorro, Jason Stiffler, and Connie Bartling of Claremont McKenna College provided invaluable assistance. The encouragement of Ray Ryan of Cambridge University Press and the keen attention of Sue Dickinson in the editing of the manuscript have been essential.

CHRONOLOGY

1874   Born on March 26 in San Francisco, California to Isabelle Moodie and William Prescott Frost Jr. Named Robert Lee Frost after Confederate general Robert E. Lee. Originally from New Hampshire, his father had, as a teenager, run away to join the confederate army before being caught in Pennsylvania and sent home. A Phi Beta Kappa graduate of Harvard, he married the Scottish born Isabelle, who was brought up by her uncle in Ohio.

1875   Father named city editor of the San Francisco *Daily Evening Post*, edited by social reformer Henry George.

1876   Sister, Jeanie Florence, is born on June 25 in grandparents' home in Lawrence, Massachusetts. Returns to San Francisco in late November with mother and sister. Father, already beset by drinking and gambling problems, is diagnosed with consumption.

1885   Father dies of tuberculosis on May 5, leaving family only $8 after funeral expenses. Father's body taken to Lawrence, Massachusetts for burial. Family lives with paternal grandfather, now retired from job as a mill supervisor, and grandmother, a former leader of local suffragist movement. Family goes to Amherst, New Hampshire and stays at farm of great-aunt Sarah Frost. Family returns to Lawrence and Frost is placed in third grade.

1886   Family moves to Salem Depot, New Hampshire. Mother begins teaching fifth to eighth grades in the district school.

1889   Finishes school year at the head of the class of Lawrence High School. Befriends Carl Burell, an older student, who introduces him to botany, astronomy, and evolutionary theory.

1890   Publishes first poem, "La Noche Triste," based on episode in Prescott's *History of the Conquest of Mexico*, which appears in the Lawrence High School *Bulletin* in April.

1892   Shares valedictory honors at graduation with Elinor White, and delivers address "A Monument to After-Thought Unveiled."

Becomes engaged to Elinor. Enters Dartmouth College instead of Harvard because his grandparents blame Harvard for his father's bad habits and because it is less expensive. Leaves Dartmouth college at the end of December.

1893 Works at the Arlington Woolen Mill in Lawrence, changing carbon filaments in ceiling arc lamps. Lives with mother and sister in Lawrence.

1894 Quits job at the mill and begins teaching grades one through six in Salem. Tries unsuccessfully to convince Elinor to marry him. "My Butterfly: An Elegy" published in *The Independent* and begins correspondence with its literary editor Susan Hayes Ward.

1895 Marries Elinor White in Lawrence on December 19 in ceremony conducted by a Swedenborgian pastor. Works as a reporter for Lawrence *Daily American and Sentinal*.

1896 Son Elliot is born on September 25. Helps mother with a new school.

1897 Passes Harvard College entrance examinations in Greek, Latin, ancient history, English, French, and physical science. Enters Harvard as a freshman and moves into Cambridge apartment with Elinor, Elliott, and his mother-in-law.

1899 Concerned with his own, Elinor's, and mother's health, he withdraws from Harvard on March 31. Daughter Lesley is born on April 28. Takes up poultry farming with financial help from his grandfather.

1900 Elliott dies of cholera on July 8 and is buried in Lawrence. Frost moves family to 30-acre farm in Derry, New Hampshire. Mother dies of cancer on November 2 and is buried in Lawrence.

1901 Grandfather William Prescott Frost dies on July 10; wills Frost a $500 annuity and use of the Derry farm for ten years, after which Frost is to be given ownership of the farm.

1902 Expands poultry business. Son Carol is born on May 27.

1903 Publishes short story "Trap Nests" in *The Eastern Poultryman* (first of 11 stories and articles published in the *Poultryman* and *Farm-Poultry*, 1903–05). Daughter Irma is born on June 27.

1905 Daughter Marjorie is born on March 28.

1906 Begins full time position teaching English at Pinkerton Academy in Derry. Publishes poem "The Tuft of Flowers" in Derry *Enterprise* in March.

1907 Daughter Elinor Bettina is born on June 18 and dies on June 21, 1907.

1909 Publishes poem "Into My Own" in *New England Magazine* in May. Moves family from the farm to apartment in Derry Village.

1911   Accepts teaching position at State Normal School in Plymouth, and teaches courses in education and psychology. Sells the Derry farm in November.

1912   Family moves to England for a few years; Frost devotes himself to writing full time. Rents cottage in Beaconsfield, Buckinghamshire, 20 miles north of London. Prepares manuscript of *A Boy's Will* and submits it to London publishing firm of David Nutt and Company.

1913   *A Boy's Will* is published on April 1 and receives several favorable reviews including Ezra Pound's in *Poetry*. Through Pound, meets Hilda Doolittle ("H. D."), Ford Hermann Hueffer (Ford Maddox Ford), May Sinclair, Ernest Rhys, and William Butler Yeats. Attends weekly gatherings at homes of T. E. Hulme and Yeats. Forms close mentoring friendship with essayist Edward Thomas.

1914   Moves family to Dymock, Gloucestershire. *North of Boston* published on May 15 by David Nutt and Company to many favorable reviews. Learns that New York publishing firm of Henry Holt and Company will publish his books in the United States. Decides to return to the United States.

1915   *North of Boston* published by Henry Holt on February 20. Frost arrives in New York on February 23. *A Boy's Will* is published by Henry Holt in April. Moves to Franconia, New Hampshire in June. Meets poet Edwin Arlington Robinson and poet and anthologist Louis Untermeyer, who becomes a lifelong friend. Elinor becomes ill during pregnancy and recovers after miscarriage.

1917   Family moves to Amherst, Massachusetts in January. Edward Thomas killed by artillery shell in France on April 9 at the battle of Arras. Accepts offer to extend teaching appointment at Amherst.

1918   Awarded honorary MA degree by Amherst College in May. Reappointed professor of English.

1920   Resigns position at Amherst College in February in dispute with President Meiklejohn over teaching philosophy and to devote more time to writing poetry. Sister Jeanie arrested in Portland, Maine for disturbing the peace; Frost commits her to the state mental hospital. Sells property in Franconia and buys farm in South Shaftsbury, Vermont. Begins serving as consulting editor for Henry Holt and Company.

1921   Accepts a one-year fellowship in letters at the University of Michigan.

1923   *Selected Poems* is published on March 15. *New Hampshire* published by Henry Holt on November 15. Accepts new appointment at Amherst College.

1924   Awarded Pulitzer Prize for *New Hampshire*. Receives honorary degrees from Middlebury College and Yale University. Accepts lifetime appointment at University of Michigan as Fellow in Letters.

1925   Leaves Michigan in December when daughter Marjorie is hospitalized with pneumonia and a peri-cardiac infection.

1926   Accepts offer to return to Amherst as part-time professor of English. Participates in inaugural session of the Bread Loaf Writers' Conference in Vermont.

1927   Moves to Amherst. Marjorie enters Johns Hopkins Hospital for ten weeks of treatment.

1928   Visits Ireland and England, visiting Padraic Colum, George Russell ("AE"), and Yeats. Meets T. S. Eliot for the first time, in London. *West-Running Brook* is published November 19 by Holt along with an expanded edition of *Selected Poems*.

1929   Sister Jeanie dies in state mental hospital in Augusta, Maine, on September 7. Frost and Elinor move into 150-acre "Gully Farm" in South Shaftsbury, Vermont.

1930   *Collected Poems* published by Holt. Elected to the American Academy of Arts and Letters.

1931   Awarded Pulitzer Prize for *Collected Poems*.

1934   Marjorie dies after intensive treatment for fever at the Mayo Clinic in Rochester, Minnesota. Frost and Elinor go to Key West, Florida under doctor's orders where they are joined by Carol and his family.

1937   Wins Pulitzer Prize for *A Further Range*. Elinor undergoes surgery for breast cancer in October. Spends winter with Elinor in Gainesville, Florida.

1938   Elinor dies of heart failure in Gainesville on March 20. Frost resigns Amherst position and returns to South Shaftsbury. Kathleen Morrison becomes his secretary and arranges lecture appearances. Moves to Boston in October.

1940   Carol commits suicide with a deer-hunting rifle on October 9 in South Shaftsbury.

1941   Moves to new home at 35 Brewster Street in Cambridge, spending summers at the Homer Noble Farm and winters in South Miami. Accepts fellowship from Harvard in American Civilization.

1942   *A Witness Tree* is published by Holt on April 23.

1943   Awarded Pulitzer Prize for *A Witness Tree*, becoming the first person to receive the prize four times. Appointed George Ticknor Fellow in the Humanities at Dartmouth College.

1944   Daughter Irma afflicted by mental instability separates from husband John Crone.

1945   *A Masque of Reason* is published by Holt in March. Works on *A Masque of Mercy* during the summer. Returns to Dartmouth as Ticknor Fellow.

1946   Irma and her six-year-old son Harold stay with Frost during the summer as her mental condition deteriorates. Modern Library publishes *Collected Poems* with preface "The Constant Symbol."

1947   T. S. Eliot visits Frost in Cambridge. *Steeple Bush* is published by Holt on May 28. Frost has Irma committed to the state mental hospital in Concord, New Hampshire, in August. *A Masque of Mercy* is published by Holt in November.

1949   *Complete Poems of Robert Frost 1949*, published by Holt on May 30.

1950   US Senate adopts resolution honoring Frost on his seventy-fifth birthday (actually his seventy-sixth). Attends conference held in his honor at Kenyon college.

1953   Awarded the Fellowship of the Academy of American Poets.

1954   Attends series of eightieth birthday celebrations including one at the Waldorf-Astoria in New York sponsored by Holt. Travels with Lesley to Brazil as delegate to the World Congress of Writers held in São Paulo in August.

1957   Frost, T. S. Eliot, Archibald MacLeish, and Ernest Hemingway sign letter, asking Attorney General Herbert Brownell to drop treason indictment against Ezra Pound. Awarded honorary doctorates by Oxford and Cambridge. Revisits Gloucestershire and Beaconsfield. Returns to US and becomes actively involved in effort to free Ezra Pound.

1959   Attends dinner at Waldorf-Astoria in honor of his eighty-fifth birthday. Lionel Trilling's speech creates controversy reported in *The New York Times*.

1960   Congress passes bill awarding Frost a gold medal in recognition of his work. Testifies before Senate subcommittee in favor of a bill to establish a National Academy of Culture. President-elect Kennedy invites him to take part in inaugural ceremonies.

1961   Writes new poem in heroic couplets for inauguration on January 20. Apparently unable to read it because of glare and recites, instead, "The Gift Outright." Travels to Israel and Greece under auspices of the State Department and lectures at Hebrew University in Jerusalem. Delivers three lectures in Athens. Vermont state legislature names Frost "Poet Laureate of Vermont."

1962   *In the Clearing* published March 26 by Holt, Rinehart, and Winston, on his birthday, March 26. At invitation of President Kennedy, travels in late August to the Soviet Union as part of a cultural exchange program sponsored by the State Department. Travels to Gagra on the Black Sea and meets with Soviet Premier Nikita Khrushchev. Returns to United States and creates controversy when he tells press that Khrushchev "said we were too liberal to fight." Undergoes prostate operation on December 10. Suffers pulmonary embolism on December 23.

1963   Awarded the Bollingen Prize for Poetry on January 3. Suffers another pulmonary embolism on January 7. Dies shortly after midnight on January 29. Private memorial service is held in the Appleton Chapel in Harvard Yard, January 31, and public service is held at Johnson Chapel, Amherst College, on February 17. Ashes are buried in the Frost family plot in Bennington, Vermont on June 16.

NOTE ON THE TEXT AND LIST OF ABBREVIATIONS

Texts of all Frost poems are from *Robert Frost: The Collected Poems, Prose, and Plays*, edited by Richard Poirier and Mark Richardson, Library of America, 1995. Most of the references to Frost's essays and letters are from the selections in this edition.

CPPP   *Collected Poems, Prose, and Plays*, edited by Richard Poirier and
       Mark Richardson. New York: Library of America, 1995.
SL   *Selected Letters of Robert Frost*, edited by Lawrance Thompson.
       New York: Holt, Rinehart and Winston, 1964.
I   *Interviews with Robert Frost*, edited by Edward Connery Lathem.
       New York: Holt, Rinehart and Winston, 1966.

POEMS CITED

Note: dates cited in the text refer to first collections where poems appeared if different from dates cited below

	Date first published	Collected Poems, Prose, and Plays
		page reference
A Considerable Speck	1939	324
A Correction	1920	535
A Drumlin Woodchuck	1936	257
A Fountain, a Bottle, a Donkey's Ears and Some Books	1923	196
A Hillside Thaw	1921	218
A Hundred Collars	1913	49
A Late Walk	1910	18
A Lone Striker	1933	249
A Masque of Reason	1945	372
A Patch of Old Snow	1916	107
A Prayer in Spring	1913	21
A Record Stride	1932	535
A Reflex	1963	476
A Roadside Stand	1936	260
A Servant to Servants	1914	65
Acceptance	1928	228
Acquainted with the Night	1928	234
After Apple-Picking	1914	70
All Revelation	1938	302
An Empty Threat	1923	195
An Encounter	1916	121
An Importer	1947	360
An Old Man's Winter Night	1916	105
Asking for Roses	1913	525
At Woodward's Garden	1936	266

ROBERT FAGGEN

Introduction

If there is any truth to Emerson's aphorism "to be great is to be misunder-stood," then Robert Frost is surely one of the greatest poets. In a century in which some of the most celebrated literature seemed to follow Emerson in reverse – "to be misunderstood (or incomprehensible) is to be great" – Robert Frost's seductively limpid lines were taken as evidence of the author's simplicity or, worse, simplemindedness. Frost's popularity, as well as his will-ingness in his later years to perform as a hoary public sage, left many among the academically sophisticated suspicious. His adherence to ancient literary traditions and his disdain of political radicalism angered those with more revolutionary temperaments. A reviewer, commenting in *The New Yorker* on his *Collected Poems* of 1930, proclaimed that his "popularity can be put down to the fact that he always expressed with imaginative sincerity, American nostalgia for a lately abandoned rural background," and that he was a bard "always occupied with the complicated task of simply being sincere."

Frost mischievously invited such criticism. The character of Keeper in his late poem, *A Masque of Mercy*, said "Some people do not want you to understand them/ I want you to understand me wrong," a statement that res-onates well with Frost's own poetic practice. Years earlier in 1932 Frost wrote to Sidney Cox: "I have written to keep the curious out of the secret places of my mind in my verse and in my letters to such as you." (*SL*, 338) These comments express a doubleness, perhaps even a contradiction in his engagement with his audience; Frost reaches out but also holds back from and subverts his readers' expectations of sincerity and simplicity. Taking on many of the qualities of a trickster – innocent and sinister at once – Frost wrote "Ever since infancy I have had the habit of leaving my blocks carts chairs and such like ordinaries where people would be pretty sure to fall forward over them in the dark. Forward, you understand, *and* in the dark." (*SL*, 344) While no collection of essays could reach to the secret places of Frost's heart, this present volume is dedicated to the task of providing a context for and an introduction to the contradictions and tension that lie at the center of his poetry. The greatest innovator in blank verse after Milton and Browning, Frost cultivated an ingeniously sophisticated use of colloquial speech, giving new life to the ancient tradition of pastoral poetry. And few poets have encompassed the realms of religion, science, politics, and philosophy with as much such unassuming subtlety.

Poets have been attuned to the range of Frost's achievement perhaps longer than critics and academics. Ezra Pound lauded the publication of Frost's first two books. In the 1950s, Randall Jarrell wrote several essays about "the other Frost," a world pervaded by hate, fear, yet one inspiring mystery and awe. W. H. Auden found a kindred spirit in Frost's own desert and lunar landscapes and admired his brilliance in "argufying" in verse. In his parables and poetry, Jorge Luis Borges followed Frost's ironic twists. American poets including Richard Wilbur, Mary Oliver, and Galway Kinnell have found in Frost a crucial foundation. Attentive readers of John Ashbery can note his meditation on the ironies of Frost's "The Road Not Taken" and "Directive" in "The System" as well as other works. Frost's pastoral wit has been of great importance to Irish poets Seamus Heaney and Paul Muldoon. And the pleasure of his terrors was source of wonder for Joseph Brodsky, the Russian-born Nobel Laureate who first read Frost while a teenager in St. Petersburg. The attentive formalist criticism of Reuben Brower in the 1960s preceded the groundbreaking achievement of Richard Poirier's *Robert Frost: The Work of Knowing* (1976). In the last decade, there has been a flowering of critical attention that has placed Frost in a variety of illuminating intellectual and social contexts, and many of those critics have contributed to this volume.

Debate over Frost's biography has tended to dominate discussion of his work. Lawrance Thompson's three-volume biography presented an image of Frost as a great poet but a megalomaniac who was particularly cruel to his wife, Elinor, and to his children. Critical reviews of Thompson seized on the opportunity to sully Frost's reputation as America's national poet and alleged expositor of Yankee virtue. The personal animus and unverifiable anecdote that informs Thompson's biography received a strong corrective in William Pritchard's *Robert Frost: A Literary Life Reconsidered* (1984), a work that, among its other achievements, helped refocus attention on the dissonances and complexities of the poetry. Pritchard's contribution to this volume examines Frost's *A Witness Tree* not only in terms of Thompson but also the more recent attempt by Jeffrey Meyers to read the great poetry of this book in lurid terms of Frost's personal life; he asks what we may gain and lose by biographical readings. Frost did have a strong hand in shaping the story of his life. Donald Sheehy, who has written some of the most exacting essays on Frost biography, explores how Frost's accounts of his own life affect both biographers and critics. Was Frost a working-class youth who struggled against poverty in his early years? What attitude did he take toward laborers in the Lawrence, Massachusetts mill, and how can his experience be read in terms of a poem such as "A Lone Striker"? How attached was he to the farm life of New England? Frost eventually abandoned farming, in which he was neither terribly interested nor successful, and moved the family to England where he engaged Ezra Pound and W. B. Yeats and published his first two books, *A Boy's Will* and *North of Boston* – at the age of forty.

"Hugger-mugger farming" may not have been Frost's greatest love, but he knew it, and, more important, he knew many who lived that vanishing existence. But Frost also knew botany, astronomy, natural science, and thousands of lines of poetry, modern and ancient. Frost himself lived the existence of a farmer-poet, a tradition that extends back to the Roman poets Virgil and Horace, and his landscapes and depictions of country things are as much informed by the mythology of pastoral literature – from Virgil through Milton, Wordsworth, and Thoreau. "For Once, Then, Something," and "Spring Pools" owe their richness in part to Frost's engagement with the shifting representations of Narcissus in Ovid's *Metamorphoses*, Milton's *Paradise Lost*, and Thoreau's *Walden*. Pastoral literature has always been a mode of examining questions of political and social hierarchy, a form associated with simplicity but masking complexity. Frost's profound dialogue with the tradition of classical and Biblical pastoral literature is the subject of my own essay; his devotion to ancient Greek and Roman conceptions of poetry and poetic inspiration – Horace, Virgil, Ovid, Euripides – is the subject of Helen Bacon's "Frost and the ancient muses." Only a classicist of Bacon's immense learning could perceive the subtlety of Frost's use of the ancients. Though Frost's poetry invites longing for a lost Eden or Arcadia, his vision constantly resists the temptations of nostalgia while refusing to make grandiose claims about the difficulties of modernity. In fact, Frost's lover's quarrel with the spirit and substance of modern science distinguishes his vision of nature and man's place in it from almost all other modern poets.

Frost was hardly dismissive of his New England predecessors; he praised Edwin Arlington Robinson for his practice of "the old-fashioned way to be new." Frost's own newness is subtle, rarely seeking after shocking effect. The possibilities of ordinary language and public discourse fascinated him as he developed a suspicion and even contempt for the pretensions of religious and philosophical obscurity. The inexhaustible complexity of surfaces, the psychological interplay of individuals in dialogue, fascinated him as much as the brooding intimations of inaccessible depths. Lawrence Buell has shown the extent to which Frost conceived of himself in relation to a local tradition of New England poetry and its rhetoric that includes Dickinson and Emerson as well as Longfellow.

Any discussion of Frost has to be attentive to his ideas about prosody and his emphasis on "the sound of sense." In a letter to a friend, Frost said "I give you a new definition of a sentence as a sound upon which words are strung." (*SL*, 110) Frost believed not in making new speech tones but in capturing the essential and eternal tones of voice and playing them against the strictness of the pentameter line. Frost realized what Wordsworth had proposed, "to adopt the very language of men." But he created some of the most stunning effects in "strict" and "loose" iambic lines. Timothy Steele has been studying Frost's prosodic practice for years, and his essay reveals how to hear Frost's lines as an essential aspect of reading them. Frost himself insisted not on "reading" a poem but on "saying" it, keeping open the potential vectors of meaning. Depending on how you take the tone of a phrase or sentence, the meaning of the poem shifts and beguiles keeping its freshness while still maintaining the tension and pleasure created by the expectations of meter. Though, as Steele shows, Frost's idea of capturing the "sound of sense" is both elusive and difficult. Though we have been blessed with many recordings of Frost reading his work, his public presence always presented the risk of reducing Frost's stunning multivocality to a single tone. The voice that begins a Frost poem is not necessarily the one that ends it, and a reader has to be alert to ever-shifting tones of his verse.

As extensively as Frost thought about voice, he also thought about the nature of metaphor. Frost argued that thought was dependent upon figurative language, not as mere decoration but as the basis of conceptualization. He was also aware of how much metaphors – evolution – for example, had come to dominate aspects of our culture and do much of our thinking for us. Judith Oster maps Frost's thinking about metaphor including poems that address the question of metaphor directly – "Maple," "Birches," "Revelation," and "The Silken Tent."

Frost saw poetry as a way of psychological survival in a chaotic universe. His poetry represents a continual dialogue between control and chaos, and he saw poetry as creating "a momentary stay against confusion," a something facing the nothing. The poetic act for Frost provides order and form set somewhat heroically against chaos, "a figure of the will braving alien entanglements." As he wrote in a letter to *The Amherst Student*: "The background is hugeness and confusion shading away from where we stand into black and utter chaos; and against the background any small man-made figure of order and concentration. What pleasanter than that this should be so?"(*CPPP*, 740). Schopenhauer, Darwin, and James helped form and inform some of Frost's cosmology and psychology. Man attempts control in a universe that ignores him but the challenge provides some small recompense. But if there is in his poetic craft a rage for order, there is also a devilish love of chaos and subversion of the kind of control that borders on madness and tyranny. The essays of Mark Richardson and Blanford Parker explore the ways Frost's poems satisfy and confound our desire for order, purpose, and design. Frost took pleasure in chaos and waste, threats that inspired and limited the creation of order and meaning. No other twentieth-century poet gave so much force to the dialogue and tension of men and women. He and his fiancée Elinor were co-valedictorians at their high school commencement; his poetry often appears a continuation of her talk: "Dialogue as the Life Force." Such great blank verse narratives as "Home Burial," "The Death of the Hired Man," "In the Home Stretch," and the monologues "A Servant to Servants" and "Wild Grapes" present us with a new range of possibility for lyric poetry. Our propensity for taking sides becomes confounded by Frost's subtle and shifting representation of gender. Frost's women can no more readily be characterized than men. Frost found beauty in the unresolved conflict of equally worthy principles.

Equally misunderstood are Frost's politics, and his allegiances were complex and often seemingly contradictory. When Frost wrote that in life and poetry "strongly spent is synonymous with kept," he played on economic metaphors that seemed associated with "the trial by marketplace" but with irreverence toward its importance. Justice and mercy, freedom and equality, design and chaos remain unresolved tensions in his political, religious, and poetic thought. Frost loved the possibilities of individuality and freedom but recognized equally the limitations of environment; he regarded enforced egalitarianism with contempt but looked suspiciously and often with fear at excesses of the self-obsessed. The essays of Mark Richardson, Guy Rotella, and George Monteiro reveal the tension in Frost's responses to democracy, capitalism, the New Deal, and the Cold War – a passion for conflict and risk combined with a terrifying sense of limitation and ultimate annihilation. This tension can be seen in well-known lyrics such as "The Road Not Taken" but also in the stunning dramatic narratives, "The Ax-Helve," "The Self-Seeker," "The Housekeeper," and "The Black Cottage."

Frost looms as a giant figure in American literature. Most know or remember him for a few remarkable short lyrics, probably "Fire and Ice," "The Road Not Taken," "Stopping by Woods on a Snowy Evening." The essays in this volume discuss broad formal and thematic questions in Frost's work but also attempt to call attention to its great range – from dramatic monologues and narrative dramas to meditative lyrics. Though Frost seems an inescapable presence, his poetry represents a great achievement in negative capability. John Cunningham's concluding essay shows the extent of that negativity as human absence becomes, paradoxically, a presence in Frost's poems. Frost disappears in the multivocal dramas of his poetry and reemerges transformed in threatening and strange persistence of otherness. We have Frost's letters, his terse and brilliant prose essays, and notebooks on which to draw for insight. But it is Frost's poetry that constantly challenges readers with contradictions, ambiguity, and uncertainty. The contributors hope these essays will take readers forward and farther into the dark of some of the most compelling poetry ever written.

I

DONALD G. SHEEHY

"Stay unassuming": the Lives of Robert Frost

> You seem to reason that because my mother was religious, I must have been religious too at any rate to start with. You might just as well reason that because my father was irreligious I must have been irreligious too . . . It would be terribly dangerous to make too much of all this.
>
> To Lawrance Thompson (1948) (*SL*, 529)

> When you get around to do my biography, don't try to make it too long, too detailed, too exhaustive and exhausting. Make it somehow sprightly and entertaining so that it will have some zip to it.
>
> To Lawrance Thompson (1954)[1]

"Robert Frost was so fascinated by the story of his life that he never tired of retelling it."[2] Thus Lawrance Thompson opened the first paragraph of the introduction to the first volume of the official biography. In the thirty-three years since the publication of *Robert Frost: The Early Years*, neither have readers of Frost tired of retelling, untelling, or simply telling off Thompson. The "Frost biographical wars," as Christopher Benfey remarks in a review of Jay Parini's 1999 *Robert Frost: A Life*, continue unabated, and at the center of the conflict stand opposed the public figure of the poet as venerable Yankee sage and the figure of the private man as "monster" inscribed in Thompson's biography. The distortion in both aspects of this Janus-Frost has in recent years drawn an impressive array of critics and biographers into the fray, among them William H. Pritchard, Stanley Burnshaw, John Evangelist Walsh, Lesley Lee Francis, Jeffrey Meyers, and, as mentioned, Jay Parini.

As a composite portrait, biographical revision has given contemporary readers a richer, more intriguingly complicated, if often contradictory, image of the poet. Working from new perspectives and often with new materials, it has shed light on aspects of the poet's character and experience obscured by layers of sentimental hagiography and pseudo-psychoanalytic formulae. In taking refutation of Thompson not only as a procedural principle but also as a moral obligation, however, biographical revision has tended to look

through the official biographer rather than look at him, and thus to overlook what may be of most value in the work to which he devoted his professional life. Thompson contributes most to our understanding of Frost, I
believe, by the very terms of his failure to arrive at his own. Many reasons
there certainly are to dispute Thompson's biographical resolutions, but no
good reason to dismiss his realizations about a Frost biographer's particular
difficulties.

To an unusual extent in Frost, any consideration of the poet's life entails
a reconsideration of the many and various "lives of the poet." Having
achieved literary prominence in early middle-age, Frost spent virtually his
entire career as the conscious – and often self-conscious – subject of one or
another biographical study. Certainly, as the examples of Gorham Munson,
Sidney Cox, Robert Newdick, and a host of interviewers amply testify, the
entanglements of Frost's life-telling long antedate the appointment of
Thompson as official biographer in 1939. What an unanticipated quarter-
century of witness provided Thompson, however, was an opportunity to
compile a rich variety of Frost's self-accounting and the obligation – or so he
came to believe – to resolve them fully into accord not only with each other
but with a body of verifiable "fact." Thompson had agreed to the stipula-
tion that the official biography not be published until after Frost's death. As
a result, he spent the next twenty-five years as the most interested – and the
least disinterested – "reader" of the poet's autobiography-in-progress, an
ongoing romance in and out of verse in which telling the life and living the
tale had grown inextricably entwined.

"The traditional version of the problematic of autobiography," Paul John
Eakin observes in *Fictions in Autobiography: Studies in the Art of Self-
Invention*, "has focused on the apparently antithetical claims of truth and
fiction that are necessarily involved in any attempt to render the materials of
a life history in a narrative form." Eakin notes, however, that a paradigm
shift has occurred. "Autobiography in our time," he concludes, "is increasingly understood as both an art of memory and an art of the imagination;
indeed memory and imagination become so intimately complementary in the
autobiographical act that it is usually impossible for autobiographers and
their readers to distinguish between them in practice."[3]

Taking liberties at the border between memory and imagination was
Frost's delight – and Thompson's torment. What Eakin describes as the "play
of the autobiographical act" corresponds, of course, to what Frost called the
"freedom of the material." It enables, in a sense, "the figure a life makes":

> I tell how there may be a better wildness of logic than of inconsequence. But
> the logic is backward, in retrospect, after the act. It must be more felt than seen

ahead like prophecy. It must be a revelation, or a series of revelations, as much for the poet as for the reader. For it to be that there must have been the greatest freedom of the material to move about in it and to establish relations in it regardless of time and space, previous relation, and everything but affinity . . . All I would keep for myself is the freedom of my material – the condition of body and mind now and then to summons aptly from the vast chaos of all I have lived through.   (CPPP, 777–78)

Troubled by Newdick's biographical "sleuthing," even as he authorized it, Frost had expressed concern to John Holmes, who wrote to Newdick in March of 1939: "[Frost] said he had spent his life heaping up piles of building material – friends, experiences, memories – and leaving them behind him unused to be used sometime when, as and how he wished. He said that this material he feels is his possibly for poems, and that once shaped by another hand isn't quite his any more."[4] A concern about "rights" to raw material is still evident in 1959, when the eighty-five-year-old poet wrote to reassure Thompson that Elizabeth Sergeant's *Robert Frost: The Trial by Existence*, with which he had actively cooperated, would not steal the official biography's thunder.

I've meant to give you all the advantages, supply you with all the facts, and keep nothing back, *save nothing out for my own use even in case I ever should write my own story*. And I have left entirely to your judgment the summing up and the significance. You've had a long time to turn me over in your mind looking for some special phrase or poem to get me by. By now you may think you have plucked the heart out of my secret and I don't care if you have. All is easy between us.   (SL, 584; italics mine)

All was *not* easy with Thompson. He had cooperated with Sergeant under the assumption that her project was not biographical but critical, and he felt himself betrayed. Frost, however, could take satisfaction in Sergeant's book. *The Trial by Existence* met Frost's primary criterion by decorously rendering the particulars of personal life not for their own sake but to convey an idealized account of the tribulations and triumphs of the poet's spirit.

Tracing the course of modern autobiographical theory, Eakin locates a source in what Stephen Marcus finds everywhere implicit in Freud – that "'a coherent story is in some manner connected with mental health,'" and that "from this perspective, 'illness amounts at least in part to suffering from an incoherent story or an inadequate narrative account of oneself.'"[5] Eakin dwells at length – and in strikingly Frostian terms – upon James Olney's *Metaphors of Self: The Meaning of Autobiography* (1972): "For Olney, the dominant trope of autobiography is metaphor, a term which in his extended usage includes all the 'order-produced and order-producing, emotion-satisfying theories and equations . . . by which the lonely subjective consciousness gives order not only to itself but to as much of objective reality as it is capable of formalizing and of controlling.'"[6] Acknowledging a debt to William James, Olney defines the self in experiential and operational terms:

> The self expresses itself by the metaphors it creates and projects, and we know it by those metaphors; but it did not exist as it now does and as it is now before creating its metaphors. We do not see or touch the self, but we do see and touch its metaphors: and thus we "know" the self, activity or agent, represented in the metaphor and the metaphorizing.[7]

From a "developmental perspective," as Eakin observes, "the autobiographical act is revealed as a mode of self-invention that is always practiced first in living and only eventually – sometimes – formalized in writing" (8–9). For Frost, the practice of autobiographical self-invention and its formalization in art or rhetoric were integral and continuous, woven warp-and-woof through the fabric of his poetry, prose, correspondence, and conversation. In a remarkable letter to Lawrence Conrad in 1929, Frost touched upon the unsettling effect of being shaped by another's hand in terms that anticipate not only the Jamesian belief-into-fulfillment he would expound in his essay "Education by Poetry" (1930, *CPPP*, 717), but also the meditation on being-in-time at the heart of "Carpe Diem" (1939).

> Every little while you give me a strange picture of myself in something you say. You must be mistaken in thinking of me as ever having known what I was about. The present is least of the three times I live in. The future comes next. I live in that by a number of beliefs I want left vague – God-man-and-self-beliefs. I never know what is going to happen next because I don't dare to let myself formulate a foolish hope. Much less do I know what is happening now: I am too flooded with feeling to know. I suppose I live chiefly in the past, in realizing what happened and taking credit for it just as if I had predetermined it and consciously carried it out. But Lord Lord – I am never the creature of high resolve you want to have me. I have simply go[ne] the way of the dim beliefs I speak of dimly because I don't want them brought out into the light and examined too exactly. They wont bear it I may as well admit to forestall ridicule.[8]

Contrary to critical truism, Thompson was oblivious neither to the complexities of his subject nor to the methodological indeterminacies of his genre. While his project was finally undermined, in Leon Edel's terms, by the psychological confusion of his personal involvement with his subject and by the sheer abundance of his materials, Thompson remained acutely aware of the problematic nature of his biographical enterprise. Outlining in retrospect the praxis of the "new biography," Edel described in *Writing Lives*

(1984) a methodology "related to the methods of Sherlock Holmes and also to those of Sigmund Freud"[9]:

> The writing of lives is a department of history and is closely related to the discoveries of history. It can claim the same skills. No lives are led outside history or society; they take place in human time. No biography is complete unless it reveals the individual within history, within an ethos and a social complex.[10]

> The biographer needs to discover human self-deceptions (or defenses, which they usually are). Such deceptions may become a covert life-myth out of which lives – and biographies – are fashioned. No biography can be effective if the subject's self-concept is not studied: the private myth provides a covert drive and motivating force.[11]

In such context, it is instructive to look again at Thompson's introduction to *The Early Years*:

> Robert Frost was so fascinated by the story of his life that he never tired of retelling it. A good raconteur, he naturally varied his accounts, and whenever the bare facts troubled him, he discreetly clothed them with fictions. This imaginative process caused him to mingle self-deceptions with little falsehoods; it even caused him gradually to convince himself that some of these fictions were genuine truths. But only a few of his listeners knew the facts well enough to notice the discrepancies and even the best-informed were not inclined to challenge. They knew he resented criticism. Besides, some of his fictions amounted to mythic variations which artistically revealed this important fact: he wanted his best versions of the story to dramatize the fulfillment of ideals he had cherished since boyhood.[12]

Knowing to what end Thompson's own resentments led, it is easy to find here, in word choice and emphasis, signs of a failure of perspective. Ultimately, Thompson blurred a distinction crucial for Edel: "[T]he biographer must learn to understand man's ways of dreaming, thinking and using his fancy. This does not mean that a biographical subject can be psychoanalyzed; a biographical subject is not a patient and not in need of therapy."[13] Not yet committed fully to a diagnostic model taken from his reading of Karen Horney's *Neurosis and Human Growth*,[14] Thompson self-consciously attempts to articulate and justify a controlling metaphor – a shaping myth – for the biography.

> [Frost] had many reasons for wanting to conceal some of his most precious beliefs, even while he was trying to shape his life in accordance with his persistently mythic ideals of heroism. But in his autobiographical accounts he could not resist calling attention to evidence of his kinship with heroes. His retelling always pointed up his struggles and triumphs, in the face of almost "insuperable odds," hurts, and humiliations.

Taken loosely, as Frost would be taken, this metaphor could indeed carry us deeper and deeper into the poet's meaning, from "Into My Own" to *In the Clearing*. If the life – as rendered graceful by art – were to stand as a "constant symbol," then it was of the essence that the tale be brought "to a rounded conclusion and then be judged for whether any original intention it had has been strongly spent or weakly lost" (*CPPP*, 786). "Near the end," Thompson observes, "while he was still acting out the final scenes of the story he was also telling, Frost never missed a chance to point out mythic roundings-off and fulfillments." And if the poet was "inclined to boast when discussing fulfillments," the biographer allows that "his accomplishments exceeded his boasts."[15]

Is the biographer's task to censure? Explain? Appreciate? Expose? Diagnose? From the tangled web of his own emotional, moral, and psychological responses to Frost, Thompson was never able to extricate himself. To his credit, he attempted – albeit with an aggrieved punctiliousness – to elevate uncertainty to a methodological principle.

> It should be obvious, then, that in time certain of these details must be modified by documents or evidences which have not yet come to light. It is even more obvious that some of the interpretations, here developed, will be altered. But the primary goal, still valid, is to increase the general knowledge about Robert Frost, as man and as poet.[16]

Acknowledging the intrinsically provisional nature of biography, Thompson not only accepted the inevitability of revision but endeavored to enable it. "A properly assembled documentary biography," Edel observes, "is in effect a kind of miniarchive," and if Thompson's biography falls short of Edel's standard for "art," it certainly possesses the virtues of the "organizing imagination."[17] Although obscured by their own plenitude, the endnotes to *The Early Years* and to *The Years of Triumph* provide alternative accounts of events, supplemental texts, direct authorial commentary, and a bibliographical documentation of sources that comprised, at the time of publication, a virtual finding guide to the major Frost collections. And although economic considerations certainly figured in his decision, Thompson's preservation of his accumulated research materials and correspondence, working notes and outlines, and the more than 1500 typescript pages of "Notes from Conversations with Robert Frost," from which he had planned to abstract and publish "The Story of a Biography," stands as an invitation – and a challenge – to any who would revisit the scene of the biography.[18]

"Every bit of my career in or outside of school," Frost remarked in a 1925 interview, "began in Lawrence."[19] The fifteen years between his dislocation to Lawrence in 1885 – aged eleven and recently bereft of his father – and his relocation to Derry in 1900 were pivotal to the formation of the poet's character and convictions. Frost attended school, played, worked, courted, and came to maturity during a turbulent time in the history of the "Immigrant City," a period of untrammeled industrial expansion, unprecedented waves of immigration, and ethnic and labor strife that Donald Cole would later characterize as "decades of despair." Of the Lawrence interval, however, Frost criticism in general, and post-Thompson biographical criticism in particular, has had relatively little to say, and much of what has been said is of dubious scholarly authority.

Among the defining life episodes of which Frost never tired telling, none was more fraught with symbolic and emotional significance – nor more susceptible to continual revision – than the tale of his removal in 1900 from the environs of industrial Lawrence to a farm in Derry purchased with funds supplied by his paternal grandfather. Indeed, the complications that have attended Frost biography throughout are immanent in its first public mention. "There is perhaps as much of Frost's personal tone in the following little catch . . . as in anything else," Ezra Pound noted of "In Neglect" in a May 1913 review of *A Boy's Will*: "It is to his wife, written when his grandfather and his uncle had disinherited him of a comfortable fortune and left him in poverty because he was a useless poet instead of a money-getter."[20] Thompson recounts that Pound gave Frost a copy of the review, and Frost was horrified to discover that "his dramatic fictions concerning the inhumanities of his grandfather and uncle had been paraphrased in it."[21] In July 1913, Frost complained to F. S. Flint about the review. "But tell me I implore what on earth is a midden if it isn't a midden," he mocked, "and where in hell is the fitness of a word like that in connection with what I wrote on a not inexpensive farm." "Not inexpensive, that is, to his grandfather," Thompson mocked in turn, noting that the value of the Derry farm changed radically for Frost to suit his metaphorical purpose.[22]

Indistinct as his life and character remain, William Prescott Frost, Sr. was clearly a signal figure in Frost's life. After conversations with the poet in the 1950s, Elizabeth Sergeant noted that "When Frost speaks of his grandfather today, he looms as a sort of fateful, archetypical image in the background of his adolescent and young life: an image of severity and power, gigantesque."[23] The nature of Frost's conflicted recollections of the extent of his grandfather's sway over events in his early life loomed large as well in Thompson's judgments.[24]

Thompson's notes reveal that his knowledge of persons and incidents accumulated gradually out of Frost's retellings and his own inquiries. Disturbed by inconsistencies and contradictions, he early resolved that Frost was a self-serving liar and later that he was a self-justifying neurotic. Thompson's response to Frost's grandfather stories was particularly acute, perhaps because Frost seemed so determined to conceal certain facts about the nature and extent of W. P. Frost's financial assistance. Reviewing notes after a session with Frost in 1941, Thompson remarked on the move to England: "Of course Frost forgets that his grandfather's estate made this as much possible as his grandfather's farm." For the ten years that W. P. Frost's will required Frost to maintain ownership of the farm, he received a cash annuity of $500; thereafter, the amount was $800. Noting that the poet had never before supplied financial details about the move, he concluded that "Frost has always been disgustingly lucky for one so disgustingly lazy" and warned himself that "one must not overplay the years of poverty because they weren't really poverty at any time." In a summary of conversations in 1946, Thompson noted that "Frost is more generous toward his grandfather, and says he sees how he had to guard his means with scrupulous care because there wasn't enough to permit waste."[25] In 1939, Frost had dismissed his grandfather's wealth as a "mere competence," but when Thompson pointed out in 1951 that W. P. Frost had destroyed the notes of loans for the poet's stay at Harvard from 1897 to 1899 – having already defrayed the expense of his year at Dartmouth – Frost "grudgingly" acknowledged, "He was that decent anyway." Thompson felt the implication to be that the elder Frost had been "quite indecent in other ways."[26] Thompson's sympathies, one concludes, had come to rest with the "old gentleman."

The "years of poverty" to which Thompson refers specifically are those on the Derry farm, of which Frost's various early accounts had contributed to such misimpressions as Amy Lowell's 1917 portrait of a "young man working from morning till night to tear a living out of the thin soil."[27] Thompson's inquiry into the provisions of the estate of W. P. Frost and the financing of the Derry property dispelled any doubt that Frost had ever been required to eke out a subsistence on a marginal farm in Derry or elsewhere – a misrepresentation Frost had himself taken occasional pains to clarify in later years.[28]

Other issues, however, have remained clouded: What constituted "real poverty" in Lawrence at the turn of the century and what would Frost's experience of it have been? What did an adolescent Frost understand the socio-economic status of his family to be and by what standards and assumptions would he have construed a social identity? And finally, what light might further exploration of these questions shed upon the poet's art and thought?

In a 1937 talk published as "Poverty and Poetry" (1938), Frost prefaced a reading of "A Lone Striker" with a critique of the prevailing politics of class and a defense of those he called "my people," "the ordinary folks," "the country neighbors" among whom he had lived. "Some of them had been educated and some of them hadn't," he declared. "They were all much the same" (*CPPP*, 759). In buttressing his authority with an account of his own experience, however, he turned back not only to the accustomed terrain of rural New England but also to the streets of the mill city, to contest the legitimacy – even on that ground – of a radical social history:

> I was brought up in a family who had just come to the industrial city of Lawrence, Massachusetts. My grandfather was an overseer in the Pacific Mills. They had just come to the city from Kingston, New Hampshire, up by Exeter.
>
> The other day I was reading a book called *A Proletarian Journey* by a boy named Fred Beal. His family ran into more poverty in Lawrence than I ran into. I ran into some: I don't know how to measure poverty (I'm not boasting). His people went right down and he went to work at fourteen years of age in two of the same mills that I worked in. He talks of himself as a proletarian; he went radical. It is a very interesting book to me because he names overseers and men at the mill – and all people I knew. He was twenty years after me. We had memories of the farm and the country that I went back to. I walked out of it all one day.   (*CPPP*, 759–60)

Challenging Beal's self-avowed proletarian status, Frost scoffs genealogically:

> Now Fred Beal, who calls himself [a proletarian], is a Beal and a Hay [sic] of New Hampshire. Right away that's something a little different; he never knew the peasant life of Europe. He also counts himself a kin of Hannibal Hamlin, who was Vice-President with Lincoln in his first administration – that is another thing. For no matter how educated or poor a man is, a certain level up there in Vermont and New Hampshire stays about the same. We people just sort of fountain up, jet up out of it.   (*CPPP*, 760)

A Proletarian Journey tells a different story, for Beal had indeed dared to be "radical" when young. Convicted of murder after the Gastonia, North Carolina textile strike he had helped to organize in 1929, he had fled to the Soviet Union and remained there until disillusionment with Stalinism in the mid-30s brought him back to the United States and prison. He too, however, had been brought up in a family who had come to the industrial city of Lawrence with memories of farm and country. "Like all Yankees," he begins, "my relatives claim that our family is descended from 'pure' Mayflower stock."[29] At age fourteen in 1888, Robert Frost enrolled at Lawrence High School, choosing the "classical," or college preparatory, course of study. Living in Salem Depot, NH, where his mother had been teaching in the district school since 1886, Frost, along with his sister Jeanie, commuted daily to school by train, using passes purchased by W. P. Frost, Sr. The story of the Frost family in Lawrence had been in its main features a saga like many other successes.

When W. P. Frost, Sr. died in 1901, *The Evening Tribune* for July 11 noted on the front page the passing of a former president of the Common Council and mill overseer. Mill overseer was a position of considerable responsibility. He hired, fired, and directed the overall operations of departments or rooms with workforces that numbered in the hundreds. As long as he satisfied production standards, he exercised a virtually total discretionary authority. In Lawrence in the late nineteenth and early twentieth centuries, the position was held by English, Irish, Yankee, and to a lesser extent, German males. Although not in the same category as mill agents or others in the manufacturing elite, they enjoyed a relatively high socio-economic status. As members of an upwardly mobile managerial class, they also provided greater educational and professional opportunity to their children; W. P. Frost, Jr., for instance, was sent by his parents to Harvard.

The three-story, white-clapboard home of W. P. and Judith Colcord Frost in the thoroughly respectable precinct of Haverhill Street stood adjacent to that of Elihu W. and Lucy Frost Colcord, who had themselves enjoyed considerable success in Lawrence. After a failed adventure in the California gold fields, Elihu Colcord opened a belt manufacturing firm in 1853 to service the industries of the nascent mill city. As noted in the *Biographical Review, Volume XXVIII: Containing Life Sketches of Leading Citizens of Essex County, Massachusetts* (1898), he carried on the business in his own building from 1856 to 1873, selling out after a very successful and prosperous career.

Recollecting the relocation to Lawrence, Frost repeatedly emphasized to Thompson that Isabelle Frost and her children were perceived by the elder Frosts and Colcords to be "poor relations" and received as unwelcome obligations. Given age, occupation, and habit, W. P. Frost may very well have been stern in demeanor and even severe in his moral and fiscal economies, but Frost's complaints of cruelty seem, as Thompson concluded, unwarranted. In summarizing the years between Frost's arrival in Lawrence and his graduation from high school, Meyers evokes a scene of grim destitution and struggle in the absence of family succor.[30]

In the narrative of *The Early Years*, Thompson strikes many of the same chords, while relegating to notes his doubts about Frost's judgment of his Lawrence elders. W. P. Frost, Sr. had provided funds to bring his son's widow and children from San Francisco, and upon their arrival in the early summer of 1885 had housed them on the third floor of his home. Within weeks, perhaps motivated by tensions in the household, Isabelle agreed to spend the summer at the New Hampshire farm of Benjamin and Sarah Frost Messer, her late husband's uncle and aunt. They remained long enough for the children to enroll in a nearby school, but returned to Lawrence shortly after the fall term began. After living briefly with the Colcords, Isabelle rented furnished rooms on lower Broadway, a more congested neighborhood of commercial and residential structures, with money lent by Elihu Colcord. Early in 1886, she took a replacement position in a school in Salem Depot, NH, about ten miles to the northwest, living first in a boardinghouse and later taking rooms in the home of a local farmer. Throughout his account, Thompson emphasizes Frost's bitter resentment that neither grandfather nor uncle had helped his mother secure a post in Lawrence. Belle Frost, however, was then a teacher of limited formal credentials and slight experience – she had been an assistant teacher in a Columbus, OH high school and taught one year with W. P. Frost, Jr. at a small academy in Lewistown, PA – and had not taught in more than a decade. Her status as a widowed mother would also have been a serious obstacle in a system in which unmarried women were strictly the norm.

Over the next six years, the family's financial circumstances fluctuated with Mrs. Frost's ability to maintain classroom discipline. After two years of mounting complaints in Salem, she resigned, having been held in warm regard by those families whose aspirations extended beyond grammar school. Between 1890 and 1893, she taught at four public schools in Methuen, MA, each transfer the result of discipline problems. Paid $300 per academic year in Salem, she earned between $350 and $450 in Methuen. The average annual wage in Lawrence in the years from 1885 to 1893, by comparison, fell from $325 to less than $300. At $10 per week, Mrs. Frost's wage would have been equal to that of a highly skilled male operative in the mills.[31] The apartment on Haverhill St. to which the Frosts moved in 1890 to be nearer Lawrence High School was in a working-class neighborhood; when Mrs. Frost transferred in 1892, the family occupied a comfortable apartment on Upper Broadway in Methuen. Her resignation from the Methuen system necessitated a return to more modest lodgings at 96 Tremont St. in Lawrence. As her tutoring grew into a private school, however, she relocated first to an office building on Essex St. – where Robert and Elinor were married in December 1895 – and then to a spacious house on Haverhill St., extra rooms of which they let to boarders.

Thompson's accounts, and Meyers', of forlorn tenements notwithstanding, the Frosts were at no time slum dwellers. The abysmal living conditions for which Lawrence would become notorious during the Bread and Roses strike of 1912 had yet to develop fully while Frost lived in the city, though the process had begun. Between 1890 and 1912, immigrants from southeastern Europe would double the city's population, an influx that forced tenements to climb higher and cluster closer together. At first, most were only two stories high, but by 1895, 957 were three stories or more, the great majority in the central wards where the immigrants lived. By 1910, even the four-story building was common with 268 in the city center. While the density of population rose from 7 persons per acre to 10 between 1870 and 1890, it jumped to 20 by 1910; in the most crowded districts the figure grew to 119 per acre. A 1911 survey of five half blocks on Common, Oak, and Valley Streets, the most densely populated and poorest in the city, found that each held 300 to 600 per acre. Occupied by an average of 1.5 persons per room, the wooden tenements were often so closely crowded to the side and back that the back rooms of the front building and all of the rear had virtually no natural light.[32]

One certain indicator of social status in turn-of-the-century Lawrence was access to education beyond grammar school. The Lawrence High School Class of 1892, of which Frost and Elinor White were co-valedictorians, numbered only thirty-five students, all of whom – as the *Order of Exercises* makes evident – were of Anglo-Saxon ethnic derivation. The *High School Bulletin*, of which Frost was editor, provided in September 1891 an equally homogeneous list of seventy-two other students who had left the class over the previous three years. In the same issue, and with the pomposity of adolescent privilege, Frost editorialized about the relative distinction of his fellow scholars. While lacking the prestige of a private academy, Lawrence High School nonetheless conferred upon its graduates a real, if local, degree of social and academic distinction.

Encouraged in his studies and in such activities as the Debating Union, the *Bulletin*, and the football team, Frost was assured that family support for college waited at the successful completion of his high school career. Toward that end, and despite the immediate budgetary constraints under which Mrs. Frost maintained a household, Frost was not required at any time to work while attending school. Not until the summer of 1891, between his junior and senior years in high school, did the overseer's grandson experience life in a textile mill. As Thompson recounts, he had begun the summer doing odd jobs at a farm-cum-resort but left without being paid. Without apparent irony, Thompson describes the experience as an ideological awakening:

> Rob had not worked long in Braithwaite's mill before he found his sympathies were newly allied with the labor organizations which had been stirring up the city with protest-meetings. Never before had his mother's Socialist interest in the doctrines of Henry George or her deep admiration for Bellamy's recently published *Looking Backward* made so much sense to him.[33]

"Except for the long hours," Thompson concludes, "Rob enjoyed the new experience of mingling with the men and women at the mill. He liked the ways in which their friendliness, their harmless practical jokes, their witticisms, their laughter kept the drudgery from being unbearable."

Cheerful truisms aside, the extent of Frost's "mingling" is open to question, but his drudgery, such as it was, did not extend beyond the start of the school year. After graduation, when he more deliberately sought work in the mills, his status differed appreciably.[34] Had Frost chosen a career in industry, many similar doors in Lawrence would have opened as easily. W. P. Frost, Sr. had never hidden a hope that Robert would study law as preparation for such a career. A Lawrence High School valedictorian, grandson of a Pacific Mills overseer, and son of a schoolteacher and a Harvard Phi Beta Kappa was expected, as Frost well knew, to set his sights high, and it was by such expectations, he knew equally well, that his apparent fecklessness was measured.

Frost's last stint in the mills began in September 1893 when he was hired as a light trimmer in the Arlington Mill. Having left Dartmouth in January and taken over, until March, his mother's unruly class at Methuen Second Grammar (she was transferred to First Primary), Frost had spent the summer caretaking a country retreat to which Mrs. White brought her daughters. With no college plans – despite family disapproval – he failed as impresario for a Shakespearean reader and then looked for real employment.

"On the morning of April 12, 1893," Donald Cole reports in *Immigrant City*, "15,000 workers were out of jobs and for the first time in the memory of most citizens every mill was closed." The city wallowed in a depression until 1896. In 1894, the median weekly wage for all jobs at one Lawrence mill was $5.85; the average was $7.[35] While Frost's recollection of his wage is open to question, there is no doubt that unskilled labor was scarce and that Frost's position in the mill was, in a real sense, privileged. The contradictions in Thompson between humiliating "slavery" and lounging over Shakespeare epitomize his fundamental misunderstanding of the social economy of the mills, a misapprehension that undermines his portrayal of the poet's young adulthood.

Newdick was the first to investigate Frost's early unpublished or uncollected poems, and he took particular interest in those inspired by industrial Lawrence. "Only in his later years," he observes in a chapter entitled "The Music of the Iron," "did Frost reveal in a few published poems that he had observed as closely and as understandingly in the mill as he had on the farm and in the woods. Take, for example, the opening of 'A Lone Striker,' in which the intricacy of the spinning machines and the necessary deftness of the operator were described."

> There was a rule of the mill that latecomers be locked out for half an hour and their pay docked accordingly. Frost, once caught so, made a day of it, going to

a place in the woods where he could walk, drink from a spring, reflect on the things he loved, all of which represented for him a compelling form of action. So always he was given to rebel against merely formal and institutional claims on him . . .

From time to time *thenceforward*, Frost's manuscript portfolios contained a number of other poems embodying his observations, experience, and reflections as a mill worker.[36] (italics mine)

Citing "The Mill City" and "When the Speed Comes," Newdick contends that "Frost was a practicing American workers' poet before most of the noisy academic 'proletarians' of the nineteen-thirties were out of rompers":

Of the industrialism that dominated his day, he was conscious from his youth onwards, fully conscious, as only those who have known it at first hand can be. Steadily, too, though never exclusively and disproportionately, he wrote about it. And clearly and repeatedly, though always as an artist rather than a propagandist, he pilloried its insatiable greed, its monstrous tyranny, and its manifold oppressions of free human spirit and effort.[37]

Newdick's broadly overstated defense of Frost's social conscience is akin to those by Bernard DeVoto and others on behalf of the politically beleaguered bard of *A Further Range*. Certainly, Newdick does not distort the poet's past out of all naturalness; he does, however, allow a 1930s mythos of "The Lone Striker" to displace earlier texts and testimony in priority and authenticity. He contributes his part, in other words, toward investing with biographical legitimacy Frost's portrait of the young artist as individualist rebel. Refigured to satisfy ideological exigencies of the 1930s, this identity locates its originatory moment in a spontaneous and disinterested turn from society to solitude, from mindless and mechanical modern work to timeless play-for-mortal-stakes, from factory gate to woodland path and spring.

The symbolic efficacy of this figure for the poet-in-the-making is such that it insinuates itself inextricably, for Frost as well as for his readers and biographers, into the persona of *A Boy's Will*.[38] In *The Trial by Existence*, to cite but one instance, Elizabeth Sergeant conflates the two representative moments of poetic origin. Persuaded – so it seems – by her conversations with the poet in the 1950s, she reads "Into My Own" as complementary to "A Lone Striker":

It is known that sometime in the spring of this year 1894, R. F. gave up the mill work suddenly, as if under a new star, and found himself another elementary teaching job. As I heard the story, the youngster had arrived late, after the noon hour, and finding the mill doors closed, shouted:

"You can't do this to *me*!" and went off.

A poem ["A Lone Striker"] first printed in 1933 as a Borzoi *Chap Book*, then published in *A Further Range* in 1936, seems autobiographical. [39]

Frost has told me that this poem ["Into My Own"] represents his first desire to escape from something, his fear of something . . . Frost perhaps irrationally dreaded to be captured by the spinning mills of Lawrence or hauled back into living dependently under the tutelage of elder relatives. [40]

Which reminds me, have you anything but a sociology teacher's word for it that machine work, monotony and a life in the mills ages people any faster than the confusing variety of life on a farm or the strain of having to think up new material to teach nine hours a week in college?

To C. G. McCormick (1937)[41]

Reviewing *West-Running Brook* in 1928 and *Collected Poems* in 1930, Granville Hicks objected to a lack of attention to contemporary social conditions. What we do not find in Frost's poetically realized New England, he charged, is more important than what we do, for the unified world of Frost's poetry was achieved only through a calculated restriction of vision. Hicks elaborated in 1933:

Frost has achieved unity by a definite process of exclusion. One not only realizes that life in New Hampshire is not altogether representative of life in the United States as a whole; one has to admit that Frost disregards many elements in New Hampshire life, and especially the elements that link that state with the rest of the country. For example, northern New England has been greatly affected by the growth of industrialism, and yet one would never suspect this from Frost's poetry. Can one believe that it is by accident that he has never written of the factory towns, now so abjectly in decay, or of the exodus to the cities and its failure, now so apparent, to bring deliverance . . . ? No, Frost is too shrewd not to be well aware that he is excluding from his poems whatever might destroy their unity.

"Frost's experience is close to ours," Hicks allowed, and "we can share his appreciations and insights." To the extent that Frost concerns himself only with what is "personally congenial" and "poetically available," however, he leaves us discontented:

He has chosen to identify himself with a moribund tradition. Many poets, these hundred and fifty years, have written of mountains, fields, and brooks, and of farmers at their humble tasks; these things have become part of our imaginative inheritance, and one must be insensitive indeed not to be conscious of the beauty in them. But there are other objects now more frequently before our eyes – factories, skyscrapers, machines. We see mechanics, shop-girls, truck-drivers, more often than we do farmers . . . There is new territory that we beg the poet to conquer for us. Perhaps to-day no poet is capable of that conquest, but, if the task is ever to be accomplished, some one with the talent of a Robert Frost must make a beginning. [42]

In December 1933, Frost alerted John Bartlett to a publication impending. "I shall soon be out," he wrote in mock solemnity, "with a ponderous book of one poem on how I detached myself from the mills of Man in Lawrence Mass but without prejudice to machinery industry or an industrial age so that there will be no mistake in the record."[43] Published as a pamphlet in 1933 under the more assertive title of "The Lone Striker," and as "A Lone Striker" in *A Further Range* (1936), the poem is to be taken, in part, as a rebuttal to Hicks. Why had the criticism touched so responsive a chord? Hicks' Marxist politics were, of course, a sufficient irritant, but what rankled was the more dismissive allegation, by a fellow New Englander, of escapist irrelevance.[44] "Hicks says I'm an escapist" had become a refrain in Frost's conversation long before he complained as much in a letter to Theodore Morrison in 1938. Still setting the record straight in the 1937 talk that would become "Poverty and Poetry," Frost engaged the ideological enemy under the cover of humorous detachment:

> Suppose I begin with that very poem about me and the mills in Lawrence. This one is called, "The Lone Striker." It is all right to be a striker, but not a lone striker. You might think that I might get in right with my radical friends, but the trouble with me is that I was a lone striker; if I called it a "collectivist striker," that would be another matter. This was the way it was to me, not a very serious thing. (*CPPP*, 763)

A serious step is lightly taken, and Frost invites us to admire the casual boldness of the poet-speaker in setting off into his own, to acknowledge, again, how a solitary way can make all the difference. In the satisfaction of its sureties – "Nor was this just a way of talking/ To save him the expense of doing./ With him it boded action, deed" – the poem has tempted ironists. Thompson and others have remarked the gap between the symbolic clarity of poetic closure and the prosaic clutter of biographical fact: "The path he soon found himself walking was a bitterly familiar one. A replacement was needed for a substitute teacher in tiny District School Number Nine in South Salem."[45] Caught between its dramatic form and its didactic purpose, between character and commentary, "A Lone Striker" has raised in readers all the aesthetic misgivings common to Frost's polemical dramas from "New Hampshire" to "Kitty Hawk." Critical scruples notwithstanding, however, the poem remains fundamental to the representation of Frost's cultural identity.

By any measure, "A Lone Striker" is among the least "proletarian" – unless we strip the term of all of its historical associations – of Frost's poems about either lives of labor or the contemporary political climate. Throughout the late 1930s, as in the "Poverty and Poetry" reading, he used the poem to illustrate his distrust of activist, collectivist, or labor unionist sentiment on the political or literary left. True measure of the poem, however, can be taken only by attending to both the play of present ideological purpose and the ground of the past on which it is enacted. The hearty sententiousness of the narrative commentary makes bland parable of potential drama, but the poem retains traces of a more complex, and conflicted, experience of the scene Frost saw or thought he saw.

Early in his time at the Arlington mills, Thompson writes in *The Early Years*, Frost "had admired the deftness of the girls who worked in the wool-dusty atmosphere, the quick motions of their fingers as they reached in among taut threads to snatch up broken ends and twist them quickly together." As time passed, however, "he began to feel that these girls were forced to become human spiders; that all these threads seemed to be drawn, at a debilitating speed, from their insides. He tried to catch his own mood of resentment later, in a sonnet which did reflect his bitter disapproval of such endless mill work."[46] Transposing "When the Speed Comes" and "A Lone Striker," Thompson carries Frost from detachment to empathy, from aesthetics to ethics, from his least proletarian poem to perhaps his most sincerely so:

> When the speed comes a creeping overhead
> And belts begin to snap and shafts to creak,
> And the sound dies away of them that speak,
> And on the glassy floor the tapping tread;
> When dusty globes on all a pallor shed,
> And breaths of many wheels are on the cheek;
> Unwilling is the flesh, the spirit weak,
> All effort like arising from the dead.
>
> But the task ne'er could wait the mood to come,
> The music of the iron is a law:
> And as upon the heavy spools that pay
> Their slow white thread, so ruthlessly the hum
> Of countless whirling spindles seems to draw
> Upon the soul, still sore from yesterday.

Describing the familiar evils of textile piecework in relation to the Lawrence strike of 1912, Ardis Cameron has noted that "In almost all cases operatives worked according to the pace and rhythm of the machine that required workers to adjust to the demands of production requirements":

Seemingly controlled by swirling belts, vibrating wooden frames, and thundering looms and spindles, workers felt intensely alienated from the work process. "They call them 'devils' and not machinery," remarked a member of the strike committee. [P]ieceworkers were dependent upon speed so that wages suffered as output declined, and jobs remained in constant jeopardy.[47]

As the "straining mill began to shake," the lone striker outside finds that "The mill, though many, many eyed,/ Had eyes inscrutably opaque;/ So that he couldn't look inside/ To see if some forlorn machine/ Was standing idle for his sake." The vision that follows demonstrates how obscured for Frost the reality of the workers had become and how dimly, if poetically, perceived it had always been:

> And yet he thought he saw the scene:
> The air was full of dust of wool.
> A thousand yarns were under pull,
> But pull so slow, with such a twist,
> All day from spool to lesser spool,
> It seldom overtaxed their strength;
> They safely grew in slender length.
> And if one broke by any chance,
> The spinner saw it at a glance.
> The spinner still was there to spin.
>
> That's where the human still came in.
> Her deft hand showed with finger rings
> Among the harp-like spread of strings.
> She caught the pieces end to end
> And, with a touch that never missed,
> Not so much tied as made them blend.
> Man's ingenuity was good.

"Spinners," Cameron notes, "who worked in damp and humid rooms, were especially vulnerable to tuberculosis, the 'white plague,' and pneumonia. In the years before the 1912 strike, one third of Lawrence's spinners would die before they had worked ten years, and half of these would never reach the age of 25."[48]

Of the days in the Arlington mills, Newdick writes that Frost

discovered that human nature would somehow find playful expression even under the burdens of wages of ten cents an hour, a ten-hour day, and a sixty-hour week. "I used to think the mill people, scooting home in the dark, were sad," he once recalled, "till I worked in the mill, and heard them singing and laughing and throwing bobbins up at me as I stood up on a ladder fixing the lights."[49]

Of these workers, he continues, Frost wrote poems "full to the heart's depth with compassion," poems that "voiced his purpose really to know workers and to understand their problems":[50]

It was in a drear city by a stream,
And all its denizens were sad to me, –
I could not fathom what their life could be –
Their passage in the morning like a dream
In the arc-light's unnatural bluish beam,
Then back, at night, like drowned men from the sea,
Up from the mills and river hurriedly,
In weeds of labor, to the shriek of steam.

Yet I supposed that they had all one hope
With me (there is but one.) I would go out,
When happier ones drew in for fear of doubt,
Breasting their current, resolute to cope
With what thoughts they compelled who thronged the street,
Less to the sound of voices than of feet.

Written a decade after Frost worked in the Arlington mills, "The Mill City" depicts its somber procession in terms unrelated to "scooting" and declares its solemn purpose without any insight into laughing millhands at their labors. The change in perspective that Frost described to Newdick seems more closely related to the political positioning of the 1930s than the aesthetic posturing of the 1890s. A genre painting after the fashion of Winslow Homer's *Bell Time* (1868), "The Mill City" testifies to the divide between the poet-hero and the undifferentiated throng for whom he promises – or presumes – to speak. The studied fastidiousness of the speaker's resolution recalls the *fin de siècle* affectations of Frost's observations for the Lawrence *American* in 1895:

> I am going to betray a confidence and worse than that, a poor man's confidence, but only in the hope of compelling for him your natural if unrighteous sympathy.
>
> There are a lot of women and children that have let me see them looting coal in a yard near here. They come with buckets and gather it piece by piece under the coal cars. It is feverish work keeping warm, for such people. And the curious part of it is, they will not take the coal otherwise than from off the ground, which necessitates their twice handling it, once from the car to the ground, and again from the ground to the bucket. The moral strain attendant on such work must be excessive and one suffers to watch them skulking and stooping all day.[51]

While working as a reporter for the *American* in 1895, Thompson notes, Frost "was sent to the Arlington Mill in Lawrence to gather information about labor difficulties which had resulted in a strike, and he went directly to the main office to call on a Mr. Hartshorn, whom he and his mother knew. It was a friendly and informative visit, but Hartshorn kept interweaving so many confidences ("Don't write about what I'm going to tell you now.") that by the time Frost left the mill he saw no way of writing up the story without betraying a friendship."[52] Formerly Superintendent of the Worsted Department, William D. Hartshorn was Resident Agent of the Arlington Mills and thus, in essence, its chief executive officer. Frost's experience of Lawrence was shaped, of course, not only by William Prescott Frost's career in the mills but also by Isabelle Frost's Swedenborgian interests, which brought the family into contact, as Thompson noted in 1946, with a wide range of persons, including "several of the most prominent men in Lawrence."[53]

Frost in 1912 was teaching at the Normal School in Plymouth, NH and, having sold the farm in Derry bequeathed him by his grandfather, was planning to embark with his family upon a literary adventure to England. In June, he wrote to Wilbur Rowell, a prominent Lawrence attorney and magistrate who served as executor of the estate of William Prescott Frost:

> I felt almost sorry to be so far from Lawrence when the syndicalist strike was on. How much Lawrence has and has not changed since I left the town twelve years ago! The Letts and the Portuguese and the Greeks and the Syrians are all quite new. But at the same time they appear not to have altogether displaced the older population. I never heard of the Syrian dentist who was for dying a martyr to the cause at the hands of the militia. But I was going to say I knew all the other people the papers mentioned from Clark Carter to John Breen. I went to one college with Danny Murphy, to another with Louis Cox. I went to the Hampshire St. school with John Breen. I am proudest to have known John – as you may suppose.   (SL, 48)

At the height of the strike, Rowell had published a defense of Lawrence in *The Survey*, declaring it to be "a typical New England industrial city, with all the equipment and resources that are found in such a city for generous and noble life, and for the sympathetic relief of weakness and suffering."

With Rowell's civic and national pride and with his genteel assimilationism, Frost would have been in perfect accord.[54] Thus, Frost's use of the immigrant cycle as a shorthand for local history in his letter to Rowell was as natural as his assessment of ethnic shifts was accurate. The Syrian dentist, Dr. Haztar, had been the subject of testimony by Captain John Sullivan, Lawrence Chief Marshal, at Congressional hearings in March 1912: "I know of a Syrian doctor," said the Captain, "who had no connection with the strike, who asked for twenty-five men to go with him to throw themselves on the bayonets of the soldiers to arouse sympathy for the cause."[55]

A young Frost had forsworn industrial Lawrence and any professional career for which his grandfather would have prepared him. As the older Frost of "A Lone Striker" is at pains to make clear, however, he had had no ideological quarrel with the system.

The factory was very fine;
He wished it all the modern speed.
Yet, after all, 'twas not divine,
That is to say, 'twas not a church.
He never would assume that he'd
Be any institution's need.
But he said then and still would say
If there should ever come a day
When industry seemed like to die
Because he left it in the lurch,
Or even merely seemed to pine
For want of his approval, why,
Come get him – they knew where to search.

A lone striker is a self-made or, as is often the case in Frost, a self-unmade man, and neither version of the story readily accommodates the existence of a trust fund. The emotional complexity of Frost's relationship with his paternal grandfather defies simple explanation, but certainly the poet's self-defining narrative of independence finds a more adequate foil in the figure of W. P. Frost as austere and contemptuous authority than as a well-meaning, if severe, benefactor. In conversation with Thompson in 1940, Frost rehearsed the story with revealing purpose:

> We talked about jobs and he was much interested in an article on the editorial page of the *New York Herald Tribune*: "What is a Grape of Wrath?" He said that when he and his mother were keeping house they had left the grandfather because he was hostile; that they burned scraps of leather from the leather mill and lived on very simple food for months at a time. They needn't have done it, but they were too proud to go back to the grandfather, whose wealth was a mere "competence." Their favorite meat was a shank bone which made a good stew . . . He didn't feel sorry for himself; didn't feel as though anyone owed him a job . . . [H]e liked his freedom to proceed with his own headstrong folly without interference . . . The idea of having Steinbeck blame the whole capitalistic system for the Oakies bothers him. Believes that "the will to fail" will always keep a steady flow of people towards jails, poor houses, and insane asylums, even in the best of prosperity.[56]

In March of 1925, Frost returned to Lawrence to read his poems to an appreciative audience, his visit supported as it had been in 1916 by the White Fund for which Wilbur Rowell served as chief trustee. In a lengthy feature story and interview in the *Lawrence Telegram*, James A. Batal explained the city's claim to the celebrated poet: "Although not a native born son, Mr. Frost belongs to Lawrence for it was in this city that he spent his youth and received the education that influenced the poetry of his early career." In seeking to document the influence, however, he counsels discretion:

> I have searched through his poetry in hope of finding something that would show the effect on his poetry of his mill environment. I have found nothing that would indicate he has written about institutions.
>
> Although Mr. Frost worked for some time after his graduation from high school as a lamp-trimmer in the Arlington mills, the industrial environment in Lawrence affected his poetic creations, if at all, only by contrast – the calm and beauty of nature contrasted with the bustle and turmoil of factory machines . . . This contrast of city with country life came early to Mr. Frost, for when he was not browsing around the reading room in the library he would take long walks into the country.[57]

Batal's research is not to be faulted, for Frost had chosen to publish neither "The Mill City" nor "When the Speed Comes." When the interview turned to the importance of books, however, Frost asserted that "'One of the great books that I came near writing, but which I didn't write, was the history of Lawrence.'" He had, in fact, written such a history, but in the form of a polemical poem. Entitled "The Parlor Joke," the poem was included by Louis Untermeyer in *A Miscellany of American Poetry, 1920* but never collected by Frost.[58] As a self-described sentimental socialist, Untermeyer would be for decades Frost's ideological sparring partner, and by 1920 he had suffered Frost's barbs over the demise, for political reasons, of *The Masses* and *The Seven Arts*. Always pleased to unsettle not only Untermeyer's party politics but also any categorical expectations about his own, Frost prefaced the poem with a challenge to stay unassuming. "Dear Louis," he began, "Is it nothing to you that no longer than ten years ago I was writing town poems like this." Affixed to the end was a declaration: "Patented 1910 by R. (L.) Frost."

> You won't hear unless I tell you
> How the few to turn a penny
> Built complete a modern city
> Where there shouldn't have been any,
> And then conspired to fill it
> With the miserable many.
>
> They drew on Ellis Island.
> They had but to raise a hand
> To let the living deluge
> On the basin of the land.
> They did it just like nothing
> In smiling self-command.

If you asked them *their* opinion,
They declared the job as good
As when, to fill the sluices,
They turned the river flood;
Only then they dealt with water
And now with human blood.

Then the few withdrew in order
To their villas on the hill,
Where they watched from easy couches
The uneasy city fill.
"If it *isn't* good," they ventured,
"At least it isn't ill."

But with child and wife to think of,
They weren't taking any chance.
So they fortified their windows
With a screen of potted plants,
And armed themselves from somewhere
With a manner and a glance.

You know how a bog of sphagnum
Beginning with a scum
Will climb the side of a mountain,
So the poor began to come,
Climbing the hillside suburb
From the alley and the slum.

As their tenements crept nearer,
It pleased the rich to assume,
In humorous self-pity,
The mockery of gloom
Because the poor insisted
On wanting all the room.

And there it might have ended
In a feeble parlor joke,
Where a gentle retribution
Overtook the gentlefolk;
But that some beheld a vision:
Out of stench and steam and smoke,

Out of vapor of sweat and breathing,
They saw materialize
Above the darkened city
Where the murmur never dies,
A shape that had to cower
Not to knock against the skies.

They could see it through a curtain,
They could see it through a wall,
A lambent swaying presence
In wind and rain and all,
With its arms abroad in heaven
Like a scarecrow in a shawl.

There were some who thought they heard it
When it seemed to try to talk
But missed articulation
With a little hollow squawk,
Up indistinct in the zenith,
Like the note of the evening hawk.

Of things about the future
Its hollow chest was full,
Something about rebellion
And blood a dye for wool,
And how you may pull the world down
If you know the prop to pull.

What to say to the wisdom
That could tempt a nation's fate
By invoking such a spirit
To reduce the labor-rate!
Some people don't mind trouble
If it's trouble up-to-date.

NOTES

1 To Lawrance Thompson in 1954 ("Notes from Conversations with Robert Frost" in the Manuscripts Department of the University of Virginia Library [Accession Number 10044] 532T).

2 Lawrance Thompson, *Robert Frost: The Early Years* (New York: Holt, Rinehart, and Winston, 1966), p. xiii.

3 Paul John Eakin, *Fictions in Autobiography: Studies in the Art of Self-Invention* (Princeton, NJ: Princeton University Press, 1985), pp. 4–6.

4 Robert S. Newdick, *Newdick's Season of Frost: An Interrupted Biography of Robert Frost*, ed. William A. Sutton (Albany: State University of New York Press, 1976), p. 230.

5 Eakin, *Fictions in Autobiography*, p. 170.

6 James Olney, *Metaphors of Self: The Meaning of Autobiography* (Princeton, NJ: Princeton University Press, 1972), p. 187.

7 *Ibid.*, p. 188.

8 David H. Lowenherz, *Letters, Manuscripts, and Inscribed Books by Robert Frost from the Collection of David H. Lowenherz* (New York: Grolier Club, 1999), pp. 45, 46.

9 Leon Edel, *Writing Lives: Principia Biographica* (New York: Norton, 1984), p. 161.
10 *Ibid.*, p. 14.
11 *Ibid.*, pp. 17, 173.
12 Thompson, *Frost: The Early Years.*
13 Edel, *Writing Lives*, p. 28.
14 See Donald G. Sheehy, "The Poet as Neurotic: The Official Biography of Robert Frost," *American Literature* 58 (October 1986), 393–410.
15 Thompson, *Frost: The Early Years*, p. 14.
16 *Ibid.*, pp. xxiii–xxiv.
17 Edel, *Writing Lives*, p. 14.
18 Lawrance Thompson's "Notes from Conversations with Robert Frost" are in the Manuscripts Department of the University of Virginia Library (Accession Number 10044).
19 James A. Batal, "Poet Robert Frost Tells of His High School Days in Lawrence," *Lawrence Telegram* (March 28), 1925, p. 14.
20 Ezra Pound, "A Boy's Will," review of Robert Frost, *A Boy's Will, Poetry*, 2, 72–74 (May 1913), p. 73.
21 Thompson, *Frost: The Early Years*, p. 412.
22 *Ibid.*, p. 421.
23 Elizabeth Sergeant, *Robert Frost: The Trial by Existence* (New York: Holt, Rinehart and Winston, 1960), p. 17.
24 Thompson, *Frost: The Early Years*, pp. xvii–xviii.
25 To Lawrance Thompson in 1954 ("Notes from Conversations with Robert Frost"), p. 209.
26 *Ibid.*, p. 458.
27 Amy Lowell, *Tendencies in Modern American Poetry* (New York: Macmillan, 1917), p. 96.
28 One way to look at Frost's problem with his grandfather was not that he required assistance and his grandfather refused. Rather it was that his grandfather provided assistance Frost would have preferred not to have needed. Since Frost did not refuse his grandfather's financial aid, he found it necessary to convince himself that the assistance represented a means of controlling him. Indeed, the money did carry implicit obligations and explicit stipulations, but benefactor became enemy because acknowledging assistance would undermine a sense of self-reliance that initially served as a defense against failure and a loss of self-esteem and later became a philosophical and political tenet. In any case, Frost consistently distorted accounts of his dealings with trustees of his grandfather's estate and its executor, Wilbur Rowell.
29 Fred Beal, *Proletarian Journey: New England, Gastonia, Moscow* (New York: Hillman-Curl, 1937), p. 29.
30 Jeffrey Meyers, *Robert Frost: A Biography* (New York: Houghton Mifflin, 1996), pp. 16–19.
31 In 1894, the median wage for all jobs studied at one mill was $5.85/ week; the average wage for all jobs at the same mill was $7.00/week (see Donald B. Cole, *Immigrant City: Lawrence, Massachusetts, 1845–1921* (Chapel Hill: University of North Carolina Press, 1963), pp. 118–20).
32 *Ibid.*, pp. 68–71.

33 Thompson, *Frost: The Early Years*, p. 106.

34 Thompson, *The Early Years*, pp. 134–35.

35 Fred Beal, *Proletarian Journey: New England, Gastonia, Moscow* (New York: Hillman-Curl, 1937), pp. 119–20.

36 Newdick, *Newdick's Season of Frost*, p. 41.

37 *Ibid.*

38 Louis Mertins summons Thoreau as witness to the pastoral turn.

> Some days he would stroll out to the top of Cemetery Hill, which complacently looked down on the low-lying town. Its three-hundred acres of factories (each with uncounted thousands of spools, bobbins, shuttles, and human machines weaving cloth for far-flung markets) made a forest of smokestacks belching flame and soot, poisoning the pure oxygen of the air. Here must have come to his imagination all the horrors of what one inside at work there would have to come to at last. It was a place where
>
> > *The air was full of dust of wool,*
> > *A thousand yarns were under pull.*
>
> The young Frost, gazing from his eminence at the sinuous Merrimack winding below, recalled the comforting words of Thoreau concerning the same town and the same river, yes, the very site on which his eye at the moment rested.
>
> When at length it has escaped from under the last of the factories, it has a level and unmolested passage to the sea, a mere waste of water as it were, bearing little with it but its fame; its pleasant course revealed by the morning fog which hangs over it, and to the sails of a few vessels which transact the commerce between Haverhill and Newburyport. It was at this place, at this point that the future poet took account of himself. (In *Robert Frost: Life and Talks-Walking* [Norman: University of Oklahoma Press], 1965, p. 38.)

39 Sergeant, *The Trial by Existence*, p. 38.

40 *Ibid.*, p. 57.

41 Frost's letter to Charles G. McCormick, dated January 1937, is in the Robert Frost Collection of the Amherst College Library [Correspondence #90]. I thank The Estate of Robert Lee Frost, Peter Gilbert, Executor, and the Amherst College Library for permission to publish this material.

42 Granville Hicks, *The Great Tradition: An Interpretation of American Literature Since the Civil War* (New York: Macmillan, 1935), p. 246.

43 Margaret Bartlett Anderson, *Robert Frost and John Bartlett: The Record of a Friendship* (New York: Holt, Rinehart, and Winston, 1963), pp. 170–71.

44 American pastoralists, as Lawrence Buell remarks, have been "hard put to deal with the Peter-Pan side of themselves even at the very point of indulgence." And harder put, of course, when interrogated by those readers of pastoral texts who find disturbing the "seeming insouciance with which the persona turns away from social confrontation for the sake of immersion in a simplified green world" (7). "But I wasn't escaping," Robert Frost protested in 1927 to his then-biographer, Gorham Munson, recounting his removal (at age twenty-six, and at the very advent of the twentieth century) from the industrial city of Lawrence to the rela-

tive isolation of the Derry farm. "No escape theory will explain me. I was choosing when to deliver battle" (Thompson, *The Years of Triumph*, p. 323). See: Lawrence Buell, "American Pastoral Ideology Reappraised," *American Literary History*, 1 (Spring 1989), 1–29.

45 Edward Connery Lathem and Lawrance Thompson, *Robert Frost and the Lawrence, Massachusetts, High School Bulletin: The Beginning of a Literary Career* (New York: Grolier Club, 1966), p. 75.

46 Thompson, *Frost: The Early Years*, p. 158.

47 Ardis Cameron, *Radicals of the Worst Sort: Laboring Women in Lawrence, Massachusetts, 1860–1912* (Urbana: University of Illinois Press, 1993), pp. 118–19.

48 *Ibid.*, p. 99.

49 Newdick, *Newdick's Season of Frost*, pp. 39–40.

50 *Ibid.*, p. 41.

51 *Ibid.*, p. 305.

52 Thompson, *Frost: The Early Years*, p. 194.

53 Thompson observes that "Mrs. Frost's Swedenborgian interests in Lawrence brought her into contact with . . . several of the most prominent men in Lawrence – one family of Hales, who either owned the water-works or were high up in mill ownerships there, attended meetings in their Methuen homes" ("Notes," 268). In a recollection of the period written in 1963, Susan Holmes identifies Horace Hale Smith – who was later the architect of the Central Bridge – as "a pal of Frost's," and lists among other prominent guests at Robert and Elinor's wedding both Horace Hale Smith and "Richard Hale (of the Essex Company)." Tom Holmes, Susan's father, was gate tender for the Essex Company and oversaw the operations of the North Canal gatehouse. A typescript of "Robert Frost in Lawrence" is in the Lamson Library of Plymouth (NH) State College.

54 Frost's nationalist and assimilationist views are pervasive. Passages from a 1923 interview are representative (see *I*, 50).

55 "Police Say Women Led Lawrence Mobs," *New York Times*, March 3, 1912, 6.

56 To Lawrance Thompson in 1954 ("Notes from Conversations with Robert Frost"), pp. 7–8.

57 Batal, "Poet Robert Frost Tells of His High School Days in Lawrence," p. 14.

58 While Frost never publicly declared the poem to describe Lawrence, the evidence is compelling. By dating the poem to *circa* 1910 for Untermeyer, Frost places it on the eve of the Bread and Roses strike. A manuscript version of the poem in the Robert Frost Collection of the Jones Library is more forthright. In parentheses beneath the title, Frost wrote "When you think that this was written at the time of the I. W. W. strike in Lawrence in nineteen eleven."

2

WILLIAM PRITCHARD

Frost Biography and *A Witness Tree*

In a 1975 essay, where I proposed Frost's "The Wind and the Rain" as his best "unknown" poem, I also claimed that the opening ten poems in *A Witness Tree* (1942) ("The Wind and the Rain" is one of them), is the most impressive sequence of poems to be found anywhere in the poet's work.[1] The sequence, I wrote, contained "extremes of delicate tenderness and of shocking brutality," and its pervasive melancholy reached a depth not hitherto encountered, or to be encountered again, in Frost.[2] Recently two accounts of the biographical circumstances out of which *A Witness Tree* emerged have caused me and perhaps others to think again about that book, especially its opening sequence, and about the degree to which a poet's art can be more fully understood and appreciated when we learn more about the life experiences that surround and motivate it. My comments here are directed toward clarifying, or at least exploring further, these matters of literary and biographical criticism.

I

I should begin by acknowledging with gratitude the first of these two accounts, Donald Sheehy's essay, "Refiguring Love: Robert Frost in Crisis, 1938–1942," by far the most subtle and penetrating treatment of Frost's life in the years following his wife Elinor's death in 1938, up through the publication of *A Witness Tree* in 1942.[3] Those years include, most saliently, his relationship with Kathleen (Kay) Morrison, officially his secretary, unofficially and surely his lover, and the most important "other" in his life during those four post-1938 years. During them, Frost composed some of the best poems in *A Witness Tree*, also his great essay "The Figure a Poem Makes" that prefaced his *Complete Poems* (1949). Mr. Sheehy's claim for the opening sequence in *A Witness Tree* is similar to mine, but sets it more richly within the biographical nexus:

Taken in its entirety, the opening section of *A Witness Tree* is a major triumph of Frost's career, rivaled in its sustained power and human complexity only by *North of Boston*. To read it exclusively as a record of personal experience is, of course, to diminish its poetic accomplishment, but to approach it without recognizing it to be a poetic chapter of personal crisis and resolution is finally to devalue the emotional and psychological achievement that it represents. If a career is a progress both public and private, then for no poet more than for Frost were the two moments so inextricably linked.[4]

This is admirably and tactfully said, and it invites us to investigate more fully the extent to which it is possible to read this sequence "as a record of personal experience."

The other recent effort to make a case for *A Witness Tree* in its biographical circumstances is to be found in Jeffery Meyers' biography of Frost, whose most revelatory chapter is one that treats Frost's relations with Kay Morrison. What Sheehy's essay did with tact and complication, Meyers approaches in his typically blunt, free-swinging way, providing us with a you-are-there glimpse of the poet and his new love. In a key paragraph he describes the consummation of their relationship, and the single footnote to this paragraph refers us to Robert Newdick's unfinished biography of Frost – in which Frost spoke to Newdick about being "fearful" of the "arrangement with Kay" – also, more germanely, to Lawrance Thompson's unpublished "Notes on Frost." It is presumably the latter source, unless Meyers is inventing things, that enables him to write as follows: "Troubled and excited by their long walks in the woods, [Frost] took along condoms (which he had been reluctant to use with Elinor.)"[5] There follows, and in quotation marks, "Then Frost began making passionate love to her and found that she was willing . . . All he had to do was to take off her drawers and consummate an urge that seemed mutual."[6] Meyers makes things even more exciting by alluding to a figure from "The Figure a Poem Makes": "Frost rode on her own melting."[7] Meyers concludes the paragraphs with two sentences I am quite unable to fathom: "Frost wrote that no one could object to being legally wed when the marriage was consummated naked in bed. But it is an entirely different matter when you have sex out of doors with no clothes off but drawers."[8]

At the conclusion of this chapter about Kay Morrison – whose love affairs with Bernard DeVoto, a hired man named Stafford Dragon, and with Thompson himself are detailed – Meyers writes three-and-a-half pages in which he reveals "the real meaning of *A Witness Tree*."[9] Of course such a phrase as "real meaning" should in itself be enough to alert readers that some activity other than sensitive criticism of lyric poetry is likely to go on. As usual Meyers is of no two minds in his judgments, telling us that the first ten poems of *A Witness Tree* under the rubric "One or Two," take up "the question of whether Frost will be alone or joined with Kay."[10] (Meyers neglects to mention that Frost's previous collection, *A Further Range* (1936), organized its poems under the rubrics "Taken Doubly" and "Taken Singly.") "The ten poems express, directly or indirectly," Meyers goes on, "his love for Kay."[11] Meyers thinks that the first of them, "The Silken Tent," "describes, with the greatest possible delicacy, the conflict between Kay's bondage and freedom as she is pulled, loosely by Ted in marriage or tightly by Frost in love."[12] By way of indicating an aspect of the poem's great delicacy, Meyers instances Frost's use of the word "guys" ("So that in guys it gently sways at ease") as "a triple pun on ropes, mockery, and men."[13] So much for delicacy. Among other poems mentioned by the biographer is "The Most of It," which "describes Frost's longing for and response to Kay."[14] Presumably Frost identified with the great buck who "creates an orgasmic waterfall, so that his mate can make The Most of It." As for "Never Again Would Birds' Song Be the Same," its final line – "And to do that to birds was why she came" – "concludes on a bold sexual pun," suggesting that "as the lady's voice intensified the birds' song, so Kay's sexual passion inspired the words that made this poem."[15]

"The poem must resist the intelligence/ Almost successfully," wrote Wallace Stevens, and Frost himself either as man or poet had no wish to be too easily found out. In a letter of 1929 he addressed the question of how much personal material should go into one's poems:

> Everybody knows something has to be kept back for pressure and to anybody puzzled to know what I should suggest that for a beginning it might as well be his friends, wife, children, and self . . . Poetry is measured in more senses than one: it is measured feet but more important still it is a measured amount of all we could say an we would. We shall be judged finally by the delicacy of our feeling of where to stop short.   (*SL*, 361)

The trouble with Meyers' account of these *Witness Tree* poems is that it does not know where or when to stop short. The poems do not resist his intelligence "almost successfully," indeed they do not resist it at all. Or so he presumes, insofar as their real and true meaning can be grasped and stated as easily and quickly as it takes to desubtilize them by plugging their lines and imagined situations into real-life equivalents named "Kay," or "orgasmic waterfall." The question remains, what exactly has one understood by so penetrating the poems' language in order to extract their real meanings? The answer is, I am afraid, not very much. And even Meyers would probably agree that establishing the crucial biographical importance of the love between Frost and Kay Morrison does not mean perforce that we must put a high value on the poems supposedly resulting from it. We might remind ourselves that *A Further Range,* dedicated to Elinor Frost, contained poems as major to the Frost canon as "Two Tramps in Mud Time," "Desert Places," "The Strong are Saying Nothing," "Neither Out Far Nor In Deep," "Design," "Provide, Provide," and the lovely, under-appreciated "Iris by Night." It is not as if Frost in the 1930s had entered or declined into some rut in which he did no more than rework old themes or perform his bardlike functions as public entertainer.

Yet the sequence in *A Witness Tree is* something special. After two epigraph-like and rather enigmatic short poems, "Beech" and "Sycamore," we have the following: "The Silken Tent," "All Revelation," "Happiness Makes Up in Height For What It Lacks in Length," "Come In," "I Could Give All to Time," "Carpe Diem," "The Wind and the Rain," "The Most of It," "Never Again Would Birds' Song Be the Same," and "The Subverted Flower." After this sequence the final four poems in "One or Two," are a falling-off, although "The Quest of the Purple-Fringed," written much earlier, is exquisite. Perhaps the use of that adjective about this poem in praise of the orchis (or rather, as George Monteiro has suggested, the gentian), may suggest the difference between it and the earlier ten poems:

> Then at last and following him I found –
> In the very hour
> When the color flushed to the petals it must have been –
> The far-sought flower.
>
> There stood the purple spires with no breath of air
> Nor headlong bee
> To disturb their perfect poise the livelong day
> 'Neath the alder tree.

With reference to the man's discovery of the flower he has been seeking, Frank Lentricchia called it "the purest celebratory moment in Frost's poetry,"[16] surely it is a lovely one, a lyric instance of song that ends itself as fully as Frost ever ended any poem: "Then I arose and silently wandered home,/ And I for one/ Said that the fall might come and whirl of leaves,/ For summer was done." It does not invite a search for some key that might unlock it; it is not a "conflicted" poem, and if, as Frost claimed, everything written is as good as it is dramatic, I take "The Quest of the Purple-Fringed" to be a small exception to that rule. Or at least its dramatic component – in the sense of some argument or complication going on between voices in the poem – is small: it has an "I" whom we can trust, who is telling us a small story of discovery that has a beginning, middle, and end. It *settles*, admittedly in a slightly melancholy way, rather than unsettles; in this it is distinguished from the earlier sequence in *A Witness Tree*.

Those ten poems are neatly divided in half, five of them with an "I" speaking out of a dramatic situation whose level of realization varies, though in none of them is it as strongly located in place and time as is "The Quest of the Purple-Fringed," or as it was in earlier Frost poems like "The Tuft of Flowers," "The Wood-Pile," or "Two Look at Two." Perhaps the most conventionally "dramatic" of the first-person poems from "One or Two" is "Come In," with its familiar prop of man confronting dark woods ("Into My Own" began all that) and debating whether or not to enter them. What is most familiar about "Come In" is the play of tone by which the speaker declines the thrushes' blandishment, first by making much of their song, although in a way that hedges slightly – "Almost like a call to come in/ To the dark and lament" – then more emphatically declining the invitation in two stages: "But no, I was out for stars:/ I would not come in." followed by the admission that it was not an invitation at all – "I mean not even if asked,/ And I hadn't been." Recently Joseph Brodsky made much of the poem, in a line-by-line exposition, but ended up with translating, disappointingly, the title into a meaning – "I am afraid, the expression 'come in' means die" – rather than pointing out how Frost the trickster once more, in the language of "One Step Backward Taken," "saved myself from going."[17] For all its cleverness, I find "Come In" perhaps the least interesting poem in the sequence.

Of course thinking sequentially about the ten poems is not an inevitable or even necessary way of proceeding: they could be read individually, without regard to juxtapositions; or they could be put with poems from earlier volumes by way of establishing thematic and other relationships. But if we care at all about Frost's literary career with its order of published volumes, and if we take seriously the order in which, within the individual volume, Frost arranged the poems, then there appears to be visible a grouping of these ten poems by way of how they approach subject and reader. The first two, "The Silken Tent" and "All Revelation," are impersonal pronouncements that propose universal or mythic, revelatory disclosures. They are followed by five more personal disclosures, especially as concerned with the lyric speaker's feelings about present and past, time, change, and death told in the first person. (Even though one of these five, "Carpe Diem," is not in the first person, it belongs with the others in tone and theme.) Then follow "The Most of It," "Never Again Would Birds' Song . . .", and "The Subverted Flower": large, parable-like declarations that refuse to declare themselves quickly or unambiguously.

As for how these poems have been valued, relative to one another, the nod goes clearly to the third-person ones, which tend to get anthologized.

(Interestingly enough Randall Jarrell, in "To the Laodiceans," where he made lists of Frost's best and second-best poems, included only "The Most of It" and "I Could Give All to Time.") Richard Poirier has made the strongest case for the closing three poems, claiming that they suggest, as did Frost's earliest ones in *A Boy's Will*, "That consciousness is determined in part by the way one 'reads' the response of nature to human sound."[18] He also claims that by placing "Never Again . . ." between "The Most of It" and "The Subverted Flower," "Frost once again revealed his deep commitment to married love as a precondition for discovering human 'embodiments' in nature." Poirier is eloquent about both "The Most of It" and "Never Again . . ." and his phrase, in referring to "The Most of It," about that poem's "large but wavering mythological context"[19] suggests to me that, especially with reference to the second adjective, the formulation may be of use in thinking about not just "The Most of It" but the whole *Witness Tree* sequence.

"Wavering" – restless, playing or moving to and fro, swaying, hesitating, faltering, unsettled in opinion – these filial relatives in the wavering family have often been invoked by readers of Frost who are responding to the moral and human doubleness that informs his situations and concerns. The principle of wavering informs the last poem from Frost's earlier volume *Mountain Interval* (1916), "The Sound of the Trees." From the beginning of his career, it was not only the sound of trees, but more centrally the sound of sense that the real poet cultivated and the good ear-reader attended to, having acquired a listening air. There is no diminishment of this commitment to sound in the *Witness Tree* poems; indeed, the more we reread them, the more familiar we become with their content, the more we marvel at the rhythmic life and variety of their sentence sounds. And the more they add up to an achieved "wavering," from one poem to the next and within individual poems. Which makes biographical accountings for them, such as Meyers' (how "Kay" inspired this one, how that one is "about" Frost and her) less and less to the point.

II

By way of demonstration, in the remainder of this chapter I shall make some remarks about the prosodic rhythms of some of these poems, neglecting – perhaps to the point of folly – their content, my purpose being no more or less than to bring out the strange originality, even for the always original Frost, of their aural inventiveness. In "The Silken Tent," we have an Elizabethan sonnet, consisting of a single sentence which, like the tent's central cedar pole, is "loosely bound," at least to the extent where Judith

Oster, at the outset of her rigorously exhaustive grammatical analysis of it, admits that "the sentence comes perilously close to going out of control with the multiplication of subordinate clauses." Attempts to paraphrase "The Silken Tent," by way of unpacking its content, inevitably feel lame and uninteresting and tend to sound like this one: "The ties to 'everything . . . the compass round' reveals her awareness and concern for all people and the whole scope of experience." Let us call it rather a poem that is extremely beautiful as you perform it, say it aloud, but from which there is nothing to take away, at least insofar as thoughts about either a woman or a tent. In fact you could even say there is no woman in the poem, and no tent either. For "The Silken Tent" is fictive music played out through a grammar complicated and elusive enough so as to provide no easy and direct way out to the world, to action, to human beings, to a woman – whether she is named Elinor Frost or Kathleen Morrison. In his preface to *King Jasper* (*CPPP*, 741) Frost once considered the question of how or whether a poem leads to action. "Surely art can be considered good only as it prompts to action," says a young man to Frost. "How soon, I asked him. But there is danger of undue levity in teasing the young."

"All Revelation," which Reuben Brower writes well about in his still useful book, *The Poetry of Robert Frost*, is an especially challenging poem, certainly one I have never spoken about with confidence. In calling it Frost's "most symbolist poem" Brower seems to acknowledge the air of equivocation that characterizes it.[20] Brower calls the final line – "All revelation has been ours" – an achieved answer "to the doubts and wonders expressed in the exclamation that concludes the second stanza – "Strange apparition of the mind!" But though he thinks "All Revelation" is "Frost's most vigorous answer to the larger question of the relation between mind and reality," he immediately qualifies the claim by finding an "irony" that remains in asserting so limited a revelation."[21] And he warns us not to suppose Frost "has reached a firm conclusion or final position in this or any poem."[22]

This lack of a firm position is of course what so annoyed Yvor Winters about Frost's poetry generally, and though few of us are likely to accept his strictures on Frost's limitations as a poet, Winters identified something crucial to the poetry. It may be indicated by some words from a letter Frost wrote to Leonidas Payne in answer to Payne's question whether, in "Mending Wall," Frost's intention was fulfilled "with the characters portrayed and the atmosphere of the place." "I should be sorry," wrote Frost in reply, "if a single one of my poems stopped with either of those things – stopped anywhere in fact. My poems . . . are all set to trip the reader head foremost into the boundless." (*SL*, 344) He went on in the same letter to speak of his "innate mischievousness," a mischievousness that we find in programmatically playful poems like "Mending Wall" or "Departmental," but just as much in the lyric soundings of affirmation – the large declarations, in *A Witness Tree*, about "countless silken ties of love and thought," or of how "All revelation has been ours." A reader who does not "trip" over them, not just on a first or second reading, but permanently, will not be propelled into the boundless, a place where it is not reassuring to be but which is our true and real destination in Frost's best work.

In "I Could Give All to Time," fifth poem in the sequence, a propelling into something like the boundless occurs in the third stanza, two earlier ones having described the inexorable levelling action of "Time" on all things. Now the man, just because he knows all about Time's effects, is impelled to resist them:

> I could give all to Time except – except
> What I myself have held. But why declare
> The things forbidden that while the Customs slept
> I have crossed to Safety with? For I am There,
> And what I would not part with I have kept.

In that final stanza we see those capital letters, hear that ringing human affirmation (which Randall Jarrell compared to the affirmation at the close of Yeats' "Dialogue of Self and Soul"[23]) but get tripped up when we attempt to specify or analyze exactly what has been declared. We are left instead with the mischievous, double-edged Customs metaphor and the unparticularized "what" of the final line – "And what I would not part with I have kept."

In that same essay of Jarrell's on Frost, he speaks of how some Frost poems might be considered "slight," yet says that the sigh we give after we read them is not a slight one.[24] In these terms, perhaps the two slightest poems in the sequence are "Happiness Makes Up in Height For What It Lacks in Length," and "Carpe Diem." Both are slim poems to the eye, twenty-four and twenty-six lines long respectively, written in trimeter – "Happiness" in trimeter couplets; "Carpe Diem" unrhymed. Especially as we encounter it in couplets, trimeter seems unpromising as a vehicle for lyric depth, although Yeats uses it (without couplets) in some of his finest verse – in "Easter, 1916," "The Tower," section III, and "In Memory of Eva Gore-Booth and Con Markiewicz." Frost had exploited trimeter with success in "The Sound of the Trees," and in "Happiness Makes Up in Height . . ." he also manages to portray a meditative imagination at work, arriving at "wisdom" over the course of, through the figure of, the poem. ("It begins in delight and ends in wisdom. The figure is the same as for love," – from the essay, "The Figure a Poem Makes," *CPPP*, 776.) He achieves his effects, in "Happiness . . .", mainly by playing the sense units against the couplet rhyme and overriding the couplet's closure. It is an excellent meter for poems designed to "trip the reader" since it has in its feel, a "tripping" rhythm, reluctant (in Frost's words) to "stop anywhere":

> Oh, stormy stormy world,
> The days you were not swirled
> Around with mist and cloud,
> Or wrapped as in a shroud,
> And the sun's brilliant ball
> Was not in part or all
> Obscured from mortal view –
> Were days so very few
> I can but wonder whence
> I get the lasting sense
> Of so much warmth and light.

It is a poem of three sentences, the first completing itself with line eleven, the second with line seventeen, then sweeping on to end the third in line twenty-four. As with the way the couplets succeed one another, there is a sense of irregularity about the sentence units, and both these qualities help to create the illusion of a mind exploring the past, rather than owning an attitude toward it all made up in advance:

> I verily believe
> My fair impression may
> Be all from that one day
> No shadow crossed but ours
> As through its blazing flowers
> We went from house to wood
> For change of solitude.

No punctuation at the ends of lines; slightly off rhymes like ours/ flowers and wood/ solitude: it is an example of what Milton in the note he added to *Paradise Lost* called "the sense variously drawn out from one Verse into another." In Frost's words from "The Figure a Poem Makes," a "clarification of life" has been achieved, but just barely, and not one "such as sects and cults are founded on."

Similarly with "Carpe Diem," which Poirier treats sketchily and rather condescendingly as "inadequate to the mixed complications it proposes to sort out."[25] On the contrary, it seems to me a highly adequate way of thinking about time present and time past, and as with "Happiness . . ." its adequacy – call it rather its beauty – is intimately connected with the movement of its verse. Instead of rhyming couplets, each line has a feminine ending (stress on the penultimate syllable) that contributes to the irregularity and informality of rhythm. There is also a playful jamming-up of words that echo, sometimes duplicate, one another – both within and at the ends of lines – perhaps by way of suggesting the crowding, confusing present that defeats our imagination. The poem opens with a rather creaky personification, "Age," who takes it upon himself to instruct a pair of youthful lovers (though not to their faces) on how to seize the day. After Age does his number, Frost takes over the poem and instructs Age on the way things happen in real life, rather than in the commonplaces and conventions of literary wisdom. Simple enough, but it is made complicated and complexly satisfying by the way the language is worked:

> Age saw two quiet children
> Go loving by at twilight,
> He knew not whether homeward,
> Or outward from the village,
> Or (chimes were ringing) churchyard.
> He waited (they were strangers)
> Till they were out of hearing
> To bid them both be happy.
> "Be happy, happy, happy,
> And seize the day of pleasure."
> The age-long theme is Age's.

Three "happy"s succeeding one another in a line is almost enough in itself to demonstrate the fatuity of Age's advice, and immediately after he says his little piece Frost plays with Age's personified status by turning it back on him – "The age-long theme is Age's" – before delivering a seven-line, unpunctuated sentence that makes a tricky, quite unobvious sound of sense:

> 'Twas Age imposed on poems
> Their gather-roses burden
> To warn against the danger
> That overtaken lovers
> From being overflooded
> With happiness should have it
> And yet not know they have it.

The play with overtaken/ overflooded, the repetition at line ends of "have it," guarantees that Frost's sense will be sounder than Age's simple "Be happy, happy, happy." The play continues in the poem's final eight lines – another sentence – with "the present" concluding three of the lines and introducing something of an aural vertigo ("Too crowding, too confusing") from which we emerge only in the final line. There "present," now no longer "the present," becomes instead an adjective nested within the line and replaced at its end with the weighted verb "imagine." One thinks, by contrast, of the weighty, toneless annunciation of Eliot in the opening lines of "Burnt Norton" – "Time present and time past/ Are both perhaps present in time future,/ And time future contained in time past." Indeed a comparison between Frost and Eliot could well be conducted by juxtaposing "Carpe Diem" and the beginning of "Burnt Norton." Frost said of Eliot: "We are both poets and we both like to play. That's the similarity. The difference is this: I like to play euchre. He likes to play Eucharist."[26]

No wonder then that Frost critics often look up from the analytical task, clear their throats and admit how difficult it is to perform that task without heavy-handedness. Even so resourceful an interpreter as Poirier says at one point that some of Frost's poems are beyond us, not quite understandable. A recent essay on the poet by Jason Mauro speaks of how hard Frost makes us work, how the reader "must strain to keep things from splitting apart," and Mauro notes that Frost's genius "works at teasing out the duplicitous, complex nature of any utterance, any sentence, any word."[27] Judith Oster, before launching her commentary on "The Most of It," says "This is a poem that eludes any definite interpretation or response."[28] This elusiveness, which I believe to be part of the greatness of these *Witness Tree* poems, is there in "The Most of It" not despite but because of its forthright, declarative sequence of assertions, right down to "And that was all," – which says everything, and nothing in particular. It is there as well in "Never Again Would Birds' Song Be the Same," through the opposite of declarative forthrightness, in a sonnet that begins, cagily, "He would declare and could himself believe," then follows such conditionals with subtle qualifiers like "Admittedly," "Be that as may be," "Moreover," and "probably."

"As for "The Subverted Flower," final poem in the sequence, Frost liked to say – in his "devilish" way and while not reading the poem aloud – that it was about "frigidity in women." The poem may have originated from an incident involving him and Elinor, though Poirier suggests that it is more a nightmare, a symbolic dream-enactment of something terrible. Meyers says that it "obliquely describes their passionate sex life" but does not demonstrate how it does so "obliquely."[29] An important part of that obliqueness I take to attribute to its meter, which is again trimeter (not the four-stressed line Poirier hears), here rhymed in an irregular, off-balanced way that gives it the shimmering strangeness of fairy tale (I quote roughly the poem's second half):

> It was then her mother's call
> From inside the garden wall
> Made her steal a look of fear
> To see if he could hear

> And would pounce to end it all
> Before her mother came.
> She looked and saw the shame:
> A hand hung like a paw,
> An arm worked like a saw
> As if to be persuasive,
> An ingratiating laugh
> That cut the snout in half,
> An eye become evasive.

Brower, in his remarks on the poem, says that the girl's "discovery" of her lover's bestiality (if these are the right words) is rendered with some of D. H. Lawrence's hard purity.[30] Yet when he quotes to illustrate this, Brower omits the very lines that are to me supremely and relentlessly memorable:

> A girl could only see
> That a flower had marred a man,
> But what she could not see
> Was that the flower might be
> Other than base and fetid:
> That the flower had done but part,
> And what the flower began
> Her own too meager heart
> Had terribly completed.

In one of his best formulations, Frost has said that there should be more than disagreement and debate in a classroom: "Clash is all very well for coming lawyers, politicians and theologians. But I should think there must be a whole realm or plane above that – all sight and insight, perception, intuition, rapture . . . Get up there high enough and the differences that make controversy become only the two legs of a body."(SL, 324) I have written before about Frost's "elevated play" and these lines from "The Subverted Flower," for all the terror of their content, are a great instance of both elevation and play, in the face of the unspeakable. At such a moment, and in these poems from the section of A Witness Tree most clearly connected to Frost's life-experiences of love and death, he reaches the realm or plane where a reader, rather than explaining things biographically or otherwise, must prepare to be tripped head foremost into the boundless.

NOTES

1 William Pritchard, "Bearing Witness: 'The Wind and The Rain,'" in *Gone Into if Not Explained: Essays on Poems by Robert Frost*, ed. Greg Kuzma (Crete, Nebraska: The Best Cellar Press, 1976), pp. 129–34.

2 *Ibid.*, p. 187.

3 Donald G. Sheehy, "The Poet as Neurotic: The Official Biography of Robert Frost," *American Literature* (October 1986), pp. 393–409.

4 *Ibid.*, p. 394.

5 Jeffrey Meyers, *Robert Frost: A Biography* (Boston: Houghton, Mifflin, 1996), p. 246.

6 *Ibid.*, p. 246.

7 *Ibid.*

8 *Ibid.*

9 Meyers, p. 264.

10 *Ibid.*

11 *Ibid.*

12 Meyers, p. 265.

13 *Ibid.*

14 Meyers, p. 266.

15 *Ibid.*

16 Frank Lentricchia, *Robert Frost: Modern Poetics and the Landscapes of Self* (Durham: Duke University Press, 1975), p. 86.

17 Joseph Brodsky, "On Grief and Reason," *Homage to Robert Frost* (New York: Farrar, Straus & Giroux, 1996), p. 243.

18 Richard Poirier, *Robert Frost: The Work of Knowing* (New York: Oxford University Press, 1984), p. 169.

19 *Ibid.*, p. 165.

20 Reuben Brower, *The Poetry of Robert Frost: Constellations of Intention* (New York: Oxford University Press, 1963), p. 139.

21 *Ibid.*, p. 144.

22 *Ibid.*, p. 145.

23 Randall Jarrell, "To the Laodiceans," *No Other Book: Selected Essays*, ed. Brad Leithauser (New York: HarperCollins, 1999), p. 32.

24 *Ibid.*, pp. 37–38.

25 Poirier, *Frost: The Work of Knowing*, p. 204.

26 Quoted in *The Letters of Robert Frost to Louis Untermeyer* (New York: Holt, Rinehart, and Winston, 1963), p. 321.

27 Jason Mauro, "Frost and James: The Gaps I Mean," *South Carolina Review*, 28, 2 (1998), p. 112.

28 Judith Oster, *Toward Robert Frost: The Reader and the Poet* (Athens: University of Georgia Press, 1991), p. 84.

29 Meyers, *Frost: A Biography*, p. 161.

30 Brower, *The Poetry of Robert Frost*, pp. 120–21.

3

ROBERT FAGGEN

Frost and the Questions of Pastoral

To call Robert Frost a pastoral poet is at once to say too much and too little. Frost himself said that "he first heard the speaking voice in poetry in Virgil's *Eclogues*."[1] Virgil's ten *Eclogues* are models of pastoral poetry, dialogues or dramatic monologues of shepherds dwelling in a mythic Arcadia, a land of innocence and beauty. Frost's relation to Virgilian pastoral, as Reuben Brower has observed, "is so deep and pervasive that it is nearly impossible to describe."[2] Ezra Pound shrewdly called Frost's poems "modern georgics."[3] He was referring to Virgil's four great didactic poems about farm work that form the basis of a tradition that stands in contrast to pastoral; it is a type of didactic poetry extolling hard labor and a scientific approach to nature. Pastoral itself is a rich and complex tradition. Not only a genre or set of conventions, it is often a mode by which authors from Theocritus and Virgil to Dante and Milton as well as Wordsworth and Thoreau have explored questions of human equality, man's place in nature, and the nature of faith. If by pastoral one means a mode that emphasizes the beauty and simplicity of country life, then Frost's poetry seems decidedly dissonant. But Frost's dissonant renewal of this ancient tradition allowed him to explore complex, modern attitudes about democracy, science, and faith.

Pastoral has an important place in American ideology.[4] The Puritan pursuit of renewal through rebellion against ecclesiastical corruption often invokes the pastoral longing of perfection through simplicity. Thomas Jefferson's praise of the way of agrarianism echoes Greek ideals even if his prophetic fear of the destruction of agrarian life sounded prophetic Hebraic chords. Shortly after his *Collected Poems* were published in 1930 (for which he received his second Pulitzer Prize), Frost affirmed the relationship of his poetry to a fundamental pastoral idea, the praise of rustic over urban life:

> Poetry is more often of the country than the city . . . Poetry is very, very rural
> – rustic. It might be taken as a symbol of man, taking its rise from individual-
> ity and seclusion – written first for the person that writes and then going out
> into its social appeal and use. Just so the race lives best to itself – first to itself,

storing strength in the more individual life of the country, of the farm – then
going to market and socializing in the industrial city.   (I, 76)

Frost's analogy between the ideal development of poetry, the individual, and
race based on agrarian beginnings has strong grounding in the development
of ancient Greek democracy.

In his landmark study *The Other Greeks: The Family Farm and the
Agrarian Roots of Western Civilization*, Victor Hanson has shown that "we
owe our cultural legacy to Greeks outside the walls of the polis, forgotten
men and women of the countryside, the 'other Greeks.'" Hanson's particular emphasis is on the success of having small, individual farms rather than
collectives, and this form of agrarianism also leads to developments in technology. "The buildings and circuit walls of the city-state were a testament to
the accumulated bounty of generations, its democratic membership a formal
acknowledgment of the unique triad of small landowner, infantry soldier,
and voting citizen . . . The real Greeks are the farmers and infantrymen, the
men and women outside the city, who were the insiders of Greek life and
culture."[5] Jefferson's romantic praise of agrarian ideals recalls ancient
Greece. But neither the agrarian world of ancient Greece nor of Frost's New
England is a democratic utopia; it is a place of labor, struggle, and warfare.
Its emphasis on the urgencies and uncertainties of the moment militate
against too much contemplation or theorizing. Frost's agrarians appear at a
time of great threat of extinction from highly developed technology and
industry as well as social upheaval from immigration. But these threats yield
in Frost neither nostalgia nor messianic longing. Rather, Frost's rural world
becomes a metaphor for the kind of forces and challenges that continually
test the limits and balance of human freedom and equality.

Pastoral has been recognized as a mode that encompasses many genres
including poetry. Its mythic contents have been shown to include the search
for a peaceful and beautiful landscape (a *locus amoenus*), the dialogue and
singing of shepherds, and the praise of contemplation over work (*otium* over
labor). If we adhere to strict definitions then Frost definitely appears out of
place: his landscapes are often barren, his shepherds seem to be rather tough
farmers, and contemplation always appears threatened and mingled with
hard labor. Is Frost, then, satirizing the pastoral? Not if we recognize that
pastoral literature has been filled with irony from the beginning and that its
ideals of innocence and perfection are often seen through the lens of experience and failure. Frost plays on these old tensions and adds to them in ways
that encompass more modern concerns about work, play, class, and gender
in the context of a modern democracy. His poetry depicts retreat, rather, than
escape from universal chaos as a way to reflect upon and strengthen the self.

The poems often poke fun at the pretenses of urbanity and sophistication. But they also reveal the brutal and sinister qualities of country folk, deflating romantic fantasies of natural innocence and virtue. Frost's characters embody more "ragged individualism," as he liked to call it, than rugged individualism; they dramatize "the paradox that you become more social in order that you may become more of an individual."(I, 78) The pastoral in Frost represents the power of the social to save the individual from the excesses of isolation as well as the power of the individual will to resist what he called "alien entanglements." As he wrote in "The Constant Symbol":

> We must be preserved from becoming egregious. The beauty of socialism is that it will end the individuality that is always crying out mind your own business . . . The ultimate commitment is giving in to it that an outsider may see what we were up to sooner and better than ourselves . . . Every poem is an epitome of the great predicament; a figure of the will braving alien entanglements.
>
> (CPPP, 787)

Retreat is a crucial topos of the pastoral mythology. Renato Poggioli offered an engaging definition of pastoral as "a double longing after innocence and happiness, to be recovered not through regeneration but merely through retreat."[6] The speaker of Frost's "One Step Backward Taken" feels his "standpoint shaken/ In the universal crisis," and asserts that "with one step backward taken/ I saved myself from going." The figure of retreat or, perhaps, "backward motion to the source," primordial and original, can be found throughout Frost's work. Frost insisted, however, that retreat should not be considered escape but "pursuit" and that life was "a pursuit of a pursuit of a pursuit of a pursuit."[7] But the seeker in Frost becomes disillusioned by both fear and the interminable chain of longing; no landscape provides innocence or happiness except, perhaps, "a momentary stay against confusion," as we find in the figure of the cord of maple decaying in a swamp in "The Wood-Pile." Two poems that frame his complete *oeuvre*, "The Pasture" and "In Winter," reveal the importance and complexity of retreat in his work. Frost used "The Pasture" as the prefatory poem for his *Complete Poems* (1949) and he announces his retreat to the pastoral source: "I'm going out to clean the pasture spring;/ I'll only stop to rake the leaves away/ (And wait to watch the water clear I may)/ I sha'nt be long – You come too." Innocent and inviting, it seduces and lures the unsuspecting reader into a troubling journey, a retreat in search of clarity but which is haunted by the fragility and brevity of experience. Frost made the parenthetical phrase of "The Pasture" into the title and epigraph of his final book *In the Clearing*. The last poem in that volume provides a haunting coda to a whole mythology of pastoral retreat:

In winter in the woods alone
Against the trees I go.
I mark a maple for my own
And lay the maple low.

At four o'clock I shoulder axe
And in the afterglow
I link a line of shadowy tracks
Across the tinted snow.

I see for Nature no defeat
In one tree's overthrow
Or for myself in my retreat
For yet another blow.

In contrast to the shepherd of "The Pasture" who tells us that he is "out to fetch the little calf," the speaker of this poem retreats "in the woods alone," purposive, possessive, and violent: "I mark a maple for my own/ And lay the maple low." Frost complicates the mythology of retreat in the penultimate line. Does the speaker "retreat" from the woods or to the woods? And is "another blow" what he will give to Nature (embodied in a tree) or what Nature (and life) gives to him, driving him back to the woods. Retreat here describes not a return to innocence or happiness but an endless and circular process of giving and receiving "blows."

Almost everything in Frost is figurative and metaphoric but in the suggestive ways of parable or proverb. The act of chopping wood appears ordinary enough until Frost invests it with mythic suggestion in "The Wood-Pile," "The Ax-Helve," and "Two Tramps in Mud Time." In those poems a narrator contemplates woodchopping as an activity of liberating pleasure and power, an artful violence spent for its own sake. Frost reanimates the ancient pastoral tension between work and play, *labor* and *otium*, attempting to bring the power and necessity of the former to a seemingly effete process of contemplation. In "Two Tramps in Mud Time," the speaker, too often simply conflated with Frost, claims pure love as the motive for "the blows that a life of self-control/ Spares to strike for the common good" that he "spent on the unimportant wood." The longing for heroic and possibly violent expenditure is withheld from a "common good" in which he neither cares nor believes. His attitude towards the "tramps," whom he depicts as Yahoos in search of mere work for hire, is one of condescension. They represent the social and basic need; his motives, putatively, are less obvious and higher. He knows them but they do not know him: "except as a fellow handled an ax/ they had no way of knowing a fool." Here, as in so many poems by Frost, the power of secrecy and the covert may be more obvious and worthy of skepticism than supposed. Are our narrator's hopes foolish or subversive? He proclaims that his "object in living is to unite / My avocation and my vocation," "where love and need are one/ And the work is play for mortal stakes." This pastoral hope is set, however, in "mud time," not a *locus aemoenus* but a space-time of change and deception. Even the narrator warns us of "the lurking frost in the earth beneath/ That will steal forth after the sun is set/ And show on the water its crystal teeth."

"Two Tramps in Mud Time" as well as "The Ax-Helve" and "Mending Wall" reanimate a kind of poem found in Virgil's ten *Eclogues*, known as amoebaean dialogue, a type of competition between shepherds (the even-numbered eclogues tend to follow this form). Frost was conscious of Virgilian models when he assembled *North of Boston*, his second book and the one that defined his place among modern poets. He claimed it "was not written as a book nor towards a book. It was written as scattered poems in a form suggested by the eclogues of Virgil . . . Some of them are a little nearer one act plays than eclogues but they seem to have something in common that I don't want to seek a better name for. I like its being locative."[8] The "something" in Frost may have much to do with self-definition in terms of origin, the locative voices of his characters. Those voices are numerous and conflict; the attempt to find a monolithic Frostian voice misses the subtlety of the many. It is possible to see Frost masquerading behind many of his characters, particularly women, as a way of playing out dramatically the contradictions of his own moods and thoughts as well as racial and sexual conflicts among the speakers. Doubleness and irony pervade these masterful dramatic poems. William Empson's politically astute definition of pastoral as the "process of putting the complex into the simple" helps in considering Frost's characters. Empson explained that "the essential trick of the old pastoral, which was felt to imply a beautiful relationship between rich and poor, was to make simple people express strong feelings (felt as the most universal subject, something fundamentally true about everybody) in learned and fashionable language."[9] If he creates a "beautiful relationship" among rich and poor, educated and uneducated, high and low, it is by the ironic turn on Jefferson that "all men are created equally funny." By funny Frost meant innocent, playful, and sinister. The trick of Frost was to subvert our sense of hierarchy by making "simple people" as complex, cruel, and wise as their putatively regarded sophisticated interlocutors.

Frost's own relationship to his readers and to his characters may also reflect pastoral conflicts. Though he often seemed an off handed farmer-philosopher, it was a posture that was calculated to fool his readers. He wrote that "It takes all sorts of in and outdoor schooling/ To get adapted to my kind of fooling." Frost's poetry while it seems to possess a democratically appealing simplicity and clarity also embodies extraordinary sophistication and learning. A superb student of classical literature in the original Greek and Roman, Frost spent two years at Harvard studying philosophy, literature, and geology. He was a tireless student of botany and astronomy. It should not be surprising that Frost creates meaning in a dialogue with his predecessors – Virgil, Shakespeare, Milton, Donne, Marvell, and Wordsworth – as well as by his insights into his neighbors in rural New Hampshire and Vermont, in and outdoor schooling. As a chicken farmer, his neighbors were no doubt suspicious of a man whose primary interest was poetry.

The depiction of "country things" in Frost often involves both experience and observation as well as literary and scientific feats of association. Pastoral and georgic traditions merge in Frost's imagination. Clear definition of these two genres is difficult but still useful. The term "eclogue" denotes dialogue between and among shepherds. It often is associated with a retreat into a natural landscape into colloquy free from labor and strife. "Georgic," taking its name for the Greek word for farmer, connotes a tradition that begins in Greece with Hesiod's *Works and Days* and continues into Rome in Lucretius' *De Rerum Natura* and Virgil's *Georgics*. The emphasis in those works is on labor, knowledge (*scientia*), and struggle. He combines the colloquy of pastoral with the didactic and the scientific that characterizes georgic. To be sure, works in both modes have rarely proved to be pure. The blend of pastoral and georgic in Milton's poetry is crucial to any understanding of Frost. Milton's early masque *Comus* was a favorite of Frost's, and he called it "the greatest poem of Puritanism."[10] The tension between a sensuous existence and the demands of discipline, labor, and government find expression in that masque and throughout Milton's poetry. In *Paradise Lost*, "perfect" Eden is a place that demands labor and care; the future is born out through the dialogues of Adam, Eve, Satan, and Raphael. It is also important to recall the figure of Comus himself, a sophisticated rhetorician and reveller who masquerades as a "harmless villager." This kind of pastoral trickster appears frequently in Frost–Lafe of "A Hundred Collars," Baptiste of "The Ax-Helve" (a poem also inspired by Thoreau's French-Canadian woodchopper of *Walden*) or the farmer of "The Code," all playful and sensuous but also threatening and subverting the unsuspecting around them. In "Snow," we are confronted with a baffling minister named "Meserve," whose maddening rhetoric requires hard work to find "the snow white beneath the frost." In Frost's world the fool enters to confound hierarchies of ethics and values, the American fantasy with both agrarian life and with nature and wilderness, and to help us comprehend the range of suffering in all ranges of life. Humor is often a mask for seriousness, as he once said, "I am never so serious as when I am fooling."[11]

If it has been difficult for some to see Frost in the rather serious context of Virgil, Marvell, and Milton, it has much to do with Frost's subtlety and his extremely sly humor. Frost often appears to many the uncritical advocate of country and nature, as did Thoreau, another American pastoralist whom Frost greatly admired. But Thoreau, of course, can be relentlessly ironic. While appearing to praise the reality of nature (placing him in the tradition of the georgics and of Lucretius), he can wink at us with the suggestion that even "reality" is a construct: "Shams and delusions are esteemed for soundest truths, while reality is fabulous."[12] In the little poem "Dust of Snow" we have Frost at his trickiest:

> The way a crow
> Shook down on me
> The dust of snow
> From a hemlock tree
>
> Has given my heart
> A change of mood
> And saved some part
> Of a day I had rued.

The sudden appearance of the black crow shaking the white snow suggests a saving revelation. But other aspects of the poem remain troubling, especially the associations we have with crow, dust, and hemlock but also the mythic resonance of Satan as the cormorant alighting on a tree in *Paradise Lost*: "Thence up he flew, and on the Tree of Life,/ The middle tree and highest there that grew,/ Sat like a cormorant; yet not true life/ Thereby regained, but sat devising death/ To them who lived; nor on the virtue thought/ Of that life-giving plant, but only used/ For prospect, what well used had been the pledge/ Of immortality . . ." (Book IV, lines 194–201). Crows eat hemlock seeds that burst forth in winter; hemlock trees prevent others from growing in their shade. We begin to wonder what of a day the speaker had "rued" is really saved? Is non-human nature more or less cruel or kind than our perceptions of it? What kind of innocence can ever be recollected after experience? Frost often lures readers to read nature as an edifying scripture but leaves us only with suggestions of uncertainty.

The philosophical stance of pastoral poetry has often been associated with Epicurus and Epicureanism, a life of unreflective and simple pleasure free from torment and fear. This Epicurean philosophy informs Lucretius' great poem *De Rerum Natura*, but here the sense of pleasure becomes complicated by science, a science that abolishes fear of the supernatural even while it leads to a sense of the demands and limitations of the natural, material world. The praise of the pleasures of the country life and country deities combined with the need for knowledge of how the world works so that one can live in it informs Virgil's second *Georgic*:

> How lucky, if they know their happiness,
> Are farmers, more than lucky, they for whom,
> Far from the clash of arms, the earth herself,
> Most fair in dealing, freely lavishes
> An easy livelihood . . .
>   For my own part my chiefest prayer would be:
> May the sweet Muses, whose acolyte I am,
> Smitten with love, accept my service,
> Teach me to know the paths of the stars in heaven,
> The eclipses of the sun and the moon's travails,
> The cause of earthquakes, what it is that forces
> Deep seas to swell and burst their barriers
> And then sink back again, why winter suns
> Hasten so fast to plunge themselves in the ocean
> Or what it is that slows the lingering nights . . .
> Blessed is he whose mind had power to probe
> The causes of things and trample underfoot
> All terrors and inexorable fate
> And the clamour of devouring Acheron;
> But happy too is he who knows the gods
> Of the countryside, knows Pan and old Silvanus
> And the sister nymphs.[13]

The tension here between knowing the causes of things and believing in the Gods of the countryside finds its own particular form in Frost's early pastorals, particularly of *A Boy's Will*. In the masterful "Mowing," there is an unresolved tension between labor and contemplation, reality and dream. Haying, like woodchopping, is a form of pastoring, of tending to meditation as well as labor. Critics have also seen it as a figure of writing, of the creation of sound and for the poem as a resolution of the contradictions of labor and leisure. The speaker alludes to the traditional pastoral trope of "the noonday hour," but here it appears more ominously as an inescapable "heat of the sun," an environmental force that mutes singing so that the scythe can but "whisper" instead of "speak." The scythe cultivates even though its destructive motion suggests time and death, as it did in Spenser's "Mutability Cantos" and in Shakespeare's sonnets XII, LX, and CXXIII. Whatever meaning can be derived from the sound of his solitary labor, it "is no easy gold at the hand of fay or elf." Frost evokes, as he often will, the hard demythologizing of Lucretius who poked fun at ideals of Arcadian leisure:

I have observed places tossing back six or seven utterances when you have launched a single one: with their tendency to rebound, the words were reverberated and reiterated from hill to hill. According to local legend, these places are haunted by goat-footed Satyrs and Nymphs. Tales are told of Fauns, whose noisy revels and merry pranks shatter the mute hush of night for miles around; of twanging lyre-strings and plaintive melodies poured out by flutes at the touch of the players' finger; of music far-heard by the country-folk when Pan, tossing the pine-branches that wreathe his brutish head, runs his arched lips again and again along the wind-mouthed reeds, so that the pipe's wildwood rhapsody flows unbroken. Many such fantasies and fairy tales are related by rustics. Perhaps, in boasting of these marvels, they hope to dispel the notion that they live in backwoods abandoned even by the gods. Perhaps they have some other motive, since mankind everywhere has greedy ears for such romancing.[14]

"The fact is the sweetest dream that labor knows," the complex, dark saying of the poem, suggests Lucretian limitations for an ear eager for "greedy romancing." Pan appears to have abandoned Frost's rural landscape, dramatized in "Pan with Us," another lyric in *A Boy's Will*. The old God's pipes "have little power to stir" than "the merest aimless breath of air." The "new terms of worth" may include both science and modern Christianity in its banishing of some of the pagan mysticism. The new Pan, half animal, half man, perhaps animalizes the human in a way disturbing to the magical powers of song. A companion poem, "The Demiurge's Laugh," finds the speaker haunted by a demonization of the Bacchic figure of Silenus. Seeking the divine in nature is driven by and perhaps ends only in self-mockery, expressed darkly when the speaker says "and well I knew what the demon meant." Humiliated and in some respects "fallen," he states "thereafter I sat me under a tree," perhaps in a moment of contemplation. This demiurge drives the world including the speaker's demonic pursuit of a phantom.

The love of nature and of beauty is everywhere threatened in Frost by the demands of environment and economics. "Rose Pogonias" from *A Boy's Will* gives praise to this colorful but rare and delicate bog orchid. The speaker and his companion cease from their labors to pick the orchids, "thus we bowed us in the burning,/ As the sun's right worship is," an interesting addition to the pastoral tradition of rest from labor and indulgence in contemplation at the noonday hour. This poem echoes and reverses Marvell's "The Mower Against Gardens," in which the mower seems to attack the isolated and artificial garden which man "first enclosed within the gardens square/ A dead and standing pool of air,/ And a more luscious earth for them did knead,/ Which stupefied them while it fed./ The pink grew then as double as his mind;/ The nutriment did change the kind./ With strange perfumes he did the roses taint,/ And flowers themselves were taught to paint." Marvell's tulip breeding gives way to Frost's natural bog:

> A saturated meadow,
>   Sun-shaped and jewel small,
> A circle scarcely wider
>   Than the trees around were tall;
> Where winds were quite excluded,
>   And the air was stifling sweet
> With the breath of many flowers, –
>   A temple of the heat.

Here nature creates these rare objects of beauty; their presence reflects a larger, encompassing nature that includes human labor and technology. In both Marvell and in Frost, the care for the flowers and the garden will mean "the sweet fields lie forgot." In "Mowing," the speaker appears to take orchids as beautiful aspects of annihilation's waste as well as the weeds of farming. Their "simple prayer" is that "none should mow the grass there/ While so confused with flowers." Is this only a prayer that the flowers be preserved? Is it only the grass that is "confused" with flowers or are humans "confused", perilously intoxicated, with flowers at a time when other tasks are at stake? And do we not imaginatively "confuse" ourselves with these unique specimens of beauty? *Labor* and *otium* are combined in this "temple of the heat," "the general mowing," that includes cultivation and death as well as the strong suggestion of the flowering of sexuality in this "saturated meadow." Frost's love of flowers and "botanizing" places this and other poems including "The Self-Seeker" in the context of the late-Victorian culture's orchid fetish. Orchids in the nineteenth century became an object of obsession not only for amateur collectors and professional breeders but also scientists, particularly Darwin. Darwin's study of orchids, *The Various Contrivances by which Orchids are Fertilized*, reads as parody of arguments about the relations of God's design and beauty, focusing instead on orchids as machines with wonderfully fluid apparatus for reproduction and survival.

The tension between the pursuit of pure beauty and the demands of the ordinary rituals of life finds powerful expression in "A Prayer in Spring," in which the speaker hopes not to think too much about the "uncertain harvest" but hopes to "keep us here/ All simply here in the springing of the year." Love here is the procreative love associated with Venus and not the wild eroticism of Bacchus. It avoids the imprisonment of passion but insists on an eros that fosters continued blossoming. "Too Anxious for Rivers," a later poem, makes reference to the legendary torment of Lucretius, the poet who professed liberation from passion, unable to cope with lust because of the torment caused by a potion given to him by his wife Lucilia. In Tennyson's "Lucretius," the Roman poet dreams of a "storm in the night! for thrice I heard the rain/ Rushing; and once the flash of a thunderbolt–/ Methought I never saw so fierce a fork – / Struck out the streaming mountain-side, and showed/ A riotous confluence of watercourses/ Blanching and billowing in a hollow of it,/ Where all but yester-eve was dusty-dry." An orderly universe becomes one of chaos, atom, and void. Frost echoes this torment in the destructive and apocalyptic images that begin his poem but with far more ironic detachment. Frost's poem explores the hell of a desire that knows no satisfaction and seeks only self-annihilation. He alludes to Lucretius' praise of Epicurus, a hero who "longed to smash the constraining locks of nature's doors. The vital vigour of his mind prevailed. He ventured far out beyond the flaming ramparts of the world and voyaged in mind throughout infinity."[15] Frost believed it unnecessary to venture so far out in the world to learn the "essay of love" and the freedom from fear that leads to the "momentary stay against confusion" that makes possible the keeping of home and life. But home in Frost is more often than not a place of fear or of battle than of comfort. If, in "Desert Places," the speaker heroically rebukes those who invoke the interstellar gloom against humanity – "They cannot scare me with their spaces between stars where no human races" – his conclusion undermines expectations of comfort with a terrifyingly bravado: "I have it in me so much nearer home/ To scare myself with my own desert places." Frost's individualist can take pride only in the freedom and equality of his own inner and outer hell.

The barren and threatening landscape of "Desert Places" is a mirror of the self. Unlike Emerson, Frost does not take nature as merely the externalization of the soul. Both human and non-human nature spring from the same source, and we are deeply attracted to our common origins. Our attraction to nature is an inevitable part of our desire to find ourselves free and godlike without the oversight of religious or moral hierarchy. But what we find through "downward comparisons" ("The White-Tailed Hornet," *CPPP*, 253) leaves us questioning our motives and emotions as little more than superfluity in a vast, indifferent world.

The very moment of delight and recognition in "downward comparisons" with the natural world initiates the possibility of imminent dissolution. Though less stark than "Desert Places," "Spring Pools" creates a lovely spring scene only to undermine it with the threat of mutability and extinction. The pools are metaphors of our reflective consciousness, and the speaker soon recognizes his own limitations as he contemplates the pools. Here, as in "For Once, Then, Something," Frost evokes the premonition of danger and metamorphosis of paradisiacal perfection that visited narcissistic

Eve as she became too fascinated by her own reflection in Book IV of Milton's *Paradise Lost*. The interpenetration of organic and inorganic worlds, of spirituality and materiality, is represented in the chiastic phrase "[t]hese flowery waters and these watery flowers." The speaker's threat to the trees to "think twice" before they drink up the waters makes us think twice about our place in nature: we participate in its competition and battle even as we wish to arrest its transient beauty. But consciousness, too, owes its embodiment to "snow that melted only yesterday," as the last line mutes with acceptance of change the preceding feeling of discontent and loss.

Our emotions of loss and "dwelling on what has been" are rebuked, for example, by the phoebes that take over and keep a burned-down barn in "The Need of Being Versed in Country Things": "You had to be versed in country things/ Not to believe the phoebes wept." In the end, "country things," a wry allusion to *Hamlet's* "country matters," include the birds' indifference to our grief and our longing for home, a contradiction in which we must become, oddly, "versed." "The Most of It" leaves man's cry for response answered only by a mysterious "embodiment," "[a]s a great buck," as we are reminded of the inhuman theophany from the whirlwind as God rebuked Job.

"The Oven Bird" remains one of the greatest poems on the tension between the human and natural world, a tension that has long been part of pastoral poetry. If one regards pastoral as an embodiment of creatures on an equal plane with humans in nature, Frost's apparent anthropomorphism in the poem greatly complicates the tradition. The reader is lured by the speaker to the oven bird, "a singer everyone has heard." But this singer, we learn, "knows in singing not to sing," and what he "says," particularly in the sestet, remains disturbing:

> And comes that other fall we name the fall,
> He says the highway dust is over all,
> He would cease and be as other birds
> But that he knows in singing not to sing.
> The question that he frames in all but words
> Is what to make of a diminished thing.

The optimism into which we were lured in the octave, the sound "that makes the solid tree trunks sound again," gives way to a tentative skepticism. The bird "knows" and "The question that he frames in all but words" reveals a consciousness which may be different in degree but not in kind from the human. That consciousness and voice, "all but words," may also suggest that the human is at best a minor addition to the vast non-human world. What he knows should be the sadness left unsaid, not unlike the whisper of the scythe in "Mowing." The fact that oven birds build their nests on the ground, exiled from heights in the trees, and feel "the highway dust is over all," reflects a lament over the way progress moves despite the consequences to individuals, the instability of any moment of perfection giving way to inevitable change. The close and fragile relation between "home" and "nature" is underscored here and throughout Frost's work – from "The Death of the Hired Man" and "Home Burial," to "The Black Cottage" and "The Generations of Men." In the final phrase, the question, "what to make," can be taken as "how to interpret" or "with what to do," in such a situation, the elusive "diminished thing?" This last phrase has the elegiac sense of belatedness without the grandeur of "the Fall." Like Pan in "Pan with Us," we are left with an uncertain sense of the worth of making, from the Greek word *poesis*, anything much less music or poetry. The oven bird, a North American warbler, was also an important figure in one of Frost's favorite books, Darwin's *The Voyage of the Beagle*. The oven bird of Darwin's investigations suggested the interrelations of all creatures past and future. This kind of "indoor schooling" adds to the ulteriority and mythic dimension of the poem. "The Oven Bird" presents a world of threat and uncertainty shared by all creatures and one in which the lowly speak the highest wisdom.

Frost's conception of himself as an "Old Testament Christian" also gives us insight into the Biblical aspects of Frost's pastoral thought. Jesus himself is, of course, a great pastoral figure, a lowly figure embodying the highest power. So was King David, the shepherd boy and youngest of Jesse's sons, who became King and was also a poet. But it was just the incarnatory thrust of spirit into matter, of the high into the low that held so much power in Frost's imagination. In the brilliant late poem "Kitty Hawk," Frost delights in the subversive and heroic venture that produced the fall into matter:

> Pulpiteers will censure
> Our instinctive venture
> Into what they call the material
> When we took that fall
> From the apple tree.
> But God's own descent
> Into flesh was meant
> As a demonstration
> That the supreme merit
> Lay in risking spirit
> In substantiation.

Frost took care to distinguish materialism from materiality, and his mode was to emphasize that a passion for matter and the world is more admirable than any attempt at transcendence. The wit of the phrase "that fall/ From the apple tree" highlights the tension between the old Biblical story of origins and the modern theory of our possible descent from arborial creatures.

"After Apple-Picking" is the only lyric or poem that "intones," as Frost said, in *North of Boston*. Stories from the Old and New Testaments merge in this pastoral lyric of penetration into matter and acceptance of limitations and of labor. Elegiac in tone, it seems quite overtly to address the virtues of work in the orchard. The speaker loves the sensuous attraction to the beauty of the apples "Stem end and blossom end,/ and every fleck of russet/ showing clear." But all of the contemplation is connected to a dramatic mythology of seeking after completion, after perfection, a movement "toward heaven" through the tree, through the technology of the ladder, and the passionate preference of "picking." Paradise, a word of Persian origin that means walled-in, was derived from the attempts to cultivate apples, hard work at the least. Labor and cultivation to the point of exhaustion are virtues extolled in Hesiod and also in Virgil and a fact of existence in Milton's super-fecund garden of *Paradise Lost*. Frost obviously plays with the mythology of the *felix culpa* or fortunate fall, Jacob's ladder, as well as the Pauline (1 Corinthians 1: 12) aspiration of seeing God face to face instead of through a glass darkly. But all hopes of perfection suggested in the poem appear to be circumscribed by the imminence of failure, exhaustion, limitation. One of the crucial themes in this poem is the importance of what remains unpicked and unharvested, magnificent waste beyond our control. He concluded "Unharvested" with jovial prayer:

> May something go always unharvested!
> May much stay out of our stated plan,
> Apples or something forgotten and left,
> So smelling their sweetness would be no theft.

The fact of waste and of superfecundity is Frost's version of Thoreau's ideal that in "wildness is the preservation of the world." In "The Last Mowing," "the meadow is finished with men. Then now is the chance for the flowers/ That can't stand mowers and plowers." The praise goes to "you, oh tumultuous flowers,/ To go to waste and go wild in,/ All shapes and colors of flowers,/ I needn't call you by name." Our attempts to control through cultivation or the nomenclature of botany are happily subverted by waste and wild. Here and in "After Apple-Picking," the lure and sensuousness of the flowers and apples is cultivated and loved beyond their value in the marketplace and worth much more. But the pursuit of aesthetic perfection, even beyond the demands of survival and environment, comes to loss. Even in "The Last Mowing" as in "Spring Pools," fragile, reflective beauty lasts only a moment in the general competition that will produce trees: "It must be now, though, in season/ Before the not mowing brings trees on,/ Before trees, seeing the opening,/ March into a shadowy claim." All of nature competes, and our lack of participation in cultivation "brings trees on" (a treason to our desire for control and sympathy for the flowers). We cannot control an orchard and the revelation at the end of "Good-by and Keep Cold," a reversal of human expectations, is that "something has to be left to God." Though, in Frost, both the morality of God and his oversight appears doubtful.

Another "mythology" inherent in this poem is the Darwinian story of the "Tree of Life," one in which there are apples that are saved, survive, and others that go to waste, good and bad apples completely naturalized in a process of selection in which we participate. The apples which the laborer cannot harvest will go to the "cider apple heap as of no worth" no matter "if bruised or spiked with stubble." And one must wonder about the speaker himself who flouts seasons and the crucial principle in agriculture of "timeliness" (also part of Hesiod's advice). Out of season, when winter sleep is coming on, the laborer persists on the ladder. The woodchuck who, as in the case of many creatures, lives off the seed of others and has the preservative instinct to hibernate, lives in contrast to "human sleep," which may be little more than the contemplative fantasy of dreams.

"After Apple-Picking" provides a suggestive commentary to many of the other eclogues in *North of Boston*. Competition of various kinds and conflict mark almost all of the poems, from "Mending Wall," a new amoebaean dialogue, to the creation and destruction of barriers and moral hierarchies in "Home Burial." The contrast between the desire to lead a life of contemplation in nature and the absolute hazards of doing so are an integral part of "The Self-Seeker," "The Death of the Hired Man," and "The Housekeeper." "A Servant to Servants," a dramatic monologue, presents a woman justifying her life against hard labor and insanity. The title echoes the Biblical curse on Ham, Noah's son, for having seen his father naked, a curse later used to justify racism. This woman has seen the hollowness, the nakedness of her husband Len and the cruelty of a world that has ascribed her pain as madness worthy only of the asylum. She speaks to women on a botany outing, and her speech and life story become one of nature's dark flowerings.

In spite of the traditional association of flowers with beauty and innocence, flowers in Frost participate in a universal competitive machinery. In the early poem "In Hardwood Groves," fallen leaves, like all individuals, "must go down past things coming up,/ They must go down in the dark decayed." Those "things" include flowers:

They *must* be pierced by flowers and put
Beneath the feet of dancing flowers.
However it is in some other world
I know that this is the way in ours.

The "pale orchises" of "Mowing" or the flowers in "A Star in a Stone-Boat" are the weeds of cultivation, the persistent part of nature that grows in spite of our efforts at control as well as figures of ephemerality and fragility as they seem to be in "Spring Pools."

The literal descent of fruit from flowers becomes analogous to the precarious relation of knowledge to love. In "The Rose Family," the speaker appears to be wistful about the ever-ramifying trees of both knowledge and descent that threaten unity of knowledge and understanding. Every act of naming, every signification may slip over time as family resemblances grow and develop in different directions. The Shakespearean realism of "A rose by any other name would smell as sweet," becomes part of a corrosive palimpsest of "sayings" that includes Gertrude Stein's parodic nominalism "a rose is a rose is a rose":

The rose is a rose,
And was always a rose.
But the theory now goes
That the apple's a rose,
And the pear is, and so's
The plum, I suppose.
The dear only knows
What will next prove a rose.
You, of course, are a rose–
But were always a rose.

The speaker attempts to reaffirm an essential figurative relation of rose and love, despite the ramifications of the ever-changing tree of knowledge and of life.

The attempt to find or keep an exclusive realm of identity or meaning can lead to as much madness as the failure to do so. Metaphors in Frost are limits and boundaries that must be built up but also allowed to break down. "The Self-Seeker" provides the figure of a mill owner whose legs are crushed in an accident in the mill's wheel pit. He wishes to get the insurance money to "get settled" but nothing can make up for his loss or the losses of those around him. His true love, however, was not people but the orchids that grow on his property, and we have the sense that his great attention to his orchid fetish and to seeking himself in non-human beauty has led to the carelessness about life that has left him lame. He will, like Oedipus, hobble as a result of his blindness to the interdependence and fragility of life around him. A little girl named Anne brings him flowers, but mocks his lack of interest in orchids that are "too common." The girl, who has in traditional fashion pressed flowers into a book, has been "broken of gathering flowers" by the "self-seeker" who wants them left for himself. He arrives at the dark revelation that "pressed into service means pressed out of shape." Though he refers to the girl's being "broken" of gathering flowers, the saying circles back to himself and the way he, too, has been broken, his legs pressed out of shape, by a larger machinery. In "Birches," Frost makes an analogy between trees and people as he shows the way "ice storms," the blunt reality of environment, bends the unyielding trees down to stay. Only the flexibility of a boy's play with birches can "take the stiffness" out of trees as he represents a limited and temporary creation of form amidst terrifying chaos.

Frost explores with neither sentiment nor nostalgia for a pre-technical world the analogy between humans and mechanical instruments, both used and discarded by larger forces of time, environment, and change. In "The Grindstone," the narrator observes a once useful machine that now sits useless "under a ruinous live apple-tree." The tree becomes a figure for knowledge and for biological change and the grindstone itself suggests the decay of Plato's world-machine or demiurge in the *Timaeus*. Frost allows the analogy between technological perfection and natural history to break down. The antagonism of the narrator and "a Father Time-like man" in grinding a perfect blade, one that could be either a tool or a weapon, have contributed to destruction of this instrument. Its "pride had failed to get him anywhere" (Frost's deliberate anthropomorphizing collapses human and non-human worlds in vicious circles of analogy). But failure "is not a sin," it is an inevitable and ineluctable expense of life that includes hate and struggle as well as love and play devoid of moral certainties. God becomes entrapped by creation as mankind becomes entrapped by its technology in a vicious circle of creation and waste.

The ruinous tree of life becomes a figure in Frost for both the common roots of human understanding and the divisions that drive us apart. This is particularly the case in "The Generations of Men," "The Ax-Helve" (a branch of the human division), and "The Code." In the last of these poems, the traditional contrast between country and town becomes intensified in a series of jokes. Although it appears to be a cautionary tale of a farmer telling a city-bred interlocutor about what might happen to him should he fail to respect his workers, one wonders whether his claims of possessing a particular code of language or of ethics is anything other than a pretext for confusing or visiting violence on whomever he pleases. The same may be true of the herdsman in "The Mountain," whose toying with the wanderer pokes fun at his earnestness as well as the leisure he has to climb the mountain just for the fun of it. But is he really a worker, or does he simply enjoy toying with the expectations of his interlocutor who is prying where he has no business?

This problem of pastoral also reveals itself in the gender conflict in one of Frost's greatest poems, "Home Burial." Amy does set up barriers to her husband, so much so that he begs "let me into your grief if it's something human." She complains that humans make only pretense of grieving and that she has a comprehension of the world beyond death that her husband cannot possibly understand. She appears superior in her sensibilities, higher in her moral demands. But are these really about the child and loss or about her power in the marriage, a barrier to protect her from her husband whom she deems brutish? The husband may be more subtle than she suspects when she recounts his saying, "'Three foggy mornings and one rainy day'/ Will rot the best birch fence a man can build." A dark saying but not simply the "everyday concern" Amy takes it to be. Indeed, it can be seen as a figurative way of talking about loss, including the loss of a child who acted as a barrier between himself and Amy and a bleak and extinguishing future. The terror in Frost is often the extent of internal and external threat to establishing home, order in a chaotic universe. A tension emerges in Frost between the need for design and the need to uproot and abandon it as soon as it becomes too comfortable and comforting.

The competition between singer-shepherds that occurs in pastoral poetry in both Theocritus and Virgil becomes transformed in Frost into philosophical dramas highlighting tensions about equality both of race and of gender. In "The Generations of Men," for example, a boy and girl, both with the family name "Stark," meet at a cellar hole where a grand family reunion was rained out. Their courtship dance, playful and witty, is troubled by the problem of establishing the basis of kinship and family. The drama becomes a figure for the drama of sexual selection and the power of women to make men dance as well as the uncertainty and wisdom of maintaining pride of ancestry within the annihilating chaos of natural history. The figure of the family tree had become in the nineteenth century the governing conceptual metaphor for the development, the descent of languages. The figure was carried into biology. But establishing lines of descent backward from the present demanded an imaginative leap to posit a single, common ancestry or to establish common origins. Frost's pastoral drama of courtship becomes a figure for the epistemological and ethical problems that modern science had brought to understanding human relations.

The title evokes in parody the repeated phrase from Genesis, "these are the generations of men." But Frost's poem suggests an ironic distance between the world of the Hebrew Bible and the new text of natural science in which genealogies can be invoked with far less pride and in which women play as great a role as men. Both Eden and Arcadia appear as Bow (an amusing reference to the covenant made with Noah after the world-destroying flood), a town showing the ruins of a lost way of farm life:

> And those of the name Stark gathered in Bow,
> A rock-strewn town where farming has fallen off,
> And sprout-lands flourish where the ax has gone.
> Someone had literally run to earth
> In an old cellar hole in a by-road
> The origin of all the family there.
> Thence they were sprung, so numerous a tribe
> That now not all the houses left in town
> Made shift to shelter them without the help
> Of here and there a tent in grove and orchard.

The image given here is literally of the womb of the earth sprouting what has grown to numerous descendants. No one else shows up in Bow because of the rain. The boy and girl attempt to figure out their relations by means of elaborately drawn family trees, but they are surely "laborious device[s]" used to ensure "passport," a dark reference to turn-of-the century anxiety over immigration and race:

> Provision there had been for just such meeting
> Of stranger cousins, in a family tree
> Drawn on a sort of passport with the branch
> Of the one bearing it done in detail –
> Some zealous one's laborious device.

The difficulty they have is in figuring out the precise nature of their kinship. But it becomes a game, a ritual of courtship through which the girl demands displays of imaginative prowess from the boy. The insoluble problem of establishing essential "Starkness" becomes a drama and dance about hierarchy and power. The girl teases the boy with riddles:

> "You know we might not be and still be cousins:
> The town is full of Chases, Lowes, and Baileys
> All claiming some priority in Starkness.
> My mother was a Lane, yet might have married
> Anyone upon earth and still her children
> Would have been Starks, and doubtless here today."
> "You riddle with your genealogy
> Like a Viola. I don't follow you."
> "I only mean my mother was a Stark
> Several times over, and by marrying father
> No more than brought us back into the name."

Her point is only that her grandmother, who married a Lane, was still a Stark by descent and so was her daughter. Marrying a Stark merely brought her back into "the name" but since everyone was hypothetically descended from an original pair, they cannot help but be Stark. Names become arbitrary fictions and demarcations in the wild descent of nature. The boy's invocation of Viola of Shakespeare's *Twelfth Night*, a woman masquerading as a man and then pretending to be a woman underscores a fluidity of characteristics of gender that often occurs in Frost's dramatic pastorals. The "pride of ancestry" and "the family tree" do not provide shelter from the confusing contingencies of history, represented metaphorically by an obscuring "mist":

> "One ought not to be thrown into confusion
> By a plain statement of relationship,
> But I own what you say makes my head spin.
> You take my card – you seem so good at such things–
> And see if you can reckon our cousinship.
> Why not take seats here on the cellar wall
> And dangle feet among the raspberry vines?"
> "Under the shelter of the family tree."
> "Just so – that ought to be enough protection."
> "Not from the rain. I think it's going to rain."
> "It's raining."
>   "No, it's misting; let's be fair.
> Does the rain seem to you to cool the eyes?"

In conjuring what "great, great, great, great Granny" must have looked like, the boy is deflated by the girl's assertion of mere projection: "It's as you throw a picture on a screen:/ the meaning of it is all out of you;/ The voices give you what you wish to hear." Voices are a "purer oracle" (though not pure oracle) in Frost's world in which tones of voice bear the inheritance of primordial gestures. In a letter of 1915 Frost wrote "All I care a cent for is to catch some tones that haven't been brought to book. I don't say to make them, mind you, but catch them. No one makes them or adds them. They are always there living in the cave of the mouth. They are real cave things: they were before words were."(*I*, 91) Vocal gestures are neither eternal forms nor mere illusions in Plato's cave but are "real cave things" that have been inherited from our ancestral past. The girl leaves suggesting they ought to meet again "tomorrow . . . if it rains" but "if we must, in sunshine." The future of their love rests in the play and inexplicable attraction between them without recourse to ideals or knowledge.

"Directive" also plays on a quest for origins that begins with the evocation of a traditionally pastoral landscape of simplicity, but one existing in a lost past, a ruin not unlike the cellar hole of "The Generations of Men." Frost also treats us to lines that seem to parody Eliot's style in both *The Wasteland* and in *Four Quartets*:

> Back out of all this now too much for us,
> Back in a time made simple by the loss
> Of detail, burned, dissolved, and broken off
> Like graveyard marble sculpture in the weather,
> There is a house that is no more a house
> Upon a farm that is no more a farm
> And in a town that is no more a town.

This pastor-poet narrator toys with our nostalgia and our longings for home and simplicity, foundations that become uprooted and destroyed over time. He has only "at heart your getting lost." Whatever one finds there is something we project onto the vast expanse of natural history from which "two village cultures faded/ Into each other. Both of them are lost." Perhaps this is an echo of Thoreau's wisdom in *Walden* that we need to become lost in order to find ourselves. But the retreat from confusion to simplicity appears an illusion and joke. At this source (a strange Parnassus similar to the spring in "The Mountain") is a spring and a Grail-like goblet "Under a spell so the wrong ones can't find it,/ So can't get saved, as Saint Mark says they mustn't." The tone and ultimate meaning of the parenthetic reference to St. Mark's account of Jesus' parable about why he speaks in parables says a great deal about Frost's attitude toward religion and poetry. In St. Mark's account, Jesus speaks in parables to exclude, to keep the wrong ones out. In the parallel account in St. Matthew, Jesus justifies speaking in parables as a means of education, to heighten attention and thought.[16] Frost loved indirection as a means of education. In "Revelation," he laments that it would be "a pity if the case require/ (Or so we say) that in the end/ We speak the literal to inspire/ The understanding of a friend." And in "Mending Wall" the narrator also enjoys hinting, "I could say 'Elves' to him,/ But it's not elves exactly, and I'd rather/ He said it for himself." But the idea of parable in St. Mark underscores exclusion and exclusivity rather than education. This does not so much represent an attack on all Christianity but certainly a recognition of the underlying persistence of the will to power. Frost repeatedly brings the passage from St. Mark into question in relation to democracy, revealing his own preference for parable as a wall to be built up and then to be subverted and broken down:

> But this thing that I've brought up before here. I've quoted it, I think, in a couple of places, and it's always coming into my head: that these things are said in parable so the wrong people can't understand them and so get saved.

It says that twice in the New Testament. It sounds very harsh and undemocratic, doesn't it. Sounds esoteric. And one of my good friends went forth from my saying that to say that I was esoteric – that my thinking was esoteric. But not at all. Because it also says in the New Testament that except you become as little children, you know. That meant that so professors won't understand it. It's so simple and so foolish that only little children can understand it.[17]

In his notebooks, he is even more explicit about the deeper relation of parable to "dark sayings" of both Hebrew wisdom literature and ancient Greek wisdom literature. Frost's comments suggest that wisdom can come from many unexpected sources, all of whom have or can make claims to power and authority:

> Athens was the headquarters of philosophy but Sparta of wisdom. Plato is my authority. He says the Spartan had the wisdom and when he felt it coming over him to talk wisdom he ordered all the strangers out of the room so they couldn't profit by it. (How like Mark's saying Christians in their exclusiveness must talk in parable so the wrong people won't understand and so get saved.) Many people consider Plato infallible. Sometime I mean to round up a lot of wise sayings such as we have from the Spartans such as "Good fences make good neighbors." My guess would be we owe most of these to the wise woman of the tribe or family.[18]

Frost complicates how we read the ultimate "mystery" of "Directive" but he also underscores the tension in "Mending Wall." Surely he regarded the "old-stone savage's" dark saying, "Good fences make good neighbors" as much as the saying of the speaker "Something there is that doesn't love a wall." This "savage" is engaged literally and figuratively in putting up a barrier (as St. Mark's Jesus was). But this has nothing to do with religious mysticism and cultishness that Frost found to be mere obscurity. "Some people don't know the difference between obscurity and what are called in ancient times 'dark sayings,' that you go into deeper, darker in your life. But obscurity isn't that. Obscurity is a cover for nothing. You go looking for it and it comes out 'A stitch in time saves nine.' But there are dark sayings."[19] Frost's poetry moves us to a "higher plane of *regard*" (not a higher plane) in enabling us to consider different surfaces or aspects of a recurrent and very old problem.

Frost throughout his work expresses skepticism toward "metaphysical profundity." The dialogue in *A Masque of Reason* is also a pastoral dialogue of competing shepherds. Job rebukes aspects of Christian mysticism. For God's descent into matter through the incarnation as well as his suffering is not more but almost less than we can understand. The more obscure aspects of theology and mysticism fail to explain the mystery of suffering and existence. But even skepticism comes full circle to doubt itself:

I've come to think no so-called hidden value's
Worth going after. Get down into things
It will be found there's no more given there
Than on the surface. If there ever was,
The crypt was long since rifled by the Greeks.
We don't know where we are, or who we are.
We don't know one another; don't know You;
Don't know what time it is. We don't know, don't we?
Who says we don't? Who got up these misgivings?
Oh, we know well enough to go ahead with.
I mean we seem to know enough to act on.

Knowing what principles in which to believe or foundations to act on is at the core of "The Black Cottage," a pastoral (reflecting on Wordsworth's "The Ruined Cottage") in which the narrator listens to a minister wavering between extreme skepticism and faith. He is troubled by the memory of a woman who lived in the cottage who had an unwavering faith in Jeffersonian ideals of equality, the principle that "all men are created free and equal," as he ponders the fifty years since the end of the Civil War. Her adherence to Jeffersonian principles enabled her to justify the Civil War and all its waste. The minister is strangely condescending and patronizing toward her, treating her as a sentimental abolitionist who associated with Garrison and Whittier. His skepticism may mask his desire to assert his own arid fantasy of utopia against the encroachments of life. He proposes at once a vision of perfection in the past – the nativity – and his own desert monarchy in the future as a preserve against change:

"As I sit here, and oftentimes, I wish
I could be monarch of a desert land
I could devote and dedicate forever
To the truths we keep coming back and back to.
So desert it would have to be, so walled
By mountain ranges half in summer snow,
No one would covet it or think it worth
The pains of conquering to force change on.
Scattered oases where men dwelt, but mostly
Sand dunes held loosely in tamarisk
Blow over and over themselves in idleness.
Sand grains should sugar in the natal dew
The babe born to the desert, the sand storm
Retard mid-waste my cowering caravans–
There are bees in this wall."

The speech is inspired and lyrical but ultimately untenable, at odds with time and the movement of life. For all her alleged simplicity, the woman's adherence to that "hard mystery" of Jefferson may possess more wisdom than the tortured doubts of the minister. Frost's own public comments about the Jeffersonian ideal reveal his own playful ambivalence about the progress of democracy:

> In 1897 I was sitting in a class in college when I heard a man spend quite the part of an hour making fun of the expression that we were all free and equal. So easy to dismiss. Let's have a look at it. All men were created free and equally funny. Before you laugh too much at that, take another look at it. Four hundred years ago the only people who were funny were yokels . . . Now, today, even kings are funny. We've come a long way.[20]

The renewal of a phrase fascinates Frost as does the power of change and time to unsettle hierarchies and to keep us unassuming. We wonder in Frost how free an individual can be before challenging another's freedom and sense of equality. Frost remained uneasy about abandoning a sense of hierarchy: "I am a great equalitarian: I try to spend most of my time with my equals."[21]

The sudden intrusion of the bees in "The Black Cottage" suggests a natural process of change through which all monarchies and authorities suffer banishment and reconstitution. The bees in Frost's poem interrupt the high poetry of the minister even as they participate in making the old woman's home a ruin; like Darwin's earthworms in his last book, *The Formation of Vegetable Mould, through the Action of Worms* (1881), they represent a naturalized and somewhat frightening version of Jesus' pastoral beatitude that "the meek shall inherit the earth." In the fourth *Georgic*, Virgil presented bees as figures of the power to bring the future into being:

> Thus it is
> That though a narrow span of life awaits
> Each individual (for none of them
> Outlive their seventh summer) yet the stock
> Remains immortal, and for many years
> The house survives in fortune, and its annals
> Count generation upon generation.[22]

In "The Black Cottage," "The Generations of Men," and many other poems, Frost presents a world in which "waste is the essence of the scheme," one that forces us out of our gardens as we go forward into the dark.

NOTES

1 Reuben Brower, *The Poetry of Robert Frost: Constellations of Intent* (New York: Oxford University Press, 1963), p. 156.

2 *Ibid.* Other critics have commented upon Frost's pastoralism but John F. Lynen's *The Pastoral Art of Robert Frost* (New Haven: Yale University Press, 1960) remains the only full-length study. Lynen's approach focuses primarily on poetic form. Paul Alpers devotes a chapter to Frost in his monumental study *What is Pastoral?* (Chicago: University of Chicago Press, 1996). Thomas G. Rosenmeyer provides some interesting comments about Frost in his study of Theocritus, *The Green Cabinet: Theocritus and the European Pastoral Lyric* (Berkeley: University of California Press, 1969), as does Theodore Ziolkowski in *Virgil and the Moderns* (Cambridge: Harvard University Press, 1990).

3 Ezra Pound, "Modern Georgics," *Poetry* (December 5, 1914), 127–30.

4 For a general discussion of American pastoralism see Leo Marx's landmark study, *The Machine in the Garden* (New York: Oxford University Press, 1966). Another important approach is Lawrence Buell's *The Environmental Imagination: Thoreau, Nature Writing, and the Formation of American Culture* (Cambridge: Harvard University Press, 1995).

5 Victor Davis Hanson, *The Other Greeks: The Family Farm and the Agrarian Roots of Western Civilization* (New York: The Free Press), pp. 2–3.

6 Renato Poggioli, *The Oaten Flute: Essays on Pastoral Poetry and the Pastoral Ideal* (Cambridge: Harvard University Press, 1975), p. 1.

7 Frost in "On Taking Poetry," in *CPPP*, 821.

8 "Preface to an Expanded 'North of Boston'," in *CPPP*, 849.

9 William Empson, *Some Versions of the Pastoral* (London: Chatto and Windus, 1935), pp. 11–12.

10 *Robert Frost: A Living Voice*, ed. Reginald L. Cook (Amherst: University of Massachusetts Press, 1974), p. 91. Frost also arranged student productions of *Comus* when he taught at Pinkerton Academy.

11 From a recorded talk, *Robert Frost Reads From His Own Work*, Carillon Records (1961), Yale Series of Recorded Poets Produced by the Yale University Department of English and Audio Visual Center, ed. R. W. B. Lewis, recorded May 19, 1961 in the Pierson College Lounge, Yale University.

12 Henry David Thoreau, *Walden* (Princeton: Princeton University Press, 1973), p. 95.

13 Virgil, *Georgics*, trans. L. P. Wilkinson (London: Penguin Books, 1982), pp. 91–93.

14 Lucretius, *On the Nature of the Universe*, trans. Ronald Latham (London: Penguin Books, 1951), p. 148.

15 *Ibid.*, p. 29.

16 See Frank Kermode's study of the origin of parable, *The Genesis of Secrecy* (Cambridge: Harvard University Press, 1979).

17 "On Taking Poetry," in *CPPP*, 819. See also Frost's remarks in a later essay, "On Extravagance": "Some people can't go with you. Let them drop; let them fall off. Let the wolves take them. And, you see, in the Bible twice it says – and I quote that in poem somewhere, I think, yes – twice it says, 'these things are said in parables' – said in this way that I'm talking to you about, see, extravagance said in parable – 'so the wrong people won't understand them and so get saved.' Thoroughly undemocratic, very superior – . . . 'Taint everybody. It's just those only – the few that have done every thing, sacrificed everything, bet their sweet life on what they lived, you know . . .", *CPPP*, 910.

18 *Prose Jottings of Robert Frost*, ed. Edward Connery Latham and Hyde Cox (Lunenberg, VT: Northeast Kingdom Publishers, 1982).

19 Frost speaking about critical commentary on "Spring Pools" from a reading recorded at Yale University, 1961.

20 "What Became of New England," in *CPPP*, 757.

21 "Preface to 'A Swinger of Birches,' by Sidney Cox," in *CPPP*, 838.

22 Virgil, *Georgics*, Book IV, p. 131.

4

HELEN BACON

Frost and the Ancient Muses

Robert Frost repeatedly warns his readers, sometimes openly, often mischievously, to look for further implications in his poems and not to stop with their obvious associations. In 1927 he said, "I almost think a poem is most valuable for its ulterior meanings . . . I have developed an ulteriority complex."[1] This view about his writing has been increasingly acknowledged by his more critical readers from the second half of the twentieth century as they explore the deceptively homespun New England persona and subject matter of many of Frost's poems and discover the many subtle ways that they embody and play with the forms and thought of our literary tradition, including the Bible, as well as much of the theological, philosophical, and scientific thought of an increasingly global world. It is clear from his critical writings and from his talks that he wanted the public to recognize this aspect of his work and was annoyed by how slow most of his readers were to grasp it. The question to ask a poet, he said, is "not what he means but what he's up to"(*CPPP*, 823). His readers failed to see what he was up to, how large a world of forms and ideas he was drawing on. He admonished them against mistaking the agricultural New England scene for his whole subject matter, and him for a rustic New England sage, saying, "I talk about universals in terms of New England . . . I talk about the whole world in terms of New England. But that's just because I have it all around me."[2]

One aspect of this "whole world" not often given the recognition it deserves is the thoughts and literary forms of classical antiquity, with which he was saturated in high school and college and which remained throughout his life part of his perspective on art and the human condition. There is of course general recognition of his fairly solid grounding in the Greek and Latin languages and literatures. Direct allusions to classical material (words, names, ideas) have been identified and commented on; but the many less obvious ways in which such material pervades his work tend to go undetected. In general, critics have treated it as a relatively minor aspect of his writing, of mainly academic interest, if any. In fact it is a large part of that "ulteriority" that he thought of as the very heart of poetry, part of his theory of the "renewal of words" that he regarded as poetry's main function.[3] This "renewal" occurs when, through the use of metaphor (in Frost's very flexible definition), we are led to perceive affinities between apparently unrelated, often commonplace, words and experiences. In doing so, we see again the inherent life of words and their content, which has been dulled by over-familiarity or distance in space or time.

Even at the high school in Lawrence, Massachusetts, the college preparatory program that Frost followed was based mainly on the classics, as was the curriculum at Dartmouth (where he walked out after less than a semester), and Harvard (where he spent almost two years with some distinction). The classics and the world of humanistic thought have been almost totally supplanted in the modern curriculum by a bevy of practical, technical, and scientific fields, required for success in the modern economy. It is clear from Frost's letters that many of his contemporaries shared his tradition and easily picked up on his most glancing references that would mean little or nothing to the more recent generations of even college-trained minds.

"The Pasture," first published in 1914 as the first poem of *North of Boston*, is an example of the way an utterly simple poem, apparently restricted to rural New England realities, can talk about "everything" in terms of New England. In this case Frost has included a reminder that he is affiliating himself with poets of classical antiquity by borrowing one of their own familiar devices.

Lawrance Thompson had recognized, even in 1942, some of the wider, more universal references of "The Pasture," which he described as evoking the delight of lovers in sharing the experience of rustic beauty. In Thompson's biography, this insight is reinforced by a quotation from Frost himself (*CPPP*, 756). Others, too, have felt the upwelling spring and the tottering calf as embodiments of life, and seen the fellowship of lovers who view them as part of the larger human fellowship of art. The many layers of such seemingly simple poems, even when not consciously grasped, make them mysteriously moving. This linkage of particular with general is a notable element of Frost's power.

In 1973, Kiffin Rockwell suggested still another way in which one may understand the poem's tender vignette of rustic chores. He points out that by evoking the tradition of a whole string of Greek and Roman poems – poems that go back as far as the Homeric Hymn to Apollo – Frost is announcing a new poetic program for *North of Boston*.[4] In 1975, Lowell Edmunds, picking up on this brief and somewhat elliptical statement, expands on the recurrent use of "The Pasture" throughout the rest of Frost's life as an epigraph to many of his selected and collected poems from 1923 to 1949.[5] In

1962, the year before he died, in his final selection, *In the Clearing*, the epigraph occurs as the single line, "And wait to watch the water clear, I may –," an expressive leave-taking from one who talks "about everything in terms of New England." This epigraphical reappearance before every major volume of Frost's poetry affirms, according to Edmunds, Rockwell's original perception that Frost had already announced at the opening of *North of Boston*, "reticently but with his Classics in mind," a program for a completely new kind of poetry, which, as Edmunds goes on to point out, the poet reaffirmed for the rest of his life, by recalling "The Pasture" in all subsequent collections.

In this simplest of rural poems, at the very beginning of his publishing career, Frost evokes one of the oldest conventions of Western poetry. As it does in the work of his Greek and Roman predecessors, this convention proclaims both his affiliation with that tradition and his own original contribution to it. The additional depth and range that this twofold application gives to his little poem is quite typical of what Frost's incorporation of classical literature gives to many of his poems.

Frost's well-known belief in the metaphor as being the heart of poetry – indeed, the heart of all thinking – caused him to refrain from the kind of obvious learning, sometimes accompanied by footnotes, that impressed readers of Pound and Eliot. "Success in taking figures of speech," Frost asserted, "is as intoxicating as success in making figures of speech"(*CPPP*, 814). He despised footnotes because they "robbed the heart of the chance to see for itself what a poem is all about" and so to arrive at the "clarification of life," that poetry can achieve. He claimed to write for his equals, namely, "those I don't have to write footnotes to. The footnotes, if I used them, would be a condescension to the people that can't keep up with me." It irritated him that, as time went on, fewer and fewer of his readers could rise to the challenge of keeping up with him. Too many failed to recognize the depth and range of the intellectual background he drew upon.

Almost as slight and apparently rustic as "The Pasture" is "Hyla Brook," published in *Mountain Interval*. An awareness of how it interacts with an almost equally slight poem of Horace (*Odes* III, 13, often referred to as *Fons Bandusiae*, "The Spring of Bandusia") deepens and enlarges both its charm and its frame of reference to reveal previously unexpected implications. Horace's poem has its own kind of ulteriority, not generally known to classical scholars until pointed out by Steele Commager in 1962: an ulteriority confirmed and elaborated on by Gordon Williams in 1969. In 1916, Frost had already noticed and built into "Hyla Brook" this "ulteriority" of *Fons Bandusiae*, that apparently had escaped two millennia of Horatian scholarship. *Fons Bandusiae*, like many of Horace's poems, celebrates a ritual, an offering to a perpetual spring, on his rustic farm in the Sabine hills, to which Horace often escaped from the crowds and sophisticated society of Rome to enjoy the simpler and more peaceful life of the country. On the following day, the spring will be honored not only with the usual rustic offering of wine and flowers but also with the sacrifice of a kid whose prospect of love and war will be cut off when his red blood stains the icy waters. Horace praises the spring for the coolness and surrounding shade that it offers to straying sheep and oxen weary from the plow in the savage heat of August. He ends by declaring,

> You too shall become one of the renowned springs
> When I tell of the ilex that overhangs your hollow
> Rocks, whence your voluble
> Waters leap down.　　　　*Odes* III, 13 (author's translation)

It is clear from the offerings of flowers and wine and the promise of a sacrificed kid that the spring is a rustic deity. Horace's audience would also have realized that his little poem is in standard hymnal form, which reinforces the idea of celebration and worship. Nor would they have had trouble, as some modern critics do, in seeing the implications: a kid cut off before realizing his destiny in lovemaking and war. Here is a variation on the theme of loss transmuted into art, such as we see in the myth when Pan plucks the reeds into which the nymph Syrinx had been changed as she fled his embrace, and makes them into Pan pipes (syrinx), on which he then plays music. Horace's audience would also have known that the goat is sacred to Dionysus – the god of lyric and dramatic art. The never-failing spring under a spreading tree that offers refuge from the ferocious August heat is still a familiar Mediterranean scene today. When Horace tells of the ilex tree that overhangs its rocks, he declares that his spring too will become one of the "renowned" ones. Horace's "renowned" founts can only refer to the several springs of the Muses (Castalia, Hippocrene, Peirene are the most renowned) that are scattered throughout Greek literature. The gushing life of these year-round springs symbolizes the sphere of the Muses – the unfailing creativity of art and its capacity to make the dead past live again. Even as Horace claims membership for his spring in this august group whose cult pervades Greek literature, he seems to distinguish it as belonging to an Italian rather than a Greek world. Castalia, Helicon, and Peirene are all in places made famous by myth, known and visited by worshippers and travelers throughout antiquity. Horace's Italian spring is known only to Horace and the few rustics in the Sabine hills who honor it with rustic offerings. Generally, throughout Greek literature, and even today, it is a giant plane-tree that shades Greek springs; but Horace's spring is shaded by the ilex, or live oak, as though to underline the fact that *his* Muses have migrated from their more famous homes to his humble farm in Italy's Sabine hills. However, like the waters of the Greek springs, they suggest renewed life and song as their chattering (*loquaces*) waters leap down (*desiliunt*) across the rocks.

Though Frost's "Hyla Brook" runs out of "song and speed" by June, it is, as we shall shortly see, a celebration of the Muses, evoking many of the themes of Horace's poem. In a fifteen-line poem (Horace's poem is sixteen lines), Frost describes a short-lived watercourse on his New Hampshire farm. It is quite typical of Frost's borrowings that he should claim for his brook the same properties that Horace claims for his Sabine farm spring – though at first glance, the brook is the opposite of Horace's spring, whose leaping, chattering waters are a never-failing source of coolness and shade, even in the dog days of August.

By June *our* brook's run out of song and speed. As it vanishes, it evokes the past, first May and the "spring peepers" (Hylas), whose call pervades the spring nights,

> (And taken with it all the Hyla breed
> That shouted in the mist a month ago.

The Hylas in turn evoke the more remote past of winter,

> Like ghost of sleigh-bells in a ghost of snow) –

Or perhaps the brook has

> gone groping underground
> Or flourished and come up in jewel-weed.

Even as the poem moves forward to July and August, the brook manifests itself as jewel-weed, which also looks to the past as it bends backward towards its source, rather than forward towards what was once the brook's course. This image reminds us once again of the brook's past, whereas in the present, in its summer manifestation, it exists in memory only –

> A brook to none but who remember long.

Its appearance, however, as a

> faded paper sheet
> Of dead leaves stuck together by the heat –

reminds us of a book. Only three poems before in the collection, in "A Patch of Old Snow," Frost compares the snow to a "blow away paper," that

> is speckled with grime as if
> Small print overspread it,

a nearby reminder that Frost can see books in unexpected places. Books can be an even more effective reminder of the past than the remains of the brook. Horace's poem, like Frost's, plays with the theme of memory and confirms *his* spring's place amongst the company of renowned springs – for which he uses the adjective *nobilis*, derived from a root that means "to know." This word *nobilis* is another indication of the presence of the Muses in his poem. The Muses are the daughters of Memory, and it is through their song that the past, which would otherwise be lost, becomes *nobilis*, known, renowned.

Frost's list of evocations of the past culminates with a reminder of a "faded paper sheet." The remains of the brook suggest a book. Through memory, the vanished brook soundlessly carries on its function of preserving and celebrating the past.

What follows echoes Horace's claim that he has brought the august Greek goddesses to his humble farm, for Frost goes on:

> This as it will be seen is other far
> Than with brooks taken otherwise in song.

(CPPP, 115)

Frost's brook is "other far" than brooks sung about elsewhere. Horace's spring, even as it joins the "renowned springs" of Greek literature, remains part of a far simpler Italian world. With Frost, the Muses have migrated once again from Italy to New England. Different though his short-lived brook is from Horace's never-failing spring, it is still the poet's source of inspiration. It too gives life through song to the otherwise vanishing past. So Frost honors *his* brook in a characteristically less ceremonious way with,

> We love the things we love for what they *are*.

In the paradoxical Frostian world, his brook is *both* a New Hampshire brook that runs dry in June *and* a home to the Muses – an eternal source of life and inspiration.

Many critics have recognized and written feelingly about the many springs in Frost's poems that symbolize life and creativity. But on the basis of these two very early (1914 and 1916) evocations of the Muses in association with water, it seems probable that for him, whenever watercourses represented life and creativity, they frequently, if not always, suggested the Muses – the sources of art and inspiration in both Greek and Roman literature.

A relatively late (1945) example of this theme is "Directive," which seems to be a more concise retelling (62 lines) of "The Mountain" (1914) (109 lines). Both poems deal with a mountain, wildness, harmony, and a mysterious journey on a hidden path to a spring at the very top of the mountain – a journey that suggests to most some kind of initiation. Harmony and wildness are for Frost two essential and complementary aspects of poetry to which he often refers. In "The Figure a Poem Makes" (1939), he speaks of the mystery of "how a poem can have a tune in such a straightness of meter" and "how a poem can have wildness and at the same time a subject that shall be fulfilled." And he goes on to say that a poem "begins in delight and ends in clarification of life – not necessarily a great clarification . . . but in a momentary stay against confusion."

For anyone as steeped in antiquity as Frost, the setting of these two poems (in spite of the obvious Biblical allusions) brings to mind (with its suggestions of initiation and revelation) Mount Parnassus where, near the town of Delphi, the sacred spring Castalia, one of the homes of the Muses, gushes out between its twin peaks. There, Apollo and Dionysus, both gods of music and inspiration, appropriately share a cult. These two gods are embodiments of Frost's two basic principles of poetry. Apollo represents harmony and order; Dionysus represents wildness and instinct. But Dionysus does not represent instinct run wild, as he so often appears to do in modern interpretations. Though he dances with his barefoot Maenads in the wilderness, he also tames and harnesses savage leopards and panthers to his chariot. He is the god who transmutes impulse into art as already described in the myth of the Syrinx. Harmony and order brought to bear on the chaos of impulse result in a "clarification of life," which is a "momentary stay against confusion."

It is interesting that the opening lines of Wordsworth's sonnet:

> The world is too much with us; late and soon,
> Getting and spending we lay waste our powers;

is echoed in Frost's "this now too much for us" (near the beginning of "Directive") with a typical Frostian twist. The whole sonnet longs for a retreat to antiquity, where, rid of the distractions of the present, the poet might experience the freshness of an encounter with ancient divinities. It ends:

> Have sight of Proteus rising from the sea;
> Or hear old Triton blow his wreathèd horn.

Frost's allusion to Wordsworth reinforces the need expressed in "Directive" to return to our origins in antiquity and thus affirm the timelessness and universality of our inspiration.

In each of these poems about New England springs or watercourses, separated as they are in time over more than thirty years, Frost looks to the antique sources of his poetic inspiration. These and many other images and symbols that date from his early saturation in the classics stayed with him and continued to generate potent poetry throughout his life. The poems that recall this ancient world share with his other poems the suggestion of many possible meanings. Though often one may barely guess at them one feels the mystery and power of unplumbed depths. The more they are pressed the more they reveal analogies beyond analogies. Their many meanings make them as unpredictable as life itself. A poem for which one can discover the one and only meaning is a dead poem.

In drawing attention to the way Frost incorporates antique images and forms into his poetry throughout his life, I do not pretend to have found the only meaning of any of the poems I discuss. I hope only to point out another dimension, another depth, to a few of his multi-faceted poems – and also, perhaps, a more far-reaching aspect of his work than many readers and critics are aware of. Frost confesses, in a 1916 letter to Louis Untermeyer, what he calls "a very damaging secret" that he has only confided to one other person, namely, "The poet in me died nearly ten years ago." That would be a few years after the end of his formal, largely classical, education in 1899, when he withdrew from Harvard, and during the period of his early teaching ventures in various secondary schools, well before *A Boy's Will* (1913). Frost goes on to claim,

> The calf I was in the nineties I merely take to the market. I am become my own salesman . . . The day I did "The Trial by Existence" [first published in 1906 in *The Independent*] says I to myself says I, this is the way of all flesh. I was not much over twenty, but I was wise for my years. I knew then . . . I must get as much done as possible before thirty.

This claim or boast, that he had laid the basis for his whole prospective *oeuvre* by age thirty, is, as Poirier points out, literally absurd and involves a good deal of attitudinizing in a typically Frostian manner; it does, however, if not taken too literally, tend to bear out my suggestions that the ongoing source of his later poetic creativity is an imagination formed largely by his intense contact at a very impressionable age with the writers of antiquity, and some of their successors among English writers. When asked in 1942 to list and comment on sixteen of his own favorite poems, he described his poems as "all written by the same person out of" a restricted region (north of Boston) and "out of" a limited group of books. Among these he singles out "a few in Greek and Latin," the rest in English, intimating that his creative imagination developed out of and continued to be inspired by the same twofold source – a narrow landscape and a small core of books. To this New England landscape and this core of reading he returns again and again for the rest of his life as to an inexhaustible source.

The sense of fellowship in art going back to its early originators in classical antiquity is implicit in "The Pasture" and in other poems such as those we have been discussing that involve membership in the cult of the Muses. The sense of relatedness to the past generations of artists going back to our literary beginnings is poignantly expressed in an early poem, "The Tuft of Flowers" (1906). There a laborer comes "to turn the grass" of a meadow where in early dawn a previous laborer had laid flat both grass and flowers with his scythe. A straying butterfly leads the latecomer's eye to a tuft of flowers.

> A leaping tongue of bloom the scythe had spared
> Beside a reedy brook the scythe had bared.

The latecomer perceives that the unseen mower has saved the tuft of flowers because

> The mower in the dew had loved them thus . . .
> from sheer morning gladness. . .

The sight of the flowers later in the day puts him in mind of the mower's morning joy – the birdsong and the sound of the scythe. The "message from the dawn" brings the past to life, as the Muses do across the generations. In connecting to the morning mower he feels,

> a spirit kindred to my own;
> So that henceforth I worked no more alone.
>
> And dreaming, as it were, held brotherly speech
> With one whose thought I had not hoped to reach.

This fellowship across the generations is the fellowship of art that unites men by their participating in and contributing to the tradition of poetry. This is what makes it possible to be in touch with the dawn.

> "Men work together," I told him from the heart,
> "Whether they work together or apart."

For Frost, this feeling of being part of the long succession of poets is not one of rivalry but of fellowship in the service of the Muses. And here too as in many of his other poems, he finds the image for this experience in the New England landscape.

Up to now we have been considering the way ancient ideas of the Muses and their followers pervade the way Frost thinks of the art of poetry and himself as a poet in relation to poets past and present. I will only show how two of Frost's poems – "Wild Grapes" and "One More Brevity" – rely for their "ulteriority" to a large extent on two extended individual ancient poems, one Greek and one Latin.

"Wild Grapes" was written at the request of Susan Hayes Ward, the poetry editor of *The Independent* magazine. Frost referred to her as "my first discoverer" because she was his first publisher ("My Butterfly," 1894). From then on, she and her brother, who was editor-in-chief of *The Independent*, were friends and encouragers of the young Frost. Miss Ward asked Frost to write her a poem that would do for girls what "Birches" did for boys – a poem to be based on her own childhood experience. Her older brother had bent down a birch tree so that she could reach the wild grapes entangled on vines in its upper branches. When he released it, she was carried heavenward as she grasped the vines, only getting back to earth when her brother bent the tree back down again. Riding heavenward and back to earth on a birch tree is the central motif of "Birches" and "Wild Grapes." In the case of the boy, both the ascent and the descent are achieved with conscious mastery; in the case of the little girl both are involuntary – "run off with by birch trees into space," then rescued when her brother bends the tree back down. This same motif links "Wild Grapes" to Euripides' *Bacchae*.

The climax of *Bacchae* is the messenger's account of what happens when Pentheus, the young king of Thebes, disguises himself as a Maenad in order to spy on the Theban women who, against his orders, have followed Dionysus to revel as Maenads in the nearby mountains. Dionysus, disguised as his own priest, lures the deluded king who has repudiated him to climb to the top of a pine tree, which the god bends to earth, like the birch in "Wild Grapes," and then gently releases so that Pentheus is carried up into the sky the better to witness what he imagines to be the orgies of the Theban women. When the women, who include Pentheus' mother and aunts, catch sight of a male intruder in the top of the tree peering at their rituals in honor of Dionysus, they tear down the tree and bring him to earth, where in their ecstatic frenzy they fail to recognize him and literally tear him limb from limb.

Frost is working with a twofold motif – on the one hand, that of his own poem "Birches," and on the other, that of Euripides' play with all of its complex Dionysiac lore of Maenadism in the wilderness.

This complex of motifs seems to have had a special importance for Frost. Although "Wild Grapes" was first published in *Harpers* in 1920, and "Birches" in the *Atlantic* in 1915, it appears from his unpublished papers that he was contemplating in 1958 a collection of poems (never published) that went from "Birches" to "Wild Grapes" "with an inner logic that I don't have to account for." The motif of the tree bent down to earth and in some sense functioning as an intermediary between earth and heaven is common to *Bacchae* and both Frost's poems. It is an aspect of one of his lifelong pre-occupations with the relation of matter and spirit. Already in "Birches" his longing for a retreat toward heaven is tempered by the reminder that "Earth's the right place for love." In "Wild Grapes," the little girl who is "run away with by birch trees into space" achieves a second birthday, is born again, when her brother brings her safely back to earth by bending down the birch tree. The same relation of matter and spirit is developed at length in "Kitty Hawk" – a poem that existed in several early forms, but was not published until 1962 in his final volume, *In the Clearing*. Frost chose an eighteen-line passage from it, in which he condenses his idea of the relation of matter and spirit, to affix to the dedication of the volume that contains the whole poem, as though to emphasize for his friends and for the public this lifelong concern.

As so often, when Frost appropriates foreign material, ancient or modern, he drastically modifies it. The little girl's journey heavenward on a bent-down tree has an opposite outcome to that of Pentheus. Pentheus when he rides the tree to the sky is brought to earth by the outraged Theban women and dismembered. The little girl, as she travels to the sky with the birch tree, has to be

> come after like Eurydice
> And brought down safely from the upper regions

– a second inversion, of course, because Orpheus failed in his attempt to bring back Eurydice from the nether regions. Eurydice failed to acquire "an extra life" as her little counterpart did; who, as a result of her adventure, can for the rest of her life celebrate two birthdays. She has become twice born, like Dionysus himself, whom his father, Zeus, had ripped from his mortal mother Semele's womb as she was being consumed in flames at the sight of Zeus in his full glory. Zeus then sewed his premature offspring up in his own thigh and nurtured him there until he was ready for his second birth in the sky. The twice-born are children both of earth and sky. Dionysus was the offspring of a mortal mother, Semele, and her immortal celestial lover, Zeus; whereas Frost's little heroine is both carried off to heaven on a birch branch and returned to earth. She is thereby born again, as she immediately realizes.

Pentheus, on the other hand, is only earth-born. His ascent to heaven and back results not in second birth but in being torn apart by Maenads. He has rejected Dionysus and forbidden the attempt to introduce his cult in Thebes. He does not believe in miracles and thinks the claim that the son of Semele is also a son of Zeus is just a cover-up for an illegitimate affair, and, moreover, that the celebrations in the wilderness are some kind of sexual orgy that he has a lubricious desire to witness. Dionysus plays into this delusion, persuading him to put on female dress and follow the Theban Maenads to spy on them. Because of their initial cynicism about Dionysus, they too, like

Pentheus, have fallen under his spell and have rushed off into the wilderness as Maenads. Both Pentheus and the Theban women, having self-righteously rejected the miraculous claims of the Dionysiac religion as physical impossibilities advanced by an effeminate charlatan, have lost their grip on reality. Pentheus' delusion about his own identity is revealed in his complacent reply to the taunts of the disguised Dionysus, that he does not know what he is doing or who he is, "I am Pentheus, son of Agave, my father was Echion." His blindness to the possibility of the miracle of second birth has led him to ignore the forces which, when denied, can lead to insanity. The women's delusion about reality is equally great. Though his mother, Agave, and her two sisters, his aunts, are among them, they fail to recognize him in the treetop where Dionysus has lodged him, and so take him for a lion. They drag him to earth and destroy him. His mother then carries his head home in triumph believing it to be the head of a lion. Her father, King Kadmos, brings her back from her ecstatic state to everyday life by getting her to recognize first the actual sky, then by stages to name her husband, then her son, then to say what she holds in her hand; and only finally, to look at what it is. Frost suggests a similar staged return for the little girl when her brother bends down the tree, and lowers her to earth again from where she dangled among the grapes. Frost represents her as having been as far away from the ordinary world as Euripides' Agave:

> I don't know much about the letting down;
> But once I felt ground with my stocking feet
> And the world came revolving back to me,
> I know I looked long at my curled up fingers,
> Before I straightened them and brushed the bark off.

For Agave it is the sight of the sky that triggers her return to the real world; for the little girl it is the feel of earth under her feet that brings the world "revolving back" to her. Her experience, so different from Agave's, is to have been "translated," as she herself says.

The Dionysiac context of this experience is the heart of Frost's tribute to Miss Ward. The birch tree that carries her off is an ivy-crowned Maenad.

> Wearing a thin headdress of pointed leaves,
> And heavy on her heavy hair behind,
> Against her neck, an ornament of grapes.

Frost reflects Euripides here, who implies that the pine tree that Pentheus rides skyward is a Maenad. When he describes how Dionysus gently prevents the pine tree from shaking Pentheus off, he uses a Greek verb that means literally "shake the hair while throwing back the head." This is the traditional gesture of a Maenad dancing in Dionysiac frenzy, very familiar in ancient literature, sculpture, and painting. Almost certainly Frost recognized its implications for the pine tree that carried Pentheus to his death, and adapted them to the birch tree that carried the little girl to hang among the grapes. Her brother's description of her as having been

> run off with by birch trees into space.

implies that she has been swept up and carried away by reveling Maenads. Her own perception of the grape-laden birch trees when her brother first shows them to her is also highly Dionysiac:

> Grapes, I knew grapes from having seen them last year.
> One bunch of them and there began to be
> Bunches all around me growing in white birches.

Frost must have been familiar with accounts of such miraculous burgeonings. They are commonplace in ancient literature and art about Dionysus – signs of his magical power, as when the mast of the ship in which pirates are trying to abduct him turns into a grape-laden vine and the pirates into dolphins.

The many Dionysiac motifs that I have been pointing out indicate Frost's very attentive reading of *Bacchae*, almost certainly in Greek, as his picking up the notion of the Maenad tree suggests. It is one of the signs of his deep involvement with ancient texts, his poet's awareness of their nuances of language. It is a poet's reading of a fellow poet – a reading that some scholars might not agree with. In my opinion it comes close to the heart of the play. Many further themes of Euripides that are built into "Wild Grapes" will appear in the discussion that follows.

But first, what do the cult of Dionysus and maenadism have to do with a tribute to Susan Ward? The cult of Dionysus, as represented by Euripides, is a celebration of freedom and wildness, most prominently by women, but open to men, too. Dionysus' female worshippers temporarily abandon their traditional female roles in the domestic interiors of the house and rush off in groups to celebrate him with ecstatic dances in the wilderness – the traditional province of men only. There they behave in culturally forbidden ways – clothed in fawnskins, wreathed in snakes and sprays of ivy, oak, or pine, carrying sacred wands and torches, reveling barefoot in the mountains, and forcibly attacking profaners of their rites. They revel as do Artemis and the nymphs and other woodland divinities – all virgins who resist male domination. They also briefly enjoy the freedom of the wilderness. The loss of identity that they experience in their ecstatic self-abandonment leads to a kind of second birth. The little girl of "Wild Grapes" also abandons herself. Carried away by birches, she holds on by both hands with her eyes shut against the sun and her ears deaf to her brother's advice, and throws back her head in the traditional Maenad gesture (the same gesture of throwing back the head that Dionysus stops the pine tree from making, as it carries Pentheus skyward. She feels when she returns to herself that she has acquired a second birthday. She is "a little boyish girl" who, like a Maenad, had repudiated conventional female restraints and escaped temporarily into the wilderness. Frost has turned Susan Ward's childhood anecdote into a characteristically inverted version of *Bacchae*, casting Susan Ward as a Maenad because of her untraditional role (for a female of the 1890s) as a single woman, the poetry editor of *The Independent*, functioning in the traditional male world outside the home.

Poetry, which is Susan Ward's sphere of activity, is also part of Dionysus' function. Dionysus and Apollo as patrons of music (poetry in the largest sense) share a cult on Mount Parnassus, as already described in connection with "Directive." Within that cult Apollo represents harmony or order, and Dionysus, wildness or instinct. These are the two necessary bases of poetry, which Frost describes in his projected (1958) preface to the never-published volume of poems that were to go from "Birches" to "Wild Grapes" – that is, "footbeats for the meter, and heartbeats for the rhythm" (see the discussion in "The Figure a Poem Makes," *CPPP*, 776). The little girl's transport hanging on by both hands among the grapes in the birch tree leads to her having two birthdays. Her brother points out that she has a special qualification beyond the ordinary grapes:

> "Now you know how it feels," my brother said,
> "To be a bunch of fox-grapes . . .
> "Only you have the advantage of the grapes
> In one way: you have one more stem to cling by,
> And promise more resistance to the picker."

Unlike an ordinary grape, she has "one more stem to cling by." Though her brother is joking, she interprets the experience as a sign that

> I had not taken the first step in knowledge;
> I had not learned to let go with the hands,
> As still I have not learned to with the heart.
> I have no wish to with the heart – nor need,
> That I can see. The mind is not the heart.
>
>   . . . but nothing tells me
> That I need learn to let go with the heart.

She seems to understand "the one more stem to cling by" as the instinctive knowledge of the heart. Her brother insists on her lack of knowledge:

"Don't you know anything, you girl, let go!"

His knowledge is of the mind. The same knowledge with which he mastered the trees in "Birches" and rescued her in "Wild Grapes" is what she had yet to learn, as she ignored his cries to let go, and clung instinctively with

> the baby grip
> Acquired ancestrally in just such trees
> [referring to the wild practices of
>   prehistoric times]
> I held on uncomplainingly for life.

The knowledge of the heart belongs to the sphere of wildness and primitive instinct – the sphere of Dionysus. This knowledge Susan Ward acquired during her adventure among the grapes and has not let go since. As her brother said, she had "one more stem to cling by."

This Dionysiac experience, going back to her early childhood, is a necessary part of Susan Ward's connection with poetry, but we must not forget what Frost (in that preface to the proposed 1958 collection) referred to as "footbeats for the meter," the sphere of Apollo – the world of order and harmony which is the other prerequisite of poetry. It is with this sphere, the knowing with the mind when to let go, that the little girl must still learn to deal. The comparison of her rescue to that of Eurydice implicitly links the brother with Apollo, the father of Orpheus. Orpheus, as already pointed out, failed because he succumbed to passion, whereas the brother succeeded because he kept his head. This Apollonian knowledge involves conscious self-control – good judgment about the way things work. It is not to be confused with the seeming common sense of earth-born Pentheus and the Theban Maenads that causes them to reject the miraculous claims of Dionysus and to imagine that they can master him. They are therefore carried away by powers they have already rejected. This contrast between true enlightenment and earthbound common sense that leaves no room for wildness and instinct is a central theme of *Bacchae*. Frost's earliest poetry reflects the Dionysiac/Apollonian theme, which in his 1958 unpublished preface he referred to as heartbeats and footbeats.

It is part of Frost's extraordinary ability that he sees the underlying human reality that links Susan Ward's childhood experience (at least as he imagines it) to the complex Dionysiac themes in Euripides' *Bacchae*. That discernment lifts the episode from a charming personal anecdote to a universal experience, turning it also into a tribute to Susan Ward's special gifts. We have often observed how Frost can expand from the personal and particular the stage on which his poems are enacted to take in great stretches of space and time and human experience.

"The artist must value himself," Frost said, "as he snatches a thing from some previous order in time and space into a new order with not so much as a ligature clinging to it of the old place where it was organic." In another context, he again asserts: "In the little poem it ought to be – even in a short one you know – that you can put your finger on five or six items that come from different quarters of the universe . . . I summon something I almost didn't know I had. I have command."[6] These two related descriptions of the way he combines superficially unconnected material to produce a kind of ulteriority which draws it all together come late in his career.

In "Wild Grapes" (a relatively early poem, 1920), the links with *Bacchae* extend beyond Susan Ward's personal adventure to include some implications of the ancient cult. Her allusion to bunches of grapes growing round her in the birches

> The way they grew round Leaf the Lucky's German

unexpectedly transfers the scene to a different time and place – the discovery of grapes in Vineland by Leif Erikson's German foster father Tyrker. As recounted in the *Greenland Saga*, he has the distinction of discovering the grapes growing in the New World and introducing them to his Norse companions, together with wine making, which he had learned in his native Germany. Euripides' Dionysus brought the culture of the vine and the beliefs of his cult to Greece from the ancient civilized East. Tyrker is a New World Dionysus. He introduces grapes with viticulture and all that goes with it – from the well-established vineyards of the Rhine to the wilder, more westerly worlds. Leaf, who is Tyrker's foster son, in turn brought back grapes and the culture of the vine to Greenland. He too had a Dionysiac role, and like Dionysus, can claim a second birth.

These are some, by no means all, of the "items that come from different quarters of the universe" that Frost has put his finger on in order to present Susan Ward's childhood adventure in the context of a Dionysiac experience. Dionysiac impulses go back to the Stone Age. They involve not just the world of Euripides but its diffusion westward through Europe to the cultures of Greenland and the Americas.

Finally, "One More Brevity," a really late poem (1953), also incorporates ancient material into a contemporary context. It evinces a comparable skill in snatching "a thing from some previous order in time and space into a new order with not so much as a ligature clinging to it of the old place where it was organic." As we shall see in this case the principal thing "snatched" is from Virgil's *Aeneid*. Such "snatchings" are by no means limited to ancient material. As I hope is becoming clear by now, Frost uses the same poetic techniques in his ancient borrowings as in all his other borrowings. He is at home with all the many fields which engaged his far-ranging and powerful imagination.

The unlikely subject matter of the poem is a visit from a stray dog, a Dalmatian, who unexpectedly drops in to his Vermont cabin, spends the night, and vanishes the next morning as suddenly as he appeared. The episode is described in such an endearingly and doggily appropriate way that it scarcely seems to need exploration. Except that the poet does hint that the visit has a special, not to be divulged, message for him. The brief, companionable, trusting acceptance of each other by visitor and host seems almost enough to account for the suggestion of meaning and for the poet's regret at the brevity of the encounter. When the poet opens his door for a last look at Sirius in the night sky, the dog slips in as though seeking asylum. The poet's reaction,

> and I was stirred
> To be the one so dog-preferred –

establishes the emotional tone of the visit. The welcome is unquestioning:

> I set him water. I set him food,
> He rolled an eye with gratitude . . .
> His hard tail loudly smacked the floor
> As if beseeching me, "Please, no more."

This description is so engaging that it seems almost pedantic to look further, but there are indeed suggestions to look beyond the surface impression for some ulteriority in the incident.

Sirius, the brightest of the fixed stars, the tail of the dog in the constellation Orion, is invoked even before the real dog is mentioned. The poem begins,

> I opened the door so that my last look
> Should be taken outside of a house or a book.
> Before I gave up seeing and slept
> I said I would see how Sirius kept
> His watchdog eye on what remained
> To be gone into if not explained.

Throughout Greek and Roman literature Sirius is familiar as the "dog-star" that rises with Orion and presides over the "dog days" of August (see discussion of Horace's *Fons Bandusiae* above). In New England latitudes the rising of Orion and his dog occurs considerably later, in the fall. The idea of Sirius as a watchdog or guardian is also familiar from ancient literature. Frost, quite characteristically, is checking on him to see how he is keeping his "watchdog" eye on things. The end of the poem brings us back again to Sirius. In the last line, after the visiting dog vanishes, Frost speculates that it might indeed have been Sirius who dropped in on him:

> The star itself – Heaven's greatest star,
> Not a meteorite, but an avatar –
> Who had made an overnight descent
> To show by deeds he didn't resent
> My having depended on him so long,
> And yet done nothing about it in song.

The stray dog has surprisingly become portentously symbolic. He is also the bearer of a message for Frost himself, as was implied by the affinity and mutual acceptance between dog and man at the beginning of the poem. What that message may be seems to need "to be gone into" a little further, "if not explained."

Frost's lifelong obsession with Sirius seemingly dates from a chapter in a book of popular astronomy that his mother gave him when he was a boy. In a 1935 letter Elinor Frost quotes him as saying he is "down here in Key West now to find out if Canopus is as good a star as Sirius." Up to 1953, he had done nothing about Sirius in song in spite of his lifelong concern. Though he does not name the star of "Take Something Like a Star," one feels that only the brightest of the fixed stars could be the subject of that poem. Like Keats' star and Shakespeare's star, which the poem evokes, Frost's star is a marker and guide for uncertain human beings. In other places, stars in general and meteorites appear as examples of the wondrous extent and complexity of the cosmos, but only here (in "One More Brevity"), as far as I can discover, does Frost claim a personal relationship with Sirius, so personal that he imagines the star may actually have made an "overnight descent" to pay him a visit.

But how is Sirius, the heavenly watchdog, related to Frost's "problem guest" who plops himself down exhausted as soon as he slips in the door? When Frost sees that the dog is too tired to respond to his hospitable welcome, except with a roll of his eye and a thump of his tail, he reassures him in the only triplet in this poem, which is otherwise entirely in couplets.

> So I spoke in terms of adoption thus:
> "Gustie, old boy, Dalmatian Gus,
> You're right, there's nothing to discuss . . .
> Meanwhile feel obligation-free.
> Nobody has to confide in me."

The poet's instant affinity with the dog inspires him to give him a name as a sign of adoption, and reaffirm it by repetition.

> In fancy I ratified his name
> Gustie – Dalmatian Gus, that is –
> And I started shaping my life to his
> Finding him in his right supplies
> And sharing his miles of exercise.

This affinity seems to foreshadow the feeling he expresses at the end of the poem: that his visitor *was* Sirius himself with a personal message. Near the beginning of the poem, while Frost is contemplating Sirius at the cabin door, there

> Slipped in to be my problem guest
> Not a heavenly dog made manifest –
> But an earthly dog of the carriage breed.

Already, the poet has set up some kind of correspondence between the watchdog in the sky and the visitor on earth. The end of the poem wipes out the implied contrast between the two dogs by suggesting that one is a temporary manifestation of the other.

The story of "One More Brevity" is clearly a variation on a familiar Indo-European folktale about hospitality offered to a god in disguise by a stranger without pretension to rank or power. This story is familiar in European literature from the story of Baucis and Philemon (cf. Ovid's *Metamorphoses*, VIII, 8.618–724), and from more recent tales that generally derive from Ovid. In the poem Frost suspects that his vanished guest has been Sirius,

> The star itself – Heaven's greatest star,
> not a meteorite, but an avatar.

He has clearly, without knowing it, entertained a denizen of the heavens who was bringing him a message.

Classical mythology is also full of stories of mortals who have been translated to the stars after death – like Orion and his dog, who pursue the Pleiades across the heavens. In particular there is a tradition that certain notable figures appeared in the sky after death as stars and were thought to have joined the immortals who dwell on Olympus. The tradition that Roman rulers became deified after death was publicly affirmed after Julius Caesar's murder. A comet appeared at his funeral and people immediately identified it as his soul transported to the realm of the gods. After this, Augustus (Caesar's adoptive son and successor) was saluted as the son of a god, himself to become a god after death and to join his "father" in the sky. Virgil projected this destiny onto Aeneas, the founder of the original Trojan settlement on the banks of the Tiber and ancestor of Romulus and Remus who would later found the actual city. The *Aeneid* is, among other things, the story of the ordeals which forced Aeneas reluctantly to relinquish his commitment to his life as a mortal and finally to accept his destiny as a god-to-be – the proto-founder of Rome and the progenitor of a line of mighty leaders.

In Frost's poem, hospitality was in fact enjoyed by a "heavenly dog," though the poet imagined initially that he was welcoming "an earthly dog." He had entertained a god in disguise – not only an inhabitant of the heavens but an avatar. Frost uses this word only here. He might have found it described in Bulfinch's *Age of Fable* (with which he was very familiar) as a brief manifestation of a savior god in earthly form, a temporary incarnation of deity.

The carefully indicated attitude of withdrawal that the dog adopts when he first slips in Frost's door has associations from the same world of belief. Here is a dog who has "failed of the modern speed," and is out of step with the world.

> He dumped himself like a bag of bones,
> He sighed himself a couple of groans,
> And head to tail then firmly curled
> Like swearing off on the traffic world.

Head to tail is the position of that image of detachment and eternity, the "tail eater," the *ouroboros*. The dog in this position is seeking what Frost had only recently come to understand, the state of Nirvana – "the perfect detachment from ambition and desire that can alone rescue us from the round of existence," as Frost had recently pointed out in "The Prerequisites" (*CPPP*, 814), after coming to realize that even gods long for this escape.

Who is this unfamiliar god, this star from the heavens, that appears bodily to the poet as an avatar, collapses exhausted and the next morning vanishes as unexpectedly as he came? Why does Frost feel that Sirius is the bearer of a mysterious message which the poet is reluctant to share? What metaphor unites all the disparate elements of the poem into an ulteriority which can give us some inkling of the nature of the dog? As we have seen, his host in adopting him emphasizes his name. When Frost repeats the dog's name he also repeats that name along with the name of his breed, thus "Dalmatian Gus," and in addition characterizes him as "an earthly dog of the carriage breed" reminding us yet again that he is a Dalmatian. These recurrent reminders help us to think more about this god-come-to-earth and what his message might be. Improbable as it seems, two important books of the second half of the *Aeneid*, Books VIII and X, in a typically Virgilian way, link the beginnings of Rome (when Aeneas and his refugee band founded their first camp on the banks of the Tiber) with Virgil's contemporary Rome (when the Emperor Augustus achieved his triumphant pacification of the Roman world). Virgil brings these two worlds together through his description of the gift from his mother Venus – the shield that Aeneas will carry into battle against the enemies on Italian soil of Roman destiny. Vulcan, at Venus' request, has inscribed on the shield prophecies of Rome's progress through the ages, from Romulus and Remus to Augustus. The origins of Rome and the culmination of its future are thus juxtaposed in Book VIII.

This juxtaposition of past and present is repeated with the bringing together of the image of an Augustus triumphant on the shield with that of Aeneas triumphant in Book x – the span from first to last of the many founders that will have helped to create the new civilization.

When Aeneas, a friendless exile, is welcomed by Evander (the king of the rustic village of Arcadian refugees on the future site of Rome just upstream from the Trojan camp), we already begin to realize that he is being recognized as a hero destined for future godhood because of his service to humanity. In this scene Evander evokes Heracles, the prototype in the Roman tradition of deified mortals. King Evander had entertained Heracles in his thatched hut on the Palatine (where Augustus later had built his studiedly modest dwelling) after Heracles had rescued the villagers from the fire-breathing monster Cacus, who was preying on them. Evander salutes Aeneas as a hero in the same tradition.

> Victorious Heracles crossed this threshold,
> This "royal" dwelling received him,
> Dare, my guest, to despise pomp, and make
> Yourself worthy of godhood and enter
> Without passing judgment on meager means.

In reminding Aeneas to abjure worldly pomp and make himself worthy of godhood, he is foreshadowing the future deification of Aeneas and of the many "founders" to come, particularly of Julius Caesar, already among the stars, and Augustus who will someday join him there. Aeneas shares the typology of Heracles, the hero who for his tireless labors on behalf of humanity becomes one of the Olympians. Virgil links Aeneas through this typology to many Roman leaders that follow. As we shall see, he has additional ways to associate him with Augustus.

The association of Aeneas with the heroic redeeming hero destined for godhood is extended farther in Book x by the way the description of Aeneas' first triumph in Italy anticipates on a small scale the triumphant climax to come represented on his divine shield: namely, Augustus at the battle of Actium, transfigured in the stern of his ship, flames shooting from his temples, the Julian star and the ancestral gods above his head, then celebrating in

Rome his triple triumph of Actium, Dalmatia, and Alexandria, and finally, seated gloriously on the Palatine receiving the homage of the pacified peoples of the empire.

Aeneas' first triumph on Italian soil occurs in Book x as he descends the Tiber by ship bringing reinforcements to his beleaguered comrades. He raises his shield in greeting "as he stands in the high stern," *stans celsa in puppi* – the very words that are used of Augustus at Actium on the shield. Aeneas' transfiguration is marked by comparable imagery. Flames stream from his helmet and a star, not literally present, but introduced in a typically Virgilian way via a double simile, shines over him. The flames from his helmet are compared to a comet "glowing blood red and mournful through the clear night" – a reminder of the Julian Star, the *patrium sidus* that stood over Augustus at Actium and whose connection now with Aeneas assimilates his triumph to that of his successor in Virgil's time. The two events, so far apart in time, contribute to one historical process. The second part of the simile connects Sirius with the same process by comparing the same flames to the glowing heat of Sirius which "brings thirst and sickness to mortals when it saddens the sky with sinister light." This links Aeneas to Achilles whom Homer (*Iliad*, XXII, 26ff) compares to Sirius when clad in divine armor, the gifts of *his* goddess mother, he races into battle, and instills terror in the Trojans.

The light around Achilles is baneful like the light of Sirius because it portends the death of Hector and ultimately of Achilles too, and the fall of Troy. But the positive side of this baneful light, at least for Romans, is that Rome's earliest beginnings can take place only after Troy has fallen. Then, Aeneas, bearing on his back his father, who holds the images of the ancestral gods of Troy, and leading by the hand his little son, can leave Troy to begin the search for a new homeland. The part of the simile that reminds us of the star of Julius has a similarly double message. It signals not only mourning for the death of a murdered leader but also his deification and the eventual deification of his son. Such Virgilian passages may well have been models for Frost's own charged uses of metaphor.

This abridged analysis of *Aeneid* Books VIII and x shares themes with "One More Brevity" – the major one being hospitality to a homeless wanderer, who is either destined for godhood and a dwelling among the gods, or a god in disguise (already a star) descended briefly from the heavens. Both hosts (Frost and Evander) ultimately become aware of the divine origins of their visitors. These correspondences suggest that we should look to *Aeneid* Books VIII and x for the explanation of Frost's emphasis on the name and breed of his visitor. The imagery shared by Aeneas, Augustus, and the intervening leaders (all of whom helped to create Roman civilization) affirm the exhausting effort of trying to create a Roman world of peace and brother-hood. This ideal is articulated at various stages of the epic, mainly in coun-cils among the gods. The goal, though foretold on Olympus, is not achieved in the epic. Those who struggle toward it, from Aeneas to Augustus, will be rewarded with godhood after death for their attempt to bring the Golden Age to earth. The exhaustion of Dalmatian Gus is like theirs. Like them, he has done all he can in this world and belongs among the stars.

Gus is short for Augustus. Dalmatian Gus has much in common with Augustus Caesar, whose defeat of Antony and Cleopatra at Actium was fol-lowed by his triple triumph, whose celebration included not only Actium and Alexandria, but also Dalmatia. This threefold triumph appears on the shield, followed by the scene which depicts the submission to Augustus of the subject peoples of the Empire and his attempt to establish the Golden Age of peace and brotherhood on earth with pacification of the Roman world. If Dalmatian Gus is really Augustus Caesar, then the undisclosed message for the poet must be something about the pain and struggle involved in trying to give social and political reality to a political ideal.

This sampling of ways Frost drew on the literature and concepts of the Greek and Roman world at every stage of his life indicates how imbued with it he was. The intense exposure of his high school and college years was forma-tive for him, providing both literary material and ideas about poetry that he drew on for the rest of his life. It is clear from the poems discussed how resourcefully and variously he drew on his knowledge of antiquity and with what art he used it to add breadth and depth to the apparently simplest of poems. The fact that he was able to continue to draw on it throughout his life indicates how inexhaustible a source it was for him for his poetic theory and practice. It was of course only one of many of Frost's uses of *Metamorphoses*.

An adequate discussion of the varied ways that Frost adopted or adapted Plato's thought and imagery would fill another chapter. "The Trial by Existence" (first published in 1906, even before his first book) is an example of the way a passage of Plato with its many far-reaching implications can dominate a poem and enlarge its scope. Frost's poem actually paraphrases the "myth of Er" that closes Plato's *Republic* (Book x, 614ff). Some aware-ness of this passage and its relation to the main argument of the ten books of the *Republic* is necessary in order to understand, let alone grasp the rich-ness of "The Trial by Existence." Earlier critics have acknowledged that the main structure of Frost's poem is unmistakably determined by specific fea-tures of Plato's myth. More recent critics often do not mention Plato's account. Either they are unfamiliar with it, or consider it irrelevant.

Like many other of Plato's "myths" that appear here and there throughout the *Dialogues* (the most familiar being the "myth of the cave" – also in the *Republic*, VII, 514–21), the "myth of Er" restates in poetic form arguments the speakers have previously presented philosophically. The speakers in the *Republic* are seeking, throughout its ten books, to discover what kind of man will attain the greatest happiness – whether the most just man, that is, the philosopher, or the most unjust man, the tyrant. The basic discourse is structured around the discussions of the proponents of one or other of these two types, in what Socrates more than once calls a "contest for happiness." The argument ends when Socrates proclaims the philosopher to be the victor.

Socrates, when he tells the "myth of Er," widens the range of the contest. Now included is the well-being and happiness of souls traveling their many cycles of birth and death. For a reader who is not aware of this myth and of the whole argument that it sums up poetically, Frost's poem becomes imaginatively diminished.

The "myth" tells the story of a man named Er who comes back to life after having died in battle and reports as follows to the living. After a period of rewards and punishments in the next world for lives already lived, souls are summoned for rebirth to a meadow where they will select the life they will live in their coming transmigration. Frost reproduces the main features of Plato's scene of the gathering of souls for rebirth. He describes on the right hand a path up into the sky by which the souls pass to be rewarded, and also a road down from the sky by which they return eventually to choose a new life. On the left is the path leading down into the earth by which souls descend for punishment, along with an upward path out of the earth by which they return after punishment to choose their next life. Thus there is a continual coming and going of souls enacting this cycle of rebirths. This scene anticipates by hundreds of years the outlines of the familiar Christian version of the Last Judgment which depicts souls rising to Heaven on the right and descending to damnation on the left. Plato's version postulates many cycles involving thousands of years for each soul's punishments or rewards; the Christian version coalesces the process into one apocalyptic judgment.

In most of the poems I have discussed, the source of the image that governs the poem's structure is far less obvious than it is in "Directive" or "Wild Grapes." In "The Trial by Existence," all the critical elements of Plato's myth, even beyond what we have mentioned, are in Frost's version – for example, the eyewitness account, the openings to heaven and the underworld thronged by souls coming and going in both directions, the majestic enthroned authority that oversees the choice of lives (the goddess called

Necessity for Plato, God with a capital G for Frost), the display of the many patterns of life to choose from, the distribution of the lots that determine the order of choice, and the stern proclamation that though the order is determined by necessity, the responsibility for the life chosen is the chooser's alone, not god's.

Plato dwells on the soul that having drawn the last lot gets to choose last of all. This is Odysseus, whose previous life of heroic struggle has taught him to give up on the rewards of ambition. After long search he chooses the life of an obscure private citizen which other souls have overlooked. Frost picks up on the meaning of this repudiation of worldly glory.

> Nor is there wanting in the press
>> Some spirit to stand simply forth,
> Heroic in its nakedness,
>> Against the uttermost of earth.
> The tale of earth's unhonored things
>> Sounds nobler there than 'neath the sun.

In Frost's version, the assembled souls greet the daring choice with a shout of joy. Though he does not name Odysseus, he clearly understands the choice as a wise one.

Though Frost christianizes some aspects of Plato's account of the inexplicable pivot of the human condition, he also reproduces the atmosphere of mystified reverence and awe with which Plato presents it. The reader shares Frost's stunned awareness that the very basis of human existence is the seemingly contradictory fact that whatever one must endure in this world one has brought upon oneself.

> Tis of the essence of life here,
>> Though we choose greatly, still to lack
> The lasting memory at all clear,
>> That life has for us on the wrack
> Nothing but what we somehow chose;
>> Thus are we wholly stripped of pride
> In the pain that has but one close,
>> Bearing it crushed and mystified.

The poem ends with this affirmation of the thought that governs the "myth of Er" – that is (in Plato's own words): "The responsibility [for the life chosen] belongs to the chooser. The god is not responsible." Frost, by choosing the image of the transmigration of souls over aeons of time to present this dilemma of the human condition, though almost certainly thinking metaphorically, gives this thought the same kind of solemnity and cosmological weight that it has had for Plato. Without this parable that furnishes the context, the poem is reduced from an impassioned statement about all human life to a quirky and self-centered assertion of Frost's personal control over everything in his own destiny.

Plato as a young man sacrificed a burgeoning career as a poet to devote his life to philosophy. His works are permeated with passages of poetry, in the form of myths and parables, like the story of Er, which give expressive form to his theoretical arguments. In addition, his *Dialogues*, as Aristotle (*Poetics* 1447 b7) early noted, are to be classified as works of art – poetry in its highest sense. The *Dialogues* should be recognized as dramas in prose, not technical treatises. Plato's gifts as a poet are one reason for his notorious distrust of the seductiveness of poetry. The combination of philosophy and poetry are clearly one of the causes of Plato's pervasive appeal to Frost as reflected both in his imagery and thought. Frost too had a comparable combination of poetic gifts and a mind powerfully engaged with scientific and philosophic ideas – something like Plato's synoptic grasp of poetry and philosophy. Plato himself comes from a tradition which began with poets (such as Pythagoras and Parmenides), who were also sages and philosophers. In later times, the tradition carries on with the Epicurean Lucretius and Virgil, who was also trained and deeply involved in philosophy; and in a lesser way with Horace, who saw himself as a prophet-poet and moral leader. Later still, Dante, who claimed Virgil as his master, built his epic around Aquinas' version of Aristotelian thought. Frost shared with these poets their ability to incorporate the ideas of philosophy and science into a comprehensive vision of the human condition. His thinking and writing in prose and poetry belong in this same grand tradition.

NOTES

1 Quoted from the Buffalo (NY) *Evening News*, November 11, 1927, p. 27, in a report of a reading given by Frost at the Grosvenor Library, Buffalo, November 10, 1927.
2 Quoted in Reginald L. Cook, *Robert Frost: A Living Voice* (Amherst: University of Massachusetts Press, 1974), p. 23.
3 "But the whole function of poetry is the renewal of words, is the making of words mean again what they meant," from "What Became of New England," Oberlin College Commencement Address, June 8, 1957 in *CPPP*, 756.
4 Kiffin Rockwell, *Classical Journal*, December 1972–January 1973, 182–83.
5 Lowell Edmunds, *Classical Journal*, 70, 3 (February–March 1975), 36–37.
6 Quoted in Cook, *Frost: A Living Voice*, p. 117.

5

LAWRENCE BUELL

Frost as a New England Poet

To classify Robert Frost as a poet in a traditional New England vein can be dangerously misleading or entirely proper, depending on how you define your terms.[1] Biographically, he was a New Englander not by birth but by adoption – or rather readoption: the first canonical writer to return from the New England diaspora to his parental region and claim it as his literary home. By the same token, artistically, Frost's tastes were cosmopolitan, not strictly regional. His first favorite poet was Poe; he was an able and zealous student of the classics, especially Virgil's *Eclogues*; he once described himself as "car[ing] most for Shakespearean and Wordsworthian sonnets"[2]; the one significant fellow poet to whom he dedicated a poem was the English Georgian, Edward Thomas; and in the formation of his mature poetic styles no writers of the New England Renaissance era were more important to him than Matthew Arnold and Robert Browning. Yet Frost was also acutely conscious of his relation to his New England precursors. Sometimes he showed it by explicit claim or allusion, more often obliquely, by imitation, repossession, echo, or parody – and not just by means of the written word. Also important to the construction of the Frost image was visual iconography: photographs like the one facing the title page of his 1949 *Complete Poems* (New York: Holt), which depicts the grizzled sage as serene Brahmin in a work shirt.

I shall unfold Frost's New Englandism in four stages, laying particular emphasis upon what links him to Emerson and other significant New England poetic precursors from William Cullen Bryant through Edwin Arlington Robinson: first, a capsule summary of literary affinities; second, a narrative of the emergence of the regional sensibility that followed from those affinities; third, an analysis of some major dimensions of that sensibility; and finally an anticipation of the "So what" question – What justifies lingering on this somewhat unfashionable subject?[3]

I

Here, in summary, is what we think we know about Frost's cognizance of fellow New England writers. (I hedge somewhat because a good bit of the evidence comes in the form not of hard proof but of assertion, often from that notorious trickster Frost himself.)[4] Emerson's *Essays and Poems* and Thoreau's *Walden* Frost once listed among his favorite ten books. Emerson's poetry Frost knew better and relished more than Emerson's prose – a striking reversal of what has always been the dominant view of Emerson's relative merits. Emerson was the one premodern writer about whom Frost wrote extensive formal criticism, not one essay but two (*CPPP*, 814–16, 860–66). Indeed, Frost went so far as to claim on several occasions that a particular twenty-two-line passage in "Monadnoc" "meant almost more to me than anything else on the art of writing when I was a youngster" (*CPPP*, 693) – of which more later. Thoreau's *Walden* was the only other regional literary work that Frost credited with such a crucial influence on his own formation, remarking that a particular passage therein (unspecified) "'must have had a good deal to do with the making of me,'" and later affirming that *Walden* "'surpass[es] everything we have had in America.'" But whether Thoreau inspired Frost stylistically as well as by force of his ideas and his persona is uncertain.[5] Frost read Emily Dickinson enthusiastically after her first (posthumous) *Poems* appeared in 1890; experimented with her compressed gnomic lines in some early poems; in later life compared his sensibility to hers; and praised her as "'the best of all the women poets who ever wrote.'"[6]

Discussions of Frost in relation to "classic" New England writers tend to stop with these three precursors. That is understandable enough. After all, they have been the canonical figures in the history of New England poetics since the time Frost achieved eminence in the 1920s; Frost's critics, memorists, biographers, and live audiences have thus taken special interest in his affinities with them; and Frost himself was usually willing to play along. But the life-story of his connections with his New England precursors hardly ends there. In particular, Frost read the poetry of Henry Wadsworth Longfellow early and eagerly, and he defended it well after it had become unfashionable. As a turn-of-the-century teacher Frost assigned *The Courtship of Miles Standish*, *Evangeline*, and other works; and he wrote an imitation-Longfellow commemorative poem for the school's commemoration of the centenary of Longfellow's birth in 1907.[7] He encouraged his children to memorize several Longfellow poems; he attended the Bowdoin College centenary of Longfellow's graduation in 1925; and he selected the little-known Lawrance Thompson as his official biographer partly on the strength of Thompson's 1938 biography of Longfellow. Although Frost did not specify what pleased him about that book (if indeed he inspected it closely), it is striking that *Young Longfellow* – the most penetrating and incisive study of that poet ever written – already evinces the Melvillian probing of the demonic underside of the writer's persona that Thompson went on to pursue more famously – and very controversially – in a critical book on Melville (*Melville's Quarrel with God* [1952]) and his three-volume biography of Frost. Since Thompson was also a younger colleague and friend at the Bread Loaf School of English, Frost may not have realized that he was inviting psychography, not hagiography; but in any case it tells us something both about Frost and about latter-day obliviousness to Longfellow's range that Longfellow was one of the bridges that brought the two men together.

New England's other "Fireside" or "Schoolroom" poets[8] mattered less deeply to Frost, although he certainly knew their work to some extent. By the eldest among them, William Cullen Bryant, "the American Wordsworth," who was one of Frost's mother's favorite poets, he memorized when young at least one piece, "To a Waterfowl" (*APNC* 1: 125–26); and he alluded to Bryant occasionally in his mature work. Frost enjoyed John Greenleaf Whittier's poetry selectively but distanced himself from Whittier's moralism. The two other figures in the standard constellation, James Russell Lowell and Oliver Wendell Holmes, seemingly did not interest Frost much, if indeed he read them at all beyond his schoolboy exercises, despite Lowell's experiments (and Holmes' to a lesser extent) with backcountry New England intonations.

With one exception, the other nineteenth-century New England verse and prose poets who died before Frost reached maturity he did not know or care much about. Emerson's sometime protégés, Jones Very and Ellery Channing, did not exist for him, nor did their hinterland contemporary, Frederick Goddard Tuckerman. Nathaniel Hawthorne mattered to Frost only in the general sense of being as a precursor in the regional gothic line, and by the 1920s he retained only the most shadowy recollection of Hawthorne's work. And Frost paid no attention at all to such less canonical writers of antebellum regional prose as Catharine Maria Sedgwick, Sarah Josepha Hale, and Lydia Maria Child. Harriet Beecher Stowe meant "abolitionist" to him rather than "regionalist." The one exception mentioned above was the Connecticut-born adoptive Californian Edward Rowland Sill, whose poems collected in the 1880s (cf. *APNC* 2: 397–400) impressed the youthful Frost for their restrained philosophic expression of elegiac melancholy.

With the later nineteenth-century local colorists or "regional realists," whose careers were ending about the time Frost began publishing, his work has close affinity, particularly his many dramatic monologues and dialogues of regional life: the New Hampshire writer Alice Brown (whom Frost thought of as a friend), Rose Terry Cooke, Mary Wilkins Freeman, Sarah Orne Jewett, Rowland Robinson, and Celia Thaxter. Both early reviewers and later critics have sometimes defined his originality as a contributor of poems to a then predominantly prose genre.[9] But although Frost was well aware of the vogue these writers had created for New England outback scenes, replete with "abandoned farmhouses, the miles of stone walls gridding whole townships long since reverted to forest, and the tottering and fallen stones of family graveyard,"[10] it is not clear that their writing much interested him, even though several of them also wrote poetry, Thaxter especially. The one elder regional contemporary whose work Frost is known to have read faithfully was Maine poet Edwin Arlington Robinson. Robinson figured for Frost first as an admired, senior, more established presence ("'the best of the moderns,'" Frost called him in the 1930s: a telling indication of his own conservatism), then as a rival whom he increasingly criticized, although he wrote a gracious introduction to Robinson's posthumously published last book, *King Jasper* (1935) (*CPPP*, 741–48).[11] Indeed Frost later declared that this was "the nearest I ever came to getting myself down in prose" (*CPPP*, 773).

The other New England poet of Frost's own era now reckoned as truly great, Wallace Stevens, published his first book only after Frost's mature style crystallized and his international reputation was secured; and despite half-hearted attempts at making acquaintance (including recollection of Harvard ties), they did not get along either biographically or artistically, but wound up patronizing each other. Frost was flustered by Stevens' urbanity, and Stevens was acutely self-conscious of Frost's being (and knowing himself to be) much more of a literary lion than he. Poet-critic Amy Lowell mattered mainly to Frost for her condescending commendation of him as an authentic New England primitive.

So much for "the facts" about Frost's regional literary affinities. Now for a look at his exfoliation as a regional bard.

II

The sequence of volumes that formed the basis of Frost's first *Poems* (1923) shows an initially hesitant but increasingly assertive embracement of a regional persona that was to empower, define, and by the same token delimit him.

The title of *A Boy's Will* (1913) is taken from the first part of the refrain of Longfellow's "My Lost Youth" (*APNC* 1: 406–08), a reminiscence of boyhood scenes in Portland, Maine ("'A boy's will' is the wind's will/ And the thoughts of youth are long, long thoughts"); but the collection as a whole is hardly place-specific. New England figures chiefly as "a setting for [the poet's] sentimental education," as Kemp shrewdly puts it.[12] Tellingly, Frost lifts the least "local," the most "archetypal" part of "My Lost Youth": a scrap Longfellow himself quoted from an old Finnish poem. Lost-youthishness is certainly a distinctive Longfellow motif (cf. the young lovers of *Evangeline*, separated in the forced Arcadian diaspora reunited only in old age) but no more so than for Wordsworth or Byron or Arnold. Again, the pastoral ambiance of most of the poems in *A Boy's Will* ("In a Vale," "Mowing," "The Tuft of Flowers," "My Butterfly" [*CPPP*, 24, 26, 30, 36], is vague enough to suggest any number of rural places. And the book's most ambitious piece, "The Trial by Existence" (*CPPP*, 28), is literally out of this world: an allegorical Shelleyan dream vision of metempsychosis. Frost was clearly still – and never wholly ceased to be – the poet who at the age of twenty affirmed to his first literary editor that his favorite poems were Keats' "Hyperion," Shelley's *Prometheus*, Tennyson's "Morte d'Arthur," and Browning's "Saul."[13]

A Boy's Will does also show Frost starting to bond to more recognizably New England subjects. Its seasonality, for instance the fall colors celebrated in "October" (*CPPP*, 35), had been for three-quarters of a century a canonical hallmark of New England nature writing, as had the sereness of brown November. A number of the poems ventriloquize specific New England voices. "A Late Walk" in autumn "through the mowing field" amidst falling leaves across "the headless aftermath" which "Half closes the garden path" (*CPPP*, 18) reprises Longfellow's "Aftermath," which also treats the moment when "the Summer fields are mown" and "dry leaves strew the path" as symbolizing the poet's own slim pickings (*APNC* 1: 426). "To the Thawing Wind" (*CPPP*, 21) tries out the jaunty trochaic tetrameter with which Emerson invokes "The Humble-Bee" as a muse (*APNC* 1: 272):

> Bring the singer, bring the nester;
> Give the buried flower a dream;
> Make the settled snowbank steam   [Frost]

> Let me chase thy waving lines,
> Keep me nearer, me thy hearer,
> Singing over shrubs and vines.   [Emerson]

In "Stars" (*CPPP*, 19), Frost both echoes Emerson in stanza one ("tumultuous snow" recalls the "tumultuous privacy of storm" in Emerson's "The Snow-Storm" (*APNC* 1: 274) and experiments with Dickinsonian laconics in stanza two:[14]

> As if with keenness for our fate,
>   Our faltering few steps on
> To white rest, and a place of rest
>   Invisible at dawn, –

Altogether, the regionalism of *A Boy's Will* was persuasive enough to set the Yankee farmer-poet image-making going among his reviewers. But without the hindsight advantage of knowing Frost to be a New England bard, these echoes do not seem much more telling than others from "the worn book of old-golden song" mentioned in another poem (*CPPP*, 24) (doubtless Palgrave's *Golden Treasury* of English poetry: Frost's favorite anthology, which as a teenager he had read "literally to rags and tatters")[15] – a poem whose rhetoric is redolent of Keats and even the preromantic William Collins ("the bat's mute antics") (*CPPP*, 23).

The poems in *North of Boston* (1914) announce themselves far more explicitly as products of a regional imagination, although the chief genres (dramatic monologues and dialogues in blank verse) is rather in the vein of Shakespeare and Browning.[16] The volume provides a kind of anthology of familiar upcountry New England workways, landforms, and psychographs. Wall-building, blueberrying, apple-picking, hay-making. Reclusive bottled-up neurotic cottagers, rural poverty, strange bumpy contours. The poetic language has a more "oral" quality than in *A Boy's Will*, especially in the fictive voices, but also in the poet's "own" voice, as in the "I sha'n't be long" of the opening poem, "The Pasture," which eventually became the preface to the *Complete Poems* as a whole (*CPPP*, 3). Though Thoreau never wanted to be a dialect poet, he did strive for a counterpoint between poetic rhythm and prose syntax, complicating this further in his dramatic poetry with a second counterpoint between formal and vernacular; and *North of Boston* achieves both breakthroughs.

The world portrayed therein is pretty much that of late-century regional realism: a world otherwise today chiefly known, now that Robinson's Tilbury Town poems are less and less read, through the stories and sketches of Sarah Orne Jewett, Rose Terry Cooke, and Mary Wilkins Freeman. It is an intensely local agrarian world that time has passed by, a world populated by reserved folk either inarticulate or nervously garrulous, a world where city people and institutions figure as largely absent aliens and/or exploiters. In a predictably male vein, Frost stresses solitude more than sociality and portrays female community not at all; but – possibly through osmotic absorption of the female local colorists – he is also more critical than not of male harshness or failure of understanding of women and sympathetic to female impatience with male stolidity and narcissism. "Home Burial" shows that Frost, unlike all the men in Susan Glaspell's story "A Jury of Her Peers," would definitely have understood if not approved the emotions of the farm-wife who killed the husband who strangled her canary.

Frost places "himself" most fully in the context of that turn-of-the-century upcountry world in "The Black Cottage" (*CPPP*, 59–62). A garrulous local "minister" takes the persona on a tour of a "forsaken" "little cottage" inhabited for decades by a Civil War-widowed dowager of strict, demand-ing old-time rectitude.

> She had her own idea of things, the old lady.
> And she liked talk. She had seen Garrison
> And Whittier, and had her story of them.
> One wasn't long in learning that she thought
> Whatever else the Civil War was for,
> It wasn't just to keep the States together,
> Nor just to free the slaves, though it did both.
> She wouldn't have believed those ends enough
> To have given outright for them all she gave.
> Her giving somehow touched the principle
> That all men are created free and equal.
> And to hear her quaint phrases – so removed
> From the world's view today of all those things.

The minister proceeds to muse inconclusively about that "hard mystery" of Jefferson – whether the Declaration's free-and-equal clause really is true – caught between his own dubieties and his respect for the widow's indom-itable "innocence," which might just "at last prevail" in the wider world just as it did in his parish, where the old lady's opposition kept him from liber-alizing the language of the worship service.

From the minister's rambling talk, the dead woman emerges as a figure whom the neighborhood has consigned to an antiquity so remote that it takes this spokesperson a great effort to conjure it up, and even then she remains a mysterious and ghostly figure for all her personal staunchness and residual power as a cultural superego. For the persona-interlocutor, that bygone world, the glorious New England Renaissance moment of righteous eloquence in poetry (Whittier) and oratory (Garrison) must feel all the more distant. An additional measure of the distantiation is that the poem's central image, the ruined cottage, is obviously not New England-specific but trans-atlantic, indebted whether directly or indirectly to the dialogue at Margaret's ruined cottage in Book I of Wordsworth's *The Excursion* (1814), the long poem by which America's favorite British Romantic was best known in the nineteenth century. Yet despite such stylizations, even as the poem reduces Whittier almost to a cartoon figure of bygone zealotry, it seems teasingly to reinvoke him when the minister discovers a nest of bees in the wall and they abruptly exit. Might this seriocomically allude to one of Whittier's most sensitive and touching poems, "Telling the Bees"? – in which the lover returns after an absence to find the servant-girl telling the bees that his sweetheart has died (so they will not desert the farm) (*APNC* 1: 468–70). Might the minister's monologue be a fumbling unconscious equivalent of this ritual of propitiation; or, even if that is too rarefied, might the poem be wanting to keep at arm's length the stiffish side of its precursor (Whither the "Quaker Militant") while honoring Whittier the humanitarian? However this may be, the poem clearly wants to offer an image of visitors standing bemused amidst the relics of a cultural tradition that continues to exert a certain force and authority upon those who listen closely to it, but which takes a great effort even to begin to understand.

During the next decade, Frost planted himself solidly within that New England world. Whereas in *North of Boston*, except for "The Pasture," the persona pictures himself as less embedded in its premises than his local characters are, in *Mountain Interval* (1916) the persona starts to become another character in the dramatic ensemble, the local who refuses to sell his balsam firs to a city slicker ("Christmas Trees" [*CPPP*, 103]), the farmer who stops mowing to help his child save a nest of birds he almost cut through ("The Exposed Nest" [106]), or one rustic meeting another on equal terms ("The Gum-Gatherer" [134]). In these poems, the posture of witness to outback obsolescence partially gives way to that of the naturalized villager, with an old-timer's hostility to creeping commercialism, even to basic technology like telephone and telegraph ("An Encounter," "The Line-Gang" [121, 135]). Frost has begun more actively to play the inheritor of the lost world of the widow of "The Black Cottage." As one reviewer of his next collection put it, "where Lowell and Whittier observed and reported the New England peasant, Frost has become one."[17]

The process of regional identification reaches an end point of sorts in *New Hampshire* (1923), whose title and lead-off poem, the longest in Frost's canon except for the two late-life dramatic "masques," wryly but assertively declares allegiance to that state (and to Vermont as well) (*CPPP*, 151–62). This is a poem Frostians like to dislike, and for good reason. It teeters awkwardly between genial humor and ingratiating self-irony ("when I asked [a Boston poet: Amy Lowell] what ailed the people,/ She said 'Go read your own books and find out'" [*CPPP*, 157]), and the kind of self-focused complacency into which one too easily gets drawn once one becomes conscious of becoming publicly defined as a spokesperson of a certain sort. Kemp judges "New Hampshire" "an excruciatingly ostentatious and affected attempt on Frost's part to come to terms with his adopted regional personality":[18] a harsh but understandable verdict. Failures, however, are often revealing performances, and so here. "New Hampshire" highlights at least three things about Frost's "reinhabitation" of New England – to borrow an apt term from ecocriticism.[19] First, it was a process involving continual self-revision. For example, he tries to counter, without retracting, the image of himself (warranted, he realizes) as an anti-New Hampshire gothicizer by a combination of boosterism and portrayal of himself as a perpetually hyper-sensitive person who would be disaffected in any environment. (Frost does not explicitly link his ingrained disaffection to his adopted New Hampshireness, though the link is strongly implied and elsewhere exploited more piquantly.) Second, regional self-implacement means a certain dis-placement of forebears as well as rapprochement with them. The poem takes aim at two eminent Victorians Frost particularly admired: Matthew Arnold and Ralph Waldo Emerson, with sideswipes at Bryant and Whittier along the way.[20] Indeed, "New Hampshire" largely turns on the charge laid down in Emerson's quasi-abolitionist "Ode, Inscribed to W. H. Channing" that "'The God who made New Hampshire/ taunted the lofty land with little men'" (*APNC* 1: 283), against which Frost wants to argue that this goes to show that between the two neighbors the provincial is Massachusetts, not New Hampshire. Third, implacement will always remain performative and thereby somewhat factitious. The speaker does not, it turns out, want to make a choice that irrevocably boxes him in; and even if he did, at most he would be "a plain New Hampshire farmer/ With an income in cash of say a thousand/ (From say a publisher in New York City)" (*CPPP*, 162); and even if he could stay put as a plain New Hampshire farmer, he would not be satis-fied because the disaffected side of him recognizes the partial truth of Emerson's charge. Altogether the poem is a classic example of self-conscious belatedness about cultural identity: of identity being not "natural" but con-structed; of identity being asserted in the context of having been defined pre-viously by others; of identity as a role one wants to act out without being bound by – though amidst and despite that self-consciousness he cannot but be aware that it must entail binding himself down in some fashion.

So Frost's pilgrimage toward regional identification, entailed a double movement: from one form of "naivete" to another (from more-or-less ungrounded romantic pastoralism to a more grounded local character or sage persona) and, concurrently, from one form of poetic self-consciousness (earnest romantic aestheticism of the "I dwell with a strangely aching heart/ In that vanished abode there far apart" variety [*CPPP*, 16]) to another (affec-tionate-satirical regionalism of the "trust New Hampshire not to have enough/ Of radium or anything to sell" variety [*CPPP*, 154]). The typical weaknesses of his mature repertoire, both of which mar "New Hampshire," are sententiousness on the first wavelength and triviality on the second.

Though Frost has a unique historical place as New England's first great returnee after the invention and canonization (only now being seriously contested) of New England as the nation's dominant culture region, virtually all the traits so far described, and more, are already visible in the work of his regional forebears, notwithstanding his swerves in "The Black Cottage" and "New Hampshire" away from Whittier, Emerson, Bryant, and others – as we shall now attempt more fully to assess.

III

There are at least five ways of situating poetic practice *vis-à-vis* regional identity. (1) Biographically, via the writer's life-experiences, including the evidence of reading in attentiveness to sociality with other regionalist practitioners. (2) Geographically, via the cultural-environmental repertoire of the writer's represented world, including (for the traditional New England hinterlands) rustic villages with their standard spatial layouts, meeting houses, and other architectural landmarks together with the civic and religious rituals associated with them, ethnically homogeneous populace, church-related rituals, small-scale agrarianism, stone walls, and other folk architectural motifs, typical flora and fauna both cultivated (apple trees, elms, and oaks as decorative or commemorative trees) and the fortuitous (steeple bush, blueberries). (3) Ideologically, via attitudinal traits like town-centeredness, self-sufficiency (post-)protestant religiosity, moralism, the work ethic, historical and genealogical self-consciousness. (4) Linguistically, via distinctive idiom ("interval" for narrow valley between mountains), pronunciation ("sh'an't" in "The Pasture"), syntax ("What I like best's the lay of different farms/ Coming out on them from a stretch of woods" (*CPPP*, 53), and tonality (wry, dry, laconic restraint). (5) Formally, via preferred genres and metrics, as well as allusions to particular precursor works. The first dimension we covered reasonably well in section I. Concerning the second and third, far more can be said than was said in section II about both the typicality and the idiosyncrasy of Frost's New England thematics. Very broadly speaking, he stays away from village centers and public rituals, concentrates on privatistic experience, takes georgic scenes and rustic character to a new level of textured particularity relative to earlier poets, and in the area of nature imagery extends the range and subtlety of his precursors particularly in the areas of regional flora and – rarely noted in Frost criticism – the look and feel of sky and stars. But in order to grasp Frost's *poetics* in their New England context, and specifically in relation to the "Fireside" group that comprised the first American poetic canon, it is best to concentrate especially on criteria four and five.

Given that most of Frost's Brahmin precursors have been ignored for decades by literary scholars and are likely to remain so for the indefinite future, the results may seem surprising. Although virtually none of Frost's "major" poems could have been written by any of them, virtually everything in Frost's poetry is anticipated here and there in their work. The fuller significance of that point I shall develop in the final section of this chapter. But first, let us sift the textual evidence.

Like his New England precursors, Frost favors either bound prosodic forms (meter, rhyme, stanza) or blank verse. When he praised Robinson for staying "content with the old-fashioned way to be new" (*CPPP*, 741) he was both being true to the taste that prompted him to rate Whitman's poetry below Emerson's because Whitman could not write good conventional verse, as well as to his own poetic practice.[21] One marks that this commitment was a faith in the possibilities of highly formal verse structures like the rondeau ("Stopping by Woods on a Snowy Evening" [*CPPP*, 207]), the narrative sequence in stanzas of couplets ("The Tuft of Flowers" [30]) or triplets ("A Star in a Stone-Boat" [162]), and especially the sonnet ("Mowing," "Design," "For Once, Then, Something," and so on [26, 275, 208]), which was a well-established New England genre thanks to Longfellow, Lowell, and Robinson (not to mention Very and Tuckerman).

It might seem a revisionary swerve on Frost's part that he also tried to some extent to "open up" or "subvert" the sonnet. The burden of "Design," for instance, is to turn the traditional theme of providential and, by implication, aesthetic design into a question; and "For Once" is an inverted sonnet (6–8, not 8–6), about the failure of a hoped-for epiphany (and by extension the poem itself) to yield a clear vision. But Frost's "subversions" are nothing compared to his younger contemporary Cummings' modernist contortions of sonnet form and, more to the point at hand, Frost's predecessors had been there before him. One common mark of Fireside sonneteering is a diminuendo in the sestet that threatens to unravel what came before, like the "– Though" in Longfellow's "Mezzo Cammin" when his aspiration to fulfill his dream to build a "tower of song" is chastened by the vision of Death (*APNC* 1: 382). Emerson's "Days" (*APNC* 1: 324) is formally a truncated sonnet, thematically about foreshortened vision. One of Frost's favorite poems by Robinson, sometimes considered an influence on "Nothing Gold Can Stay" (*CPPP*, 206) is a sonnet that develops a beautiful tableau of green wheat metamorphosing into "a thousand golden sheaves," only to pull the plug at the end with an autumnal metaphor – "As if a thousand girls with golden hair/ Might rise from where they slept and go away."[22] Frost's own sonnet, "The Oven Bird" (*CPPP*, 116) thematizes this diminuendo tradition and articulates its premise at the close ("what to make of a diminished thing").

As these examples suggest, the theme of cultural or spiritual "aftermath" was by no means something Frost derived from turn-of-the-century upcountry ethnography or from the local colorists alone. One of Emily Dickinson's best critics has identified the aftermath of mysterious trauma as "the crucial" experience in her poetry.[23] Aftermath in the sense of lonely senescent decrepitude, which Frost wrote about feelingly in "An Old Man's Winter Night" for example (*CPPP*, 105), had also been a favored theme of Robinson before him (Frost particularly admired "Mr. Flood's Party") and before that Oliver Wendell Holmes' "The Last Leaf," Longfellow's "My Books," and in a more reverential mood Whittier's "To My Old Schoolmaster."[24] Aftermath in the more culturally contexted sense that *North of Boston* and a number of later poems imagine it – the vision of a regional Yankee culture past its apogee, however admirable for wit, stoicism, and rectitude – had been quite fully unfolded by Whittier, especially in his immensely popular nostalgia piece *Snow-Bound*, which memorializes farming family life in the preindustrial era across the chasm left by the Civil War (*APNC* 1: 476). Like Frost, Whittier was also the wistful memorializer of roads not taken ("of all sad words of tongue or pen, / The saddest are these: 'It might have been'" (*APNC* 1: 462), of lost intellectual vitality ("How has New England's romance fled"), and of the need to make the best of sparse local cultural resources – as the world sees it, anyhow ("Here swells no perfect man sublime, / Nor woman winged before her time, / But with the faults and follies of the race, / Old home-bred virtues hold their not unhonored place").[25] Like Emerson and Dickinson and like Frost after them, Whittier was repeatedly protesting that despite the harshness of the landscape and the provincialism of the culture compared to Europe and various other dream-places, he loved his piece of earth anyway. In short, a Frost poem like the masterful "Directive" (*CPPP*, 341–42), which leads its readers back through the ruined landscape of hill country memory in what proves also to be a dream-reinvention of childlike arcadia, is a distillation from a regional imaginary long set in place.

Sonnet and elegiac disposition were by no means the only traditions that tied Frost to the Fireside poets. Another was ballad. "Brown's Descent" (*CPPP*, 132), for example, recalls various seriocomic efforts like Whittier's "Cobbler Keezar's Vision."[26] In later years, Frost also turned out numerous short sententious epigrammatic wisdom poems like Emerson's mottoes and epigrams. Emerson's haunting conclusion to "Brahma" ("But thou, meek lover of the good/ Find me, and turn thy back on heaven," which Frost said haunted him for many years (*APNC* 1: 319; *CPPP*, 815–16), is reprised in Frost's own "We dance round in a ring and suppose/ But the Secret sits in the middle and knows" (*CPPP*, 329). Still another shared genre was the short lyric in rhymed symmetrical stanzas on a discrete natural object, in which the meditation proceeds from composition of the image to a moral inference.

The first New England poem Frost is known to have memorized, Bryant's "To a Waterfowl," follows that very pattern. The first seven stanzas chart the flight of the waterfowl in a mood of joyous pensive affirmation, then the last points the pious moral (*APNC* 1: 125):

> He who, from zone to zone,
> Guides through the boundless sky thy certain flight,
> In the long way that I must tread alone
> Will lead my steps aright.

The genre extends back, of course, to the British romantics and thence to Donne, Herbert, and Vaughan – but then so does much else in traditional New England poetics, of which more in section IV. Longfellow's "Snow-Flakes," Emerson's "The Rhodora," Holmes' "The Chambered Nautilus," and Lowell's "To the Dandelion" are all variations on this same pattern, as is Bryant's own "To the Fringed Gentian."[27] Within this tradition, Frost innovates to the extent of stressing descriptive texture relative to moral reflection and ambiguating the latter so as to undermine the sense of moral or metaphysical certainty. For instance, by "resolving" the eerie tableau in "Design" of dead fly caught by fat dimpled spider with the question "What but design of darkness to appall?" rather than an assertion; or dissolve the incipient allegory of snowscape as cosmic wasteland that "Desert Places" starts to build into a confession of its status as personal fantasy, that he's scaring "myself with my own desert places" (*CPPP*, 275, 269). Yet to distinguish between the Fireside poets and Frost in terms of "traditional closure" vs. "modernist openendedness" is too cut-and-dried. For example, in the "closure" to Bryant's "To the Fringed Gentian," which compares this late-blooming native woodflower to the end of human life, an element of modernist dubiety is already evident: "I would that thus," pleads the speaker, "when I shall see/ the hour of death draw near to me/ Love blossoming within my heart/ May look to heaven as I depart" (*APNC* 1: 125). He *hopes* that his life-closure will be as tidily secure as the gentian's, but he cannot be sure; after all, this was the same poet whose career was launched with the resolutely stoical "Thanatopsis" (122), who later wrote that "Ahaz"-like neopagan tribute to the groves as "God's first temples" (*CPPP*, 161, *APNC* 1: 153). Frost, for his part, when he came to write his own poem about the same flower, on the one hand secularized his pursuit into an almost purely narrative-descriptive affair, but on the other hand ended his quest with a much more cozily reassuring closure (*CPPP*, 311):

> And I for one
> Said that the fall might come and the whirl of leaves,
> For summer was done.

Only the tiniest disquiet is residually present here, in the mismatch between the alternating pentameter and dimeter lines. The effect recalls the last of his "Hill-Wife" poems, "The Impulse," where the same meter is used to register the snapping of the bond between husband and wife. This willed asymmetry of lineation, however, is itself anticipated in such Fireside efforts as Whittier's "Ichabod," decrying the fall of Daniel Webster (tetrameter-dimeter quatrains) and Longfellow's lament for the untimely death of "Hawthorne," his work incomplete (pentameter-trimeter).[28] One of the traits for which Frost admired Longfellow was his wry modesty; "he took himself with the gentlest twinkle."[29] As evidence Frost cited, among other works, "The Birds of Killingworth," a poem from *The Tales of the Wayside Inn* that narrates the story of a Connecticut town that resolved to kill its birds as pests to crops despite the local schoolmaster's eloquent plea – for "Men have no faith in fine-spun sentiment/ Who put their trust in bullocks and in beeves" – but then suffered a plague of insects, repented, and welcomed the birds back.[30] Here and in many other poems – *The Courtship of Miles Standish* being another – Longfellow loved to set up quietly satiric contrasts between stolid linear-minded practicality and a more complex aesthetic-intellectual sensibility, and to chasten the former by according the latter moral if not literal victory. Frost loved to do the same, most famously in the face-off between the poet and his neighbor in "Mending Wall," the stolid countryman who cannot "go behind his father's saying" and therefore does not get the benefit of even hearing the speaker's playfully anarchic musings, shared with the putatively sympathetic reader alone, about the desirability of dismantling walls (*CPPP*, 39–40). Frost was similarly drawn to Emerson's tones of bemused detachment. Indeed, possibly the single most important service these two precursors performed for Frost was to help him figure out the right tone to set as a New England sage: the right balance between satire and sympathy, between the passionate and the cerebral, between explanation and insinuation, as well as the right balance between colloquial and formal utterance. In his comments about poetry, nothing preoccupied Frost more than the necessity of coordinating prose syntax with metrical form. A late epigram encapsulates his leading idea (*CPPP*, 329):

> The sentencing goes blithely on its way,
> And takes the playfully objected rhyme
> As surely as it keeps the stroke and time
> In having its undeviable say.

Poetry should read like unaffected prose, but it should also keep "stroke and time" in a way that interanimates both by the concurrent pleasures of how "natural" it feels ("blithely on its way") and resistance to/within the grid ("playfully objected rhyme"). Frost could have derived this article of his artistic conscience from any number of the great English or Roman poets,[31] but the proof text to which he kept returning was that twenty-two line passage in Emerson's "Monadnoc" on the vernacular wellsprings of good (regional) poetry.[32]

> Now in sordid weeds they sleep,
> In dulness now their secret keep;
> Yet, will you learn our ancient speech,
> These the masters who can teach.
> Fourscore or a hundred words
> All their vocal muse affords;
> But they turn them in a fashion
> Past clerks' or statesmen's art or passion.
> I can spare the college bell,
> And the learned lecture, well;
> Spare the clergy and libraries,
> Institutes and dictionaries,
> For that hardy English root
> Thrives here, unvalued, underfoot.
> Rude poets of the tavern hearth,
> Squandering your unquoted mirth,
> Which keeps the ground and never soars
> While Jake retorts and Reuben roars;
> Scoff of yeoman strong and stark,
> Goes like bullet to its mark;
> While the solid curse and jeer
> Never balk the waiting ear.

Judging both from Frost's reflections on poetry and from his poetic practice, at least four things would have appealed to him about this passage. First, the Wordsworthian commendation of peasant speech as the vital force behind good poetry, and the aesthetic of pithy simplicity underlying it, discommoding both pedants and aesthetes. "I want to be a poet for all sorts and kinds," Frost affirmed in 1913, not to "make a merit of being caviare to the crowd the way my quasi-friend Pound does" (CPPP, 668). Frost wanted to be a "public poet," much in the way that William Charvat characterizes Longfellow in a wonderfully instructive essay that sheds much light on the craftsmanly ethos of the whole Fireside group and Frost as well.[33] It was fitting that Frost became the nation's first professional poet-pedagogue, pioneering the artist-in-residence idea, and in such a way as to make that post serve as a platform for communicating far beyond the academy's confines.

Second, however, it was no less important to Frost that "Monadnoc" does not go all the way in the direction of the vernacular: does not itself talk the language of Jake and Reuben, though it begins to suggest the force of such language through the "bullet-like" briskness of the tetrameter couplets with their terse end-stopped lines, folksy contortions of meter (not by chance is "libraries" metrically twisted into doggerel), and pithy monosyllables – "scoffs," "rude," "mirth," "balk," "stark." Emerson's performance both gave Frost a mandate for developing a more grainy vernacular of his own, as he did especially in his dramatic monologues and dialogues, and a model for a more distilled, distanced celebration of vernacularism – which remained Frost's own primary wavelength as latter-day regional sage, not the dialect poetry James Russell Lowell pioneered in his *Biglow Papers*.

Third, and similarly, as we have seen already, Frost would have relished "Monadnoc"'s amused detachment from the objects of its commendation, typical of many Emerson poems and the drift of his later prose style from "New England Reformers" on. Unlike Wordsworth's exalted defense of the speech of humble rustics in his Preface to *Lyrical Ballads* (and unlike Coleridge's equally solemn refutation of Wordsworth's doctrine in *Biographia Literaria*), Emerson can take Jake and Reuben with a twinkle as well as himself, the "schoolman."

Fourth, Frost himself was deeply precommitted to fathoming the implications behind Emerson's notion of "our ancient speech" – for reasons we shall review in the next and final section.

IV

Any thinking person at the turn of the twenty-first century who starts to press the connection very far between Frost and traditional New England poetics must confront a host of real or imagined adversaries. Who wants to listen, anyhow? Who cares about Longfellow and Whittier anymore? And as for Emerson and Thoreau, has it not been established that their real poetry was in their prose and that their verse was "klunky" by comparison? And even if we can find a certain amount of really good verse in that traditional New England archive, why bother? Is not the American poetic tradition that really counts a more experimental form-resistant tradition – the Whitmanian tradition, particularly? And among poets who favored more traditional metrics is not Dickinson a far more interesting case of form-resistance than Emerson or Frost? Is it not the case that an examination centered on Frost and the Brahmins leaves us in an anti-modernist cul-de-sac of white male Anglo-Saxon Protestants? Surely, if we want to do right by Frost – and maybe we cannot, because everybody knows that his stock has sunk since the 1970s – what we ought to stress are his quasi-affiliations with the modernists instead: we ought to do our best to establish Frost as an inhabitant, albeit uneasy, of the moment of Pound, H. D., Williams, Stevens, Crane, Cummings, and that laureate of African American urban folklife, Langston Hughes.

Yet there are also cogent reasons for reversing the medal and insisting on the unacknowledged significance of the unfashionable Fireside–Frost continuum instead. For one thing, Frost's commitment to "the old-fashioned way to be new," to repeat what he wrote about Robinson, has never really become obsolete despite whatever can be said about the modern salience and "American" distinctiveness of Whitmanian open-form poetics or form-breaking modernist avant-gardism more generally. Not only can we point to a continuation of talented if subgalactic latter-day poets who are self-consciously Frostian, like Robert Francis, Wendell Berry, and Philip Booth, but also to the fact that some of the most significant voices in twentieth-century American poetry have been at least as attracted to bound forms as open forms, even some of those typically arraigned on the other side like T. S. Eliot, who expressed a fastidious skepticism about "free verse" oddly resonant with Frost's. Elizabeth Bishop, John Crowe Ransom, Sterling Brown, the young Theodore Roethke and the young Gwendolyn Brooks, Richard Wilbur, Robert Lowell, Sylvia Plath, Robert Hayden, William Stafford, and the eventual American W. H. Auden to name just a few. If we change our central criterion for defining that continuum away from matters of prosody to matters of language and tone, to an aesthetic of emotionally guarded expression rendering prose syntax in measured lines within a modulated tonal register ranging from sententious to wryly ironic, a number of these same names again basically fit (Bishop, Wilbur, Stafford, for example) and we can add many others: Marianne Moore, James Wright, John Haines, Simon Ortiz, Rita Dove.

This is, be it noted, by no means an androcentric or an ethnocentric list, notwithstanding the male Yankee homogeneity of the Fireside poets and Frost; and by the same token it shows the risks of trying to correlate "progressive" politics with "progressive" poetics. On the contrary, just as Frost and his Brahmin antecedents favored traditional metrics, retention of prose syntax within those forms, modulated passion, and shareable vocabulary partly that they might be accepted as public poets, so too for more "marginal" voices with more "subversive" agendas, as intimated by Langston Hughes in *Montage of a Dream Deferred*:[34]

> Cheap little rhymes
> A cheap little tune
> Are sometimes as dangerous
> As a sliver of the moon.

A cheap little tune
To cheap little rhymes
Can cut a man's
Throat sometimes.

The same aesthetic is no less well adapted for purposes of personal or communal self-defense, as Frost demonstrated at the personal level in his homely totem animal poem "A Drumlin Woodchuck" (*CPPP*, 257) and Paul Laurence Dunbar demonstrated at the level of cultural assertion in his great poem about the necessary agony of protective deception, "We Wear the Mask." Nor have the potential uses to which the Fireside aesthetic has been put by non-WASP poets been confined to "the political" in the ordinary senses of the term, as Hughes reveals in the epigrammatic poem he contributed to a late-life poetic gathering in Frost's honor:[35]

God, in His infinite wisdom
Did not make me very wise –
So when my actions are stupid
They hardly take God by surprise.

Hughes might, of course, have chosen primarily for strategic reasons to depoliticize his rhetoric here, to strike the cosmic rather than the activist note here out of deference to the mainstream sage, to preserve decorum by resort to moral abstraction. Yet it is also the case that Hughes was by disposition a poet who habitually wrote in many different registers including this one and that it is specious in any case to try to disaggregate "moral abstractionism" from "the political" in Fireside aesthetics. Although their work is conventionally believed (and often appears) to want to evade political engagement to the "privatistic" realm of family life, nature, and moral abstractions, virtually all of them (from Bryant down to Frost himself) wrote a goodly number of explicitly political poems and – more directly to the point at hand – they looked, with considerable justice, upon moral abstractionism as a potential form of political intervention, not as a separate sphere. Frost's "The Black Cottage," examined in section II above, shows this very clearly: although it has nothing specific to say about the American political process as such it is deeply preoccupied with its key ethical mainspring: the troubled legacy of the Declaration's "free and equal" clause.

All this is by no means to say that most of the poets listed above were profoundly touched by Frost, much less by Emerson and the Brahmins (although certainly Dunbar was), only that the prism of the Fireside–Frost aesthetic refracts a wider spectrum of poetic possibilities than we are conditioned to think, beginning, among the unshakably canonical poets of the United States, with the *oeuvre* of Emily Dickinson.

To stress the Fireside–Frost continuum has the further advantage of reopening the broader issue of what counts as national poetics. Frost wanted no less than Whitman or William Carlos Williams to write in an "American grain" that would be faithful to vernacular idiom and rhythm, but he followed Emerson's notion in "Monadnoc" that the path to recovery of "our ancient speech" in the hinterlands led not to a dictionary of regional dialect but to the discovery of "that hardy English root" lost in the parlance of "clerks" and "statesmen." This was more a "classist" than a "culturalist" conception of vital language – or, rather, an "anti-classist" conception, since the vision of an accessible poetic was basic to it – and it led Frost to take a position at first sight paradoxical but on second thought quite self-consistent: "that the colloquial is the root of every good poem" but that "colloquial as I use the word" might extend not only to "the beauty of the high thinking in Emerson's Uriel and Give All to Love" but "all the lyric in Palgrave's Treasure for that matter," like Herrick's "To Daffodils" (*CPPP*, 693).

In short, Frost believed, as for the most part did the Fireside group as a whole, in a species of poetic colloquiality which would be locally nuanced, but which would also, and by the same token, take its place in an Anglophonic symposium to which Yeats and Hardy and Robinson, Emerson and Longfellow and Arnold, Shakespeare and Wordsworth and Keats, all rightfully belonged. The assumption of a shared Anglophone poetic (without sacrifice of local particularity) and the goal of a publicly accessible poetic communication (without sacrifice of complexity) were the two most basic coordinates of Frost's conception of what the historical and social position of poesis should be. This ethos of cosmopolitan localism, or localist cosmopolitanism may not, as doctrine, sound particularly striking or glamorous; but its best poetic results have been admirable, and in a deeply divided but intractably global world it merits a fresh look.

NOTES

1 My sincere thanks to my research assistant Ansley Dalbo for her help in preparing this chapter.
2 Quoted in *Robert Frost on Writing*, ed. Elaine Barry (New Brunswick, NJ: Rutgers University Press, 1973), p. 75.
3 References to the traditional New England poets are from *American Poetry: The Nineteenth Century*, ed. John Hollander, 2 vols. (New York: Library of America, 1993) (abbreviated in the text as *APNC*).
4 The most extensive critical studies to date are John C. Kemp, *Robert Frost and New England: The Poet as Regionalist* (Princeton: Princeton University Press, 1979), which emphasizes Frost's strategic fabrication of a New England identity and George Monteiro, *Robert Frost and The New England Renaissance*

(Lexington: University Press of Kentucky, 1988), which, to the contrary, stresses inherent affinities of sensibility and practice between Frost and selected New England precursors. More specialized influence and affinity studies are cited below. Also indispensable is Frost biography, especially Lawrance Thompson's richly documented but contentious trilogy *Robert Frost: The Early Years, 1874–1915*, *Robert Frost: The Years of Triumph, 1915–1938*, and (completed by R. H. Winnick) *Robert Frost: The Later Years, 1938–1963* (New York: Holt, 1964, 1970, 1976); William H. Pritchard, *Frost: A Literary Life Reconsidered* (New York: Oxford University Press, 1984); and Jeffrey Meyers, *Robert Frost: A Biography* (New York: Houghton Mifflin, 1996). Both the biographical and critical studies often anchor their claims of Frost's New Englandism to his rather copious *ex cathedra* statements, written and oral, about poets and poetry, a good number of which (but by no means all) have been collected in *CPPP*.

5 Quoted from letters of 1915 and 1922, respectively, by Eric Carl Link, "Nature's Extra-Vagrants: Frost and Thoreau in the Main Woods," *Papers on Language and Literature*, 33 (1997), 182, which proceeds to stress plausible affinities but judiciously leaves the influence question open.

6 Quoted from the report of a 1959 conversation in Monteiro, *Robert Frost and the New England Renaissance*, p. 25. See also Elizabeth Wahlquist, "You Don't Have to Go to Niagara To Write about Water: Robert Frost's Defense of Emily Dickinson," *Literature and Belief*, 10 (1990), 90–102, the notes of her 1959 experiences studying Dickinson with Frost and Stephen Whicher at Bread Loaf School of English.

7 "The Later Minstrel" (*CPPP*, 511) wistfully opens: "Remember some departed day,/ When bathed in autumn gold,/ You wished for some sweet song, and signed/ For minstrel days of old."

8 "Schoolroom," because together with Emerson and Longfellow they comprised the "first canon" of important American poets as defined by late nineteenth-century critics and publishers in the northern United States; "Fireside," because they were promoted and accepted as edifying family entertainment. I shall use both terms interchangeably below. In conventional twentieth-century usage the group includes specifically Bryant, Longfellow, Whittier, Lowell, and Holmes. In this chapter, I blur the border between them and Emerson, whose poetry came to be placed in the same authorial constellation (although justly considered more ruggedly original), as well as Emily Dickinson and E. A. Robinson, who were never considered part of that group but whose own poetry was strongly influenced by it.

9 Amy Lowell, "North of Boston," *New Republic*, February 20, 1915, rpt. *Critical Essays on Robert Frost*, ed. Philip L. Gerber (Boston: Hall, 1982), p. 22; Perry D. Westbrook, "Robert Frost's New England," *Frost: Centennial Essays* (Jackson: University Press of Mississippi, 1973), pp. 239–55.

10 Westbrook, "Robert Frost's New England," p. 244.

11 Quotation from Meyers, *Robert Frost*, p. 172. The fullest study is Robert P. Tristram Coffin, *New Poetry and New England: Frost and Robinson* (Baltimore: Johns Hopkins University Press, 1938); one of the most judicious is Barton Levi St. Armand, "The Power of Sympathy in the Poetry of Robinson and Frost: The 'Inside' vs. the 'Outside' Narrative," *American Quarterly*, 19 (1967), 564–74, which contrasts the two as the cultural insider who tried to wean himself away vs. the cultural outsider who consciously worked his way in.

12 Kemp, *Robert Frost and New England*, p. 87, overall a strikingly intelligent demystification of Frost's New England spokesperson persona (and the public image of such), weakened only by a tendency to take a good thing too far. I follow Kemp's account at a number of points in this section.

13 22 April 1894 to Susan Hayes Ward, Literary Editor of *The Independent*, SL, 20.

14 According to Wahlquist, "You Don't Have to Go to Niagara," p. 94, Frost himself said of this poem that "'some say [it] has an accent of the lady from Amherst.'"

15 Quoted in Barry, ed., *Robert Frost on Writing*, p. 75.

16 The Fireside poets as a group did not favor blank verse for either lyric monologue (except for Bryant) or dramatic poetry, except when they turned their hands to poetic drama, as in Longfellow's *Christus* trilogy, of which Frost is known to have admired portions of Part Two, *The Golden Legend*. Indeed, they wrote few dramatic monologues or conversation poems at all. As to lyric monologue in blank verse, notable examples include Bryant's "Thanatopsis," "Forest Hymn," and "The Prairies" (*APNC* 1: 122, 153, 162); Emerson's "Musketaquid" (308), and Lowell's "Under the Willows" (695).

17 Anon., "Robert Frost," from *The Literary Spotlight*, rpt. *Critical Essays on Robert Frost*, ed. Gerber, p. 59.

18 Kemp, *Robert Frost and New England*, p. 199.

19 See Gary Snyder, "Reinhabitation," *A Place in Space* (Washington, DC: Counterpoint, 1995), pp. 183–91; and John Elder, *Reading the Mountains of Home* (Cambridge: Harvard University Press, 1998), pp. 25–26, a sensitive and searching literary–critical–autobiographical essay about the author's own construction of regional identity, from Californian to Vermonter, using Frost's "Directive" (*CPPP*, 341–42) as one of his chief guides. "Reinhabitation" for Snyder implies especially the principled outsider's aspiration to "become native" to a place insofar as possible, to approximate the commitment to it integral to the traditional folkways of its aborigines, the first "inhabitors"; but for Elder and a number of other bioregional writers (and for Snyder too) settlers can, in principle, effectively become "natives."

20 The Bryant reference is a gently satiric allusion to the opening line of "The Forest Hymn" (*APNC* 1: 153): "Even to say the groves were God's first temples/ Comes too near to Ahaz' sin [pagan tree-worship] for safety" (*CPPP*, 161) – one of many instances where Frost canon disowns the romantic pantheism to which he is also intermittently attracted. Matthew Arnold, in a much lengthier previous passage, is made to play Bryant's opposite number: the neurotically anti-nature person (161) (Richard Poirier discusses Frost's quotations from Arnold in *Robert Frost: The Work of Knowing* [1977; rpt. Stanford: Stanford University Press, 1990], pp. 46–48). Earlier, Frost takes a bizarre droll-affectionate-satiric poke at Whittier, remembering how Salem, New Hampshire, used to have "a company we called the White Corpuscles/ Whose duty was at any hour of night/ To rush in sheets and fools' caps where they smelled/ A think the least bit doubtfully perscented/ And give someone the Skipper Ireson's Ride" (154–55). Frost could not have failed to realize the ironic discrepancy between the borderline KKK charivari troupe of Salem, New Hampshire, and the Marblehead women's tarring and feathering of Skipper Ireson (in a ballad whose rollicking meter is meant to jar against its very serious core), who in direct violation of the code of captaincy ethics had fled his sinking vessel and abandoned their loved ones to their deaths.

In pretending to praise New Hampshire here, the poem, whether deliberately or not, trivializes Whittier and incriminates New Hampshire – and perhaps itself as well.

21 *Robert Frost and Sidney Cox: Forty Years of Friendship* (Hanover, NH: University Press of New England, 1981), p. 111.

22 Edwin Arlington Robinson, "The Sheaves," *Tilbury Town: Selected Poems*, ed. Lawrance Thompson (New York: Macmillan, 1953), p. 119.

23 David Porter, *Dickinson: The Modern Idiom* (Cambridge: Harvard University Press, 1981), pp. 9–24.

24 Robinson, *Tilbury Town*, p. 102; Holmes, *Poetical Works* (Boston: Houghton Mifflin, 1895), p. 1; Longfellow, *Complete Poetical Works*, ed. Horace Scudder (Cambridge: Houghton Mifflin, 1886), p. 357; Whittier, *Poetical Works* (Boston: Houghton Mifflin, 1888), p. 173.

25 Whittier, *Poetical Works*, pp. 127, 210.

26 *Ibid.*, p. 270.

27 *APNC* 1: 423, 272, 557, 161; Lowell, *Poetical Works* (Boston: Houghton Mifflin, 1885), p. 83.

28 *APNC* 1: 454; Longfellow, *Complete Poetical Works*, p. 289.

29 *SL*, 299.

30 Longfellow, *Complete Poetical Works*, p. 242.

31 Or from Longfellow's "Birds of Killingworth," for example, where the notorious awkwardness of ottava rima stanza (*abababcc*) in English, is not flaunted as in Byron's *Don Juan* but subsumed to prose rhythm to a remarkable extent.

32 *The Complete Writings of Ralph Waldo Emerson*, ed. Edward W. Emerson, vol. IX (Boston and New York: Houghton Mifflin, 1903–4), pp. 66–67.

33 William Charvat, *The Professor of Authorship in America, 1800–1870*, ed. Matthew J. Bruccoli (Columbus: Ohio State University Press, 1968), pp. 106–54.

34 "Sliver," *Collected Poems of Langston Hughes*, ed. Arnold Rampersad and David Roessel (New York: Knopf, 1994), p. 425.

35 *Collected Poems of Hughes*, p. 455.

6

TIMOTHY STEELE

"Across Spaces of the Footed Line": the Meter and Versification of Robert Frost

Robert Frost was an immensely skillful and conscientious poet, and he was fascinated by the technical aspects of versification. The magical paradox of fine verse is that it marries fixed measure with fluid idiomatic speech, and no poet more keenly relished and embodied this paradox than Frost. For more than sixty years, he wrote in a manner that was both utterly conventional and brilliantly idiosyncratic. Further, he was a thoughtful analyst of his art and made many just and original observations about it.

Unfortunately, however, Frost's talents and insights as a craftsman have seldom been adequately acknowledged. There are two reasons for this neglect. First, Frost is a poet's poet. His art conceals art. It is easy to overlook his dexterities because he appears to achieve them effortlessly. Second, though Frost made many sparkling perceptions about versification, they are not conveniently accessible in any one place, but are scattered here and there in his correspondence, in the handful of short essays and prefaces he published in his lifetime, and in transcripts of interviews with him and of public lectures he delivered. Moreover, when people have looked at Frost's criticism, they have tended to concentrate on his remarks about "the sound of sense." These are arresting and valuable and concern an issue close to Frost's heart. But they are also in certain respects confused and have left some readers, especially those unfamiliar with the depth and breadth of Frost's writing and thought, with the mistaken impression that he was, as a theorist at least, naive or eccentric.

This chapter attempts to focus Frost's practical and critical genius and to discuss his versification both in light of his poems and in light of his written and recorded comments about poetry. The chapter's main purpose is to increase the appreciation of Frost's artistry, but there are additional benefits of examining Frost's verse and ideas about verse. For one thing, Frost is a comprehensive technician in the same way as Shakespeare, Milton, Pope, or Wordsworth. As they do, he modulates meters in a style that is entirely his own and that sensitive readers would never mistake for anyone else's; yet at the same time he is in the center of the historical tradition of English-language versification. To comprehend his metric is to comprehend the larger metric of our poetry from Gower and Chaucer's time to ours.

Another benefit of studying Frost's craft involves its variety. While Frost does not engage such larger genres as epic or tragedy – genres that had drifted, by the end of the eighteenth century, from verse to prose and to the novel – he writes in many meters and stanzas and is equally adept at lyric and narrative. Frost's collected poems supply a survey of English verse forms and types that is almost as extensive as, and is much more enjoyable than, that contained in any manual or encyclopedia of poetry.

Finally, to study Frost's art is to experience the hope that poets of the future may be able to heal the terrible breach between rhythm and meter that occurred in twentieth-century poetry. As do all outstanding poets, Frost delights in putting personal rhythm and impersonal meter into, as he says to John Cournos, "strained relation" (*CPPP*, 680). But unlike such younger contemporaries as Ezra Pound and T. S. Eliot, Frost never suggests that rhythm and meter get a divorce. Frost is preeminently the modern poet who demonstrates, memorable poem by memorable poem, that the rhythms of colloquial speech can vitally coexist with normative metrical structure. If metrical writing, as it has been practiced for several millennia, is to survive in the twenty-first century, poets will have to recover and sustain Frost's love for the dialectic between prosodic rule and individual tonality.

1. Frost and the Interplay of Meter and Rhythm

In his preface to Edwin Arlington Robinson's *King Jasper,* Frost speaks of poetry's having a "metric frame on which to measure the rhythm"; and in his aphoristic essay, "Poetry and School," he remarks: "Poetry plays the rhythms of dramatic speech on the grid of meter" (*CPPP*, 741, 809).

These statements capture the essence of traditional versification, which involves the concurrent but distinguishable phenomena of meter and rhythm. Meter is the basic norm or paradigm of the line. It is an analytical abstraction. It is, to use Frost's terms, a "frame" or "grid." In the case of the iambic pentameter, for example, the frame or grid is

one two, one two, one two, one two, one two

Rhythm, on the other hand, is the realization in speech of this pattern. Only very rarely will a poet write a line in which the realization exactly mirrors the paradigm – a line, that is, that consists of successive two-syllable, rear-stressed phrasal or verbal units. Indeed, not one of the thousands of Frost's iambic pentameters is so shaped, though the thirty-seventh line of his tetra-metric "Brown's Descent" is:

He reeled, he lurched, he bobbed, he checked

More frequently, the rhythm may involve an alternation of weak and strong syllables that approximates the norm fairly closely:

The *birch* begins to *crack* its *outer sheath*
("A Young Birch," line 1)

However, most iambic pentameters do not feature such uniform fluctua-tions. Though the type with five obvious off-beats and five obvious beats is the most common, it can claim only a smallish plurality in Frost's or almost any other poet's verse. Poets write not only in feet, but also in larger phrases, clauses, and sentences. These feature syllables which do not all fall neatly into the categories of minimal accent and maximal accent, but which rather display an infinite range of stress-shadings. Hence the fluctuation between lighter and heavier syllables is not absolutely regular, but is instead some-times more emphatic, sometimes less.

In this respect, we might think of iambic lines in light of the Frostian image of mountain ranges. Peaks and valleys alternate. But not every peak is an Everest, nor is every valley a Grand Canyon. Frequently, a peak or two is not as high as the others:

And melting further in the wind to mud
("The Star-Splitter," line 81)

The tribute of the current to the source
("West-Running Brook," line 70)

Frequently a valley or two is not as deep:

The winter owl banked just in time to pass
("Questioning Faces," line 1)

Squire Matthew Hale took off his Sunday hat
("The Gold Hesperidee," line 45)

Further, because the iambic line requires only the maintenance of the lighter-to-heavier fluctuation – and because the only requirement of an iamb is that its second syllable be weightier than its first – a metrically unstressed syllable at one point in the line may carry more speech emphasis than a met-rically stressed syllable at another point.

Of dead leaves stuck together by the heat
("Hyla Brook," line 11)

Here, that is, "leaves" (the metrical off-beat of foot two) actually has more speech stress than "by" (the metrical beat of foot four). Even so, the line maintains the fluctuation of lighter to heavier syllables and scans conventionally:

$$x \quad / \quad x \quad / \quad x \quad / \quad x \; / \quad x \quad /$$

Of dead ‖ leaves stuck ‖ togeth ‖ er by ‖ the heat

(Some authorities scan feet like "leaves stuck" as spondees, which consist of of two metrically accented syllables, and feet like "-er by" as pyrrhics, which consist of two metrically unaccented syllables. However, from a linguistic standpoint, routinely scanning pyrrhics and spondees into English iambic verse is doubtful, since successive syllables in our language hardly ever feature equal degrees of accent. From a prosodic standpoint, the procedure can lead to unnecessary complications and confusions, because it suggests that feet whose syllables are relatively close in weight are variants, whereas such feet occur all the time in any naturally and competently written iambic poem. The simplest course, then, is to treat as an iamb any foot whose second syllable is heavier than its first syllable. The degree of difference much affects the rhythm of a line, but is irrelevant to the meter.)

In writing in meter, then, Frost modulates the measure from within, laying various and vital segments of speech across the grid so as to adhere to the paradigm without mechanically or monotonously replicating it. The fundamental pattern is constant, but the individual verse lines embody it in ever-changing ways. As Frost remarks, in a conversation with Cleanth Brooks, Robert Penn Warren, and Kenny Withers, the aim of good verse is "to break the doggerel [i. e., the absolute regularity of the metrical norm]. And it mustn't break *with* it . . . [T]here's both the meter and the expressiveness on it – and so we get a poem" (*CPPP*, 854, 856). Likewise, he comments to John Freeman: "All I ask is iambic. I undertake to furnish the variety in the relation of my tones to it. The crossed swords are always the same. The sword dancer varies his position between them."[1]

As Frost emphasizes on several occasions, meter and rhythm coexist inextricably in actual verse. When we read poems, we do not hear the meter at one level of the brain and the rhythm at another. Rather, our experience of the two is integrated. We hear at once the comprehensive metrical pattern and the individual rhythmical realizations of it. Frost makes this point in an interview with William Stanley Braithwaite. The poet speaks of his desire to convey meaning by tone and "sound-posture" as well as by the literal sense of words, and when Braithwaite interjects, "[D]o you not come into conflict with metrical sounds to which the laws of poetry conform?" Frost replies: "No, . . . because you must understand this sound of which I speak has principally to do with tone. It is what Mr. Bridges, the Poet Laureate, characterized as speech-rhythm. Meter has to do with beat . . . The two are one in creation but separate in analysis."[2]

Because Frost so keenly appreciates how meter and rhythm support each other – rhythm giving meter life and energy, meter giving the rhythm shape and focus – he is suspicious equally of prosodists who disparage the simple frame element of meter and of prosodists who try to reduce the complex rhythmical element to false simplicity.

On the one hand, Frost is skeptical of the vers-libristes. "They use the word 'rhythm' about a lot of free verse," he says to Brooks, Warren, and Withers; "and gee, what's the good of the rhythm unless it is on something that trips it – that it ruffles? You know, it's got to ruffle the meter." Frost views Pound as a particularly dubious theorist, and he tells Brooks, Warren, and Withers: "Ezra Pound used to say that you've got to get all the meter out of it [poetry] – extirpate the meter. If you do, maybe you've got true free verse, and I don't want any of it!" And one of Frost's best known observations about his own taste is, "For my pleasure I had as soon write free verse as play tennis with the net down" (CPPP, 854, 856, 809).

On the other hand, Frost is distrustful of those who, hungry for prosodic exactitude, seek to establish laws not only for meter, but also for the variable rhythms of speech. However much Frost admires Bridges, he is disturbed by Bridges' interest in assigning to English vowels and syllables the specific values of length that ancient prosodists gave to syllables in Greek and Latin. Frost knows that English prosody measures syllabic stress rather than syllabic length; and he acutely appreciates, as we shall see, that stress is not entirely classifiable by phonemics and phonetics, as length is in ancient prosody, but instead varies with grammatical and rhetorical sense. And in a letter to Sidney Cox, Frost takes Bridges to task for "his theory that syllables in English have fixed quantity . . . Words exist in the mouth not in books. You can't fix them and you don't want to fix them" (CPPP, 670, 671).

In much the same vein, Frost criticizes Sidney Lanier's view that spoken syllables have, or should be treated as having, the precise durational properties of musical notes. To be sure, Frost dislikes Lanier's theory partly because it prizes musical tones of speech more than the colloquial tones which Frost was so deft at conveying; but Frost is also troubled by the way in which the specious exactitude of Lanier's analysis deforms and limits the play of rhythm. Alluding to Lanier's Science of English Verse and to Carlyle's statement that if you "think deep enough you think musically," Frost comments to Braithwaite: "Poetry has seized on this [musical] sound of speech and carried it to artificial and meaningless lengths. We have exemplified it in Sidney Lanier's musical notation of verse, where all the tones of the human voice in natural speech are entirely eliminated."[3]

Because post-Modernist poetic practice has largely followed the Pound–Eliot anti-meter extreme, whereas the Lanier–Bridges reduce-rhythm-to-rule extreme has had negligible effect, we today think of Frost as one of the twentieth century's most eloquent defenders of meter against the looseness of free verse. If, however, Frost had lived and written in the sixteenth century, when the strongest attack on the native metric was launched by neo-classical writers seeking to quantify English speech and versification, we would remember him as a defender of rhythm against a factitiously strict prosody.

Frost's appreciation of rhythm has many applications to his own versification, the most important of which concerns monosyllabic words. Frost realizes that all our monosyllabic words can, given the right context, serve as either metrical beats or metrical off-beats. Admittedly, light articles, prepositions, and conjunctions are mostly metrically unaccented, but they not uncommonly appear in metrically accented positions, as "in" does in the line we cited from "The Star-Splitter." And though monosyllabic verbs and nouns tend to appear in metrically accented positions, they often turn up in metrically unaccented ones as "bank" does in the line from "Questioning Faces." Frost summarizes this issue in the same letter to Cox in which Bridges' theories are addressed. (When Frost mentions different musical notes, he does so merely to indicate that a word may assume different stress properties in different contexts: he is not suggesting, à la Lanier, that he has analytically determined precise durational values.)

> The living part of the poem is the intonation entangled somehow in the syntax idiom and meaning of a sentence . . . It is the most volatile and at the same time important part of poetry. It goes and the language becomes a dead language the poetry dead poetry. With it go the accents, the stresses, the delays that are not the property of vowels and syllables but that are shifted at will with the sense. Vowels have length there is no denying. But the accent of sense supersedes all other accent, overrides and sweeps it away. I will find you the word "come" variously used in various passages as a whole, half, third, fourth, fifth, and sixth note. It is as long as the sense makes it. (*CPPP*, 670)

Frost gives no examples of this various use of "come," but attentive readers can point them out in his poems. For instance, in "Fireflies in the Garden," Frost employs "come" as metrically accented in the first line, but as metrically unaccented in the second:

```
     x    /   x   /   x /  x  /  x   /
   Here come ‖ real stars ‖ to fill ‖ the up ‖ per skies
     x    /   x   /    x   /   x /  x   /
   And here ‖ on earth ‖ come em ‖ ulat ‖ ing flies
```

When, that is, "come" first appears, it carries considerable weight, since in English we stress words at the ends of phrases like "here come," unless context demands contrastive emphasis (*"here* come," as opposed *"there* come."). This initial "come" assumes stress as well on account of being situated between two words that are grammatically subordinate: the adverbial "here" goes with "come," and the adjective "real" modifies "star." When, in contrast, "come" appears in the second line, the word is weaker because it is situated between two strong syllables. "Earth" not only has lexical weight to begin with, but also is a key element of the earth-skies/stars-flies contrast that governs the poem; and "em-" is the primarily stressed syllable of "emulating." And as linguists have observed, when we have three fairly strong syllables in a row, we tend to "demote" the middle syllable.

Thus are the stress qualities of "come," "shifted at will with the [syntactical and rhetorical] sense."

In another letter to Cox, Frost suggests a phenomenon which is related to the one in "Fireflies in the Garden," but which is even more unusual. Discussing "sentence sounds" – the tones that different sentences carry – Frost remarks: "You recognize the sentence sound in this: *You*, you! – It is so strong that if you hear it as I do you have to pronounce the two you's differently" (*CPPP*, 681). A practical application of this point is that a poet can place, in an English iambic foot, the same repeated monosyllable so that it serves as both a metrical beat and offbeat. To illustrate this application, we could analyze line 3 of "Beyond Words," in which Frost sets "you" into the meter four times in a row, or line 116 of "The Generations of Men," in which "great" appears four times in succession, or line 30 of "Home Burial," in which Amy peppers her husband with four consecutive "don'ts." (Frost was fond of this last legerdemain, remarking of it to Cournos: "I also think well of those four 'don'ts' in Home Burial. They would be good in prose and they gain something from the way they are placed in the verse" [*SL*, 130]). However, two other cases more plainly illuminate the matter.

The first occurs at the end of "Acceptance" where Frost suggests (13–14) that the bird who has just found a perch for the night is resigned to whatever the future may bring. Frost pictures the bird's thinking that it does not wish "to see

Into the future. Let what will be, be."

Here "be" supplies both the offbeat and beat of the final foot of the line. The first time the word appears, it follows "will," which not only is the metrically accented syllable of the fourth foot, but also is conceptually crucial, indicating the futurity with which the bird and poem are concerned – what *will* be. Hence the voice drops when it moves from "will" to the first "be."

Yet the voice gives prominence to the second "be," since here the focus shifts from the sense of the future to the very order of existence and the bird's acceptance of it. The second "be" also receives weight because it is the culminating word of the sentence (and the poem) and because it is the line's rhyme-syllable.

$$x \quad / \quad x \quad /$$
Into ‖ the fu ‖ ture. Let ‖ what will ‖ be, be.

A comparable case occurs in lines five and six of "The Egg and the Machine," in which Frost describes a railroad-hating man who regrets not having sabotaged some track when he had the chance:

He wished when he had had the track alone
He had attacked it with a club or stone

Because Frost is writing in the past perfect tense, "had" changes its metrical nature in the third foot of the first line of this couplet. The first "had" is merely auxiliary, whereas the second "had" – the past participle of "have" – is the main verb:

$$x \quad /$$
He wished ‖ when he ‖ had had ‖ the track ‖ alone
He had attacked it with a club or stone

(In the couplet's second line, the auxiliary "had" is promoted to a metrical beat because it is preceded by the light pronoun "He" and is followed by a past participle, "attacked," whose word-accent is not on its first but its second syllable.)

If Frost uses variable speech rhythms to enliven fixed metrical patterns, he also sometimes employs meter to direct us to a correct interpretation of rhythm. For example, in line 15 of "The Housekeeper," the title character says to a visitor that it is odd that he should have come to see the man of the house, when the latter has just left to go see him. She comments, "Strange what set you off

To come to his house when he's gone to yours.

If we are reading inattentively, we may give a metrical accent to the fifth syllable, since prepositional phrases like "to the house" usually take strong stress on the object of the preposition and accord only light stress to the preposition and the article or attributive pronoun that precede the object. Yet skimming over "his" and coming down heavily on "house" produces false meter. Even worse, it misses the tonal quality of the speaker. It gives us the sense of her words without, to adapt Frost's phrase, the sound of her sense. If, however, we read with our ears open to the meter, the voice leaps into tonal clarity. We hear that the speaker is emphasizing "his" and contrasting the word with the other attributive pronoun, down at the end of the line:

x / x / x / x / x /
To come to *his* house when he's gone to *yours*.

There is a related case in which Frost uses metrical pattern to direct rhythmical interpretation. Sometimes, he repeats in a line the same monosyllabic noun, stressing it in one place and, in the other, subordinating it to a modifier. This effect appears relative to "stone" and "arm" in these lines:

x / x / x / x / x /
Where they have left not one stone on a stone   ("Mending Wall," line 7)

x / x / x / x / x /
You link an arm in its arm and you leave   ("To a Young Wretch," line 5)

Though they may initially appear odd, the readings that the meter suggests are natural. "Where they have left not *one* stone on a stone" is natural, since Frost is talking about rabbit-hunters who, in their monomaniacal lust to kill, totally destroy walls and anything else that might shelter prey. (Frost returns to this subject in his late poem, "The Rabbit-Hunter.") By the same token, the reading of "You link an arm in *its* arm" is appropriate. The "its" refers to one of the speaker's spruce trees, which the young wretch of the poem's title has chopped down and poached for Christmas. And by stressing the attributive pronoun, Frost reinforces our sense of the comic–bitter spectacle of the wretch's heading off with the tree as cavalierly as a playboy waltzing off with a mistress. In the Caedmon recording of "Mending Wall," incidentally, Frost reads the line from the poem iambically. (I have not heard a recording of Frost reading "To a Young Wretch.")

Examining these lines clarifies a matter that might otherwise puzzle us in Frost's criticism. Frost associates doggerel with polysyllabic words, as in his comment to his old friend and student, John Bartlett: "Verse in which there is nothing but the beat of the metre furnished by the accents of the polysyllabic words we call doggerel" (*CPPP*, 665). To be sure, excessive use of long words can produce insipid rhythm, but wooden uniformity of movement can result from any number of other causes. For instance, the numbing effect of Chaucer's "Sir Thopas" – the mother of all doggerel poems in English, and the one that moved the Host of the Tabard to coin the term "rym dogerel" (*Canterbury Tales*, B[2] 2115) – has nothing to do with polysyllabic words. Rather, the clip-clop jog-trot of "Sir Thopas" results from Chaucer's intentionally unimaginative handling of the romance-six stanza and from his habitually pausing after syllable four in his tetrameters and after syllable six in his trimeters. What is more, Frost himself frequently builds from long words perfectly natural lines:

By psychological experiment ("At Woodward's Garden," line 19)

Collectivistic regimenting love ("A Considerable Speck," line 25)

Indeed, because any word, regardless of its length, has only one primarily stressed syllable – the other syllables receiving varying amounts of secondary, tertiary, or weak stress – polysyllabic words can give verse pleasing rhythmical modulation, as long as they are not overly exploited.

However, in words of two or more syllables, one syllable customarily takes primary accent, and if secondary and tertiary accents exist, these too are conventionally disposed. And this customary and conventional *word-accent* overrides and diminishes the possibilities of playing with *sense-accent*. The internal accentual contour of a polysyllabic word may well be complex. The currently conventional pronunciation of "psychological," for example, places strong stress on the third syllable, secondary stress on the first, tertiary on the fifth, and weak stress on the second and fourth syllables. But no ambiguity exists in this contour, as might exist when five monosyllabic words appear in succession. And while polysyllabic words can modulate the meter, they never tug it in the way that Frost sometimes likes to tug it. They do not allow him to shift sense off and on words, nor do long words require the reader to listen sensitively to the syllables to hear how they conform to the iambic meter, even as at points their stress properties shade almost levelly into each other:

You tell her that it's M-A-P-L-E ("Maple," line 7)

Not only is Frost a master, as has been observed often, of the striking line comprised of monosyllabic words; he derives, as much as any other poet in our language, interesting rhythmical effects from manipulating monosyllables. And he feels, more acutely than other poets might, that verse which relies excessively on polysyllables is rhythmless, is doggerel.

Frost's fascination with interplay of meter and rhythm occupies him throughout his career. In 1914 he makes the statement to which I alluded in my introduction and which may be cited more fully now: "My versification . . . is as simple as this," Frost says of the unrhymed iambic pentameters of his *North of Boston* narratives: "there are the very regular preestablished accent and measure of blank verse; and there are the very irregular accent and measure of speaking intonation. I am never more pleased than when I can get these into strained relation" (*CPPP*, 680). Decades later, Frost repeats this idea, giving it a figurative twist, in lines 213–15 of his last big blank-verse poem, "How Hard It Is to Keep from Being King When It's in You and in the Situation." (Since the poem's title consists of a pair of iambic pentameters, it should always be printed as two distinct lines.)

> Regular verse springs from the strain of rhythm
> Upon a metre, strict or loose iambic.
> From that strain comes the expression *strains of music.*

2. Frost and Iambic Verse

The excerpt from "How Hard It Is to Keep from Being King When It's in You and in the Situation" recalls a comment Frost offers in "The Figure a Poem Makes": "All that can be done with words is soon told. So also with meters – particularly in our language where there are virtually but two, strict iambic and loose iambic" (*CPPP*, 776).

What Frost says of English verse in general applies also to his own verse in particular. Admittedly, he occasionally composes in non-iambic meters, and we shall in due course take note of them. But virtually all of his verse is iambically based.

Though the prevalence of iambics in our poetry results from their accommodating the normal rhythms of English better than any other rhythm does, this flexibility is less a consequence of the structure of our individual words than it is of the relatively uninflected character of our language. Many of our most common words are in fact uniambic. They are heavy monosyllables like "love," "shout," "green," and "well," or fore-stressed disyllables like "table," "offer," "ready," and "very." Yet English customarily introduces words, phrases, and clauses with lightly stressed articles (that is, "a," "an," "the") or pronominal forms (for example, "her," "our," "we," "you," "it,"); and English often connects or relates words, phrases, and clauses with lightly stressed conjunctions (for example, "and," "but," "so," "if") and prepositions (for example, "by," "to," "in," "of"). And these little functional words are apt to catch up the lexically weighty words, however uniambic they may be by themselves, into iambic rhythm.

Because iambic structure often is compounded of non-iambic elements of English word-shape and phraseology, a poet like Frost can initiate, within the basic iambic rise-and-fall movement, all sorts of counter-currents to the prevailing rhythm. An exemplary instance of these modulatory West-Running Brooks occurs in stanza three of "Stopping by Woods on a Snowy Evening":

> He gives his harness bells a shake
> To ask if there is some mistake.
> The only other sound's the sweep
> Of easy wind and downy flake.

In the first two lines, Frost uses mainly monosyllabic words, and of the two two-syllable words, one is rear-stressed. As a result, divisions between feet and those between words largely coincide, and this in turn produces a strong sense of rising, iambic rhythm:

> He gives ‖ his har ‖ ness bells ‖ a shake
> To ask ‖ if there ‖ is some ‖ mistake.

In contrast, the remaining two lines feature four fore-stressed disyllabic words. Consequently, words more often cross foot divisions than end at them. Even as the iambic fluctuation continues, the lines have a falling, trochaic character, which in turn suggests the sweeping movement of wind and snow:

> The on ‖ ly oth ‖ er sound's ‖ the sweep
> Of eas ‖ y wind ‖ and down ‖ y flake.

Frost's first version of the line about the wind and flake read, "Of easy wind and fall of flake."[4] He may have made the change not only because he wanted a more descriptive word for the snow, but also because he intuited that the rhythm would benefit from a more descending flow than "and fall of flake" could give.

Frost secures expressive rhythmical effects in iambic meters not only by shifting between words of different rhythmical contours, but also by shifting between words of different lengths. Consider, for instance, the passage (lines 6–8) in "The Most of It" in which he describes the young man who, living alone by the lake, longs to hear a human voice other than his:

> He would cry out on life, that what it wants
> Is not its own love back in copy speech,
> But counter-love, original response.

Frost fills the first two pentameters with mostly monosyllabic words. In the third line, however, he sets across the metric frame four words that are largely unlike those in the previous lines. Further, these four words are all unlike each other. "But" is monosyllabic. "Response" is disyllabic. "Counter-love" is a trisyllabic compound, and "original" has four syllables. The lines all scan conventionally:

> x / x / x / x / x /
> He would ‖ cry out ‖ on life, ‖ that what ‖ it wants
> x / x / x / x / x /
> Is not ‖ its own ‖ love back ‖ in cop ‖ y speech,
> x / x / x/ x/ x /
> But coun ‖ ter-love, ‖ orig ‖ inal ‖ response.

But the third line is, rhythmically, worlds apart from its two predecessors, as perfectly suits Frost's context. Just when the person in the poem demands something different – something more than "copy speech" – Frost changes his diction. He switches from a slow succession of short words to a more rapid and supple mixture involving longer words.

If Frost sometimes introduces longer words into his iambics to speed them up, he on other occasions loads the line with heavy monosyllables to slow it down or to suggest an obstructed effect. Such an effect occurs in that passage (lines 41–43) of "Our Singing Strength," where Frost describes spring birds coping with an unseasonal snow storm and flying about congestedly. The birds made, Frost says,

> A whir among white branches great and small
> As in some too much carven marble hall
> Where one false wing beat would have brought down all.

After the first two lines' easy current, facilitated by the four disyllabic words ("among," "branches," "carven," and "marble"), the monosyllables jammed in the third line give aural emphasis to the crowding that the birds experience.

Frost achieves diverse rhythms by setting across the meter not only words of miscellaneous lengths and shapes, but also phrases and clauses of mixed extent and character. At times, he slots short phrases into the measure:

> We stand here dreaming. Hurry! Call them back!
> ("In the Home Stretch," line 77)

> No footstep moved it. "This is all," they sighed.
> ("Two Look at Two," line 13)

At other times, he slides longer and more freely running phrases and clauses into the grid. In regard to these latter cases, he has a gift for oddly canted phrases that at first look ungainly, but that are nicely expressive when said aloud:

> Professor Square-the-circle-till-you're-tired?
> ("A Hundred Collars," line 44)

> A light he was to no one but himself
> ("An Old Man's Winter Night," line 15)

Frost expressively manages as well the larger relations between sentence structure and the metrical structure. When he seeks emphatic tones, as he does, for instance, in "Once by the Pacific," he tends to end each line with a full or partial grammatical stop. He makes the metrical and grammatical units correspond. On the other hand, he will, when it suits his purposes, place meter and grammar at variance, and run his lines on. For example, in lines four and five of "The Wood-Pile,"

> The hard snow held me, save where now and then
> One foot went through. . . .

just as the snow-crust cannot hold the speaker's weight, the line-end cannot contain the clause, which breaks through the measure to the next verse.

Something similar happens in "The Exposed Nest" when (lines 17–19) the speaker and his daughter discover baby birds whose field-nest has been destroyed by a mowing machine. The daughter tries to build a shelter out of the fresh-cut hay, and the father says:

> You wanted to restore them to their right
> Of something interposed between their sight
> And too much world at once . . .

That the sentence runs on – and that the grammatical import is divided between two lines – reinforces our feeling of the division between the little birds and the great world, which overwhelms their weak sight.

Frost is no less expressive in handling the conventional variants of the iambic line than he is in handling its customary regularities. One such variant occurs in "The Death of the Hired Man" in those lines (100–01) where Mary comments on Silas' plight:

> And nothing to look backward to with pride,
> And nothing to look forward to with hope

Because the only requirement of an iamb is that the second syllable be weightier than the first, poets can, as Frost does in each of these lines, follow a light iamb with a heavy one, so as to produce four degrees of rising stress over two feet:

$$\begin{array}{cccc} 1 & 2 & 3 & 4 \end{array}$$
And noth ‖ ing to ‖ look back ‖ ward to ‖ with pride,
$$\begin{array}{cccc} 1 & 2 & 3 & 4 \end{array}$$
And noth ‖ ing to ‖ look for ‖ ward to ‖ with hope

And here the twin rises through the second and third feet (and the falling-offs to a light fourth foot) throw into rhythmical relief the words "backward" and "forward" and throw into thematic relief Silas' desolate past and empty future.

Another common variant in English poems in iambic pentameter is the occasional introduction of an alexandrine (that is, an iambic hexameter); and as he does with the rise-over-two-feet, Frost sometimes strikes apt effects with this variant. A good example occurs at line 80 of "Wild Grapes," where the frightened narrator describes herself hanging in the air from a birch tree:

> My small wrists stretching till they showed the banjo strings.
> My small ‖ wrists stretch ‖ ing till ‖ they showed ‖ the ban ‖ jo strings.

Just as the girl's wrists are extended by her exertion, so the meter is elongated.

Frost even expressively employs the two most familiar, workaday metrical variants in iambic verse – the trochaic inversion of the first foot and the feminine ending (that is, an extra unaccented syllable at the end of a line). As Roman Jakobson has suggested[5] these variants probably evolved and received sanction because they are not very noticeable: there is usually a suspension of movement and sense at the beginnings and ends of lines, and, under these conditions, rhythmical modification is less disruptive than it would be in the middle of a developing phrase or clause. (An additional reason the variants gained acceptance is their convenience: they enable poets to begin iambic lines with strong syllables and end them with weak ones.) Now and again Frost employs these variants not just by-the-bye, but for the delight of slotting into the line at different points the same word, so as to make it serve different metrical functions. For example, in this line (507) from *A Masque of Mercy,*

> Failure is failure, but success is failure

Frost has "failure" initially figure in a trochaic first foot, then as an element integrated into the line's iambic frame, and finally in a feminine ending:

> / x   x /   x   /   x /   x / (x)
> Failure ‖ is fail ‖ ure, but ‖ success ‖ is failure

So, too, in line 115 from Frost's "The Generations of Men,"

> Making allowance, making due allowance

we find a pair of repeated words engaged in different metrical functions. When the fore-stressed disyllabic word "making" initially appears, it comprises a trochaic first foot. The second time it appears, it is integrated iambically into the interior of the line. The first time "allowance" appears, Frost merges it into the iambic rhythm of the line's interior. However, with its second appearance, Frost disposes the word so that its final syllable is a feminine ending:

> / x   x /   x   /   x /   x / (x)
> Making ‖ allow ‖ ance, mak ‖ ing due ‖ allowance

And, to return to our point about Frost using his medium expressively, we can see that the poet is having a metrical joke here. This line about allowances avails itself of the two most common in English versification.

Frost uses feminine endings and trochaic first feet for other expressive purposes. In rhymed verse, feminine endings have a song-like quality, and Frost puts them to musical advantage in, for instance, his Herrickesque "Asking for Roses," all of whose rhymes are feminine. Feminine rhymes can also produce a sense of comic strain, and the humor of "Departmental" results partly from such wild pairings as "any" and "antennae" and "Formic" (Frost's coinage for "the language of ants") and "Jerry McCormic." (Because feminine rhymes call attention to themselves, Frost uses hypermetrical endings sparingly in his rhymed work; probably fewer than five per cent of his rhymes are feminine. However, feminine endings are less noticeable in unrhymed poems and approximately a third of Frost's blank verse lines feature feminine endings.)

As regards trochaic first feet, Frost sometimes introduces these to communicate a sense of heaviness in keeping with his subject, as when he describes, in line six of "Birches," the way the trees are bent,

/   x
Loaded with ice a sunny winter morning

And in the next-to-last line of "The White-Tailed Hornet," the trochaic first word and foot emphasize the spiritual desolation that ensues when we forget that we are related to higher as well as lower life forms:

/   x
Nothing but fallibility was left us

At the risk of pleonasm, we might observe that Frost's strict iambic is strict. Rarely do we find extra syllables. Those that do appear are often subject to elision (i.e., metrical contraction); and in his recordings of his poems, Frost generally elides where the metrical context calls for contraction. For example, when he reads, in the Library of Congress recording of "The Mountain," the poem's forty-eighth line, he clearly pronounces, for meter's sake, "interest" in the disyllabic, syncopated manner ("ín • trist"):

x   /   x   /   x   / x   /   x   /
But what would interest you about the brook

As adept as Frost is, he occasionally fudges a pentameter. He occasionally writes a decasyllabic line that fails to maintain the iambic fluctuation, but instead has a swingy four-beat rhythm. Robert Francis has noted this aspect of Frost's practice and has used the word "crumbling"[6] to describe the effect of such lines. Usually, the problem is that neither lexical structure nor rhetorical context attract a metrical beat to syllable two or syllable four, whereas syllable three is heavily stressed. Consequently, the first six syllables in the line have a pattern of light-light-heavy, light-light-heavy:

And the back of the gig they stood beside

("The Fear," line 6)

> But suppose she had missed it from the Creed
>
> ("The Black Cottage," line 101)

Sophistry might salvage such lines by dividing them into disyllabic feet and scanning them as exotic pentametric variants. We might, for instance, treat the line from "The Fear" as having a light trochaic first foot and a trochaic second foot:

> / x / x x / x / x /
> And the ‖ back of ‖ the gig ‖ they stood ‖ beside

But the effect on the ear is of a semi-anapestic, semi-iambic four-beat line:

> x x / x x / x / x /
> And the back of the gig they stood beside

Because Frost is such a master, one feels like a Zoilus in pointing out these slight slips. Nor do they occur often. Indeed, Frost once challenged Lewis Chase, "Find ten lines in North of Boston that won't scan."[7] We will find maybe half that number among the 1983 lines of the collection.

If Frost is extraordinarily resourceful in strict iambic verse, he is scarcely less inventive in "loose iambic," which is iambic verse that features extra metrically unaccented syllables. These extra syllables produce (or can most conveniently be scanned as producing) anapests. Loose iambic mostly appears in Frost – as it mostly does in English verse overall – in measures of less-than-pentameter length. Extra syllables are less problematic in such measures than they are in longer measures. The brevity of a short measure allows the ear an easier purchase on the beat-count, and we can more readily absorb the extra syllables in the shorter line, especially when the poet reinforces the line's identity by means of rhyme.

The nature of loose iambics is illustrated by Frost's "Neither Out Far Nor In Deep," which is written in iambic trimeter. This poem examines our fascination with the unknown and explores its theme by means of a contrast in which the sea symbolizes the unknown, the land the known.

> The people along the sand
> All turn and look one way.
> They turn their back on the land.
> They look at the sea all day.
>
> As long as it takes to pass
> A ship keeps raising its hull;
> The wetter ground like glass
> Reflects a standing gull.

The land may vary more;
But wherever the truth may be –
The water comes ashore,
And the people look at the sea.

They cannot look out far.
They cannot look in deep.
But when was that ever a bar
To any watch they keep?

A number of the poem's feet (eleven of forty-eight) are anapests instead of iambs. Yet the beat count is clear, and the rhymes help us hear the line-endings distinctly.

The poem also well demonstrates the expressive potentials of loose iambic verse. Particularly skillful is Frost's coordination of his intermittently lilting rhythm with his theme. For example, in each of the first two lines of the second stanza he introduces an anapest, and these suggest the instability of the sea and the rocking of the passing vessel on the horizon:

$$
\begin{array}{ccccccc}
x & / & x & x & / & x & / \\
\end{array}
$$
As long ‖ as it takes ‖ to pass
$$
\begin{array}{ccccccc}
x & / & x & / & x & x & / \\
\end{array}
$$
A ship ‖ keeps rais ‖ ing its hull

Then in the stanza's third and fourth lines, Frost returns to regular iambics to suggest the stability of the land:

$$
\begin{array}{cccccc}
x & / & x & / & x & / \\
\end{array}
$$
The wet ‖ ter ground ‖ like glass
$$
\begin{array}{cccccc}
x & / & x & / & x & / \\
\end{array}
$$
Reflects ‖ a stand ‖ ing gull.

A related effect appears in the final stanza. The first two lines are not only iambic. Their regularity is metronomic. The light syllables are very light, the heavy ones very heavy. And this is appropriate. Frost is making an emphatic statement. Oceans – literal and figurative – lie out far and in deep in the universe. They are beyond our knowing. Of their mysteries, we can get only distant and incomplete glimpses.

$$
\begin{array}{cccccc}
x & / & x & / & x & / \\
\end{array}
$$
They can ‖ not look ‖ out far
$$
\begin{array}{cccccc}
x & / & x & / & x & / \\
\end{array}
$$
They can ‖ not look ‖ in deep

Yet this does not lessen the mind's curiosity about the unknown. And when Frost, in the stanza's third line, voices this counter-idea – "But when was that ever a bar . . ." – the rhythm shifts away from the straightforward regularity of the previous lines, almost in defiance of them and the truth they express:

$$x \quad / \quad x \quad x \quad / \quad x\,x \quad /$$
But when ‖ was that ev ‖ er a bar

It is an exquisite touch, and sets up the return to the norm in the final line:

$$x \quad / \quad x \quad / \quad \quad x \quad /$$
To an ‖ y watch ‖ they keep?

Because of its lilting quality, loose iambic has limited capacities for modulation. It would be hard to write something with the extended gravity and grace of "The Census-Taker" in loose iambic, and certain of Frost's great short poems – including "Spring Pools," "Once by the Pacific," "The Most of It," and "Never Again Would Birds' Song Be the Same" – require the sure grace and framing power of the stabler line. Nonetheless, in the hands of masters like Frost, the loose iambic mode is a wonderful one.

To get a feel for Frost's loose iambic measures, one can do no better than to read poems that embody them alongside poems in the same measure's stricter manifestation. Read the loose dimeters of "Dust of Snow" and "Gathering Leaves" in conjunction with the strictly dimetric "Pertinax" and "The Rabbit-Hunter." (The apparent extra syllables in lines eight and thirteen of the latter are resolvable by elision). Read the loose iambic trimeters of "They Were Welcome to Their Belief" and "A Drumlin Woodchuck" in connection with the strict trimeters of "Happiness Makes Up in Height for What It Lacks in Length" and "Closed for Good." Read the loose iambic tetrameters of "The Road Not Taken" (a poem in which the wavering rhythm reflects the regretful condition of the speaker and his memory of his indecision) and "The Need of Being Versed in Country Things" in conjunction with the strict tetrameters of "Revelation," "Stopping by Woods on a Snowy Evening," and the first poem of the two-part "The Wind and the Rain." Frost adopts loose iambic less often when he works in iambic pentameter, but once in a while he relaxes that line, too, as in "Mowing," "On Looking Up by Chance at the Constellations," and "Willful Homing."

Meters other than iambic exist in English, and Frost uses several of these. For instance, "Clear and Colder," "An Importer," and "A Correction" feature trochaic tetrameters; and Frost also uses trochaics for "To the Thawing Wind," "The Hardship of Accounting," "A Reflex," "Four-room Shack Aspiring High," though in these poems the lines are chiefly catalectic (that is, the final unaccented syllable is dropped from the line). "Blueberries" and "Too Anxious for Rivers" are in four-beat trisyllabic meters. Because trisyllabics admit alternative foot-division, nomenclature is arguable in these cases. Probably the best course is to say that "Blueberries" is in anapestic tetrameters (with occasional iambic substitutions) and to call "Too Anxious for Rivers" an amphibrachic tetrameter poem whose second and twenty-sixth lines are catalectic. "For Once, Then, Something" imitates, in accentualized verse, classical Phalaecean hendecasyllabics.

Frost also sometimes experiments with astrophic iambics. He writes poems, that is, which have rhymed, iambic lines, but in which the rhymes appear in irregular sequence and in which the line-lengths vary, unusually running from monometer at the low end of the scale to hexameter at the high end. "After Apple-Picking" is the masterpiece in this mode, which Frost evidently got from Coventry Patmore, who had made it his special métier and whose "Magna est Veritas" was one of Frost's touchstones.[8] "Storm Fear" and "The Telephone" are other Frost poems of this type. "The Lovely Shall Be Choosers," Frost's powerful tribute to his mother, represents a rhymeless version of the type. A final – and beautifully profound – poem in an unusual iambic measure is "Carpe Diem," which Frost composes in rhymeless iambic trimeters with feminine endings.

Writing in the early 1920s to John Gallishaw, Frost summarizes his verse by saying, "I have written very little except in perfectly regular iambic."[9] We should place next to this statement his answer to the question of why he writes poems: "To see if I can make them all different." Commenting on this response, Richard Wilbur well observes, "There are no two lines alike in Frost."[10] Frost's measures are simple and few, but his effects are complex and many. His work shows the breadth and vitality of the iambic tradition, and confirms his own maxim, "The possibilities for tune from the dramatic tones of meaning struck across the rigidity of a limited meter are endless" (*CPPP*, 776).

Because "the sound of sense" has attracted more attention than any other facet of Frost's criticism, I should like to examine it briefly before moving to the concluding section of this essay.

Between 1913 and 1915 – that period when his work at last is receiving book-publication and recognition – Frost endeavors, in a series of letters, interviews, and public talks, to explain his aesthetic position to others and, one suspects, himself. In particular, he wishes to justify his use of colloquial speech in his work and to assert his originality in doing so. And in a well-known letter of July 4, 1913 to Bartlett, he says: "I am possibly the only person going who works on any but a worn out theory (Principle I had better say) of versification . . . I alone of English writers have consciously set myself to make music out of what I may call the sound of sense" (*CPPP*, 664).

What is this "sound of sense"? It is tone of voice. It is the power of vocal tone to communicate meaning in addition to or independent of words in their merely definitional function. It is sound that makes sense purely as sound. In his letter to Bartlett and in his 1915 interview with Braithwaite, Frost demonstrates the existence and communicative capacity of pure tone by, as he puts it to Braithwaite, "the example of two people who are talking on the other side of a closed door, whose voices can be heard but whose words cannot be distinguished. Even though the words do not carry, the sound of them does, and the listener can catch the meaning of the conversation."[11] The listener can catch, that is, "[the] tone of meaning but without the words," to quote a line from Frost's "Never Again Would Birds' Song Be the Same." Or, as Frost says in his letter to Bartlett, "The sound of sense, then. You get that. It is the abstract vitality of our speech. It is pure sound – pure form" (CPPP, 665).

To understand further Frost's ideas about the sound of sense, we must explain the reasons that he is so interested in tone of voice generally and in colloquial tone specifically. For one thing, Frost simply loves talk and the human voice. "I like the actuality of gossip, the intimacy of it," he writes Braithwaite in 1915. "Say what you will effects of actuality and intimacy are the greatest aim an artist can have" (CPPP, 685). In much the same spirit, he tells Chase in 1917, "I can't keep up any interest in sentences that don't SHAPE *on some speaking tone* of voice."[12] And it is telling that when Frost performs his poems in public, he does so in an almost conversational manner and often uses the verb "say" rather than "recite" or "read" to describe his presentation of his work. Prefacing "Stopping by Woods on a Snowy Evening," he tells one audience, "I'll say this little one"; and later, before concluding his performance with "Come In," he remarks. "I'll say one of the old ones Doc Cook asked me to say" (CPPP, 822, 829).

Frost's interest in colloquial tone also has a slightly defensive aspect. When he was a budding writer, an early reader judged his work to be "too near the level of talk."[13] And when in 1894 William Hayes Ward and Susan Hayes Ward of *The Independent* discovered the young poet and accepted "My Butterfly" for publication, they nevertheless questioned his diction and his metric and mailed him a copy of Lanier's *Science of English Verse* to help him out (SL, 21, 22). Frost was always grateful to the Wards, especially Susan Hayes Ward, for their support; but he rightly felt misunderstood when they sent him to school to Lanier, just as he felt misunderstood when the other early reader questioned the colloquial quality of his writing. Such responses implied criticisms of what Frost most cherished in speech and verse.

Frost's concern with the tones of actual speech represents as well reaction against the excessively mellifluous qualities of the work of such late-Victorian poets as Tennyson and Swinburne. In this regard, Frost's views are not unlike those that Robinson, Pound, Eliot, and the later Yeats are expressing during the same period; and his views are not unlike those expressed by any number of earlier literary innovators and renovators who had sought to reform poetic diction. And although Frost at times suggests that his interest in colloquial tone is unique, he at other times acknowledges the connections between his ideas and those of his predecessors. For instance, in a letter in 1914 to Cox, Frost observes of his theories: "Of course the great fight of any poet is against the people who want him to write in a special language that has gradually separated from spoken language" (*CPPP*, 682). And in the 1915 interview with Braithwaite, Frost correlates his preoccupation with the sound of sense with Wordsworth's desire to restore natural speech to poetry when its diction was still largely dominated by the model of Pope's *Iliad*. "As language only really exists in the mouths of men," Frost tells Braithwaite, "here again Wordsworth was right in trying to reproduce in his poetry not only the words – and in their limited range, too, actually used in common speech – but their sound."[14]

Frost's theory of the sound of sense is additionally, I suspect, a reaction against Imagism and the cult of the Image that T. E. Hulme, F. S. Flint, and Pound were encouraging in England when Frost arrived there in 1912. Frost values sharply observed detail as much as any poet does, but he worries that the concentration on the visual in poetry is undermining its aural aspect. "We value the seeing eye already," he remarks to Cox in 1914. "Time we said something about the hearing ear – the ear that calls up vivid sentence forms" (*CPPP*, 682). In the same year, he tells Cournos: "I cultivate . . . the hearing imagination rather than the seeing imagination though I should not want to be without the latter" (*SL*, 130). And in 1925 he writes to John Freeman: "Fool psychologists treat the five sense elements in poetry as of equal weight. One of them is nearly the whole thing. The tone-of-voice element is the unbroken flow on which the others are carried along like sticks and leaves and flowers."[15]

In his verse, Frost's sensitivity to the tones of living speech contributes to a style that is fresh and idiomatic. It is a style that involves, as Wilbur notes in connection with "After Apple-Picking," "colloquial language, but a beautifully refined and charged colloquial language."[16] In his letters, interviews, and lectures, however, Frost at times loses sight of the "refined and charged" element of his writing and makes dogmatic statements that come dangerously close to equating colloquiality with poetic speech *per se*: "All poetry," he asserts at one point, "is a reproduction of the tones of actual speech" (*CPPP*, 701). Frost, moreover, repeatedly goes beyond the sensible position that poetry always should maintain some contact with living speech to the unreasonable position that phrases and sentences on the page can and must exactly communicate specific tones of voice.

This latter view is evident in his letters to Bartlett. In the July 4, 1913 communication, he says, "The reader must be at no loss to give his voice the posture proper to the sentence" (*CPPP*, 665). On February 22, 1914, he writes, "The voice of the imagination, the speaking voice must know certainly how to behave how to posture in every sentence he [the poet] offers" (*CPPP*, 675). On May 30, 1916, he adds, "A sentence *must* convey a meaning by tone of voice and it must be the particular meaning the writer intended. The reader must have no choice in the matter. The tone of voice and its meaning must be in black and white on the page" (*SL*, 204). Reading such remarks, one feels that Frost is standing on its head Alexander Pope's dictum that "sound must seem an echo to the sense" and is urging that "sense is a mere echo of the sound."

To his credit, Frost recognizes the difficulty of precisely establishing, on the page, tone of voice; but he suggests, in an address he delivers in 1915 to the Browne and Nichols School, that a writer can resolve the difficulty by providing a context from which tone can be inferred. He also on this occasion illustrates his ideas by citing the opening stanza of his poem, "The Pasture."

> [I]t is a fundamental fact that certain forms depend on the sound; – e.g., note the various tones of irony, acquiescence, doubt, etc. in the farmer's, "I guess so." And the great problem is, can you get these tones down on paper? How *do* you tell the tone? By the context, by the animating spirit of the living voice . . . And my poems are to be read in the appreciative tones of this live speech. For example, there are five tones in this first stanza,

> *The Pasture*
> I'm going out to clean the pasture spring;   (light, informing tone)
> I'll only stop to rake the leaves away   ("only" tone – reservation)
> (And wait to watch the water clear, I may):   (supplementary, possibility)
> I sha'n't be gone long. – You come too.   (free tone, assuring)
>   (after thought, inviting)
>   (*CPPP*, 687, 688)

Although this is interesting analysis, it is unlikely that many readers, if asked to guess how many tones were in the stanza would answer five, or, if told that there were five, would guess them to be those Frost designates. If it be objected that his example ill suits his argument, and that it is hard to infer any but a sketchy context from the opening lines of a lyric poem, we might respond that even when poets minutely particularize their contexts, tone may remain elusive or subject to interpretation. For example, Shakespeare clarifies, with extensive circumstantial detail, the political and personal issues that surround Prince Hal, Hamlet, and Prospero, but fine actors have offered equally plausible but very different readings of these characters and of the tones appropriate to particular lines and passages.

Skeptical of Frost's assertion that writers can precisely convey tone, Gamaliel Bradford remarks to the poet in 1924: "It is probable that every writer hears his own composition as well as sees it. But the subtle possibilities of variation in the matter are so wide, that I can hardly feel that you are right in feeling that any one interpretation out of many can possibly be imperatively indicated" (*SL*, 298–99). This seems a sensible assessment of the issue. Writers should compose, as Frost does so magnificently, with their ears sensitively attuned to the resources of the live voice. But it is overstating matters to demand that writing consistently specify vocal tone.

Frost himself sometimes appears to doubt his theory of the sound of sense. In discussing it, he keeps fiddling with his terminology in a way that suggests he cannot focus his meaning to his own satisfaction. What begins, in the first letter to Bartlett, as "the sound of sense," becomes, in the second letter to Bartlett "sentence sounds." And we may well feel that these phrases indicate somewhat different things – pure tone in the first case, sentence as tone in the second – even though Frost indicates in his letter of March 1915 to Braithwaite that the terms are synonymous: "[M]y conscious interest in people was at first no more than an almost technical interest in their speech – in what I used to call their sentence sounds – the sound of sense" (*CPPP*, 684). Other phrases Frost employs to indicate the sound of sense include "sound-posture" (e. g.,[17]), "vocal posture" (e. g.,[18]), "sentence tones" (e.g., *CPPP*, 690), and "vocal imagination" (e. g., *CPPP*, 789).

Moreover, in his February 1914 letter to Bartlett, Frost remarks of his ideas about tone, "This is no literary mysticism I am preaching"; and he says shortly afterwards, "I wouldn't be writing all this if I didn't think it the most important thing I know. I write it partly for my own benefit, to clarify my ideas for an essay or two I am going to write some fine day (not far distant)" (*CPPP*, 675, 677–78). And in February 1915, after saying to Cox, "Words are only valuable in writing as they serve to indicate particular sentence sounds" – a statement that overlooks the essential if untonal value of words as communicators of denotative meaning – Frost immediately adds: "I must say some things over and over. I must be a little extravagant too" (*SL*, 152). That Frost realized that his ideas might puzzle others, that he never wrote the essay or two he hoped to write, that he recognized that he was being "a little extravagant" – all of this may indicate that he intuited that this aspect of his thought was not wholly workable.

If "the sound of sense" gives pause as a "theory" or "principle," we should stress in Frost's defense that he manages, as well as any poet, to *suggest* tone.

In such story-poems as "The Death of the Hired Man" and "The Code" the dialogue is vividly realized, and many lines among his lyrics carry similar tang or bite. The following tercet from "Provide, Provide" is typical:

> Some have relied on what they knew;
> Others on being simply true.
> What worked for them might work for you.

To mix a metaphor, one can almost hear the twinkle in the poet's eye as he says the tercet's final and culminating line.

We should also note that Frost's interest in the sound of sense ties into his love of the paradox mentioned at the beginning of this chapter: good verse can fuse vivid and variable speech with the fixed units of meter. Nowhere is Frost's love of this paradox and of colloquial tone clearer than in a letter which he writes in 1915 to Walter Pritchard Eaton:

> I am only interesting to myself for having ventured to try to make poetry out of tones that if you judge from the practice of other poets are not usually regarded as poetical. You can get enough of those sentence tones that suggest grandeur and sweetness everywhere in poetry . . . I have tried to see what I could do with boasting tones and quizzical tones and shrugging tones (for there are such) and forty eleven other tones. All I care a cent for is to catch sentence tones that havent been brought to book . . . But summoning them is not all. They are only lovely when thrown and drawn and displayed across spaces of the footed line. (*CPPP*, 690–91)

3. Feats of Association: Frost's Rhymes and Stanzas

In addition to being a fine metrist, Frost is a remarkable rhymer. Like Aristotle, Frost believes that one of the surest signs of genius in a poet is a gift for metaphor – for making unexpected but illuminating connections between things. And Frost regards rhyme as an acoustic equivalent of metaphor, or an extension of metaphor into sound. "[A]ll there is to thought is feats of association," is the way Frost sums up the matter. "Now, wouldn't it be a pretty idea to look at that as the under part of every poem: a feat of association, putting two things together and making a metaphor . . . Carry that idea a little further, to think that perhaps the rhyming, the coupling of lines is an outward symbol of this thing that I call feats of association."[19]

Like good metrical composition, good rhyming entails an element of similarity and an element of dissimilarity. Just as versification fuses the fixed units of meter with the variable rhythms of speech, so rhyming involves syllables which, on the one hand, sound alike, but which, on the other hand, denote different things and serve different grammatical functions. Rhyme audially folds syllables into each other, while lexically opening them outward to connect with conceptual categories remote from their own.

To grasp this point, and its relevance to Frost, we can examine the first two stanzas of "Good Hours":

> I had for my winter evening walk –
> No one at all with whom to talk,
> But I had the cottages in a row
> Up to their shining eyes in snow.
>
> And I thought I had the folk within:
> I had the sound of a violin;
> I had a glimpse through curtain laces
> Of youthful forms and youthful faces.

These lines are graceful and fluid in part because of the effective variety of their rhymes. Frost matches not only nouns with nouns (as happens in lines three and four and in lines seven and eight), but also a noun with a verb (talk/walk) and a preposition with a noun (within/violin). Likewise, though the rhymes in the first stanza all entail monosyllabic words, in the second they concern words of other lengths and shapes. We have a rear-stressed disyllable ("within") chiming with a trisyllable with significant stress on its third syllable ("violin"). And we have two fore-stressed disyllables (laces/faces) that comprise a feminine rhyme.

Frost takes many small and tactful pains to keep his rhymes as interesting as possible. For example, he realizes that if a poet rhymes a common word with an unusual one, it is as a rule best for the unusual word to come second. This understanding is evident in the couplet (lines 15–16) of "Evening in a Sugar Orchard," in which Frost describes sparks that, rising from a sugarhouse chimney, catch in the bare maples above it and form sublunary constellations:

> They were content to figure in the trees
> As Leo, Orion, and the Pleiades.

What reader, hearing the initial "trees" termination, would anticipate its being answered by "Pleiades"? Yet this word is just right. It is visually apt. It is, moreover, intellectually striking, concluding as it does the arresting comparison between the small, transitory sparks in the trees and the vast and virtually immutable stellar groups in the heavens. And it is important that "Pleiades" clinches rather than sets up the rhyme. If we reversed the lines, they would still make prefect grammatical sense:

> As Leo, Orion, and the Pleiades,
> They were content to figure in the trees.

But the rhyme would not startle us with the same pleasure.

At the same time, Frost is careful not to show off. He never lets the rhymes run away with the poem. More important, Frost appreciates that when good poets rhyme they are coupling not only similarly sounding syllables, but whole phrases, sentences, and thoughts. In his essay "The Constant Symbol," he remarks: "No rhyming dictionary for me to make me face the facts of rhyme. I may say the strain of rhyming is less since I came to see words as phrase-ends to countless phrases just as the syllables *ly*, *ing*, and *ation* are word-ends to countless words" (*CPPP*, 790–91). And Frost knows that, contrary to what is sometimes alleged by critics, there are no intrinsically banal rhymes. There are no rhymes that cannot be redeemed by the appropriate context. The first poem in Frost's first book begins with a couplet that employs what many consider one of the tritest of rhymes in our language.

> One of my wishes is that those dark trees,
> So old and firm they scarcely show the breeze . . .
>
> ("Into My Own," lines 1–2)

However, few of us feel that the rhyme here is feeble. Rather, we are simply struck by the memorable image of the rigid, ancient trees – stiff even when the breeze blows through them. The rhyme is fine.

Frost often arranges his rhymed poems into stanzas, and he does so for two reasons chiefly. The first is musical. Stanzas enable Frost to fashion verbal harmonies difficult to achieve in non-stanzaic verse. Stanzas permit him to play with patterns of rhymes and to mix together lines of different lengths. Consider, for example, the second and third stanzas of "A Late Walk," a poem in ballad stanza. (A ballad stanza is a quatrain whose first and third lines are unrhyming iambic tetrameters and whose second and fourth lines are rhyming iambic trimeters. In this poem, the iambics are slightly loosened, with occasional extra unaccented syllables within the lines.)

> And when I come to the garden ground,
>   The whir of sober birds
> Up from the tangle of withered weeds
>   Is sadder than any words.
>
> A tree beside the wall stands bare,
>   But a leaf that lingered brown,
> Disturbed, I doubt not, by my thought,
>   Comes softly rattling down.
>
> ("A Late Walk," lines 5–12)

Frost could have written this passage in blank verse and said something like

> And when I'm visiting the garden ground,
> The birds that rise from tangled, withered weeds
> Make sounds as sad as words could ever make.
> A bare tree standing by the wall lets fall
> A brown leaf (troubled by, it seems, my thought),
> And it comes softly rattling to my feet.

But deprived of the rhymes and the varying line-lengths (and of course Frost's inimitable phrasing), the verse loses its wistfully pointed quality.

The second key function for which Frost uses stanzas is indicated by the origin and history of the term. "Stanza" comes from an Italian word meaning "stopping place" or "room." Just as architects divide buildings into rooms to help people organize various aspects of their lives, so Frost stanzaically partitions poems to help the reader find a way through their components. Consider Frost's eight-line poem, "Fragmentary Blue":

> Why make so much of fragmentary blue
> In here and there a bird, or butterfly,
> Or flower, or wearing-stone, or open eye,
> When heaven presents in sheets the solid hue?
>
> Since earth is earth, perhaps, not heaven (as yet) –
> Though some savants make earth include the sky;
> And blue so far above us comes so high,
> It only gives our wish for blue a whet.

This poem consists of a question and an answer. Frost devotes the first stanza to the former and the second to the latter. He asks, "Why make so much of the beauty of the color blue, wherever we find it here on earth, when there's such an abundance of blue in the sky above us?" Then he answers, "However abundant the blue above us is, it is inaccessible; and though it stimulates our love of beauty, we prize the fragmentary earthly blue because we can see it closely and feel part of it." And thanks to Frost's putting the question in one stanza and the response in another, we can readily grasp the poem's dialectical nature.

In addition, Frost at times expressively opens up his stanzas and lets the sense run from one to another. "To Earthward" well illustrates this technique:

> Love at the lips was touch
> As sweet as I could bear;
> And once that seemed too much;
> I lived on air

> That crossed me from sweet things,
> The flow of – was it musk
> From hidden grapevine springs
> Down hill at dusk?
>
> I had the swirl and ache
> From sprays of honeysuckle
> That when they're gathered shake
> Dew on the knuckle.
>
> I craved strong sweets, but those
> Seemed strong when I was young;
> The petal of the rose
> It was that stung.
>
> Now no joy but lacks salt
> That is not dashed with pain
> And weariness and fault;
> I crave the stain
>
> Of tears, the aftermark
> Of almost too much love,
> The sweet of bitter bark
> And burning clove.

Notice how the transversal of the first stanza into the second – "I lived on air / That crossed from sweet things" – communicates the happy sensory "flow" the poet experienced when young. By the same token, the movement from the fifth to the sixth stanza – "I crave the stain/ Of tears, the aftermark / Of almost too much love" – gives us the sense of the emotional effects that excessive passion leaves in its wake. Finally, the way that the argument drives through the end of the next-to-last stanza, and into the concluding stanza, reinforces the impression of the speaker's desire:

> When stiff and sore and scarred
> I take away my hand
> From leaning on it hard
> In grass and sand,
>
> The hurt is not enough:
> I long for weight and strength
> To feel the earth as rough
> To all my length.

Just as the speaker voices dissatisfaction with the limits of his feeling, so the sentence expressing that dissatisfaction bursts the boundary of its stanza. "The hurt is not enough," and neither is the stanza.

One other notable quality of Frost's stanzaic verse is syntactical variety. In the same way that Frost varies the rhythms playing across his meters, he modulates the kinds of phrases, clauses, and sentences he sets across his stanzas. As he says in an interview with *The Paris Review*: "I'm always interested, you know, when I have three or four stanzas, in the way I *lay* the sentences in them. I'd hate to have the sentences all lie the same in the stanzas" (*CPPP*, 890). Even "To Earthward," with its tight trimeter-trimeter-trimeter-dimeter stanza, features considerable syntactical diversity. For example, the third stanza consists of a relatively straightforward sentence, following the common subject-verb-object pattern, with additional predicate matter that clarifies the object, which is in this case compound ("the swirl and ache").

> I had the swirl and ache
> From sprays of honeysuckle
> That when they're gathered shake
> Dew on the knuckle.

The seventh stanza, in contrast, is an introductory dependent clause,

> When stiff and sore and scarred
> I take away my hand
> From leaning on it hard
> In grass and sand,

that attaches to the main clause ("The hurt is not enough") only in the succeeding stanza.

Frost, then, enacts with his stanzas the same timeless dialectic of art that he enacts with his meters and his rhymes, balancing likeness and unlikeness, coherence and diversity.

Any discussion of Frost's versification would be incomplete if it failed to speak of the pleasure his poems give. The most significant feature of his technical skill is that it serves not itself but its subjects. Whether weighty or light or both, his poems exhibit a spirited engagement with language and an enchantingly exact observation of the world. Thanks to their strong and honest technique, they enable us to perceive beauties and joys that we might otherwise overlook or imperfectly appreciate; and they enable us as well to confront darker aspects of experience, aspects from which, but for his mediating grace, we might turn away in fear or emotional cowardice.

Discussing the process by which he wrote a poem, Frost once said: "What do I want to communicate but what a *hell* of a good time I had writing it?" (*CPPP*, 892). And there is no better way to end this discussion of Frost's versification than by citing an exchange between the visitor and the farmer in

"The Mountain." At one point earlier in the poem, the farmer has told the visitor that at the top of a mountain is a brook that is "always cold in summer, warm in winter" (49); and toward the close of the poem (100–04) the visitor recurs to the subject, asking, "Warm in December, cold in June, you say?" to which the farmer replies:

> "I don't suppose the water's changed at all.
> You and I know enough to know it's warm
> Compared with cold, and cold compared with warm.
> But all the fun's in how you say a thing."

NOTES

* My analysis of Frost's handling of the stanzaic structure in "To Earthward" is indebted to Kenneth Fields, who years ago in conversation perceptively remarked on the expressive opening up of the first stanza into the second. I am indebted as well to Kevin Durkin and John Ridland, both of whom read an early draft of this chapter and made helpful suggestions and corrections.

1 Elaine Barry, *Robert Frost on Writing* (New Brunswick: Rutgers University Press, 1973), p. 81.

2 *Ibid.*, p. 153.

3 *Ibid.*, p. 154.

4 Charles W. Cooper, in consultation with John Holmes, *Preface to Poetry* (New York: Harcourt Brace, 1946), pp. 604–07.

5 Quoted in Thomas A. Sebeok, ed. *Style in Language* (Cambridge, MA: MIT Press, 1960), pp. 363–64.

6 Robert Francis, *Frost: A Time to Talk: Conversations and Indiscretions* (Amherst: University of Massachusetts Press, 1972), p. 97.

7 Barry, *Robert Frost on Writing*, p. 73.

8 *Ibid.*, pp. 80–81.

9 *Notes by Robert Frost on His Life and Early Writings*, with an introduction by William H. Pritchard (Amherst: The Friends of The Amherst College Library, 1991), p. 11.

10 *Speaking of Frost*, Richard Wilbur and William H. Pritchard, interviewed by Donald G. Sheehy (Amherst: The Friends of The Amherst College Library, 1997), p. 13.

11 Barry, *Robert Frost on Writing*, p. 153.

12 *Ibid.*, p. 70.

13 *Ibid.*

14 Barry, *Robert Frost on Writing*, p. 154.

15 *Ibid.*, p. 81.

16 *Speaking of Frost*, Wilbur and Pritchard, p. 9.

17 In Barry, *Robert Frost on Writing*, p. 153.

18 In *ibid.*, p. 94.

19 Robert Frost, *Poetry and Prose*, ed. Edward Connery Lathem and Lawrance Thompson (New York: Holt, Rinehart, and Winston, 1972), p. 380.

7

JUDITH OSTER

Frost's Poetry of Metaphor

"Metaphor is the whole of poetry." "Poetry is simply made of metaphor . . . Every poem is a new metaphor inside or it is nothing."(*CPPP*, 786) Such are the burdens Robert Frost placed upon metaphor, and on himself as a poet. He went even farther in his claiming that metaphor is the whole of thinking, and that, therefore, to be educated by poetry – note: *by* poetry – is to be taught to think (*CPPP*, 786). In "Education by Poetry," an essay that originated in a talk at Amherst, he says:

> [T]he teacher must teach the pupil to think . . . We still ask boys in college to think, . . . but we seldom tell them it is just putting this and that together, it is saying one thing in terms of another. To tell them is to set their feet on the first rung of a ladder the top of which reaches to the sky . . . The metaphor whose manage we are best taught in poetry – that is all there is of thinking. It may not seem far for the mind to go, but it is the mind's furthest. The richest accumulation of the ages is the noble metaphors we have rolled up.
>
> (*CPPP*, 723; 725)

But he also cautions that all metaphors break down somewhere, as of course they must because a metaphor, no matter how rich or how apt, is not an identity, never an exact correspondence. On one hand, this means that one must be wary when thinking by means of metaphor, and one must be wary when reading or hearing the metaphors of others. As examples he gives scientific theories such as evolution (a plant metaphor), a mechanistic universe (a machine – all right – but where's the lever, or button, or pedal?), and concludes: "Unless you have had your proper poetical education in the metaphor, you are not safe anywhere. Because you are not at ease in figurative values: you don't know the metaphor in its strength and its weakness . . . You are not safe in science; you are not safe in history" (721). We must understand that a metaphor will take us only so far before it "breaks down." My love may be a rose in her softness, her sweetness, her beauty, or even her tendency to hurt me. But she does not grow outside in the garden on a stem. The human lover is infinitely more complicated than the rose.

On the other hand, the fact that metaphors are not merely correspondences or strict analogies is their glory. In their richness, great metaphors enlarge our thinking and our imaginations as we "play" with their possibilities, but also test their limits. How far can we take one up that ladder before we fall? How good are we at creating our own metaphors, and what do we risk when we do so? This is very serious "play" – to Frost, "play for mortal stakes," as he writes in "Two Tramps in Mud Time." The "game" in "Mending Wall" ("Oh, just another kind of outdoor game,/ One on a side. It comes to little more"), as well as the playfulness of its tone, never successfully masks the seriousness of that poem or its mysteries. What is the "something" that does not love a wall? What can be meant by "know[ing] what I was walling in or walling out"? What is it that requires "walling in"?

Possibly related to reading and writing metaphors is one of Frost's metaphors of poetry: "I wouldn't have a poem that hadn't doors. I wouldn't leave them open, though."[1] The basic conceptual metaphor,[2] is that of a structure (which a poem, after all, is). If a poem has doors that open and close, it may be represented as a house, where leaving doors open could leave the resident vulnerable to intrusion, even theft or harm. We may ask once again whether closing the door means walling in or walling out, or both. On the other hand, a house with doors can also be inviting; the one standing outside may be invited in. A door, after all, is meant to be opened as well as shut. A word like "something," for example, used as Frost uses it, opens it at least a crack: "Something there is that doesn't love a wall" ("Mending Wall," *CPPP*, 39); or: "What was that whiteness?/ Truth? A pebble of quartz? For once, then, something" ("For Once, Then, Something," *CPPP*, 208). A poem, then, can be an invitation, but not an unlimited one, not always, and not to everyone. We may get invited in and challenged to play the game, but we are not assured of a perfect score.

A person who does not realize that this is an open-ended game with no one "correct" answer may be too timid to accept the challenge. This is true of many who "fear" poetry, and this can include serious students of literature. It is true of a woman whose mother had named her Maple. "Maple" is a long poem, not anthologized, that dramatizes these issues of metaphor – its functions, its demands, its rewards, and its traps. To summarize the poem briefly: Maple is a girl's name, but teachers and friends usually insist on calling her Mabel. Her father confirms, when she is still a young child, that "Maple" was indeed correct: her mother had given her that name before she died in childbirth, and the father assumes it bid her "Be a good girl – be like a maple tree./ How like a maple tree's for us to guess." He had promised to tell her more about the different trees and more about her mother later, when she was older. She never forgot this discussion, as he assumed she would; the seeds he sowed merely slept and came to life when she grew older and pondered her name once more:

> Its strangeness lay
> In having too much meaning . . .
> Her problem was to find out what it asked
> In dress or manner of the girl who bore it.

She grew up searching for herself and educating herself in the process. Her secretarial education brought her to the city, where, raising her eyes while taking dictation one day, she reminded her boss of a maple tree. Since he had thought her name to be Mable,

> They both were stirred that he should have divined
> Without the name her personal mystery.
> It made it seem as if there must be something
> She must have missed herself. So they were married
> And took the fancy home with them to live by.
>
> (*CPPP*, 170–1)

They went to her girlhood home on a pilgrimage to see if there were some special tree, but they found none, and so clung "to what one had seen in the other/ By inspiration. It proved there was something." They "kept their thoughts away from when the maples/ Stood uniform in buckets," relating her, rather, to autumn maples. Eventually, they gave up their search. The poem concludes with the judgment: "Better a meaningless name."

Surely ironic is ending a poem of failure to find meaning by disparaging names with meaning. True, it is much easier to have a name that is simply a label, yet the name had brought Maple together with a man who intuited her essence. To live by fancy is not all bad; to search for meaning creates a more meaningful life, whether one finds the "correct" meaning or not. What Maple saw as a "problem" requiring *a* solution, Frost would surely have seen as a glorious opportunity to enter into a poetic game. To analyze the ways in which the couple "failed" is to enter into the whole question of how to read a metaphor: the danger of overreading, and the opposite pitfall of being too literal, or even too narrowly analogical. To be good like a maple, or scarlet like a maple, or beautiful like a maple is not to *be* a maple. Finding a point of similarity with a maple is far narrower than finding the essence of "mapleness."

Her husband recognized her "mapleness," and she responded to that recognition, yet neither one could define it or understand it. Instead of really looking at maples, they kept looking for clues, for a particular maple, the particular message.[3] They had rejected one because it would not have been there when her mother named her.

Could it have been another maple like it?
They hovered for a moment near discovery,
Figurative enough to see the symbol,
But lacking faith in anything to mean
The same thing at different times to different people.

Could we have a better lesson than this on poetic interpretation – clearer permission from the poet not to be bound by another's interpretation of a "symbol" or figure? Surely Frost is criticizing the inability to be figurative enough, to allow metaphor some flexibility. The father begins the interpretive process by assuming that the name was "after *a*" tree ("Well, you were named after a maple tree."), but it was probably not with *a* tree in mind, nor was the intent to "name *after*." In saying "Be a good girl – be like a maple tree," he creates a simile that leaves unclear how maples are good, and how a "good" maple tree is analogous to a good girl. The mother seemed only to say, "Be a maple – or like one." In this case, the presence or absence of "like" or "as" would make no difference, for in their deep structure they could be the same, with an analogical connection either way. Rather the real difference is between specifying a single property or feature as opposed to leaving open the possibility of any number of analogous features. The father goes on to say *How* like a maple tree's for us to guess" (emphasis mine), but it is this range of possibility they fail to explore. They are too afraid, or too lacking in imagination to "guess." In *Models and Metaphors* Max Black argues for an interaction view of metaphor. Rather than viewing metaphor as simply a comparison between two things, or of one substituting for the other, he sees metaphor as dynamic – the principal subject (here, the girl Maple) and the subsidiary subject (here, the maple tree) interacting along a system of shared commonplaces and newly created implications. Interaction implies that the view enriched by metaphor can go both ways – we see both the girl and the tree in new ways as a result of the association. Likewise, Mark Turner no longer relies solely on "projection" from what he calls the source domain (loosely, the metaphoric image) to its target (that which the image expresses or describes). He finds enrichment and dynamism of meaning made possible in the "blending" that occurs when inferences and meaning are carried across at least two "mental spaces," coming from both the source space and the target space to create a "blended space" that makes possible the construction of inferences which simple projection from source to target could not achieve.[4] In "Maple," for example, we do not rest simply in realizing that the subsidiary subject, maple, affects our view of the principal subject, girl, insofar as it shares attributes in common with a human (beauty, for example, or sweetness); and it is not simply that she seeks maples better to understand herself, rather the subsidiary subject – maple – has an *effect* on the principal subject – girl. As the reader explores the metaphor and the ways it shares commonplaces with its "target," or the possibilities of meaning that can arise in a newly created space blending maples and girls, the reader sees newly created implications, but only if she opens herself to the fullest range of shared attributes, meanings, and implications. This is what Maple-the-reader-of-metaphor failed to do. Her problem lay in insisting that the metaphor be tied too firmly to one attribute, or one tree.

There are various attributes of a maple which we can think of and which the couple see. The problem is only that they fail, for one reason or another, to apply them to her. The mother named the baby at her death, but it was also in her season of bearing; yet the couple could only focus on the image of the maple in fall – season of death. In keeping their thoughts away from the sap season, they missed the "steam," the rising sap. They missed the inner sweetness, looking as "she [had always] looked for herself . . . more or less outwardly." That the maple's inner sweetness occurs at a time of minimum beauty, and that the greatest outward beauty occurs at the time of death, is a paradox that escapes them entirely. Even in fall, though:

> Once they came upon a maple in the glade,
> Standing alone with smooth arms lifted up,
> And every leaf of foliage she'd worn
> Laid scarlet at her feet.

One reason they failed to relate her to this tree was "a filial diffidence [that] partly kept them/ From thinking it could be a thing so bridal" – too beautifully undressed – again missing the fact that this, like the spring maple of rising sap, sweetness, and bearing may have been exactly what her mother would have wished her to be and to have. That and the beauty and the upturning, up-reaching that had attracted Maple's husband to her.

Since all these are attributes of a maple, any maple, any time, Frost seems to be demonstrating that to be too literal, or to remain at the level of one-to-one analogy is to limit the range of one's understanding. At the same time, however, to be too analytical, trying too hard to find the "secret," can be the stumbling block to finding the secret. Simply coming upon those maples – any maples – and relating to whatever it is that is magnificent at that time, that is what Maple was too self-conscious to be able to do.[5] She also seemed unable to reconcile herself to mystery – the mystery of her own being, the mystery of her husband's intuitive apprehension of her essence, what Karsten Harries considers the transcendent possibility of metaphor to express the not-present. Her husband's one great contribution was his inspired and intuitive recognition of the "inner mystery" of her being, and their marriage became a combination of his perception and her mystery – the ideal relationship between reader and poem.

To understand poetry – come close to it, as Frost would say – is to know it at its strongest and largest, but to know it at its weakest as well; to know how far one may take it, where it breaks down, and where it breaks out and soars beyond itself. To read poetry like much of Frost's is to keep open the widest range of possibilities, but, as Frost says elsewhere, to "stay unassuming," not daring to close down or be conclusive where the poem stays open. This is especially true in poems where we can only suspect that we are reading metaphor, or, where we are not given a second term or situation with shared attributes, but are somehow convinced that this image or small drama has meaning beyond itself, that it is indeed metaphor, and because its referent is left open, can be "about" many things, none of them mutually exclusive. Winifred Nowottney speaks of this as symbolism:

> With metaphor, the poet talks about object x as though it were a y . . . With symbolism, he presents an . . . x, but his way of presenting x makes us think that it is not only x, but also is or stands for something more than itself – some y or other, or a number of 'y's . . . It is as though . . . the poet were trying to leap out of the medium of language altogether and to make his meaning speak through objects instead of words. Even though he does not tell us what . . . x stands for, or even that it stands for anything, he makes us believe that it means, to him at least, something beyond itself.[6]

A poem like "Birches," for example, practically forces us to ask: what is this poem *about*? Not "what does it mean" or "what do birches stand for?" or "what is the poet telling us?" but what is the poet asking us to explore or connect with; think about, and feel? While those birches may present us with a beautiful New England image, the real picture we are given is not a static tableau of trees, but a powerful, dynamic drama of *climbing* birches, of a boy testing the limits of his daring, keeping his balance in a precarious position of his own choosing. Too far from town to play baseball, too alone to be challenged by others, he challenges himself. It is true that the trees and the boy's actions are described metaphorically:

> You may see their trunks arching in the woods
> . . .
> Like girls on hands and knees that throw their hair
> Before them over their heads to dry in the sun.

>   he always kept his poise
> To the top branches, climbing carefully
> With the same pains you use to fill a cup
> Up to the brim, and even above the brim.

We must also keep in mind that even the literal description of the boy and his actions are being imagined wistfully by the speaker – the trees have, in reality, been bent down to stay by ice storms; and these are also described metaphorically in terms of crazed enamel, broken glass, and the inner dome of heaven. Ironically, that magnificent picture is called "matter-of-fact" because it is Truth – ice storms, not boys – even though it is expressed in language that is not matter-of-fact at all. There is no lack, then, of metaphor, even metaphor within metaphor and metaphoric playing *in* the poem, but what of the significance of that whole scene and its drama – the whole poem as metaphor, or, in another word, the story-as-metaphor we term "parable"? What are those arching girls doing there? Why, suddenly, does the speaker declare: "Earth's the right place for love," when he has just been talking about pain and weariness, memories of being himself a swinger of birches, of a pathless wood, and a weeping eye?

By the time he says "It's when I'm weary of considerations,/ And life is too much like a pathless wood" it is clear that we are not just talking about trees and boys climbing them; the question is, at what point before this did the poem begin to push toward parable?[7] That the poem encompasses more we would probably all agree, but we would have trouble agreeing on, or even identifying the exact line where we began to feel those larger meanings – life and death, the risks and costs and joys of love, or art, or climbing in every sense – the absolute need for both daring and balance when we do so. In fact, even in our own subsequent readings we would most likely point to different places. But that is the strength of the poem. Its supreme art lies precisely in the way it blurs the distinctions between concrete fact and imagination, between catching us up in the experience of the poem and forcing us to contemplate it in a more detached manner – the same tension, of course, between experience and contemplation that is everywhere *in* the poem.

In some poems we need to ask a question more fundamental even than where metaphor begins or what it signifies: are we in the presence of metaphor at all? Perhaps the most debated work in the Frost canon is that best-known and best-loved poem "Stopping by Woods on a Snowy Evening" (CPPP, 207). It has been read as "simply" a beautiful lyric, as a suicide poem, as recording a single autobiographical incident, and everything in between.[8] Ours is not to adjudicate, nor to "fix" a meaning, but to allow the poem its openness, its fullest possible range; at the same time, to ask how such a delicate lyric, so satisfying in its perfect blend of description, sound, feeling, and form, has still prompted its readers to find, or seek, something more. Why hasn't it just been taken literally? What triggers those readings? To choose just one of any possible starting points, the word "promises."[9] In this context of beautiful scene the word "pulls down" the experience from the merely aesthetic and sensual, but does so without diminishing that beauty or that feeling, without weighing down the poem. What results is a conflict between two undiminished forces: "promises" that would lead the speaker onward, and his desire to give in to his intoxication with the beauty and peacefulness of the woods. The pull between those alternatives can be seen as that between obligation and temptation, or most literally, between stopping and going on.

If we decide to look at the situation literally, we would think about what staying might mean. Most obvious is simply that it's too cold to stay there safely. The restfulness – the "ease" of "easy wind" and the "down" of "downy flake" begin to suggest an implicit metaphor, especially when combined with the "sleep" which must be postponed until promises are kept ("and miles to go before I sleep") – that of a bed. Sleeping before stopping, then, adds to the notion of not-yet-doing the danger of no-longer-being.[10] Whether a beautiful momentary diversion from "promises," a fleeting wish that one *could* postpone promises, or a more dangerous temptation, the scene offers escape, aided by the hypnotic effect created by the beauty of the scene. The reader, too, is lulled by the scene, and by the rhythmic perfection of the poem.

What *does* the poem mean? Frost would probably say "Read it. It means what it says." What *can* the poem mean? That is another issue: whatever those words in those combinations will allow without distorting their meanings, without introducing elements that cannot fit in the context of the poem as a whole. What will it mean to a particular reader at a particular moment of reading? That must be flexible: one could follow Frost's advice to a graduate student to take his poetry "all the way." Or one could feel chastised by Frost's ridicule of those who say this is a "suicide poem." Or one could ignore Frost altogether.

It is just such questions, fueled by our desire to make meaning, or to explore the possibilities and limitations of words, that make Frost such a challenge to his readers despite the accessibility of his language and his "dramas." What does "The woods are lovely, dark and deep" mean? Can a line be more literal than this? But then we might be influenced by other associations we have built up with a word like "dark." Our everyday discourse uses "dark" metaphorically with no reference to poems, for example: we are kept in the dark (ignorance of the situation); we have deep, dark secrets (those we are ashamed to divulge, perhaps); someone gave me a dark look (menacing or unfriendly); theologians write of a dark night of the soul. On the most literal level, children are often afraid of the dark, most probably because they cannot see what is there, and nothing is more frightening than the unknown, than imagining what might be there that we cannot see. Even the least imaginative adults are afraid when they cannot see their way, for they might trip over some object, or bang into it, or get lost.

Poetry, of course, is filled with metaphors of darkness, and Frost's is no exception. The question here, though, is how we suspect metaphor where a word, despite its resonant connotation, could be read only as literal. In "The Oft Repeated Dream" (*CPPP*, 123–24), we read of a dark pine, which, alone, could remain nothing more than physical description – pines *are* dark, especially at night. But put into its context – "She had no saying dark enough/ for the dark pine," we recognize that its darkness could have other meanings. "Sayings" can only be dark metaphorically; pines could go either way. Given the context of the whole phrase, though, we are not too surprised as the poem continues, that the pine is seen as menacing, even animated in the mind of the woman who "had no saying dark enough for" it, who invests the tree with "tireless but ineffectual hands," with the ability to "try the window latch," and who fears "what the tree might do." Interpreting her fear, of course, is taking our reading of the poem another step, perhaps a psychological one.

"Desert Places"(*CPPP*, 269) can serve as another example of description that depends on context to force a metaphorical reading.[11] Desert places can be just landscape.

> Snow falling and night falling fast, oh, fast
> In a field I looked into going past,
> And the ground almost covered smooth in snow,
> But a few weeds and stubble showing last.

In this poem of going by woods there is no temptation to stop. The scene is bleak, and loneliness does not seem to be the pleasure of being alone that one can feel in "Stopping by Woods on a Snowy Evening." But even though we are given bleakness and loneliness, we could take the words "desert places" literally even in the poem's last lines:

> They cannot scare me with their empty spaces
> Between stars – on stars where no human race is.
> I have it in me so much nearer home
> To scare myself with my own desert places.

Clearly, there is emotion here – fear and loneliness exacerbated by the bare winter landscape, but the speaker who feels this way could still be referring to his own frozen fields where nothing is growing. What renders this "desert" an interior as well as an exterior one occurs in the middle of the poem: "I am too absent-spirited to count;/ The loneliness includes me unawares." Any further interpretation that would follow must take such inner barrenness into account.

One poem that contains no contextual clues within it, no language loaded with emotional weight, is "The Pasture" (*CPPP*, 3), that invitation to join the speaker as he goes "out to clean the pasture spring," to "rake the leaves away/ And wait to watch the water clear." Both stanzas end with "You come too." The speaker issues an invitation and repeats it. We need make nothing more of it. But once we notice that this poem stands at the front of every one of Frost's collections, we assume it has a greater significance to him. We see this poem in a context, even though the context is outside the poem itself. We may assume (as others have) that it is either a love poem, or an invitation into his poetry. And once we assume that, the words, so innocent of metaphorical weight up to that point, are open to re-examination – where else does he write of pastures, and water (clear or in need of clearing); where else of leaves, and mothers, of being gone long? The answer: in many places. One has only to peruse his body of work to find a broad range of experiences, emotions, speculations, and conflicts expressed through and among leaves, or water, or clearing, or wandering. Still, the poem, like "Stopping by Woods," remains a lovely lyric.

What if there are no contextual clues to guide us, or to force us into metaphor? Usually, we can take an image or leave it, seeing a poem more, or less, richly, fearing under- or over-reading, with nothing very much at stake. In "Home Burial," however, there is a moment when everything could depend on whether or not the words were metaphor, and if they were, on what an "interpretive reading" might have been able to achieve. The grief-stricken wife, it will be remembered, cannot reconcile herself to the death of her baby, and cannot forgive her husband for his failure to grieve. The poem does indeed dramatize the burial of that home and that marriage, bringing the reader into a frustratingly anguished scene of confrontation and failed (or non-existent) communication. After much urging, the wife has finally given voice to what has been upsetting her so much – her husband's digging of the infant's grave:

> "If you had any feelings, you that dug
> With your own hand – how could you? – his little grave;
> . . .
> I thought, Who is that man? I didn't know you.
> . . .
> Then you came in. I heard your rumbling voice
> Out in the kitchen, . . .
> . . .
> You could sit there with the stains on your shoes
> Of the fresh earth from your own baby's grave
> And talk about your everyday concerns.
> . . .
>
> I can repeat the very words you were saying:
> 'Three foggy mornings and one rainy day

Will rot the best birch fence a man can build.'
Think of it, talk like that at such a time!
What had how long it takes a birch to rot
To do with what was in the darkened parlor?"   (*CPPP*, 58)

The answer, if he had been speaking metaphorically, could have been "Everything!" Wetness rotting a birch fence, talked of "at such a time," could have been his way of commenting on death, projecting onto a fence what would happen to the best coffin one could build, and to whatever it contained. But she did not see that possibility; he did not explain it, and even though we readers understand what such a metaphor could have meant, we can also understand how callous he either seemed to one who could not think metaphorically, or how callous he really was, if the words were, literally, about his everyday concerns.

We cannot resolve in any definitive way which of the alternatives is "right." The husband's obtuseness elsewhere in the dialogue would not lead us to suspect him of much poetry; still, he reacts to her accusations by saying, "I'm cursed!" Again, does that mean for his wrongs, or in his having a wife who cannot understand *him* any better than he understands her. He has, after all, made some effort. But the issue of not "getting" a metaphor, as if some sort of test has been failed, can be looked at quite apart from the drama of "Home Burial." How much should have to be explained, and how much should be expected of the reader or listener? Frost's statement: "Success in taking figures of speech is as intoxicating as making figures of speech" (*CPPP*, 814) implies that the reader (or listener) must also be somewhat of a poet, must read creatively, or at least sensitively and imaginatively enough not to miss metaphors and their possibilities. For a poet to place a good reading on a par with a poet's "making" is not only a supreme compliment to readers, but to the whole process of reading. Readers have traditionally looked up to the poets they read, and here is a poet valuing what we do, implying that he may need us as much as we need him. Looked at in another way, though, such a statement places tremendous responsibility and expectation on a reader. The other side of the coin of "success" is failure – Frost would fail those who did not "take" the metaphor, those who failed his "test."

In "Revelation" the speaker seems to want friends who understand him without scorecards and translations of subtleties, but even such friends need clues. This poem has been seen as a "revelation" of Frost's own needs and expectations in his social and family relations. But it can just as easily be seen as referring to the relationship between the poet and his readers, the "maker" of metaphor and the "takers" he wants and needs:

We make ourselves a place apart
    Behind light words that tease and flout,
But oh, the agitated heart
    Till someone really find us out.

'Tis pity if the case require
    (Or so we say) that in the end
We speak the literal to inspire
    The understanding of a friend.

But so with all, from babes that play
    At hide-and-seek to God afar,
So all who hide too well away
    Must speak and tell us where they are.   (*CPPP*, 28–29)

This is a warning to the poet not to be too obscure, too subtle, not to expect too much; but it is also a cry for understanding – in friend, loved one, or reader.

In "Maple" he has done much to teach us more directly (the reason "Maple" is discussed in such detail here). In other poems the lesson is more subtle, more of a demonstration, and we may be helped by what he has written and said about poetry in conversations and on platforms. Not surprisingly, much of his poetry talk centered on the importance of metaphor. As might also be expected, the best of his comments on poetry or definitions of metaphor were themselves metaphors, for example: Frost spoke of a poem as a napkin going into a napkin ring, with the ring as the poem and the napkin spreading out again for other people.[12] Another time he used the image of a current carrying the eel grass with it, combing it like hair; it thus combs it in different directions without uprooting it from its initial clarity, its fixed meaning. What to the poet is his "fixed meaning" would most probably be, to us, the words on the page, "holding down" our readings even as they are pushed and pulled by the "currents" of possible meaning. A similar "swaying" metaphor Frost used was that of a boat at anchor: "The poetry that sways on its anchor has both deftness and definiteness."[13]

What all these metaphors of poetry/metaphor have in common is an underlying image of radiating (a term Frost also used). Words, metaphors, poems should radiate meaning(s) outward from the words on the page, becoming more than their literal selves, but never at the expense of losing their moorings, coming loose from the actual words and images that "anchor" them, or hold them "rooted" to the poet's text. One could also relate the image of radiating to Frost's metaphor of a poet's getting his ideas to "flash out new" like quicksilver rolling in a dish: just lying there it is dull, but a roll of the dish makes the quicksilver flash bright. The poet's freshness is his own knack for "breaking through" the dulling oxidation.[14]

But "radiation" is not the only conceptual metaphor of metaphor recurring in Frost. The creative and procreative possibilities of making and taking metaphor[15] were not lost on him and he was fond of expressing this in sexual terms. Frost noted that some metaphors seemed sexual – a bringing together of a male and female element to create propagation of thought. He welcomed Thompson's term "engendering," and went on to call the process "pollenating."[16] Certainly some of Frost's greatest love poetry can be seen as poems about poetry: the new creation that arises in "Putting in the Seed" (*CPPP*, 120) for example, resulting out of love "burn[ing] through" in a "springtime passion for the earth," is, literally, a seedling; but the language of its sprouting: "the sturdy seedling with arched body comes/ Shouldering its way and shedding the earth crumbs" presents us with an image that powerfully suggests both sexual union and the birth of a baby. At the same time, if, to use Frost's famous comparison, "the figure [for poetry] is the same as for love," we may view these passions and creations – love and planting – as potentially applicable to the passion for poetry and the creation that results from it. "Never Again Would Birds' Song Be the Same" (*CPPP*, 308) evokes Eve in the garden, and (a) man whose life would never be the same since "she came," but what that man "believes," hears, and "declares" seems to arise equally out of love and imagination. In so many of the poems, the loved one addressed is assumed to be sharing imagination as well as love with the speaker. In "The Telephone" (*CPPP*, 114) he "hears" (by leaning his head against a flower growing far away from their home) a message she had only thought as she faced the flower on her window sill ("Come"). In a very different vein both poetic creation and sexual procreation are fused in Sylvia Plath's "Metaphors." Her metaphors (found in every line, nine lines to the poem, nine syllables to the line!) are all of pregnancy, but at the same time this poem (aptly called "Metaphors" rather than "Pregnancy") seems to be working both ways with its metaphors of pregnancy – money in a purse, a cow in calf, yeast rising – expressing the pregnancy of metaphor, both its "fullness" and its potential for new life. Frost would surely have agreed.

More directly a love *and* metaphor poem is "The Rose Family":

> The rose is a rose
> And was always a rose.
> But the theory now goes
> That the apple's a rose,
> And the pear is, and so's
> The plum, I suppose.
> The dear only knows
> What will next prove a rose.
> You, of course, are a rose –
> But were always a rose. (*CPPP*, 225)

While there is no mistaking the barb at Gertrude Stein and other "new-fangled" practitioners of poetry, this seems to be a poem that, despite its jocular tone, is nevertheless very serious about both love and poetry.[17] What constitutes legitimate metaphor? Why is it that a woman can be a rose but an apple cannot be? We can answer that roses and apples do not trigger associations – shared commonplaces, either by analogy or convention. Women as peaches or lemons are not unfamiliar terms in our slang. But roses and plums? Such an analogy would have to be established or developed.[18] As a love poem, this compliments the woman with being, not only all that woman/rose has always been in love poetry, but with being the genuine article – the real thing, and, unlike new fads, lasting. This, in a complimentary poem that ridicules the fakery of calling anything by any other name. Only you are genuine (and only my poetry is).

Is he then trying to eliminate metaphor? How close can metaphor come to being identity? In his insistence that the rose that was always a rose really *is* a rose, Frost seems to be interrogating the metaphor's "breaking point." If the addressee is indeed a lady, we must realize, as he must, that no matter how lovely, or genuine, or traditional she is (how rose-like), she cannot really be a rose. Not unless the addressee *is* a rose.[19] In that case it is we who make the assumption that the rose is really a lady. We do so because people usually address other people, and because of all the poetry we have read. Frost would not be the first to address or speak of a rose literally; Waller's "Song" that begins "Go, Lovely Rose" does so, as does "The Romance of the Rose." But we remember that in both of those poems, we (and the ladies) are meant to see rose-as-woman. What happens to the rose will happen to you. The roses are metaphors. Can one compromise be suggested by the word "family"? Do these terms "go together" either by association, or tradition, or aptness that the listener/reader is able to see? Does "rose" radiate possibilities that plums just do not? In this scenario, the writer – or lover – is being cautioned to use metaphors judiciously, to make connections that work.

Frost's poem also plays with the possibility of denying metaphor altogether, but at the same time, questions how much we would be able to say without it. How else to "flash bright," flash genuine feeling through language long made dull, create new expression without creating a new lexicon? Putting this and that together: to Frost, we remember, this is not only metaphor, it is the whole of thinking. From "everything out of its place," it becomes "a triumph of associations"[20] – for him, a mark of intellect as it combines with imagination: "The only thing that can disappoint me in the head is my own failure to make metaphor. My ambition has been to have it said of me: He made a few connections." (*SL*, 189)

Metaphor, then, creates out of difference: items from disparate categories are associated, shown their likeness, and seen newly. To use Frost's term, they "pollenate," engender, "propagate" thought. But another way of showing "one thing in terms of another" is to show one thing becoming another – transformation rather than generation (born out in the Greek and Latin roots of the word). Frost shows both operating in his saying: "A poem is not a string but a web. It is like a sapling. Set it and watch it proliferate."[21] Frost showed this phenomenon often in poems, but did not talk about it much in lectures or prose. One famous exception, though, is his metaphor of poetic making: "Like a piece of ice on a hot stove the poem must ride on its own melting" (*CPPP*, 778). Now *there's* a becoming, a transformation: ice becomes water, a cold solid becomes a warm liquid, a static object is put into motion, and all by means of heat, which is also a metaphor, though one we have begun to use unthinkingly – the heat of passion, the heat of creative energy, the heat of a gripping idea. What we are really talking about is the transformative power of passion, whether it be for love, creation, or commitment to anything we care about deeply.

Frost's poetry is filled with transformations in nature: In "Spring Pools" (*CPPP*, 224) for example, the pools "that . . . still reflect/ The total sky . . .,/ And like the flowers beside them, chill and shiver,/ Will like the flowers beside them soon be gone." But they will neither go anywhere else nor evaporate. They will be drunk "up by roots to bring dark foliage on." While the poem paints the trees as a darkening power that "blot[s] out" pools, a lesson in the "costs" in nature of growth and process, what is actually going to occur is that the pools will become part of those trees and their leaves – pools will be transformed into the sap that makes leaves possible. In that sense, pools will become leaves. (Even the sound works to reinforce this transformation: the liquid "l" sound so prevalent in describing the pools reappears in "foliage.") More directly related to the artistic process is the transformation in "A Hillside Thaw," where "the sun lets go/ Ten million silver lizards out of snow" as if by some magic. But holding them requires the "chill effect" of the moon, who transfixes them with her "spell that could so hold them as they were." What seems to be dramatized here (besides a hillside thaw) is the way "heat" and letting go require chilling (admittedly magical) in order to be "fixed" into another shape. And we recognize that both the sun's heat and the moon's chilling spell are indispensable to the "lizard"-forming process.

"Hyla Brook" (*CPPP*, 115) at first glance combines what we have noticed in the poems discussed above – the image of water that is no longer water and a natural process figuring an artistic one. What it adds, though, is memory, as well as the image of writing: "Its bed is left a faded paper sheet

... A brook to none but who remember long." The frogs "[t]hat shouted in the mist a month ago," whose song invoked still other aural and visual images – "ghost of sleighbells in a ghost of snow," have also become memory. But the poem concludes "We love the things we love for what they are," and we are left with the question of what it is that we love, what it is that they are: is it what was (brook and frogs)? what is now (faded paper sheet and memories)? Both, I would assume, if one considers the poem (or whatever is written on paper sheets) to be loved for what it is; at the same time, we love the reality, the "are-ness" of our memories; and never would we want to forgo that original experience in and of nature – the stuff of our memory that we can transform into art.

A very different sort of passion transforms the metaphors in "The Subverted Flower" (*CPPP*, 308) even as it transforms the boy and the girl in the drama. This poem has been variously analyzed, but I see it as a youthful sexual confrontation whose sudden and newly experienced passion frightens them both with its power. What begins as a flower ("'it is this that had the power.'/ And he lashed his open palm/ With the tender-headed flower") becomes subverted, and the imagery describing the boy becomes animalistic, bestial: "ragged muzzle," "a tiger at the bone," a snout. The images are plainly there for us to see, but we, the readers, are also constantly being made aware that we are seeing them through others' eyes:

> She looked and saw the shame:
> A hand hung like a paw,
> . . .
> A girl could only see
> That a flower had marred a man,
> But what she could not see
> Was that the flower might be
> Other than base and fetid:
> That the flower had done but part,
> And what the flower began
> Her own too meager heart
> Had terribly completed.
> She looked and saw the worst.

And we are hearing the judgment of the girl through another's voice, one that has already described her "in goldenrod and brake,/ Her shining hair displaced"; described the boy's either arm stretched "as if she made it ache/ to clasp her – not to harm." In this highly charged dramatization of an encounter, we also see operating the principle of interactive metaphor, combined with the principle of metaphor as transformation; for we see not only his transformation into a beast, but hers as well: "The bitter words she spit/ Like some tenacious bit. . . . Her mother wiped the foam/ from her chin . . ." The flower has become "a brute," but how? in whose eyes? And we must ask, as we did in "Maple," to what extent her vision, her images of him effected that transformation; to what extent her own transformation was a metaphor applied to what she (and also probably he) was not yet able to understand or explain.

Of course expressing the inexpressible is one of the chief values metaphor holds for us. Putting this and that together, or saying this is like that, may be the only way we can understand or explain a "this" we cannot define, a feeling or experience or concept so abstract, or so new or so powerful that we have no adequate word for it. What the couple saw, though, was not just a flower and an animal, but a flower turning into an animal. In such cases, the analogical process of metaphor, the interactivity we have discussed between subjects, might more often be one between the reader and the drama of the transformation in the poem. Waller sends his "Lovely Rose" with a mission – to fade and die, and in so transforming to say (by showing): "You are like me – and what happens to me will happen to you." Conventionally, the rose would have been a tribute in the language of flowers, where red rose means "I love you"; this rose, however, has another function: This rose carries the "message" by *being* what it is and then changing into something no longer beautiful, no longer alive. At the same time, the rose undergoes another change: from living object to metaphor.

When the relationship between "this" and "that" is dynamic, "this" becomes "that" because some force or power, be it will or nature, an outside agent or a creative urge, has activated the process. The whole process, then, opens us up to its metaphoric possibilities; it is we who will make connections with life and death, the story of Circe, or ice cubes melted by a hot stove.

If "metaphor is the whole of poetry," where does that leave form, which Frost spoke of just as often – sound, meter, sentence-sounds; forming as a way of saving our sanity?[22] He had noted early on, in his English notebook, that "metaphor is not only in thought it is in sentence sounds as well." As one might suspect, he depended on metaphor (one of loving coupling and creation at that) to show how integral form is to the poem: "Form in language is such a disjected lot of old broken pieces it almost seems as nonexistent as the spirit till the two embrace in the sky. They are not to be thought of as encountering in rivalry but in creation" (*CPPP*, 790). One can take this the further step I suspect he wanted us to take: when they form a perfect union, the poem reaches the sky. In both a tribute to poetry and to a woman, he invokes a "heavenward" direction. "The Silken Tent" (*CPPP*, 302) he has written "in praise of [a woman's] poise"[23] has at its center a pole that is its pinnacle to heaven. This poem of woman in relation seems to me unsurpassed in the way it marries form and its central metaphor, and the way both work together as metaphor(s) of "She." Frost was very proud of his feat in creating a sonnet in a single sentence – a sentence that *as* a sentence merits very close attention along with the image:

> She is as in a field a silken tent
> At midday when a sunny summer breeze
> Has dried the dew and all its ropes relent,
> So that in guys it gently sways at ease,
> And its supporting central cedar pole,
> That is its pinnacle to heavenward
> And signifies the sureness of the soul,
> Seems to owe naught to any single cord,
> But strictly held by none, is loosely bound
> By countless silken ties of love and thought
> To everything on earth the compass round,
> And only by one's going taut
> In the capriciousness of summer air
> Is of the slightest bondage made aware.

This poem is a tribute to the kind of woman who, because of her loving and thoughtful ties to others, becomes proud, erect, and beautiful even as she exists as a shelter, creating a home, or providing a haven of privacy and emotional protection.

The silken tent swaying gently at ease presents an image not only of beauty but of dignity and free movement – the tent swaying "in guys" sways also in the "guise" of freedom of movement. But one guy going taut, a summer breeze, or increased moisture remind her occasionally of "the slightest bondage." Because these are ties of love and thought, however, because they are "silken ties," the slightest bondage is not undesirable. What is necessary and positive about such bondage only becomes fully apparent when we realize that in giving she receives; that those "ties" to others are what keep her erect; that were those ties to snap, the tent would collapse; that heavenward pinnacle signifying the sureness of the soul would fall, for nothing emanates simply from the pole. The pole stands only in relation to the guys.[24] It is important too that the ties are many, for that very diversity is what keeps the pole balanced at the center. In the relationship between heavenward pole and guys, it is almost as if the ties of love and thought are in fact her claim to heaven.

This poem of loving bondage and of an existence based upon it is a perfect example of form and words, form and idea "embracing." What seems so remarkable about this sonnet/sentence is the way in which the structure of this sentence is analogous to the metaphor itself and to the relationship the metaphor expresses. The single sentence construction provides, even more firmly than the sonnet form, a unified tightness which corresponds to the tightness of the single image and the tightness of the ropes controlling the very existence of the silken structure. At the same time, the sentence, like the tent "swaying" in the breeze, comes perilously close to going out of control with its multiplication of subordinate clauses (a guise of freedom). Sentence structure has become metaphor.

When one identifies the subordinate clauses, their subjects, verbs, and antecedents, one discovers that the sentence raises some real syntactical questions: for one, what is the main clause? For another, if "as" is used as a conjunction of comparison, it must introduce a clause – a subject and a predicate. If we assume that "tent" is the subject, what verb completes the clause – what verb that is not inside another clause and governed by its own subject? We find that "tent" actually governs no verb in the poem. It is "pole" not "tent" that is the subject of the verbs in the "and" clause; reduced to its simplest terms the sentence would read: "and its pole seems to owe naught to any single cord, but loosely held by countless ties to earth, and only by one's going taut is of the slightest bondage made aware." Grammatically, it would be the pole that is "made aware." We are made aware of "its" [the pole's] centrality to the erectness of the tent, and thus its connection to it; our intuition, though, tells us that only "she," the human subject, can be made aware. The logic of our intuition has supplied a human subject, grammar has supplied "pole" as subject, with "tent" as inseparable from it, with the result that we have a metaphoric fusion of woman, her soul, tent, and pole.

This may work as a complex metaphor, but it does not solve the issue of the subject "tent" left with no verb. Only by supplying an implied but unstated "is" can it be solved: "She is as is . . . a silken tent in a field at midday." The parallelism then is one based on existence – analogous existence, and we must see this in relation to Frost's choice of "as" over "like." There would have been no grammatical problem had Frost written: "She is like a silken tent . . .," which would make perfect sense. The way he did write the poem – with "as" – he has rejected the easier comparison between woman and tent, and forced the comparison, not of nouns, but of relationships. She is not like a tent; she exists in the same manner as a tent does, by means of the same conflicting, balancing pulls. The main clause, then, is simply: "She is." The rest of the poem shows how such existence is maintained and kept upright. In addition to the image of tent and pole being bound by ties of love and thought we are reminded that these are ties "to everything on earth the compass round." "Earth's the right place for love," after all; without the tie to earth that pole could not rise heavenward.

As with the metaphor of transformation and process, of climbing birches, what is being compared is not the more usual noun to noun, but verb to verb – in this case the verb of existence, comparing the way she *is* to the way that silken tent *is*. We do not see that second "is," though, any more than we see the pole/ soul that does the supporting. The process we undergo to "see" what is implicit but not obvious or explicit is also analogous to the way we must read a poet who expresses himself through indirection.

> Poetry provides the one permissible way of saying one thing and meaning another. People say, "Why don't you say what you mean?" We never do that, do we, being all of us too much poets. We like to talk in parables and hints and indirections – whether from diffidence or some other instinct.
>
> (*CPPP*, 719–20)

Why "permissible," and what might "some other instinct" be? Perhaps permissible because, as noted at the outset, metaphors do open doors, but not always, and not to everyone. They do not lie, they hint and veil. And veils allow us to see through them, their partial concealing, partial revealing no small part of their attraction. Perhaps "other instincts" might be both to protect the self, yet at the same time to be attractive and inviting. Frost used to mark his students according to how close they came to poetry, and it may well be that we too are being tested, or perhaps invited. But there is more to share than the feelings or insights or understanding or experience available in a poem: we are also being invited to share his considerable intellect. To use Frost's metaphor that combines these qualities: "I for my part would not be afraid to go in for enthusiasm . . . [b]ut the enthusiasm I mean is taken through the prism of the intellect . . . such enthusiasm is one object of all teaching in poetry . . . I would be willing to throw away everything but that: enthusiasm tamed by metaphor" (*CPPP*, 719). Metaphor then is the ground on which we meet a poet's "enthusiasms" and his intellect. But how shall we be marked? How shall we know if we are at least passing the test of taking metaphors, if not making them?

One test may very well be whether we are enjoying the experience – the game, the play, the seriousness, sharing both enthusiasm and intellect with the poet. This may be one way that, as Stevens says, "Poetry helps us live our lives," providing not only connection with the feeling and mind of another, but play; not only new ways of expressing our feelings and experiences, but new ways of seeing them. A good metaphor can be a lens through which we see newly; to use Frost's metaphor, a "prism of the intellect," which, as we know, not only allows us to see through it, but allows us to see a spectrum, a range of color. Our "new" vision is, in more ways than one, an enlarged vision. A fragmentary note in one of Frost's memorandum books

(English notebook) speaks of walls of books with here and there a window in them. "The books are part of what we perceive with in looking out the window." This is an arresting metaphor of how literature can work, how Frost hoped it would work: the reader seeing *through* not just *into* a text, using that text to look *out*, and not simply *in* (whether into the text, the self, or the author). Poetry, which to Frost *is* metaphor or nothing, would surely be the clearest of such windows, the sharpest of such lenses, the most color-producing of prisms.

But there is yet another "lesson," perhaps the most important of all: the glorious possibilities of language. We are encouraged to risk in it, to test and enlarge its possibilities while ever being mindful of its constraints. "Feeling free in harness" (*I*, 135) Frost used to say; swaying in the guise of freedom, at anchor – language controls and keeps us anchored, "on earth," even as it opens itself – and us – to almost infinite possibilities of perceiving and creating. Coming to realize the power of language, the beauty of it, even as we chafe at its limitations may very well be the real education by poetry. The fun begins when we accept its invitations to join in the game.

NOTES

1 Frost's English notebook, quoted in Lawrance Thompson's *Robert Frost: The Early Years, 1874–1915* (New York: Holt, Rinehart, and Winston, 1966), p. 397.

2 On conceptual metaphors see George Lakoff and Mark Turner, *More Than Cool Reasons: A Field Guide to Metaphor* (Chicago: University of Chicago Press, 1989).

3 This might be a good example of what Frost referred to as "the evil search for synonyms" (quoted in Lawrance Thompson, *Robert Frost: The Years of Triumph, 1915–1938* [New York: Holt, Rinehart, and Winston, 1970], p. 647).

4 We may notice that neither Max Black (*Models and Metaphors* [Ithaca: Cornell University Press, 1962]) nor Mark Turner (*The Literary Mind*, New York: Oxford University Press, 1996) avoid that basic metaphor of metaphor – that of transfer (Aristotle), or movement across space; "space" of course is spatial, and interaction occurs in the "movement" from one subject to another (implied in the term "vehicle" as well, although "tenor" and "vehicle" fail to capture interaction), an implied spatial concept. Both theorists have shown us the limitations of earlier theories, and analyzed the ways newness is made possible by means of dynamic interaction (Black) and creative blending (Turner). I am grateful to Todd Oakley for introducing me to Turner's theories, and to his own work on blending ("Creativity as Projection: Conceptual Integration Networks and Idioms," unpublished article).

5 Thompson explains that when Frost spoke of "the evil search for synonyms" he "was expressing his prejudice in favor of using images which imply (rather than state) analogies, images, and actions which merely hint metaphoric and symbolic extensions of meaning" (*Frost: The Years of Triumph, 1915–1938*, p. 647).

6 Winifred Nowottney, *The Language Poets Use* (London: Athlone Press, 1965), p. 175.

7 See Turner on parable as combining story and projection (5 and *passim*).

Thompson quotes Frost as saying that there is more of poetry in parable telling than in story telling. ("Notes from Conversations with Robert Frost" in the Manuscripts Department of the University of Virginia Library [Accession Number 10044] 532T 414iii.)

8 In a special section of freshman composition for foreign students, a Thai student who had never seen this poem before, had never heard of Frost, and was still struggling with the English language, suggested with great hesitation that this poem seemed to be about suicide.

9 Frost said: "You can always tell in a poem when it reaches the point of special meaning. where it is nicked for the ulterior meaning. [on 'Stopping . . .'] I've been pursued by thesis-writers as to what promises I referred to. They knew where the nick was. I'd just as soon they'd say there anything they pleased, if they would say it poetically" (speech – "The Poet in a Democracy," 1941). We could relate this as well to "Birches," as we try to decide where it has been so "nicked."

10 One could possibly see this as an example of a metaphor pushed past its breaking point too far into the literal, although I find it working within the poem's language and structure.

11 This is an example of the "very general" conceptual metaphor, STATES ARE LOCATIONS, as described by Lakoff and Turner in *More Than Cool Reasons*, pp. 49, 52, 98.

12 Lecture, University of Maryland, 1941.

13 The eel grass metaphor is quoted by Thompson in his "Notes on Frost" 415kkk. The boat metaphor is quoted in Reginald L. Cook, *Robert Frost: A Living Voice* (Amherst: University of Massachusetts Press, 1974), p. 77.

14 Thompson's "Notes on Frost", 2/18/40.

15 This may be the sort of phenomenon Black meant in speaking of "new implications" arising from metaphoric interaction. One could relate it as well to Turner's discussion of creative blending.

16 Quoted by Thompson in his "Notes on Frost" (550). He also quotes Frost as saying: something was "wrong with a writer who couldn't get into his subject and screw it to a climax: if you were going to find metaphors for the artistic process in the functions of the body, that was the way you ought to do it" (659).

17 In this combination of jocularity, love, and concern for metaphor in poetry, one is reminded of Shakespeare's sonnet "My Mistress' Eyes are Nothing Like the Sun."

18 See the section "Can Anything Be Anything'?" Turner and Lakoff, *More Than Cool Reasons*, regarding the necessity for preserving the general shape of an event, or the generic level of information (200–02).

19 Or unless her name is Rose. For one thing, Frost does not capitalize "rose"; for another, Rose would then be a label, or "stale" metaphor. Maple ruminates on the difference between her name and that of a girl she knows whose name is "Rose," a name not thought of as having meaning because of its commonness as a name.

20 *Prose Jottings of Robert Frost*, ed. Edward Connery Lathem and Hyde Cox (Lunenburg, VT: Northeast Kingdom Publishers, 1982), p. 44.

21 *Ibid.*, pp. 15–16.

22 "There is at least so much good in the world that it admits of form and the making of form. And not only admits of it, but calls for it . . . The artist, the poet might

be expected to be the most aware of such assurance. But it is really everybody's sanity to feel and live by it . . . The background is hugeness and confusion shading away . . . into utter chaos; and against the background any small man-made figure of order and concentration" (*CPPP*, 740).

23 The original title was to be "In Praise of Your Poise." (Thompson and R. H. Winnick. *Robert Frost: The Later Years, 1938–1963* [New York: Holt, Rinehart, and Winston, 1976], p. 23)

24 "Guys" is derived from the French "guier," which means to guide, another aspect of such relationship.

8

BLANFORD PARKER

Frost and the Meditative Lyric

"Directive" (*CPPP*, 344) is one of the most widely and variously interpreted of Frost's poems. Randall Jarrell in his seminal essay on Frost's poems quoted it at length, and though pronouncing it largely uninterpretable, praised its "humor and acceptance and humanity."[1] Some have connected it to the Romantic solipsism of Emerson, seeing it as a kind of guidebook that one must write for oneself without benefit of the normal moral and intellectual landmarks. But as always with Frost's audience the appearance of solipsism, sarcasm, and even contradiction could not prevent many readers from seeing the poem as good plain country truth. By the time the poem appeared Frost had long been a figure of folklore, and there is enough of his familiar folksy routine in it to preserve it from a too close inspection by most of his admirers. Even his academic readership had by the time of *Steeple Bush* (1947) accepted Frost as a poet with the limitations implied by popularity. He was not (as a recent critic announced) "tinglingly alive with a sense of the modern."

Like so many of Frost's best poems it may appear to be all things to all readers. In any case "Directive" stands out from the other poems of *Steeple Bush* as the only poem that can challenge for a place among the best of Frost's work. It may be read as an epitome of some of his most enduring themes – the origins and purpose of life, the relation of the natural to the human, and the problem of faith and knowledge. At the same time it is a kind of amorphous receptacle into which the whole panoply of rhetorical and metrical effects which Frost had accumulated over a long career could be placed. It is also his last great achievement in blank verse, a form in which he is the greatest twentieth-century practitioner.

The three customary modes of Frostian rhetoric, the prosaic, the meditative, and the lyrical, appear together in "Directive." By separating these three modes I do not want to suggest a too clear demarcation, but rather a metrical continuum. In Frost the prosaic is used as the chief mode for extended narrative poems. The homology that Frost sometimes claims between poetry and common speech is never absolute. He was capable of extraordinary flights of language.

> It could not have come down to us so far
> Through the interstices of things ajar
> On the long bead chain of repeated birth . . .
> "On a Bird Singing in Its Sleep" (*CPPP*, 275)

On the other hand, the prosaic appears as a ballast of common speech somewhere in the rhetorical mix of all but his most rarefied poems. Frost, in continuing the realistic speech experiment that Wordsworth announced in the "Preface to the *Lyrical Ballads*," treads on the boundary between traditional blank verse and mere prose. It was Wordsworth at the brink of dullness that Frost most admired, and he considered the navigation between the dull and the passionately direct to be one of his most important contributions to American letters.

> I think that's essential Wordsworth. That lovely banality and the lovely penetration that goes with it. It goes right down into the soul of man, and always, always there'll be one line in it that's just as penetrating as anything anybody ever wrote. But always this insipid tone, sweet, insipid tone. Now that's the Wordsworth I care for.[2]

In the narrative and dialogue poems of *North of Boston* Frost produces just such a sweetly insipid tone with the added tang of provincial quaintness. He replaces the Wordsworthian "spots of time," – those moments of sublime penetration – with his own kind of pungent illumination.

> He thinks if he could teach him that, he'd be
> Some good perhaps to someone in the world.
> He hates to see a boy the fool of books.
> Poor Silas, so concerned for other folk,
> And nothing to look backward to with pride,
> And nothing to look forward to with hope,
> So now and never any different.
> "The Death of the Hired Man" (*CPPP*, 40–45)

It must be recognized that the prosaic in Frost is rarely a failure of the poetic. It is always a strategic choice within a range of effects. The prosaic is never a sign of merely flat or formulaic meter as in the Arthurian narratives of Robinson. In his ten or twelve best narrative poems Frost made a metrical experiment as important, and ultimately more successful, than the "vorticism" of Pound or the "imagism" of Williams. "If meter is not the necessary adjunct of poetry," as Samuel Johnson wrote in "Milton," neither is verse to be limited to the traditional poetic genres. Frost's contribution to narrative ranks him with Anderson, Faulkner, Hemingway, and O'Connor among the great practitioners of American short fiction. It is with those great authors of prose that his prosaic pieces must be compared. His psychological and social insights, his mastery of place, and his recreation of local and realistic speech will place him very high among his peers. His novelty was neither as fashionable, nor as imitable as that of other moderns, but one imagines that it will stand the strictest test of future readers.

I have termed the second rhetorical register of Frost the meditative. In this mode Frost illustrates a certain moral or intellectual problem by means of a central (and often simple) event or image. "Mending Wall" (*CPPP*, 39), "Birches" (*CPPP*, 118), "Two Look at Two" (*CPPP*, 211), or "The Most of It"(*CPPP*, 307) may be taken as a fair range of examples. Again blank verse dominates, though many poems are in irregular rhyming stanzas. The blank verse used in this mode is more measured, elevated, and harmonious. The sources are largely Victorian, Arnold and Browning being the most obvious, though always with a personal idiom and never slavishly imitative. The subject of the poems is never historical as in the monologues of Tennyson or Browning, but always observant, immediate, and local. Eliot and Pound following the Victorian model wrote poems of historical ventriloquism *in propria persona* of Henry Adams, the Magi, Li Po, and Jefferson. The meditations of Frost always revolve around a fictional and usually contemporary speaker or scene. As in the poems of Dickinson and Stevens they do not so much embody an elaboration of character or situation as pursue a set of important problems. Dickinson, Frost, and Stevens are not America's great philosophical poets because of a mastery of the nomenclature and curriculum of modern philosophical discourse. In this Eliot was greatly their superior. They are philosophical in a more fundamental sense. They are interested in framing and even answering a narrow range of central ethical and metaphysical questions. It may seem odd to say that Eliot was not in this sense a philosophical poet at least until the opening passage of *Burnt Norton* and even there only in a very limited way. Trained as he was in academic philosophy even to the brink of a Ph.D, Eliot's poetry before the 1940s is an open repudiation of the discourse of philosophy on behalf of art at one stage, prophecy at another. In his meditative mode Frost is a philosophical poet in a way that none of the great modernists were. He is attempting with all his evasions and blind alleys to answer a few fundamental questions – and he enlists a varied cast of local and convenient characters to do so.

Of course, the prosaic and the meditative can not be too strictly separated. They serve as both metrical and thematic markers. In the prosaic or narrative poems like "A Hundred Collars" or "Home Burial" Frost pursues the logic of the narrative action with unswerving realism. Although the poem may bring home truths of great weight to the reader, those truths are not the purpose of the poems. As in the Aristotelian formulation, character is a function of action. In the meditative mode character and situation serve to illuminate an idea – the intellectual substance is given as a solvable puzzle. In "Mending Wall," for example, the narrative element is quite secondary. We are not to read the poem as either a practical georgic about fence-mending, or as a colorful recollection of an unpleasant neighbor. We are forced to consider a set of intellectual riddles including the relation of primitive to modern man, the problem of territoriality, the nature of work and ritual, and the like. If we fail to consider these matters we are bad readers. Unlike the powerful catharsis of Silas' death in "The Death of the Hired Man," the conclusion of meditations like "The White-Tailed Hornet" (*CPPP*, 253) or "The Wood-Pile" (*CPPP*, 100) demands from the reader a power of abstraction and application. For this reason the meditative poems have all the pleasures of the parable, while the narrative poems, however complicated, aim at moral transparency.

The third mode of Frost's poetry is the lyrical. I do not mean by this to group together all of Frost's shorter rhyming poems. "The Need of Being Versed in Country Things" (*CPPP*, 223) is a short piece of virtuoso rhyme and meter, but it is not in the sense I am using it, lyrical. It is a meditation on the problems of human and animal adaptation and human imagination. By the lyrical in Frost I mean the poetry of personal reflection and memory – a poetry of subjective realization. This mode is meant to preserve a private response or to memorialize an important and decisive moment.

> Love at the lips was touch
> As sweet as I could bare;
> And once that seemed too much;
> I lived on air
>
> That crossed me from sweet things,
>
> "To Earthward" (*CPPP*, 209)

"Happiness Makes Up in Height for What It Lacks in Length" is an archetypal example of the lyrical ideal of Frost. In the poem "one day's perfect weather" appears not only to epitomize but to constitute all the "warmth and light" of a long lifetime. Of course the "we" which appears unexpectedly at the end gives us a hint of ideal if momentary love as well, though the poem ends with the word "solitude." The poem makes no claim upon us as argument or action. It is pure evocation. In such moments Frost steps into a familiar Romantic situation – the poet announcing a discovery of delight or anguish which is unconditional and autonomous. We may think again of Wordsworth in "I Wandered Lonely as a Cloud" or "Stepping Westward," or more exactly of Browning in "Home Thoughts from Abroad" or "Memorabilia." "Stopping by Woods on a Snowy Evening," (*CPPP*, 207) "Come In" (*CPPP*, 304), and "Dust of Snow" (*CPPP*, 205) are representative examples of the mode. Those readers who know the common themes of Frost's meditative poems may be tempted to find them in his lyrical poems as well, but they are likely to be led astray. Frost has preserved for himself in this body of evanescent lyrics a peculiar impressionism, even at times a poetry of escape. Some of Frost's poems, like "Birches" or "The Road Not Taken" (*CPPP*, 103) hover on the boundary between the meditative and the lyrical. When Ivor Winters imagined Frost as a "Spiritual Drifter," – a poet of shifting moods and opinions – he was confusing the lyrical persona of Frost (as in "The Sound of the Trees" (*CPPP*, 150) which he quotes) with the whole work of Frost, or he was taking passages from Frost's narrative poems and plays and treating the speeches of characters as Frost's own ideas. It may have been that if Winters, who is a very great literary critic, had recognized Frost's central ideas, those the poet had spent a lifetime meditating and clarifying, he would have been horrified nonetheless, but his essay shows that he never recognized the intellectual concerns of Frost.

It will be obvious to the dedicated reader of Frost that a certain danger, a natural potential for excess, was hidden in each of his common modes of writing. The prosaic could, and sometimes as in "New Hampshire" (*CPPP*, 151) or "From Plane to Plane" (*CPPP*, 367) did sink to the folksy and banal. The narrative was Frost's main instrument for preserving his appeal as provincial poet – the representative New England curmudgeon with a gravelly Vermont accent and all the accouterments of what Robert Lowell in his sonnet "Robert Frost" called "the old act taken out of mothballs." The meditative also sometimes sank to the level of whimsical posing – a poetry of pregnant evasion, or at its worst, irascible political opinionizing. The lyrical carries with it the whole problem of the Romantic self. A poetry of mood without substance is always in danger of being trivial, and it was an unhappy example of Frost's cynical careerism that he placed one of the worst of all his lyrical pieces, "The Pasture" (*CPPP*, 3) in the front of all of his collected editions. One could list all the sins against his own art that Frost committed to remain the darling of a large public, but in listing those sins one must also recall that Frost was the single poet who was capable of entertaining and instructing the large amorphous citizenry of the modern democracy while writing poetry of the very highest order.[3]

Now if I may be excused this long excursus, "Directive," as I remarked above, comprises the rhetoric of all three of his characteristic modes, but must be considered on balance one of his finest, perhaps his last great, meditative poem. The structure of the poem is complex. There are many typically false starts and ambiguous signs on the journey of the poem. The first ambiguity is the title. A "directive" is a New England term for a guidebook, and the poem maintains the fiction of the guided tour from beginning to end. The poem in fact includes the normal sales pitches for tourists – the colorful history of the place, the beauties of a remote wilderness, a picturesque landscape, and the sense of a get away and a new beginning. The poet is serving throughout as a guide pointing out the origins, historical and geological, of the locale, and assuring the traveler of the restorative power of the trip. One way to understand the larger structure of the poem is to trace the pronominal sequence from "us" to "you" to "I." The poem begins with the communal "us," the world being too much for either the guide or the guided. It gives the impression of a shared journey in which both shall reclaim a lost world – "a time made simple by the loss of detail." But after the first line the first person plural disappears from the poem and is replaced by the second person, "you." At each stage of the journey instructions are given: "if you'll let a guide direct you," "You must not mind a certain coolness," "pull in your ladder road behind you," and in the great crescendo of the poem "Your destination and your destiny" and "Here are your waters and your watering place." In this second sense the poet is issuing "directives" which must be followed. The poet gives the impression that he is re-enacting a journey that he has already taken, going down a road which is no longer mysterious to him. In fact when the narrator returns in the final eight lines of the poem he has become a kind of master arranger of all the circumstances of the trip. He has prepared the scene for the visitor. "*I* [italics my own] have kept hidden" and "*I* stole the goblet from the children's playhouse" are the only uses of the first person singular in the text. Apparently the poet, we may safely say Frost, is the guide who "only has at heart your getting lost," and at the same time it is the "I" who finds meaning for the traveler. After all Frost is already an aged guide, a seventy-three-year-old man who recalls the twenty and more years ago to which the poem alludes. He knows the landscape and the history, he understands both the getting lost and the finding yourself. The poet is the "I," a god in the machine who arranges, and our main question is how and what does he arrange?

The poem begins with an exordium which calls the reader/traveler away from the "now" to an undetermined time in the past which is simple. The tone is at once elegiac and pastoral. We may infer at the start that we are returning to a better world – a golden world of lost youth or the lost youth of the world. The images of childhood and past history which are liberally sprinkled through the poem may lend support to such an expectation. American literature, all literature, abounds with such images of return. We may think for example of the lost world of E. A. Robinson's "Mr. Flood's

Party," or his "House on the Hill," the "Flower Fed Buffaloes" of Vachel Lindsay, the dance of Pocahontas in Hart Crane's *The Bridge,* and the whole range of poems of melancholy, remembrance, and reclamation in the nineteenth century by Bryant, Poe, and Longfellow. But we would be very wrong to hope for an Edenic return in the poetry of Frost. Frost had shattered such an expectation in many earlier poems including "Into My Own," "The Black Cottage," and "The Need of Being Versed in Country Things." In the opening poem of his first book, *A Boy's Will,* after describing his fearless quest on the open highway of the future, he announces:

> I do not see why I should e'er turn back,
> Or those should not send forth upon my track
> To overtake me, who should miss me here
> And long to know if still I held them dear.
>
> They would not find me changed from him they knew –
> Only more sure of all I thought was true.
>
> "Into My Own" (*CPPP,* 15)

Like the unseen woodsmen in "The Wood-Pile," "only in turning to fresh tasks" could Frost find value in his vocation. Over and over Frost eschews the temptation of melancholy idealizing about the personal or historical past. The reader should recognize the direction in which Frost is going by looking closely at the first metaphor of "Directive." "The time made simple by the loss/ Of detail" is "burned, dissolved, and broken off/ Like graveyard marble sculpture in the weather." The loss of detail that Frost refers to is like the obscuring of the figures of graveyard statuary and gravestones, the erasure of knowledge of the details of the past which makes it appear simple. Ignorance, that is, of the true details lead us to embrace our own fantasies. It is not unusual for Frost to have only one or two metaphors in a given poem. There are a number of Frost poems with virtually no figural content, so we must look at his selection of metaphors with particular interest. This first simile is one of razing the past by effacing sculpture, the elaborate personification of the glacier in lines 15–19 is again that of a sculptor with his chisel, but here the image is one of grinding, scraping, and rearranging the landscape. The third and final metaphor of the poem is of a "cellar hole" of a ruined house "slowly closing like a dent in dough." All these are metaphors of either active or passive destruction and decay. The metaphorical map of the poem is one of loss – of a constant rearranging and destroying of the past. From the very first simile of the effaced graveyard Frost shows a narrative of regular and continuing destruction under the guise of a vacation in a better world.

What we find in the backwards abyss of time is "a house that is no more a house/ Upon a farm that is no more a farm/ And in a town that is no more a town." The elegant parallelism which has been compared to the repetitious formulae of *Four Quartets* leads us again to a world of memory and privation. The scale of habitations from the private to the social is inverted in the structure of the fifty-four lines that follow. The larger poem moves slowly toward the private and subjectivity.

The logical structure of the poem has not till now been thoroughly described. The "guide who only has at heart your getting lost" moves through four main stages of describing the place towards which the journey leads – the geological (lines 10–19), the natural (lines 20–28), the historical (lines 29–35), and the personal (lines 36–39). Frost moves in a series of ever-contracting circles of explanation. First the Glacier personified as a mammoth sculptor bracing his "feet against the Arctic Pole" has chiseled out the space of the town. He has left behind "[G]reat monolithic knees" which embarrassed the former townsfolk with their ugliness. As in the rocky neighboring cliffs of "The Mountain" (*CPPP*, 45), there was a forbidding coolness which could not be removed. The lines of human travel ("the wear of iron wagon wheels") ran in the same grooves that the geologic titan had scraped. Human culture could not "cover" and has now been outlasted by the marks of geological time. The whole town "should have been a quarry" and is now sinking like its ruined cellars back into the earth – returning to its primeval, pre-human scene of rocky coldness.

As Frost enters the sphere of nature he admonishes the traveler that he should not worry about human ghosts staring from the abandoned cellar holes along the roadside "as if by eye-pairs out of forty firkins." The traveler enters the powerful "excitement" of the trees which "send light rustle rushes to their leaves." The sound of the woods always brings on the strongest emotion in Frost, even an odd feeling of fellowship as in "Birches," "Tree at My Window" (*CPPP*, 230), "The Sound of the Trees," or "Evening in a Sugar Orchard" (*CPPP*, 216). However beautiful they may be, the trees themselves have been competing for growing space and the hardier scrub pines "think too much of having shaded out/ A few old pecker-fretted apple trees." This is no doubt one of the innumerable references to natural selection and evolutionary adaptation which we see in Frost's poems. We are to imagine that the younger trees as they have grown have slowly eclipsed the light needed by the small apple orchard planted "only twenty years ago" by a citizen of the now defunct town. No one is there to protect the weaker fruit trees, and as they begin to lose sap and grow dry the downy and hairy woodpeckers (so numerous in Vermont and New Hampshire) peck them to their final demise. It is "upstart inexperience" that leads the traveler to fear ghosts where he should be fearing the inexorable powers of natural destruction.

Frost had sounded the same theme eleven years earlier in "There Are Roughly Zones" (*CPPP*, 278). There too the setting was a decayed house and embattled trees. The poet had warned that though human morality is unfixed, nature has definite and often punitive laws.

> Why is his nature ever so hard to teach
> That though there is no fixed line between wrong and right,
> There are roughly zones whose laws must be obeyed.
> There is nothing much we can do for the tree tonight,
> But we can't help feeling more than a little betrayed.

Frost is showing the traveler how to avoid just such a Romantic sense of betrayal. The apple trees in "Directive" planted to nourish the townsfolk are following them to early extinction. One could say more about the geological, biological, and sociological Darwinism at the heart of the poem. Robert Faggen's seminal book, *Robert Frost and the Challenge of Darwin*, has given demonstrative and sometimes startling proof of the centrality of evolutionary ideas in the whole range of Frost's poems.[4]

The reader now for the first time enters the sphere of the human community and its history. Up till now the histories have been inhuman, and the details of human memory have been effaced like weathered grave markers. The reader is not given direct physical evidence, but asked to imagine the human situation.

> Make yourself up a cheering song of how
> Someone's road home from work this once was,
> Who may be just ahead of you on foot
> Or creaking with a buggy load of grain.

The reader is told to make up a joyful song about the people who once populated the village scene; he is to celebrate those who went before him on the road. He is to imagine the products of their labor. It is here in the exact middle of the poem (line 32) that we reach the "height of the adventure." It is the place where two village cultures, probably those of the local Indians and the later European settlers, "faded into each other." It is more accurately where one village culture destroyed and absorbed another. This is not a new theme for the author of "The Vanishing Red" and "An Empty Threat." Frost had chronicled the problem of failure and extinction in those and other earlier poems. What makes this "the height of the adventure," the emotional high point of the journey, and the goal of the guide's directive, is the presence of history – the intimate if imagined struggle of the human amid the dangers of landscape, nature, and humanity itself. Yet even at the "height of the adventure" the traveler is given the disheartening message that the two cultures have disappeared – "Both are lost."

It is at the moment when the human has been swallowed up into the inhuman, preserved only in memory and imagination, that the final stage of the poem begins. Rather than a poem of elegiac emotion or of Edenic return to a lost and superior world, the poem is a studied and systematic foreclosure of human expectations. Having traveled through the stages of the past – the geologic, natural, and the historical – the reader discovers the emptiness of all teleological quests. He is left in a palpable emptiness where all seems lost. Yet the "height of the adventure" for Frost as a guide was just such a realization of human insufficiency. The guide has been a hard teacher and a thorough one. He is not a spiritual guide like the Eliot of *Four Quartets*, nor has he found the "supreme fiction" of Stevens wherein the reader may forget the naked facts of the world by engaging the imagination. His message is dispiriting and literal. The supreme art for Frost is the art of the real: "The fact is the sweetest dream that labor knows." By the time of "Directive" the real meant nothing less than a sober positivism, a thorough application of those "downward comparisons" which he had described in "The White-Tailed Hornet."[5]

But the poem is by no means a simple or direct application of Frost's maturing positivism. Not only has he presented the empirical truths of geology and biology in a sometimes playful or glancing way – Panther mountain haunted by "a certain coolness," eye pairs out of "forty firkins" following the frightened traveler through the woods, and the like; he has written a poem that intermittently courts the reader's appetite for folksy wisdom and New England reserve. The effect of the prosaic, "[A]nd there's a story in a book about it," and "a few old pecker-fretted apple trees," is to dilute the momentum of the argument of the poem, to distract the reader, or at least a certain sort of reader, to deflate the devastating implications of the meditative element of the poem. In fact, the "in and outdoor schooling," that it takes to follow Frost's logic, has been lacking in most of his critics, who have often helped to screen the reader from the ugly finalities of the text. The habit of misleading the reader was by the time of "Directive" a central part of the Frost poetic. "Directive," therefore, is anything but direct, and it becomes considerably less so when Frost turns at the beginning of the poem's remarkable peroration to the language of the personal and even the solipsist.

> And if you're lost enough to find yourself
> By now, pull in your ladder road behind you
> And put a sign up CLOSED to all but me.
> Then make yourself at home.

Just as the village worlds are lost, so the self must become lost to regain its composure. Playing with searing irony on the Christian maxim that one must lose oneself to be found, Frost, having laid waste to the traveler's hopes to find a better world, asks the reader to effect an escape from the world the poem has described. I am told that "ladder road" is a Vermont idiom for country road, but one cannot help but think of the ladder being pulled in behind the traveler as an image of surrender. The road did not prove to be the golden ladder in Book v of *Paradise Lost* which leads from the creature to God, nor any of a number of useful literary ladders leading one by degrees to happiness. The rungs of the ladders which Frost has invoked in the text are entirely backwards – the steps of geologic and evolutionary process are not teleological, and the ladder of history has led to a lost world. The guide is asking the traveler to fall back on the only thing he has left – himself – and to triumphantly announce his solitude. He is to place a sign in the wilderness marked in capital letters, "CLOSED." The unconsoling world is to be closed out and only then can the traveler "make himself at home."

The sheer willfulness of this gesture has been interpreted in a number of ways. The most ingenious, and at the same time the most serious, explanation that has been offered was that of Frank Lentricchia. The degree to which, and the way in which, I disagree with Lentricchia's solution to the seeming escapism and solipsism of the poem will help to clarify my own view. Lentricchia's argument was an attempt to save Frost from the imputation (like that made by Jarrell) that the poem was full of unresolved contradictions, and at the same time to place Frost, even if Frost had resisted being placed there, in the line of post-Kantian and Romantic thinkers who preserved a special and autonomous territory for the imagination.

Lentricchia's argument is an elegant argument and a reasonable one. It is made even more reasonable by his realization that the first thirty-one lines of the poem describe a world of abject loss and destruction. Lentricchia was the first critic of the poem to see the significance (at least in part) of the geological and natural images of the poem, and to measure the emptiness of the traveler's quest at the moment when both villages are lost. Lentricchia does not try to squeeze out of the verbal ambiguities of the poem a wholesome humanism. He sees Frost's vision as extreme and his spiritual references as ironic. On the earlier sections of the poem he makes only one important error and that is in imagining the narrator as an equal participant in the journey and too closely associating the traveler's situation with that of the poet. I shall return to this point.

Here is what Lentricchia says about the crucial passage I have just quoted above.

> In the face of the bareness, the imagination begins to infuse its life-giving powers into a long dead human scene. The isolated and wandering knight of

"Directive" needs something more than the promise of a special grail waiting for him, one of the right ones, at the end of his long journey. Bereft of community he begins to make his own song (like whistling in the dark?) . . . The height of the adventure, to put it another way, is not the verification of imagination's humanizing illusions, but the pressing of imagination to its furthest reaches by the discovery of the final evidence of the abject sadness of the human condition in a human-repelling universe. Our climb up into the higher country is a metaphor for the journey of the imagination (echoing the swinging metaphor from "Birches") and Frost is quick to seize on the conceit of the old "ladder road" to emphasize that the final stage of a journey in the mind has been reached and that it is a journey that can be completed only by solitary men. The imagination pours forth its greatest energies only after it has realized its anarchic potential, severing itself from all connections: "CLOSED to all but me."[6]

We know from elsewhere in Lentricchia's book that the notions about the imagination in this passage are derived from a variety of modern thinkers and critics – Nietszche, Sartre, William James, Poulet. From James, Lentricchia has derived both the radical isolation of each human mind and the saving communication of imagination, from Sartre the notion of the unbreachable space between the self and the other combined with the unquenchable human need to reveal and explain. "From Frost to Poulet," we are told in Lentricchia's preface, "there is really no leap at all." Frost apparently agrees with the words he quotes from Poulet:

Every thought to be sure is a thought of something. It is turned invincibly towards the somewhere else, toward the outside. Issuing from itself, it appears to leap over a void, meet certain obstacles, explore certain surfaces, and envelop or invade certain objects. It describes and recounts to itself all of these objects, and these accounts constitute the inexhaustible objective aspect of literature. But every thought is also simply a thought. It is that which exists in itself, isolatedly, mentally. Whatever its objects may be, thought can never place them, think them, except in the interior of itself.[7]

This may help us to understand the context of Lentricchia's reading. The journey of the traveler (and the poet) is to a high and solitary country, the imagination. Never does the imagination feel its powers so fully as when it sees that its reality is inward, that the world is merely the alienated realm of the other, the objective. When met with the landscapes of the inhuman, the infinite spaces of the geological and the evolutionary, it names them and in naming it also contains and tames them. The imagination gives a habitable place, a domicile for the mind stifled by the concreteness, the arbitrary nature, the fearful fixity of the world in which we live. In the battle between the two cultures of science with its objective, extra-mental facticity, and the autonomous act of internal meaning which is poetry, it is poetry which recognizes the primacy of consciousness.

Frost, according to this reading, in pulling in his "ladder road" behind him, frees himself from what Roland Barthes called "the prison of the natural."[8] The closing to "all but me" is the moment when the poet recognizes his internal and "anarchic power." He is freed from the bondage of the realms of nature and history. Lentricchia goes on to say:

> We have not finally traveled back through public history, but through private, inner time. What we recover, if we brave the various assaults that the poet has subjected us to, is the pristine moment of our childhood imagination – a moment that stands outside time – the embryo moment of our maturer imaginative faculty . . . we shall build up a universe as humanized as the inhuman universe will permit.[9]

Finally, Lentricchia indulges himself in a kind of Rousseauian/Freudian romance. Through the fusion of the child with the adult dreamer the poet returns to his sacred watering place. The brook, "too lofty and original to rage" is the gentle stream of Wordsworthian recollection. We drink again from the grail of youth and are emboldened to stand up to the worst "assaults" of the reality principle. The whole journey of the poem in fact takes place in Pouletian inner time and is merely an excuse to bring us to the baptismal (Lentricchia should have said eucharistic) moment when we are again made whole. Like Freud before him, Frost, according to Lentricchia, has described human life as an internal romance, though he is apparently more optimistic than Freud about our chances to return to childlike wisdom.

Now I do believe this is a valiant effort at explanation. It is an attempt to endow Frost with a whole range of what are, for modern academics, soothing insights. But I do not believe that the poem makes anything like these claims either consciously or unconsciously. On the other hand, the reading does point out the one weakness in a very great poem – the need to escape, or to give to the reader the illusion of escape from the implications of Frost's meditation. Generally Frost objects to the "easy gold at hand of fay or elf" or (as in the dialogue of "West-Running Brook") the escape to "lady-land" – the realm of too soothing explanations. But in playing with the reader, in offering a momentary solution or hiding place, Frost has diluted his meditation with a lyrical intermission. I have said that all three modes of Frost's rhetoric, the prosaic, the meditative, and the lyrical appear in the poem. I did not mean simply the lyrical effect – "sends light rustle rushes to their leaves," – but also the more profound lyricism which offers an autonomous moment of illumination.

For those like Frank Lentricchia who see the escape to the lyrical as the point of the poem – that which justifies the journey of the poem – my criticism will seem singularly obtuse. The problem one has in believing in the Romantic/solipsist reading of the poem is that it does not explain the lines that end the poem. It in effect ignores everything before and after the moment when the traveler closes his world.

It is at that very moment in "Directive" that we are immediately thrust into another world of loss and littleness. "The field no larger than a harness gall," "the children's house of make believe," and finally the remains of the "house that is no more a house," now "only a belilaced cellar hole/ Now slowly closing like a dent in dough." Unlike the raising up of a world supposedly lost, as in the end of Wallace Stevens' "Esthetique du Mal," William Wordsworth's "Ode: Intimations," or even Samuel Taylor Coleridge's "Dejection," Frost returns to his world of loss. If he is seeking the answer to "what to make of a diminished thing," he is not doing it in terms of the saving imagination, nor is he in the end offering an honest means of escape for the reader. When he asks the traveler to "[W]eep for what little things could make them glad," can he be asking the traveler himself to be glad? What reason for exultation is given in the poem? If this is a moment of imaginative consummation why would the reader weep for or take pity on the beliefs and ambitions of the children or the adult householders?

"The house that is no more a house" brings to mind a whole range of Frost's houses. The lost mountain house in "The Census-Taker" (*CPPP*, 164) "not dwelt in now by man or woman," which filled the poet with "no less sorrow than the houses/ Fallen to ruin in ten thousand years/ Where Asia edges Africa from Europe;" or the collapsed home (so nearly akin to the one in "Directive") in "The Generations of Men" (*CPPP*, 74) which "had literally run to earth/ In an old cellar-hole in a by-road." These, too, memorialized in earnest the fruitlessness of human endeavor and the great waring of time. Each fallen house has its compliment of dying trees, its useless furniture, the shadows of inhuman landscapes of rock. "Directive" was the summary poem of a lifetime, and this "house that is no more a house" stands in for all the lost dreams of the generations. In "The Black Cottage" written thirty-three years before "Directive" a minister discusses an old lady from the Civil War era on a visit to her decaying home. He makes it the pretext for ruing the loss of the moral and religious values of the old abolitionist Protestants who were then almost extinct.

> But what I'm getting to is how forsaken
> A cottage this had always seemed;
> It always seemed to me a sort of mark
> To measure how far fifty years had brought us.
> Why not sit down if you are in no haste?
> These doorsteps seldom have a visitor.

> The warping boards pull out their own old nails
> With none to tread and put them in their place.
> She had her own idea of things, the old lady.

It happens that the old lady had known Garrison and Whittier and was a religious moralist of the old school, a believer in equality and God; the sort of person that Frost could admire but not agree with (even then).

> I'm just as glad she made me keep hands off,
> For dear me why abandon a belief
> Merely because it ceases to be true.

That poem ends with the minister wishing he could remove himself to an untainted desert kingdom to preserve the old truths (or untruths) "worth coming back to." He wanted to preserve them not so much for as from mankind.

But "Directive" is in some ways a more extreme, an angrier poem than those earlier ones. "The house in earnest" is irretrievably lost. The traveler could not be at home there. The guide has intervened to give him instead the "children's house of make believe." He has scooped waters from the hilltop spring for the thirsty visitor. Those waters, like the aging poet, are now "too lofty and original to rage." The poet does not need to raise his voice – to pour out a torrent like the dramatic valley streams that cause so much destruction. The poet is elevated and calm; he has plumbed to the depths of the human situation.

The communion that ends the poem, like the parodic rite in "Design" (*CPPP*, 275), is not, as many critics have argued, an allusion to some saving grace of God or imagination. Frost's biographer, Thompson, and others have fallen for the quasi-religious explanation of the poem and used it as an example of Frost's theism.[10] Frost probably felt that such a notion would help to strengthen his position as national sage. I think few readers are so tone deaf as to miss the irony of:

> I have kept hidden in the instep arch
> Of an old cedar at the waterside
> A broken drinking goblet like the Grail
> Under a spell so the wrong ones can't find it,
> So can't get saved, as Saint Mark says they mustn't.
> (I stole the goblet from the children's playhouse.)
> Here are your waters and your watering place.
> Drink and be whole again beyond confusion.

The poet guide (the "I" of these final lines) has contrived a mock ceremony to mark the end of the traveler's quest. Having survived "the serial ordeal" of seeing this universal spectacle of loss, he is given the final magical draught. His Holy Grail is the toy cup of the children. It is filled with water which is in fact the rudiment of human life – of biological survival. The language of the last twenty lines is laced with Biblical and theological allusions – the chalice, the cedar, the gospel scripture, and others. That language is used not to enlighten but to disabuse the reader. A few poems later in *Steeple Bush* Frost lashes out even more nastily about the claims of revealed religion.

> If you should rise from Nowhere up to Somewhere,
> From being No one up to being Someone,
> Be sure to keep repeating to yourself
> You owe it to some arbitrary god
> Whose mercy to you rather than to others
> Won't bear too critical examination.

"The Fear of God"

Frost is bringing the traveler as close as he can to the magical truths he desires. Having sunk into himself, alone from the world, the melancholy knight is left with his careful guide. Frost is not Galahad in the poem but Merlin. The journey is contrived to show at first the raw facts of the inhuman world in which we struggle, and in the end to show the littleness of human hopes, the paltriness of the imagination with its shows of fellowship and religion. Frost exposed the bitter truth and "kept hidden" till the end the saving chicanery of the magus.

The feigning and even misleading that Frost has done is not to preserve the "impossible philosopher's dream" or the "supreme fiction." Stevens' decayed house in "Postcard from the Volcano" is a house where spirits made their mark – "cried out a literate despair" against disorder. They were the potent (if forgotten) presences of the world. Those who feel the presence of the human imagination, the "rage for order" have the better half of human experience, however deceptive. "The house that is no more a house" teaches a more sobering lesson to those who can bear it. It is a lesson with the mark of the classical – the acceptance of the inhuman as the terms and limits of human destiny. "Many towns that were thriving and powerful when I was a boy," remarks Herodotus, "are now lost to war, fire, and the sea. Such is man's lot."

Like Yeats' "The Circus Animals' Desertion," Ezra Pound's "Canto LXXXI," or T. S. Eliot's "Little Gidding," "Directive" appears to the initiated reader as both elegy and final judgment. Yet Frost reveals little about his own life; there is nothing confessional or self-lacerating, as in other poems of aged reflection. When the obscurity and peevishness of the opening of "Canto LXXXI" gives way to the sweep and power of the "Libretto," we have no doubt that Pound is pulling down his own monstrous vanity, his lifelong habit of self-idolatry and delusion, while at the same time he is attempting to save his dignity by paying tribute to the kind of poetry he created and championed over a lifetime. Likewise Yeats has confessed his own shallowness and ambition in "The Circus Animals' Desertion" while defending the claims of the human heart.

> Maybe at last being but a broken man
> I must be satisfied with my heart, although
> Winter and summer till old age began
> My circus animals were all on show,
> Those stilted boys, that burnished chariot,
> Lion and woman and the Lord knows what.[11]

Frost's great poem of old age is both angry and evasive. While the narrator remains sure of his own ironic sagacity, he lashes out at the delusions of others. Unlike other poems of moral recollection it is written in the second person. It is addressed entirely to the reader's ignorance – a guide speaking to a lost traveler. "[I]f you'll let a guide direct you," "You must not mind a certain coolness from him," and "if you're lost enough to find yourself," recall that other second-person diatribe, "Provide, Provide." Like that poem, "Directive" has the power of an accusation. Some critics have observed the poem's ironic connection to Eliot's *Four Quartets* which had appeared two years earlier. This, Eliot's last poem, was a very different kind of guidebook – participative, questing, longing. His quest ended in a saving apocalypse, "all shall be well and/ All manner of things shall be well/ When the tongues of flame are in-folded/ Into the crowned knot of fire/ And the fire and the rose are one."[12]

Looking back "Directive" does seem like an answer to Modernism's great project by offering a powerful and even bitter voice of opposition at what in retrospect was Modernism's final phase. Most of the crowning works of Modernism relied heavily on the conventions of the romance – the quest story. Joyce borrowed the Odyssean plot to enact his own myth of homecoming; Pound attempted without success to inscribe the Dantean journey through hell, purgatory, and heaven within the chaotic wanderings of *The Cantos*; all of Eliot's major work, "The Love Song of J. Alfred Prufrock," "Gerontion," *The Waste Land*, "Ash Wednesday," "The Journey of the Magi," and "Little Gidding," recreates the teleological structures of the quest; the same can be said of the later Yeats.

Frost turned away from such a project on intellectual grounds. By slow degrees he came, I believe, to see the human narrative as circumscribed by and controlled by the impersonal powers of the material cosmos. "Directive" is a monumental disavowal of the romance and of the poetic of transcendent desire on which it is built. In an age dominated by scientific realism, he was the single important poet who spoke for science. Recognizing the limitations of technology and power, he nonetheless gave life to the largely unexpressed world of creaturely existence. Although in his lyrical persona he pays high tribute to human passion and to the poetic imagination, in his meditative mask he came to doubt the sufficiency of human hopes, and of the human faculties. He was a dogged intellectual who considered the paradoxes of human community and the self with unblinking realism. In coming to see the tragic limits of the human will and imagination he left a unique legacy for the reader of modern poetry.

NOTES

1 *Robert Frost: A Collection of Critical Essays*, ed. James M. Cox (Englewood Cliffs: Prentice Hall, 1962), p. 93.
2 Borrowed from John Evangelist Walsh, *Into My Own: The English Years of Robert Frost* (New York: Grove Press, 1988), pp. 236–37.
3 For more on Frost's relation to magazine culture and a large popular readership see Frank Lentricchia, *Modernist Quartet* (New York: Oxford University Press, 1994).
4 Robert Faggen, *Robert Frost and the Challenge of Darwin* (Ann Arbor: Michigan University Press, 1997).
5 The relevant lines from "The White-Tailed Hornet" are as follows:

> As long on earth
> As our comparisons were stoutly upward
> With gods and angels, we were men at least,
> But little lower than the gods and angels.
> But once comparisons were yielded downward,
> Once we began to see our images
> Reflected in the mud and even dust,
> 'Twas disillusion upon disillusion.
> We were lost piecemeal to the animals,
> Like people thrown out to delay the wolves,
> Nothing but fallibility was left us.

6 Frank Lentricchia, *Robert Frost: Modern Poetics and the Landscapes of Self* (Durham: Duke University Press, 1975), p. 117.
7 *Ibid.*, p. 14.
8 Roland Barthes, *Barthes par Barthes* (New York: Hill and Wang, 1982) p. 83.
9 Lentricchia, *Robert Frost*, p. 119.
10 Lawrance Thompson and R. H. Winnick, *Robert Frost: The Later Years* (New York: Holt, Rinehart, and Winston, 1976), pp. 135–37.
11 M. L. Rosenthal ed., *William Butler Yeats: Selected Poems and Three Plays* (New York: Macmillan Publishing Company, 1962), p. 198.
12 T. S. Eliot, *Collected Poems 1909–1962* (New York: Harcourt Brace and Company, 1963), p. 209.

9

MARK RICHARDSON

Frost's Poetics of Control

British psychoanalyst and essayist Adam Phillips has suggested that "the contingent self enjoins us to imagine a life without blaming, a life exempt from the languages of effort and self-control."[1] To live a life without blame, and to be exempt from the language of self-control, ought to be good things. Much may be said in favor of flirtation, with its tolerations, and Phillips says it well. But notice the equation, by apposition, that informs his remarks: effort and self-control seem somehow essentially to involve blame – blame of others and of oneself. The contingent self Phillips is concerned to advance is in certain respects the opposite of the responsible self, at least from the point of view of conventional society, which is why it is usually something of a scandal. The contingent self really isn't, then, a "self" at all, as that term is properly understood. In any case, it is not a self in the legal sense: hence the concept of the "diminished capacity" of selves made contingent by neglect, abuse, insanity, poverty, immaturity. An ethics founded on the contingent self diminishes everyone's capacity: to do wrong, to be punished, to be condemned. Its language is always the language of mercy, which brings us to Robert Frost. In his poetry – its often flirtatious tendencies notwithstanding – he characteristically wants to resist exemption from the languages of effort and self-control. He always had as much interest in justice as in mercy. Something in him is wary of admitting contingencies, wary of being too much carried away, and it is a wariness associated, I believe, with the fear of insanity as Frost understood insanity: an inability to master, or to lay claim to, or to give meaning to, or simply somehow to redeem, the accidents and motives of our lives. Confusion of that sort is for him quite literally a condition of diminished capacity, a dilution of the self, and at the end of the day he will have none of it. He hated to regard himself as a merely circumstantial creature.

In "The Figure a Poem Makes," Frost speaks of the "lucky events" that befall a poet as he writes (*CPPP*, 777); that is another way of talking about contingencies of the self – or, at least contingencies of the authorial self. But his winning assurance in speaking of lucky events derives from a faith, expressed elsewhere in the essay and in "The Constant Symbol," that these contingencies are really not lucky at all, that the strong poet is what Frost calls a 'baby giant" hurling experience across later for somewhere (777). Any accident he suffers is what Kenneth Burke would call a "representative accident" – an accident characteristic of him and so in some sense traceable to his most deeply personal will and motive.[2] They are not so much contingencies as accidents on purpose, to use a phrase Frost liked. "Life has for us on the wrack/ Nothing but what we somehow chose," he says in an ambitious early philosophical poem, "The Trial By Existence" (CPPP, 30). It is one thing to be an infant or a minor. It is quite another to be a "baby *giant*."

"The Trial By Existence" encourages me to say that, for Frost, poets write poems in order to resolve accidents into events, in order to achieve a vantage point from which the casualties of their experience appear to them in a new light as accidents on purpose. And in "The Constant Symbol" Frost suggests that the experience a poet suffers in writing is like the experience anyone suffers in realizing his career in life: everyone is a baby giant, with purposes yet unrealized but working nonetheless *in potentia*. We discover "the success of [our] intention," Frost explains in "The Constant Symbol," as we go forward (CPPP, 787). We do not know our intention at the outset of the journey, but it is nonetheless for that *our* intention, something for which we are to be either credited or blamed, as the case may be. No exemption here from the languages of effort and self-control. In light of this idea I want to generalize Frost's talk about "confusion," and of poems as they stay against it, to adapt a well-known phrase from "The Figure a Poem Makes." As I have implied, confusion works in his essays as a kind of meliorating synonym for insanity, which becomes the condition of our being unable fully to own, or even sometimes merely to see, our true motives. We lose our purchase on them. We become incontinent and what we apparently no longer contain is what Frost would recognize as the self: nothing is any longer *somehow* choosing what life has for us on the wrack. We are overwhelmed, in disgrace with fortune and men's eyes. We need a therapy such as the one Frost singles out for praise in a memorial tribute to his friend the psychiatrist and poet Merrill Moore: "On a visit to Sanibel Island he had the bright idea of shovelling up from the beach with his own hands a ton or two of sea shells and shipping them North for his patients to sort out. I wish you could hear the disc recording of his speech about the therapeutic value of this exercise in beauty" (CPPP, 842–43). The aim of this discipline is to regain some kind of grip on the world and thereby also on the self in the world. The work of therapy that poetry is (at least for Frost) makes possible a point of vantage from which the poet-patient's motives can be put into some sort of order again, a point of vantage from which they may seem never at all entirely to have fallen out of order. What he discovers is that a divinity had been shaping his ends all along and that that divinity is somehow deeply personal.

Frost writes in a preface to a 1942 selection of his poems:

> I have made this selection much as I made the one from my first book, *A Boy's Will*, and my second book, *North of Boston* looking backward over the accumulation of years to see how many poems I could find towards some one meaning it might seem absurd to have had in advance, but it would be all right to accept from fate after the fact. The interest, the pastime, was to learn if there had been any divinity shaping my ends and I had been building better than I knew. In other words could anything of larger design, even the roughest, any broken or dotted continuity, or any fragment of a figure be discerned among the apparently random lesser designs of the several poems.   (*CPPP*, 783).

Frost borrows Hamlet's remark to Horatio: "There's a divinity that shapes our ends,/ Rough hew them how we will" (5.ii.10–11). For Frost – as perhaps also for Hamlet, depending on how you read him – this "divinity" is seated in the deeper self that animates the apparently chaotic happenings of his career. "Divinity" may be fatal but it may also be the "divinity" or foresight of the seer: that is to say, it can be either impersonal or personal, a sign either of fate or of power. "Divinity" in this way expresses a subtle exchange of freedom and law, of action and submission, and this is only fitting. If Frost convicts himself of having had meanings in advance there may well be justice in it. And the merger of the personal and the impersonal suggested in his wry invocation of "divinity" recalls the merger of the two "answerabilities" (as he puts it in "The Constant Symbol") to "inner" and "outer" "disciplines" – that is to say, answerabilities to what *we* determine and also to what *determines* us (*CPPP*, 787). This merger marks a tragic recognition, as I have argued elsewhere, of the essential harmony of character and fate – an idea that was apparently of great importance to Frost, who, again, would always have it that life had nothing for him on the wrack but what he somehow chose.[3] In any case, to say that he accepts the meaning "from fate" is probably disingenuous. The point is that he, the poet, had been "building better than he knew," that he had all along been somehow directing his progress through the poems. There is, there must be, a builder, a designer. Frost's remarks are written in "the language of effort and self-control," not in the language of accident or contingency. And they help us understand, as I will later suggest, Frost's hostility to social and political programs that, as he saw it, tended to limit or set aside personal responsibility.

But before we arrive at that point we have to consider another matter: namely, that if something in Frost wants to resist exemption from the language of effort and self-control, something in him also wants to open himself up to contingency and confusion. I am thinking, for example, of moments such as the one described in Frost's early poem "The Bonfire," collected first in *Mountain Interval*:

> "Oh, let's go up the hill and scare ourselves,
> As reckless as the best of them tonight,
> By setting fire to all the brush we piled
> With pitchy hands to wait for rain or snow.
> Oh let's not wait for rain to make it safe
> . . .
> Let's bring to life this old volcano,
> If that is what the mountain ever was –
> And scare ourselves. Let wild fire loose we will . . ."
>
> "And scare you too?" the children said together.
> "Why wouldn't it scare me to have a fire
> Begin in smudge with ropy smoke and know
> That still, if I repent, I may recall it,
> But in a moment not . . . ."

These lines concern a flirtation with forces the speaker may not be able to control, and the experience of it, though essentially imaginary, is exhilarating. A fine moment of balance, described as if by someone who knew the feeling, occurs precisely at the point beyond which the fire cannot be "recalled." Frost would, if only in prospect, open up to himself (and to his children) a confusion against which no stay may be possible. My point is that, with his talk about form and order, and about the "harsher discipline from without," Frost sometimes lets us see that he protests too much. True, he is interested in the poet as disciplinarian, as when, in the preface he wrote for E. A. Robinson's *King Jasper*, he rates the poet as properly a force for what he calls "correspondence." We must "correspond" to one another or be driven insane by isolation. The writing of poetry is, the essay makes clear, but an extension of our earliest experiments in correspondence, our earliest efforts to socialize the self (*CPPP*, 741–42). To write poetry well is to bring oneself (and one's reader, too, if only in sympathy) within socially accredited bounds: no disruptive heresies here – no Martin Luthers. "There is such a thing as being too willing to be different. And what shall we say to people who are not only willing but anxious? What assurance have they that their difference is not insane, eccentric, abortive, unintelligible?" (*CPPP*, 741) And yet, having said as much, Frost is nonetheless always interested in the poet as a heretic and lawbreaker – as a force for confusion rather than for stays against it – as is clear from these remarks in his 1959 essay "The Future of Man": "We become an organized society only as we tell off some of our number to be law-givers and law-enforcers, a blend of general and lawyer, to hold fast the line and turn the rest of us loose for scientists, philosophers, and poets to make the breakthrough, the revolution, if we can for refreshment" (*CPPP*, 869). Poets here are ranged among those who set loose forces that, it may well be, no discipline can contain – among those who go about flirting with bonfires that may or may not burn beyond recall. Mastery, order, form, control, choice – all these are terms of esteem in Frost's poetics. But at times they yield to other states of mind, and, by implication, possibly to other states of body and desire as well – outlaw, unaccredited states of mind and structures of feeling, "refreshing" conditions which require an exemption from the altogether more rigid, and altogether less metamorphic, language of blame.

Frost's thoughts about the confusions that attend unaccredited, heretical aspirations are strictly dubious. This dubiety has something to do with gender, though questions about gender hardly exhaust what Frost has to say. There is in Frost a specifically *masculine* imperative to dominate the scene of writing, to admit no contingencies, just as there is, in poems like "The Birthplace," a patriarchal imperative to dominate the scene of nature – to farm it, to subdue it to order, to abolish, or at least to circumscribe, its more promiscuous and uncontrollable energies. Masculinity – as Frost would have it – is what chastens the bonfire more than what sets it burning. Katherine Kearns, in one of the best books written about Frost,[4] shows how Frost generalizes this idea, associating imperatives of order with masculinity, and associating conditions of "barrierlessness," chaos, insubordination and dissolution, with "femininity" (2). She concludes that for Frost "the work of manhood" is "to urge control on the uncontrollable, to impose upon its own 'femaleness' – that which embodied in women seems too randomly destructive – moderation and orderliness" (21). The conflict in Frost's poetry between insubordinate natural forces and the forms that we impose on them is therefore also, indirectly and residually, a conflict between the feminine and the masculine. Kearns proposes to gender the dialectic that recurs throughout Frost's work – a dialectic in which "form" and "wildness," "stays against" confusion and "confusion" itself, exist in indecisive antagonism. It is in any case clear that "confusion" and "wildness" are most often gendered feminine in Frost's poetry – both at the level of theme and, if I may say so, at the level of theory. It is typically women who suffer madness in his work, as in such poems as "A Servant to Servants," "The Witch of Coos," and "The Pauper Witch of Grafton." Frost's interest in these madwomen not unreasonably suggests an identification with them. He felt the possibility for insanity in himself – after all, it ran sadly through his family, debilitating his sister Jeanie and two of his children – and he sometimes figured it, I believe, as the feminine working within and against him. I would, then, extend the terms of the antagonism just described to include the opposed, and much more general, terms mastery and contingency, action and passion, doing and suffering. The writing of poetry would be, for Frost, the experience of giving way to an instability that provocatively reaches down at times even to the very foundation of identity only to discover, as at the last minute, the resolution of identity in order and form. I am suggesting tentatively that the writing of poetry is for Frost a way to manage and control, as if by homeopathic indulgence, what might be called the woman within – a way flirtatiously to open up the rigors of the masculine self to possible confusion and instability, but to do so only the better to restore the bonds of masculinity, to achieve again a certain self-possession. It is a kind of prophylaxis. The *language* of self-control is arrived at via a tentative exemption from the *experience* of self-control. You want to manage and discipline the bonfire, but first you have to incite it – to *advocate* it.

In Frost's account, as the poet writes, his identity relaxes almost to the point of losing its figure. But it emerges from these receptive encounters with instability "only more sure of all it thought was true," to adapt the closing phrases of Frost's early sonnet "Into My Own," in which the speaker threatens to lose himself in a wilderness of imagination the better to secure his own claim to integrity and forceful will.[5] A strong and apparently autonomous self emerges from these transactions refreshed and reinvigorated, newly self-aware, with its accession to what Frost calls a "clarification of life."[6] There is in this something of the Shelleyan dialectic, as we find it in "Ode to the West Wind." "If I were a dead leaf thou mightiest bear," cries Shelley to the wind;

> If I were a swift cloud to fly with thee;
> A wave to pant beneath thy power, and share
>
> The impulse of thy strength, only less free
> Than thou, O uncontrollable!

This, too, is an imaginary flirtation with destructive forces that promise to extend beyond the point of "recall." Others have noted the sexual metaphor latent in the poem. Shelley asks that the West Wind ravish him, penetrate him, dominate him. He would "pant beneath its power." Only through submission to this larger force – only through adopting toward it what might be called, in Keats' culture, a "feminine" position – can the poet share in its power and become himself a creating agent. If he would have power he must first relinquish it. Shelley, it might be said, secularizes, or at least makes agreeably un-Christian, Donne's plea in "Batter my heart three-personed

God," where the sexual metaphor is explicit: "Take me to you," he asks of God, "ravish me" (Holy Sonnet XIV). This is the kind of paradox about losing the self in order to find it towards which Frost's own thinking tends. We encounter it also in Emerson. "It is a secret which every intellectual man quickly learns," Emerson says in "The Poet,"

> that, beyond the energy of his possessed and conscious intellect, he is capable of a new energy . . . by abandonment to the nature of things; that, beside his privacy of power as an individual man, there is a great public power, on which he can draw, by unlocking, at all risks, his human doors, and suffering the ethe-real tides to roll and circulate through him: then he is caught up into the life of the Universe, his speech is thunder, his thought is law.[7]

Later in the same passage Emerson speaks of the "ravishment" of the intel-lect. He has in view, as do Shelley and Donne in their different ways, a sur-render, a passion, in which the self welcomes penetration the better itself to penetrate. We are, here, as also in "Ode to the West Wind," at the place where action and passion merge, where doing and suffering are not really to be distinguished, where self and no-self, and where being "directed" and being "lost," are the same. Frost is not so Dionysian in his account of these transactions as are Shelley and Emerson; nor is he exactly Christian in his discovery of them, as is Donne. But they work in his thinking nonetheless, as when, in "The Constant Symbol" he speaks of the necessity on the part of the poet to open himself up to the "harsher disciplines from without" the better to realize what he calls the "*self*-discipline" from "within": "He who knows not both knows neither" (*CPPP*, 789). The poet attains a certain mas-culine force and rigor, as Frost figures these things, only by way of a passage through, or flirtation with, an essential instability. Stays against confusion are achieved only through receptive encounters with it.

I want to examine this idea further by reading two poems from Frost's 1928 volume *West-Running Brook*, "The Last Mowing" and "The Birthplace." The poems succeed one another and to my mind work together in a particularly interesting sort of counterpoint. Consider first the second of the two, "The Birthplace":

> Here further up the mountain slope
> Than there was ever any hope,
> My father built, enclosed a spring,
> Strung chains of wall round everything,
> Subdued the growth of earth to grass,
> And brought our various lives to pass.
> A dozen girls and boys we were.
> The mountain seemed to like the stir,

And made of us a little while –
With always something in her smile.
Today she wouldn't know our name.
(No girl's, of course, has stayed the same.)
The mountain pushed us off her knees.
And now her lap is full of trees.

Most remarkable is what "The Birthplace" omits to mention (as Katherine Kearns has pointed out): the mother that presumably had at least something to do with bringing a dozen girls and boys to pass. The poem concerns instead the founding father – the patriarch. Even so, the name of the mother is repressed only inefficiently in "The Birthplace," as Frost seems to acknowledge. That is to say, her role is not so much repressed as displaced onto the mountain itself, which the father husbands and makes fertile, and which "pushes" the children off her "lap" once they have grown. The allegory could hardly be clearer. This homestead is a little enclave of patriarchal order imposed on an unpredictable, unruly, but nonetheless productive, feminine landscape. There is a kind of chaos here, a kind of wild fire; but it is kept, if only for a generation or so, just this side of the boundary beyond which there is no recall. The land essentially unsettles itself, but not before at least one man has had his way with it. The feminine, this poem implies, is only partly and ephemerally susceptible to the masculine orders that would "subdue" it. The stay against wilderness and confusion figured in "The Birthplace" is therefore "momentary," which is what associates it, to my mind, with "the figure a poem makes" (*CPPP*, 777). The father of this poem, that is to say, is recognizably a father-poet – an *author*. To bring a life to pass and to bring a poem to pass are, so far as "The Birthplace" is concerned, cognate endeavors: string chains of wall round everything, whether with stanzas or with fence-posts.

But as always in Frost, something there is that does not love a wall, and it escapes the father's government. The mountain makes of us a little while, then pushes us off her knees. The written word, like the land itself, is promiscuous and metamorphic. In short, it is "feminine" – at least as "The Birthplace" figures these things. The writing of poetry is therefore the subordination to order – to the rule of the father referred to in the poem – of this feminine unruliness. It is the establishment of at least a momentary stay against confusion. And yet the masculine poet establishes it only at a certain cost, which he must not be reluctant to acknowledge: the occlusion of what was feminine, or "refreshing," in his own temperament, which necessarily recedes as the languages of effort and self-control are reasserted. Frost may associate his work as a poet with the work of the father in "The Birthplace" and of the farmer in "Putting in the Seed." But he can also imagine himself as vulnerable and unruly in specifically feminine ways. Consider in this connection an anecdote relayed in a letter he wrote to R. P. T. Coffin in 1937:

> Then there was the man who after telling me for hours about his big bold business adventures asked me toward morning what I did with myself. I staved off the confession. I likened myself to him in adventurousness. I was a long-shot man too. I liked not to know beforehand what the day might bring forth. And so till he lost patience with me and cried "Shoot!" Well I write poetry. "Hell," he said unhappily "my wife writes that stuff."

The dry humiliation recounted in the anecdote suggests that Frost felt the pressure of what he understood to be the masculine, that he chafed under it, and that he is consequently often on the feminine side of the mountain in "The Birthplace" more than on the masculine side of the father.

"The Last Mowing" bears interestingly on these questions. It precedes "The Birthplace" in *West-Running Brook* and constitutes, even at the level of form, a feminine alternative to that poem's more phallocentric implications. Katherine Kearns suggests – though not in connection with this particular poem – that "the iambic foot becomes in Frost's poetry a kind of moral baseline, a strong voice . . . The anapest and the dactyl become in this context not merely melodic variations but markers of weakness." Additionally, "feminine rhymes, with their implication of passivity, tend in this iambic context inevitably to designate a departure from seriousness or from control" (74). Astute remarks, and in light of them we can see how remarkably "The Last Mowing" differs from "The Birthplace":

> There's a place called Far-away Meadow
> We never shall mow in again,
> Or such is the talk at the farmhouse:
> The meadow is finished with men.
> Then now is the chance for the flowers
> That can't stand mowers and plowers.
> It must be now, though, in season
> Before the not mowing brings trees on,
> Before trees, seeing the opening,
> March into a shadowy claim.
> The trees are all I'm afraid of.
> That flowers can't bloom in the shade of;
> It's no more the men I'm afraid of;
> The meadow is done with the tame.
> The place for the moment is ours
> For you, oh tumultuous flowers,
> To go to waste and go wild in,
> All shapes and colors of flowers,
> I needn't call you by name.

Instead of the iambic rhythms on which Frost most often depends, we find anapestic triplets lightly supporting three-beat lines: triplets within triplets, for a delicately turned lyric waltz. We also find, significantly I think, fourteen feminine, that is to say unstressed, endings out of nineteen total lines. The levity of the meter, and of the feminine endings, contributes much to the tone of the poem, as well as to our feeling about its speaker's identity and gender. We might suppose that a child speaks here, and that we are to understand his feeling of solidarity with the flowers (as against the "mowers and plowers") as one of youth against age, or pleasure against responsibility. No doubt some of that is in the poem. But attending to the language of gender – and to the gender of prosody – suggests another, likelier possibility: that the speaker is marked more importantly by femininity than by youth. We are certainly asked to think of the mowers and plowers that oppose the speaker as preeminently, aggressively *masculine*; this is what "The Last Mowing" notices about them. And these men, these mowers and plowers, contend for dominion over the flowering field, as in a battle, with trees that are themselves grimly proprietary martial figures who "march into a shadowy claim."

My sense is that Frost is engaging, here, in some literary cross-dressing. "The Last Mowing" speaks from and to that place in Frost's personality that had been forced into occlusion by the practical and assertive mores of American masculinity (as these latter work in the business man's rejoinder to Frost: Poetry? "Hell, my wife writes that stuff"). The speaker of "The Last Mowing" likes her flowers wild and most definitely unsubdued and unproductive: "The place for the moment is ours/ For you, oh tumultuous flowers, / To go to waste and go wild in." These are what Frost might call, to refer to a letter he wrote from England to his American friend Sidney Cox, "unutilitarian" flowers, and there is nothing particularly masculine about them. "I like that about the English," Frost says,

> they all have time to dig the ground for the unutilitarian flower. I mean the men. It marks the great difference between them and our men. I like flowers you know but I like em wild, and I am rather the exception than the rule in an American village. Far as I have walked in pursuit of the Cypripedium, I have never met another in the woods on the same quest. Americans will dig for peas and beans and such like utilities but not if they know it for posies.
>
> (SL, 71–72)

So far is the speaker of "The Last Mowing" from masculinity, at least as these documents seem to understand it, that she refuses even the mildly proprietary, imperial gesture of "naming" the flowers. Alone in the woods, together with her unutilitarianly "wasted" flowers, Frost's speaker is released, if only for a moment, from the dominion and oversight of men, from the petty tyrannies of masculinity, and released, at a still more general level, from the disciplined language of self-control: "The place for the moment is ours/ For you, oh tumultuous flowers,/ To go to waste and go wild in." The release from discipline is suggested even in the rhythm of the poem, which is, for Frost, remarkably vagrant and irregular. This lyric constitutes a moment of flirtatious levity indulged in just prior to the ironic but forcefully iambic evocation of patriarchal discipline in "The Birthplace." Reading "The Last Mowing" persuades me that the burly postures Frost sometimes strikes in his accounts of the poetic vocation – a good example is his claim, in a 1921 brochure, that the poet's words "must be flat and final like the show-down in poker, from which there is no appeal" (*CPPP*, 701) – are probably maintained through considerable, or at least noticeable, exertions. In this connection there is to be considered, too, Frost's coy personification of poetry as a "spoiled actress" in a talk he gave in 1959:

> My own idea of poetry isn't of its climbing on top of the earth. Nor is it of its sitting on top of the earth nor of its standing on top of the earth but of its reclining on top of the earth and giving way to its moods . . . Like a spoiled actress, you know, the day after she has been on stage, reclining on top of the world and giving way to her moods. (*CPPP*, 262)

So much for effort and self-control. Moods are always unaccountable.

In any case, "The Last Mowing" registers the relaxation of masculine exertions and does so with a tact communicated as much in the poem's delicate form as in its theme. And if Frost identifies with plowers and mowers, he is thinking not of the ominous mowers figured in this poem (and revived in "The Birthplace"), but of the mower whom his speaker succeeds in the early poem "The Tuft of Flowers": that "mower in the dew" loves flowers so much that he unutilitarianly leaves a tuft of them behind, as a kind of signature, to "flourish" from "sheer morning gladness at the brim" (*CPPP*, 31). It is a figure, as Frost liked to point out, for the work of the poet and there is, within the terms of our culture, nothing particularly masculine about it. Frost arrives at a poetics of androgyny: his mower-poets are always also slightly feminine – as much on the side of the flowers of the field as on the side of the order that would subdue and master them. That position was very hard to hold in a cultural regime whose conception of gender was rigorously binary – a cultural regime, that is to say, which could not tolerate the idea that masculine and feminine dispositions dialectically contain one another. That Frost, for his part, could tolerate it is clear from the two poems we have been examining: here, poetry is set over against the assertion of masculinity, as in "The Last Mowing," and is at the same time associated with the assertion of masculine discipline and order, as in "The Birthplace."

One could image a theory of poetry which holds that a poem ideally marks the convergence, so to speak, of "feminine" tendencies toward irrationality and disordered associations, and "masculine" tendencies toward coherence, unity, and reason, with the latter given ultimate priority. "The Birthplace" and "The Last Mowing," when considered in the light of Frost's general proposition that a poem is "a momentary stay against confusion," suggest, to my mind at least, that his theory of poetry runs along similar lines. The further implication of Frost's theory, if such it can be called, is that the two tendencies named – toward undisciplined connotation and toward controlled denotation – are both situated in the poet. This idea helps us explain the dubiety of Frost's own literary personality, which famously comprises decisive clarity on the one hand and evasive ambiguity on the other. He is the most unavailable poet that ever made himself seem so available, as has often been pointed out. Consider, for example, the all but irreconcilable disparity of two accounts Frost gave of himself in his writing. The first is from a brochure issued in 1923 by Henry Holt and Company, Frost's publisher, and titled *Robert Frost: The Man and His Work*, the second from a 1924 letter Frost wrote to his friend Louis Untermeyer.

> Sometimes I have my doubts of words altogether, and I ask myself what is the place of them. They are worse than nothing unless they do something; unless they amount to deeds, as in ultimatums or battle-cries. They must be flat and final like the show-down in poker, from which there is no appeal. My definition of poetry (if I were forced to give one) would be this: words that have become deeds. (*CPPP*, 701)

> I have come to the conclusion that style in prose or verse is that which indicates how the writer takes himself and what he is saying . . . I own any form of humor shows fear and inferiority. Irony is simply a kind of guardedness. So is a twinkle. It keeps the reader from criticism . . . Humor is the most engaging cowardice. With it myself I have been able to hold some of my enemy in play far out of gunshot. (*CPPP*, 702–03)

In the latter example, Frost perfectly describes certain features of his own poetic and epistolary style – how he "takes himself" as a writer: he is all guardedness, humor, and twinkling irony. Nothing could be further from the evasive genius of this "most engaging cowardice" than the talk, in the first example, of ultimatums and battle-cries. In the letter to Untermeyer, Frost is thinking more of the bluff in poker than of the "showdown." And in sharp contrast to Frost's placement of poetry on a masculine battlefield are the remarks from a talk he gave in 1959, quoted above in another connection: "My own idea of poetry isn't of its climbing on top of the earth. Nor is it of its sitting on top of the earth nor of its standing on top of the earth but of its reclining on top of the earth and giving way to its moods . . . Like a spoiled actress, you know, the day after she has been on stage, reclining on top of the world and giving way to her moods." The calling of poetry is here associated not merely with femininity but with a particularly *campy* sort of femininity – a sexual persona Frost rarely adopted in print (a possible early exception is "The Last Mowing"). With these other descriptions of the work of poetry before us, the essay "Some Definitions of Robert Frost" (*CPPP*, 701) seems all the more characterized, even anxiously so, by a virile masculine ethos. And in any event, it should be clear by now that the feminine and the masculine as Frost understands them are detached from "the female" and "the male." He is characteristically concerned with gender, not with sex, which is what keeps his thinking fresh and contemporary. The authority of the poem – its stay against confusion – is arrived at dialectically through the experience of confusion itself. The assertion of self first involves a certain experience of "giving way." The poet saves his "self" by losing it. He opens himself up to contingency only the better, in the last instance, to recover and assert the language of effort and self-control.

Indeed, in the account given in Frost's poetics, writing marks a kind of fall, on the part of the writer, into contingency – into "commitments" and "answerabilities" that severely limit his freedom of movement (the terms are borrowed from Frost's essay "The Constant Symbol"). It is a lapse from transcendence into immanence, as the existentialists say, or from the "masculine" expression of self-control into a "feminine" experience of laxity and disorder. Or, to put it still another way: poetry, as Frost personifies it, ranges from the decisive poker-playing general issuing his ultimatums on the battlefield of masculinity, to the spoiled actress, who may or may not show. Poetry is at once a whimsical and a soldierly affair. Frost always sets a limit to the poet's resources for deliberate self-control. The forms of language and poetry never perfectly realize the vague sense of possibility that the poet brings to the act of writing: "Nothing he writes," as Frost puts it, "quite represents his thought or feeling."[8] There are always contingencies for which he cannot account, contingencies which manage and discipline him as much as he does them. Meaning is as much generated as expressed when a poet writes, and this process – to which the poet, at times, can feel merely incidental or catalytic – may be taken as a model for human action in general. We are always finding ourselves so "multifariously closed in on with obligations and answerabilities" that sometimes we lose our "august temper," to adapt a sentence from "The Constant Symbol" (*CPPP*, 787).

All the same, there is a promise of transcendence in Frost's poetics. I find in this promise a gesture, on his part, toward overcoming the writer's fall into contingency, a fall that necessarily becomes, to some extent, a fall out of agency and authority. It is a gesture towards mastering contingency itself, as "The Trial by Existence" suggests. Frost achieves this transcendence, at least in thought, by re-imagining agency as a force developed *out* of writing and action rather than as a force expressed *through* them: meaning and purpose are "unfolded by surprise" as the poet writes, or more generally as anyone acts (*CPPP*, 778). We come to know self-discipline and integrity only by giving way to, and by suffering, the harsher disciplines from without to which we are always contingent. The poet must be ravished in order to be chaste, must, in Shelleyan fashion, give way to something "uncontrollable" in order ultimately to achieve control. A masculine rigor such as the patriarch imagined in "The Birthplace" establishes on the land takes its meaning only in the corrosive presence of the feminine "waste" and "wildness" figured in "The Last Mowing" (corrosive, that is, from the point of view of those who would maintain order and rigor).

All of this suggests that the experience of "agency" and "authority" we usually have, in which our motives and success seem transparent and available to us before we act, is in fact rather inconsequential. Or if not exactly inconsequential, these available, premeditative motives are in any event not motives upon which a theory of authorship might be grounded. To ask a poet what he or she "means" in this limited sense is an impertinence. Frost shows us how true "authorial" agency lies much deeper, beneath the awareness even of the poet. And the partly mysterious encounter of authority and contingency on the stage of writing promises, in his poetics, to place the poet in touch with these deeper possibilities of agency. It is a powerful mythology of the self and of authorship because it holds out the possibility of a release from constriction, a new birth of the poet's "highest liveliness escaping from a succession of dead selves," as Frost says in an entry in one of his notebooks. The poet is constantly born anew into a sense of individuality and integrity. He recovers himself, his self-discipline and self-control, by way of a passage through a certain release.

An odd little poem by Emerson called "Memory," collected first in *May Day and Other Pieces* (1867), throws some further light on these matters, the more so as Emerson directly influenced Frost's line of thought, as we shall presently see.

> Night-dreams trace on Memory's wall
> Shadows of the thoughts of day.
> And thy fortunes, as they fall,
> The bias of the will betray.

The poem has to do with the idea, again, that life has for us on the wrack nothing but what we somehow choose. And it helps us understand the unusual force, in Frost's aphorism, of the adverb *somehow*. I assume that by "will" Emerson means something like "*personal* will" – in other words, the chief instrument by which we can know the motive and power of the self. Emerson's idea is that our fortunes, as they fall out, are really the unfolding of a will that we can – or *must*, in the last instance – somehow call our own. Emerson's thinking in this quatrain is vestigially Platonic. His shadows are like the shadows on the wall of Plato's cave. So, thinking of the Emersonian tradition in which Frost writes, I would paraphrase the poem like this: we discover our will, we *divine* it, even as St. Paul said we discover the light of Heaven: as through a glass darkly. We can read in the fortunes and casualties of our lives the overriding "bias" of a will that runs through them as waking themes, distorted and confused, run through the shadows of our dreams at night. We have access to that will; we have knowledge of it. But the access and the knowledge are indirect, refracted. We make the choices of our lives but can never quite say *how* we make them. Frost licenses us to draw some further inferences from these propositions: the self, the will, is a thing that understanding never entirely apprehends. The selves of which we have an apprehensive experience are apparent only, as is suggested in the notebook entry just cited: "There is such a thing as sincerity. It is hard to define but is probably nothing but your highest liveliness escaping from a succession of dead selves." The self that can be "sincer[e]," our "highest liveliness," is to be distinguished from the "selves" that merely fall away before its progress. This real self, as against those apparent ones, is always as if on the other side of a barrier from us. It is shut out from us just as the source of the light, and the forms that cast the shadows, are shut out from Plato's dwellers in the cave. But all the same we can know the *bias* of our will – its tendencies, its inflections. We can see, in the events and passages of our lives, shadows cast by our sincerest self, just as we find in our dreams the shadows of meaning and motive.

Recall Frost's remarks in the preface to that 1942 selection of his poems, which I quote again here:

> I have made this selection much as I made the one from my first book, *A Boy's Will* and my second book, *North of Boston* looking backward over the accumulation of years to see how many poems I could find towards some one meaning it might seem absurd to have had in advance, but it would be all right to accept from fate after the fact. The interest, the pastime, was to learn if there had been any divinity shaping my ends and I had been building better than I knew.

I am suggesting that, on this account, poems work in the way that dreams do in Emerson's quatrain. In his poems the poet is given access – indirect access, but access nonetheless – to the real, the deepest and sincerest, bias of his will: the divinity shaping his ends. It is there, in the poems, that he finds the shadows of himself, which is why writing is a movement toward realization of self, but also why self is never something that consciousness can altogether seize: instead, we know an experience of a succession of "dead" or merely apparent selves. We feel the real self's motives everywhere and at every moment, but it remains, to consciousness, only latent, somehow always unavailable, as the unconscious is for Freud. Returning now to the allegory of the cave, as it works in Emerson's quatrain, we may state clearly Frost's difference from the post-structuralist thinkers who have so much influenced the theory and criticism of poetry – and who have largely set the terms for any debate about literary "authority" – since his death. Let us say that to the post-structuralist – and again I borrow the figure from Emerson's poem – we live as if in a world of shadows cast by nothing. But to Frost, as to Emerson before him, there is indeed something casting at least the shadows of our own lives, and it is what we properly call the self. In other words, it may well be true that, as the post-structuralists say, the self is always elsewhere. But Frost would add a caveat: to say that the self is always elsewhere is not at all the same thing as saying that it is nowhere.

Describing the "rudimentary psychology" of what he calls the "religious man." Nietzsche explains that when such a man "experiences the conditions of power, the imputation is [always] that he is not their cause, that he is not responsible for them: they come without being willed, consequently we are not their author: the will that is not free," Nietzsche concludes, "needs an external will."[9] It is useful to think of post-structuralist critiques of "authority" as "religious" in the sense Nietzsche gives the term in the passage quoted above, paradoxical though that may seem. Post-structuralist philosophy and literary theory are, it is true, inimical to such apparently metaphysical concepts as an "external will," at least as a "religious" man might conceive of "external will." But insofar as the motives of language, of literary tradition, and of society may be said to be "external" to the will of the writing subject, that is to say, insofar as language itself, conceived of as a complex of "transindividual" codes, may be said to "speak" us rather than us, it – to this extent, in any case, post-structuralist theories of "authority" regard the poet as a kind of medium for the poem rather than as its real and only point of origin. All of his authority is apparent. And with this, we are pretty well back to Plato's *Ion*, or at least back to Donne in "Batter my heart": "take me to you," he implores his God, "imprison me, for I,/ Except you enthrall me, never shall be free,/ Nor ever chaste except you ravish me." In contrast to this, Frost's poetics is a wily – and, let us say, "impious" – effort to recover, in the name of the poet, the agency that is so easily and so often located elsewhere, whether by a mystical theory of "divine" inspiration or by a post-structuralist one of distributed subjectivity. One happy consequence of Frost's accounts of authority is indeed that they help us see what these two other theories may have in common as accounts of motivation: "piety" in both cases – to extend Nietzsche's religious metaphor – is a matter of sub-jecting the self to some will "external" to it. Frost's poetics is an alternative effort to redescribe external will as in fact internal to the subject – an effort to redescribe "the harsher discipline from without" as another (although occult) feature of what he calls *self-discipline*. The divinity shaping his end is always finally personal to him. He would reclaim, in the name of the poet, the language of self-control, and set his injunction against any exemption, in the poet's name, either from blame or from credit.

We can register quite clearly Frost's difference from the religious turn of mind, as Nietzsche describes it, by comparing his thinking on the subject of authority to that of George Herbert, a poet with whom he otherwise has much in common. I have in mind such poems as "The Altar" and "The Flower." The first two stanzas of the latter establish an analogy between the resurgent energies of spring and the onset of renewed energy, both literary and vital, in the poet himself.

> How fresh, O Lord, how sweet and clean
> Are thy returns! ev'n as the flowers in spring:
> To which, besides their own demean,
> The late-past frosts tributes of pleasure bring.
> Grief melts away
> Like snow in May,
> As if there were no such cold thing.
>
> Who could have thought my shriveled heart
> Could have recovered greennesse? It was gone
> Quite underground; as flowers depart
> To see their mother-root, when they have blown;
> Where they together
> All the hard weather,
> Dead to the world, keep house unknown.

For Herbert, the oscillations of the seasons, the oscillating seasons of the heart, and the ebb and flow of poetic power, are all bound up together into a single phenomenon: the influx and efflux of God's divinity. Herbert writes later in the poem: "And now in age I bud again,/ After so many deaths I live and write,/ I once more smell the dew and rain,/ And relish versing." In such poems as "A Prayer in Spring" and "To the Thawing Wind" Frost seems to follow Herbert, though of course he naturalizes the religion, which is never in any orthodox sense Christian. In these poems, as also in others, Frost places the creative energies of the poet in alignment with the larger impulses of renewal that reanimate the natural world. But for him the similitude affiliating natural "creation" and poetic creation is always merely that – a similitude. It is never, as it surely is for Herbert, an *identity*. At the end of the day, Frost wants to lay claim, and in his own name, to the creative power his poems manifest. His "sweet returns" are always his own, not the Lord's. He would have us say again, as always: life has for us on the wrack nothing but what we somehow choose. Frost wants to accept as his own – wants to be convicted of – even meanings it might seem absurd to have "had in advance."

As we have seen, Frost liked to quote Emerson on the question of whether or not a poet "builds better than he knows": "[A]ll through the years," he said in a talk delivered at Kenyon College in 1950, "I've been confronted with the idea . . . whether I say more than I know myself. A poet builds better than he knows." The question is *what* or *who*, in a poem, is doing the knowing and the building. The allusion, here, is to the following passage from Emerson's poem "The Problem," which concerns Michelangelo, and which marks a variation on the theme introduced in "Memory":

> The hand that rounded Peter's dome,
> And groined the aisles of Christian Rome,
> Wrought in a sad sincerity;
> Himself from God he could not free;
> He builded better than he knew; –
> The conscious stone to beauty grew.

Frost's references to this poem are shrewd and consequential. The implication in "The Problem" is that the "author" of the dome of St. Peter's or of any work of art is but an instrument for a divine super-agent that works through him. In that sense, Michelangelo "builded better than he knew." Emerson regards art as a kind of second nature: the same transcendent creative force that "built" the Andes, as he suggests in another passage in the same poem, "builds," through the instrument of human art, the dome of St. Peter. Not only the mind of the sculptor but the stone itself is "conscious," and this consciousness, whether in the stone or in the sculptor, is everywhere the consciousness of God. Frost transforms this idea, ascribing ultimate authority not to a divine agent but to a deeply *personal*, albeit initially occult, agent. To be precise, he ascribes authority to a hidden component of the artist's self that is discovered in the act of composition. He emerges from his encounters with wildness and contingency – from the Donne-like ravishment and thralldom of inspiration – only more sure of all he thought was true. He finds himself by losing himself, as if in a controlled experiment with confusion and uncertainty. Like Shelley, he would attach himself to forces he cannot, apparently, control, only the better to assert a higher self-control. And that last aspiration is what marks his difference from Herbert and Emerson. The language they use to describe the sweet returns of creative authority is religious, and would involve, as "The Altar" and "The Problem" do, the poet's exemption from both credit and blame. Frost never approaches that point.

Later in the passage quoted above from *The Will to Power*, Nietzsche suggests that "man has not dared to credit himself with his strong and surprising impulses – he has conceived them as 'passive,' as 'suffered,' as things imposed upon him: religion is the product of a doubt concerning the unity of the person, an *altération* of the personality."[10] And so is post-structuralist literary theory, in its own way, a product of these doubts: the self is always elsewhere. It may help us by way of summing up Frost's project to suggest that he impiously dares to credit himself with "authority," with his most "strong and surprising impulses," and that he does so in the face of precisely the "religious doubts" about the "unity" of the self that Nietzsche speaks of here. The writing of poetry, Frost has the audacity to suggest, actually unifies the self, actually overcomes the very *altération* or "othering" of personality that always, to some extent, undermines a poet's convictions of integrity and authority. The self of the poet certainly "alters" as he writes, but this "alteration" becomes the self – it does not oppose it. Frost tentatively makes the "divinity" shaping his end his own; whereas post-structuralist theory secularizes and distributes this "divinity." Frost personalizes it. That is why his poetics can never really be assimilated to post-structuralism, much less to *divine* theories of authority such as one encounters in the *Ion* or in George Herbert. It is as if Frost always experimentally submits his own account of authorship to a rigorous, Nietzschean critique. We have to arrive at some such formula if we are to appreciate the subtlety of his enterprise in poetry, which has both "pious" and "impious" features – both self-effacing and self-aggrandizing features.

The autonomy and the immense responsibility assigned the self in Frost's philosophy must strike some readers as regrettable, even as a bit cruel. He seems to say, in such works as "The Trial by Existence": "You built your own world, now live in it – for better and for worse." To put it very broadly – as a friend once suggested to me – this is a way of blaming the victim. It is in any event a way of affirming a life led *with* blame, a life not exempt from the language of effort and self-control. In this respect Frost's thinking is quite consistent with the free-market capitalist individualism he has often been credited with, or accused of, defending. And in its turn this connection helps explain Frost's hostility to the New Deal in *A Further Range* (1936), a book that would save the autonomy of the individual even at the expense of accepting a good deal of general purpose misery. Of course, Frost would reply to a critic of his position: "But Roosevelt saved us all from a certain amount of misery at the expense of the autonomy of the individual – the other way. Roosevelt's is a philosophy of diminished capacity." One can see how this would be the case, from Frost's point of view, by examining a bitter New Deal-era poem called "A Roadside Stand," collected first in *A Further Range*. The poem concerns what Frost takes to be an unseemly development toward centralized political and economic authority. He begins by describing "a little new shed" that has been set up alongside a rural highway in the hope of peddling fresh produce to city dwellers out for a weekend in the country. "Too pathetically," as Frost puts it, this roadside stand pleads "it would not be fair to say for a dole of bread,/ But for some of the money, the cash, whose flow supports/ The flower of cities from sinking and withering faint." And then he continues, later in the poem:

> It is in the news that all these pitiful kin
> Are to be brought out and mercifully gathered in
> To live in villages next to the theater and store
> Where they won't have to think for themselves any more;
> While greedy good-doers, beneficent beasts of prey,
> Swarm over their lives enforcing benefits
> That are calculated to soothe them out of their wits.
>
> (*CPPP*, 260–61)

The (somewhat Foucauldian) idea advanced here is that solicitude is really a technique of domination, and a calculated technique at that. Very cold indeed. Describe the situation in this way and the freedom to suffer unmolested seems a freedom essential to any broader liberty. Frost's position is Herbert Hoover's in the election year of 1936. Roosevelt's New Deal, it happens, is so pernicious a development as to bear comparison even to the fascist and bureaucratic-socialist regimes of Europe: "All the men who are seeking for mastery in the world today are using the same weapons," Hoover said in a Republican party stump speech called "This Challenge to Liberty." "They sing the same songs. They all promise the joys of Elysium without effort. But their philosophy is founded upon the compulsory organization of men. True liberal government is founded on the emancipation of men. This is the issue upon which men are imprisoned and dying in Europe right now" (*CPPP*, 350).

Readers of Frost may be reminded of the sentiments expressed in his 1936 preface to *Threescore*, an autobiography by New England-born reformer

Sarah Cleghorn. In that preface, Frost puts the following words into the mouth of a southern "Negress," as he terms her, and they are, to my knowledge, the only ones he ever ascribed to an African American in his published writings.

> Just after the great Democratic victory of 1932 I made occasion to bring the election into conversation with a Negress who had come to our door soliciting alms for a school for Negroes in the deep south.
>
> "My people don't very much like the Democrats in power again," she said. "Surely you aren't afraid of them anymore!"
>
> "I wouldn't just say we weren't afraid of them. You wouldn't think there was much they could do. But there's small things an outsider wouldn't notice."
>
> She was a poor creature, poorly clothed, but she touched her wrists with a pretty pathos for this: "Here a shackle, there a shackle, and before we know it we're back in slavery." (*CPPP*, 750)

Frost is attempting to make a point about social security. And the opening phrases of the introduction to *Threescore* make clear by implication, when we look at them in light of the entire essay, that security is itself a kind of "slavery," as Frost implies in the passage just quoted. "Security, security!" Frost exclaims in irritation. "We run in all directions for security in the game of Pussy-wants-a-corner" (*CPPP*, 749). The reference to the childish game "Pussy-wants-a-corner" is not merely incidental. Too much social security bestowed on anyone top down, so to speak, infantilizes him, diminishes his capacity, exempts him ever from becoming the dignified object of the language of blame, as children are themselves exempted. The socially secure "don't have to think for themselves anymore." All the risk is taken from the game of life. Such is Frost's belief in any case. He says in the preface to *King Jasper* that "it seems immoral to have to bet on such high things as lives of art, business, or the church. But in effect, we have no alternative. None but an all-wise and all-powerful government could take the responsibility of keeping us out of gambling or of insuring us against loss once we were in" (*CPPP*, 746–47). Security of that sort is but another name for the paternalism Frost detested. It is useful to bear in mind that, as he wrote the preface to *Threescore*, Frost had lately returned from Key West. There he had witnessed, with a chagrin expressed in his letters about the experience, the efforts of the Federal Emergency Relief Administration to make Key West, a notoriously unruly little protectorate, a much more secure place, complete with automobile mufflers, sewers, rent control, and license plates. FERA was – as Frost put it in a letter to Louis Untermeyer, and in language reminiscent of "A Roadside Stand" – "mildly and beneficently dictatorial" (*CPPP*, 251). Over against this sort of benevolence, Frost always wanted to say – as he once did in a Depression-era speech given at Amherst College – that we should endeavor to preserve and protect what he preferred to call the "privilege" to meet "emergencies" and even to fail.[11] If that sounds harsh, as it often must, we should bear in mind that Frost had the good taste not to except himself from the privilege to fail: he tolerated and even courted hardship because without it he lacked the "privilege" also to succeed – the privilege to *perform* as he liked to say. That is why, time and again, he reiterates in his work the need for obstacles, resistances, and constraints – to those "harsher disciplines from without" within which only can we come to feel the truer "disciplines" of the self: he who knows not both of these disciplines knows neither. The poet needs his immanence and contingency if he is to get his transcendence. Frost's view is therefore essentially tragic, not comic, which is simply another way of saying that the divinity shaping his end, as I already indicated, is always finally personal and individual (as in *King Lear* or *Macbeth*), never social or providential (as in *The Tempest* and many of the comedies). We begin to see just how tightly integrated Frost's thinking is: his Jeffersonian–libertarian response to the New Deal, his sense of tragedy, his Emersonian mythology of self – all of these things are intricately intertwined. And all of them work toward a single end, toward a kind of imperative: to resist at all costs exemption from the language of self-control.

By way of summing up we can say that, for Frost, poetry first involves a certain prodigality, as we know from reading "The Last Mowing"; there must be the rioting waste and wildness of flowers in bloom; there must be a certain blowsiness. But poetry always involves also a masculine mower and plower who marches in to make his shadowy claim on the blowsy fields of his endeavor. All poetical language, as William Empson says, is "debauched into associations," but never so debauched as not to constitute (or yield to) a unitary order of mind. Like the patriarch in "The Birthplace," the poet-as-mower strings chains of wall round everything and subdues the growth of earth to grass. He throws the field into shape, achieves a momentary stay against confusion which, though inevitably momentary, nonetheless holds its shape, its integrity and rigor, long enough for him to point to it, statesman-like, and to get credit for it. In Frost, there is a hatred of being controlled, disciplined, managed – in a word, a hatred of being made, apparently, "feminine." There is by the same token an admiration for those who control, discipline, and manage – whether mowers and plowers, poets, or politicians. It is not strength, even coercive strength, that Frost detests. What he seems to detest is not wielding the strength himself. Or, if a position of authority is unavailable, he detests not resisting the imposition of order. For Frost it is therefore in some sense as good to be the reluctant field as it is to be the ardent mower, and both are figures for the poet and for poetry. Great poets are neither "masculine" nor "feminine" but are, in their authority, ambivalently both. They may speak the language of discipline and self-control, asking not what their country can do for them. But they do this by knowledge, and not only in the Biblical sense, of forces whose prodigality and fertility they may not be able entirely to control. They have to like a little chaos. Indeed they have to have a little of it in themselves.

NOTES

1 Adam Phillips, *On Flirtation* (Cambridge, Massachusetts: Harvard University Press, 1992), p. 21.
2 Kenneth Burke, *A Grammar of Motives* (New York: Prentice-Hall, 1945), pp. 38–39.
3 I develop this argument at length in *The Ordeal of Robert Frost*, ed. Mark Richardson (Urbana: University of Illinois Press, 1997).
4 Katherine Kearns, *Robert Frost and a Poetics of Appetite* (Cambridge: Cambridge University Press, 1994).
5 *Ibid.*, p. 15.
6 *Ibid.*, p. 777.
7 Ralph Waldo Emerson, *Essays and Poems*, ed. Joel Porte, Harold Bloom, and Paul Kane (New York: The Library of America, 1996), p. 459.
8 William R. Evans, *Robert Frost and Sidney Cox* (Hanover, New Hampshire: University Press of New England, 1981), p. 22.
9 Friedrich Nietzsche, *The Will to Power*, ed. Walter Kaufmann, trans. Walter Kaufmann, and R. J. Hollingdale (New York: Vintage, 1968), p. 86.
10 *Ibid.*
11 Lawrance Thompson, *Robert Frost: The Years of Triumph* (New York: Holt, Rinehart and Winston, 1970), p. 417.

IO

GEORGE MONTEIRO

Frost's Politics and the Cold War

I

Shortly before Robert Frost's death on January 29, 1963, *County Government Magazine* published in its December 1962 issue the poet's response to its request for his participation in a symposium on the theme "The Cold War Is Being Won." His tone is less that of the disheartened cold warrior that he is sometimes taken to have been than of the resigned, though still optimistic, poet-diplomat he had become in the last ten years of his life.

> I hate a cold war of sustained hate that finds no relief in blood letting but prob-
> ably it should be regarded as a way of stalling till we find out whether there is
> really an issue big enough for a big show-down. We are given pause from the
> dread of the terribleness we feel capable of. I was sometimes like that as a boy
> with another boy I lived in antipathy with. It clouded my days. But here I am
> almost writing the article I was going to tell you I couldn't write. My limit
> seems to be verse and talk.   (*CPPP*, 901)

But Frost had not always resigned himself to being limited to verse and talk. And thereby hangs the tale of a poet who although he had always had his mind on politics, from the early times when his father taught him politics in San Francisco, would get an extraordinary chance in his eighty-ninth year to play the Cold War diplomat at the highest level.

In 1932, a year of increasing social pressures and widespread political turmoil, both Robert Frost and Walter Lippmann were honored at commencement exercises by the Phi Beta Kappa chapter at Columbia University. Lippmann spoke on "The Scholar in a Troubled World," and Frost read "Build Soil," a poem that branched out from his principal theme of the poet in the world to offer counsel to intellectuals, scholars, artists, and politicians. Sharing a principle he would follow for the rest of his life, Frost advised his young scholars and the rest of the world as well to slow down its rush to take action, "Build soil," he advised, depending on his audience to interpret correctly his metaphor:

Turn the farm in upon itself
Until it can contain itself no more,
But sweating-full, drips wine and oil a little.
I will go to my run-out social mind
And be as unsocial with it as I can.
The thought I have, and my first impulse is
To take to market – I will turn it under.
The thought from that thought – I will turn it under.
And so on to the limit of my nature.
We are too much out, and if we won't draw in
We shall be driven in.

Lippmann, for his part, offered advice to the scholar that seemed, at least at first look, to be in consilience with Frost's. He cautioned against the excesses of the scholar's involvement in matters "outside" the library. As the *New York Times* reported, "Mr. Lippmann contended that the 'scholar' who deserts his books and his research to heed the importunate demands of the present does not do justice to himself and the world."

> For this is not the last crisis in human affairs. The world will go on somehow and more crises will follow. It will go on best, however, if among us there are men who stood apart, who refused to be too anxious or too much concerned, who were cool and inquiring, and had their eyes on a longer past and a longer future. By their example they can remind us that the passing moment is only a moment; by their loyalty they will have cherished those things which only the disinterested mind can use.[1]

Frost might go so far as to agree that the scholar (or poet or statesman) must not leap into the middle of things in reaction to the pressures of the moment. But that he should permanently refrain from direct involvement, if that was what Lippmann advocated, was anathema to the poet who continued to harbor ancient thoughts about the poet's responsibilities to the world as he found it. If he had stoically awaited the recognition due his poems until he was nearly forty, Frost would await patiently for the time when he might be called upon to perform some meaningful public service on his country's behalf.

Meanwhile, in the 1930s, during Franklin Delano Roosevelt's first two terms as President of the United States, Frost would take on the role, at times, of the loyal opposition. He would speak out against the national government's meddling in the affairs of the individual American citizen, who should be independent of such organized manipulation and control as the Founding Fathers and as Henry David Thoreau had insisted he be. In his most strikingly political poem of the 1930s, "Two Tramps in Mud Time" (published in the *Saturday Review of Literature* in 1934), Frost questioned the basic premise of practicing social welfare to the detriment of an individual's right to well-being. For instance, should he give over the pleasurable and gratifying task of chopping his own wood to the two tramps whose creature needs staked their claim to the task and the compensation that goes with it? Or do his own, quite different needs justify his insistence on continuing with the task himself? It becomes a question of pitting the needs of spirit, aspiration, and self-fulfillment against the need for working for food. The poem's celebrated conclusion sums up explicitly the poet's answer to this antinomy.

> Nothing on either side was said.
> They knew they had but to stay their stay
> And all their logic would fill my head:
> As that I had no right to play
> With what was another man's work for gain,
> My right might be love but theirs was need.
> And where the two exist in twain
> Theirs was the better right – agreed.
> But yield who will to their separation,
> My object in living is to unite
> My avocation and my vocation
> As my two eyes make one in sight.
> Only where love and need are one,
> And the work is play for mortal stakes,
> Is the deed ever really done
> For Heaven and the future's sakes.

Only when the two rights at question here – those of love and those of need – exist apart and come into conflict will he capitulate: need comes first. But the poet will take an even higher road on the matter by revealing that the greater principle (reflecting Thoreau's basic argument "Life Without Principle") is that the needs of the self are paramount in its constant struggle against the destructive pressures of socialization – or, as Frost put it elsewhere, socialism. The aim was always to bring love and need into consilience, to turn work and play into one thing indivisible. Frost fully agreed with Thoreau when he warned: "Do not hire a man who does your work for money, but him who does it for love of it", for "if the laborer gets no more than the wages which his employer pays him, he is cheated, he cheats himself."[2] It was on this basis that Frost questioned Roosevelt's New Deal domestic policies, which were based, as the poet saw it, on unreasoned and indefensible principles of political economy that resulted in hasty, wavering, and vacillating, yet invariably dangerous measures. In *The New Frontier* for September 1934, eighteen months after Franklin Delano Roosevelt took office, Frost published "Provide, Provide," a poem inspired by the strike of charwomen at Harvard University that satires the principles, policies, and practices of the welfare state implicit in the New Deal.

> Die early and avoid the fate.
> Or if predestined to die late,
> Make up your mind to die in state.
>
> Make the whole stock exchange your own!
> If need be occupy a throne,
> Where nobody can call you crone.
>
> Some have relied on what they knew;
> Others on being simply true,
> What worked for them might work for you.
>
> No memory of having starred
> Atones for later disregard,
> Or keeps the end from being hard.
>
> Better to go down dignified
> With boughten friendship at your side
> Than none at all. Provide, provide!

Frost liked to tell the story of his having once recited the poem to an audience in Washington, with "a very important friend in front." "To rub it in," after reciting the final three lines, he repeated, "'Provide, provide!' adding ominously, "Or somebody else'll provide for you!" And then – "to make it deeper still" – he asked, "'And how'll you like that?'"[3] Frost's highly placed friend was Henry Wallace, who served as Vice-President during Roosevelt's third term, ran for the Presidency as the Progressive Party's candidate in 1948, and stood out as the most socialist-minded politician of prominence in the Washington of his day.

In the *Saturday Review* in January 1936, shortly after Roosevelt was elected to his second term as President, Frost published "To a Thinker in Office" (collected the next year, in *A Further Range*, as "To a Thinker"). His theme was the inconstancy and vacillation demonstrated by those currently exercising political power in and out of office. It was widely taken to be an anti-Roosevelt poem.

> The last step taken found your heft
> Decidedly upon the left.
> One more would throw you on the right.
> Another still – you see your plight.
> You call this thinking, but it's walking.
> . . .
> Just now you're off democracy

(With a polite regret to be),
And leaning on dictatorship;
But if you will accept the tip,
In less than no time, tongue and pen,
You'll be a democrat again,

. . .

Suppose you've no direction in you,
I don't see but you must continue
To use the gift you do possess,
And sway with reason more or less.
I own I never really warmed
To the reformer or reformed.
And yet conversion has its place
Not halfway down the scale of grace.
So if you find you must repent
From side to side in argument,
At least don't use your mind too hard,
But trust my instinct – I'm a bard.

Frost later revealed that he had not originally had Roosevelt in mind, but that he would not deny the identification when others read the poem that way. He wanted his poems put to use. In fact, "the pleasantest use of a poem," he said, was "seeing a fragment of it quoted in an editorial, we'll say, in a New York paper." "That's a very great triumph."[4] "To a Thinker" had been put to a definite political use that he approved of. As he said at the age of eighty-four, "I don't want to run for office, but I want to be a politician" (*I*, 192).

Frost's long-standing desire to be of public use, along with his hope that his work be useful to the common good, comes to the fore in the more explicit political aspects of his poetry of the 1930s. This turn away from the more purely subjective lyrics and narrative poems of his first five volumes was widely regretted and deplored by many of his critics. Indeed, so marked was the academic and intellectual repudiation of Frost, especially after the publication of *A Further Range* in 1937, that it took two brilliantly revisionary essays by Randall Jarrell a decade or more later, in the late 1940s and early 1950s, to recall Frost's readers to what Jarrell pointed to as constituting Frost's genuine contributions to poetry. Focusing on poems that showed Frost at his lyrical and narrative best, Jarrell significantly made no case for Frost's more public poetry. He did not mention "Build Soil," with its profoundly conservative message, for instance, or "Departmental," a satire on regimentation, specialization, and socialism. For a generation or more, in fact, much of Frost's political poetry was dismissed as "telling" rather than "showing." Frost's sententiousness in such poems, it was asserted, diminished the poet's overall achievement – a charge that would stick to Frost for the rest of his life and beyond. Still, while the critics disapproved, Frost continued to write his political poetry. At the conclusion of a network television interview conducted when he was serving as Consultant in Poetry at the Library of Congress, he complained that while the half-hour was up, they had not yet "settled anything!"

Frost's larger complaint about his stay in Washington was that no member of Congress ever consulted with him. He did not know, of course, that what lay ahead of him was something better than talking things over with one or two members of the United States Congress.

II

There was a long lead-time before Frost was put to his nation's use by being sent on a cultural mission to the Soviet Union. He first represented the United States, in a small way, in South America. In 1954, under the aegis of the United States Information Agency, the Department of State had sent him to South America as a delegate to the International Writers' Conference in São Paulo, Brazil. In improvised remarks to the assembly he noted that there was a tendency to see the United States as something of a monster. "I won't say anything about Russia, which perhaps does want to dominate the world," he continued, "but I do want to make it very clear that my country does not in any way want to rule the world."[5] Frost's successful mission to South America encouraged the Department of State to send him to England in 1957, which turned into a series of opportunities for Frost to visit his old friends and the places he had lived in over four decades earlier. His English tour, which saw him honored with degrees from Cambridge, Oxford, and the National University in Dublin, seemed to whet further his appetite for serving his country. Next was the Soviet Union.

The idea to send him to the Soviet Union might have begun with his friend Stewart Udall. Their friendship dated from the late 1950s when Udall was serving in Washington as a congressman from Arizona and Frost was finishing his stint as poetry consultant to the Library of Congress. When Udall heard Frost's complaint that during his term not a single member of congress had asked him for advice, he did his best to redress this slight by having Frost come to dinner. Over the next several years, largely through Udall's good offices but not entirely so, Frost would come to enjoy his closest associations ever with powerful politicians. Frost was capable of helping his own cause. He made it known that he admired Kennedy's book, *Profiles in Courage.* "That fine book, the *Profiles* is about," he would continue to insist to the end of his life, "being somewhat arbitrary, being more answerable to God than you are to your constituents . . . That's a fine idea."[6] And on his eighty-fifth birthday Frost had helped himself further by "predicting" (that is how the Press construed his not so explicit remarks) that Senator John F. Kennedy would be elected the next President of the United States. This "prediction" evoked first a letter from the young Senator Kennedy and led to what was seen later as something of a friendship. But it was not Kennedy who first thought of inviting Frost to participate in his inauguration as President. That honor falls to Udall, who was by that time Kennedy's choice for Secretary of the Interior.

The world saw Frost's performance at the Presidential inaugural ceremony on January 19, 1961.[7] The glaring winter sunlight so annoyed and distracted the seemingly disorganized, somewhat disheveled old man that he gave up his attempt to read the poem he had composed for this most public of readings before his greatest audience ever. He set his new poem aside and went on to recite "The Gift Outright," a piece – tried-and-true – that he knew by heart. But so clearly superior is "The Gift Outright" to the poem he wrote for John Kennedy that some of Frost's readers wondered whether, not only welcoming the opportunity in that moment of confusion to skip his new poem, he had somehow engineered the whole thing (if only subconsciously). Frost's popularity with politicians running the so-called New Frontier administration ran unabated into the next year. Congress voted Frost a Congressional Medal "in recognition of his contributions to American letters," which the President awarded at White House ceremonies on the poet's eighty-eighth birthday. That evening the Stewart Udalls, along with Frost's publishers, Holt, Rinehart and Winston, celebrated the poet's birthday with a dinner in his honor.

All that day, however, Frost had something up his sleeve. Nikita Khrushchev was on his mind. The premier of the USSR had visited the United States in September–October 1960, mainly to attend sessions of the United Nations General Assembly. It was at this time that, to the consternation of some of their readers but mainly to the amusement of many others, the world's newspapers reported on Khrushchev's homely, colloquial, even crude language, his generous use of proverbs, and his non-verbal shenanigans, such as taking off his shoe and pounding it on the desk before him in an effort to bring the assembly to attention.[8]

Khrushchev's use of his shoe as a parliamentary gavel was amusing. Probably only a person well used to walking would have the natural resourcefulness to see that a familiar shoe might be put to uses that had nothing to do with feet. In the poem "The Objection to Being Stepped On" Frost talks about such useful conversions:

At the end of the row
I stepped on the toe
Of an unemployed hoe.
It rose in offense
And struck me a blow
In the seat of my sense.

. . .

You may call me a fool,
But was there a rule
The weapon should be
Turned into a tool?
And what do we see?
The first tool I step on
Turned into a weapon.

Later, in an interview in Moscow, Frost's comments on the atom and war repeated the argument of his poem. "I often think about words now: weapon, tool." "A tool can turn into a weapon," he said. "When the peasants rebelled, they turned their tools of labor into weapons. I often hear that the atom has to become a tool for peace. But you always have to keep in mind that it can be a weapon for war too." (I, 284)

Khrushchev's "shoe" also recalls one of Frost's California poems from the early 1930s. In Los Angeles for the Olympics in 1932, amidst many of the world's greatest living athletes (though not the Russians), Frost remembered that he, too, had accomplished an "Olympic" feat and had only recently written a poem to commemorate it. He called it "My Olympic Record Stride," although he would later shorten the title to "A Record Stride."

In a Vermont bedroom closet
With a door of two broad boards
And for back wall a crumbling old chimney
(And that's what their toes are towards),
I have a pair of shoes standing,
Old rivals of sagging leather,
Who once kept surpassing each other,
But now live even together.

. . .

I wet one last year at Montauk
For a hat I had to save.
The other I wet at the Cliff House
In an extra-vagant wave.
Two entirely different grand children
Got me into my double adventure.
But when they grow up and can read this

I hope they won't take it for censure.
I touch my tongue to the shoes now,
And unless my sense is at fault,
On one I can taste Atlantic,
On the other Pacific, salt.
One foot in each great ocean
Is a record stride or stretch,

. . .

And I ask all to try to forgive me
For being as over-elated
As if I had measured the country
And got the United States stated.

Shoes, tools, proverbs, competition, rivalry, games, Olympics, the United States, the Soviet Union, Khrushchev and Frost – all these are counters in the story of Frost as a poet-statesman. Frost could not have been unaware that the Soviet Union had been rejected *de facto* by the 1932 Olympics committee, which refused to invite that country to participate in the games in Los Angeles. In 1962 things were different. Once, in a discussion about disarmament, Frost had thrown out the suggestion, not entirely facetiously, that the United States might consider entering into a baseball competition with the Soviet Union. Now, perhaps they – the premier and the poet – could get their respective countries on the way to what Frost called one hundred years of magnanimous rivalry. After all, Frost had said of this "a grand man," Khrushchev: "With all the fears of us, and fears of what's behind him and round him there, it doesn't seem to touch him at all . . . He's my enemy," Frost concluded, "but it takes just a little magnanimity to admire him."[9]

It is not clear whether the notion to send Frost to Russia originated with Udall or Frost himself, though most reports credit it to a third party, Anatoly Dobrynin, the Russian Ambassador to the United States. In any event, when the proposal reached the President, he approved it. Udall would accompany Frost, along with Frederick Adams, the director of the Pierpont Morgan Library in New York and a longtime friend of the poet's, and F. D. Reeve, a specialist in Russian literature and culture who taught at Wesleyan University. Ultimately, each of Frost's three companions would write accounts of the trip. Frost, who died within six months of his return from the USSR, did not. Although Frost's visit was entirely cultural – never diplomatic, of course – it is obvious that it was the possibility that he would meet with Khrushchev – or, as he might have thought it, the thing that he could believe into being – that compelled him to make this long journey and to subject himself willingly to a physically and mentally demanding schedule of public readings and events.

Shortly after arriving in Moscow, Frost began to worry that the meeting would not take place. The entire project – despite the warm and enthusiastic reception he received everywhere he went – was, he began to fear, doomed to fail. His momentous talk with Khrushchev would not take place. The story of how it was finally arranged for him to meet the Premier in the final days of the trip, though the poet was almost too ill to travel at all, has been well told elsewhere.[10] What needs to be emphasized here is that finally Frost was able to discuss – face-to-face with the Premier – matters such as cultural exchanges, negotiations over the Berlin wall, the desirability of engaging in magnanimous international rivalries in art, sports, science, and democracy, to maintaining the sterile coexistence of a Cold War. He had met with the enemy and though Khrushchev was a "ruffian" (as Frost would call him rather admiringly) he was nevertheless, Frost was certain, a statesman who understood the nature of words, language, and serious play.

Like everyone else, Frost had seen the signs of all this. On Khrushchev's visit to the United States in 1960 the newspapers had picked up on his penchant for peppering his conversation and cinching his arguments with proverbs and what Frost called "dark sayings." "We drink out of a small glass, but we speak with great feelings," he directed at President Kennedy and himself. The newspapers collected his sayings. On changes in the nature of capitalism, he said, "A black frog cannot be whitewashed." On the production of butter and meat for the Soviet Union, he came up with "A dry spoon will scrape the tongue." On nuclear weapons as a deterrent to war with the West, he said, "A gale of words will not make a windmill turn." And on the decay of Western capitalism, he prophesied, "If you cannot hold on by the man, you will not be able to hold on by the tail."[11] The American poet's own books had always been studded with aphorisms. No exception was *In the Clearing*, a copy of which he would inscribe for Khrushchev in Moscow, just as he had for Kennedy back in Washington. That, too, would be a record stride.

III

The affinity Frost first felt with Khrushchev might have come through their shared confidence in aphorisms, proverbs, and other "dark sayings." It might be useful, therefore, to look into what Frost meant when he used the term "dark sayings," along with his reasons for considering them as spirit-enhancing challenges to those who would interpret not just literature but life itself.

We might begin this investigation by looking at some lines from the poem "Mending Wall."

There where it is we do not need the wall:
He is all pine and I am apple orchard.
My apple trees will never get across
And eat the cones under his pines, I tell him.
He only says, "Good fences make good neighbors."
Spring is the mischief in me, and I wonder
If I could put a notion in his head:
"*Why* do they make good neighbors? Isn't it
Where there are cows? But here there are no cows.
Before I built a wall I'd ask to know
What I was walling in or walling out,
And to whom I was like to give offense.
Something there is that doesn't love a wall,
That wants it down."

. . .

He will not go behind his father's saying,
And he likes having thought of it so well
He says again, "Good fences make good neighbors,"

Most readings of "Mending Wall" are based on the decision as to which of the two voices in the poem – the speaker's or his taciturn neighbor's – speaks the "truth" or, at least, expresses the poet's own view of things. At Bread Loaf in 1955 Frost said this about the poem:

> It's about a spring occupation in my day. When I was farming seriously we had to set the wall up every year. You don't do that any more. You run a strand of barbed wire along it and let it go at that. We used to set the wall up. If you see a wall well set up you know it's owned by a lawyer in New York – not a real farmer. This is just about that spring occupation, but of course all sorts of things have been done with it and I've done something with it myself in self-defense. I've gone it one better – more than once in different ways for the Ned of it – just for the foolishness of it.[12]

Then Frost read "Mending Wall," only to follow its reading with more commentary. The "first person that ever spoke to me about it was at that time becoming the president of Rollins College," Frost started out.

> [H]e took both my hands to tell me I had written a true international poem. And just to tease him I said: "How do you get that?" You know. I said I thought I'd been fair to both sides – both national [and international]. "Oh, no," he said, "I could see what side you were on." And I said: "The more I say I the more I always mean somebody else." That's objectivity, I told him. That's the way we talked about it, kidding. That's where the great fooling comes in. But my latest way out of it is to say: I've got a man there; he's both [of those people but he's man – both of them, he's] a wall builder and a wall toppler. He makes

boundaries and he breaks boundaries. That's man. And all human life is cellular, outside or inside. In my body every seven years I'm made out of different cells and all my cell walls have been changed. I'm cellular within and life outside is cellular. Even the Communists have cells. That's where I've arrived at that.[13]

He noted, too, that "Mending Wall" was "very much taken as a parable."[14] Indeed, since his comments over the years suggest that he agreed with that characterization of the poem, it is profitable to approach the poem as a parable that is centered on the ambiguity of a troublesome proverb. Frost never calls "Good fences make good neighbors" a "dark saying" *per se*, but in a notebook he attributes it to the Spartans. In the same entry he links the Spartans' verbal devices for keeping their wisdom secret from outsiders with St. Mark's parable on the secrecy characteristic of parables. It is Frost's own little secret that "dark saying," related to the proverb, was synonymous with "parable." The linguistic and etymological tracing of these identifications is rehearsed by Frank Kermode in *The Genesis of Secrecy: On the Interpretation of Narrative* (1979). But the matter is put succinctly and clearly in Richard Chevenix Trench's *Notes on the Parables of Our Lord*, an important nineteenth-century study.

> Partly from the fact which has been noted by many, of there being but one word in the Hebrew to signify both parable and proverb; which circumstances must have had considerable influence upon writers accustomed to think in that language, and itself arose from the parable and proverb being alike enigmatical and somewhat obscure forms of speech, "dark sayings," speaking a part of their meaning and leaving the rest to be inferred. This is evidently true of the parable, and in fact no less so of the proverb.[15]

Now, though there is already a good deal written about Frost as a parablist, his identification of the "dark saying" with the parable has been pretty much overlooked. It is not important at this late date that, as Theodore Morrison reports, Frost's friend Hyde Cox had to point out to him, in the early 1940s, that his memory of St. Mark's explanation of why Jesus spoke in parables was faulty. "R. F. did *not* remember" recalled Cox.

> Like many other people, it was his recollection that Christ said something about parables being easier to understand. I gleefully pointed out that this was just the opposite of what Jesus had said, and I read to R. F. the 4th Chapter of the Gospel according to St. Mark. He was delighted and said at once "Does that occur anywhere else?" I then read him the thirteenth Chapter of Matthew especially verses 11–13! The rest of the evening was spent discussing the wisdom and the hardness of this thought. R. F. pointed out that it is the same as for poetry; only those who approach it in the right way can understand it.

And not everyone can understand no matter what they do because it just isn't in them. They cannot "be saved."[16]

In effect, what seems to have happened that night is that St. Mark's own parable about parables came alive for Frost in a new way. He discovered it as an old "dark saying," new to him, which he could fathom precisely because he was a poet who worked in exactly the same way. In his essay "The Prerequisites" (1954, *CPPP*, 814), which introduces *Aforesaid* (a well-made collection commemorating his eighty-fifth birthday), Frost laid out his theory of the "dark saying," along with its implications for reading and, in a negative way, for teaching. I shall limit myself to some excerpts and an observation or two. First of all, the essay is itself a parable about how not to teach poetry, or, better still, how poetry is usually mistaught. For Frost there are no prerequisites for reading poetry.

> A poem is best read in the light of all the other poems ever written. We read A the better to read B (we have to start somewhere, we may get very little out of A). We read B the better to read C, C the better to read D, D the better to go back and get something more out of A. Progress is not the aim, but circulation. The thing is to get among the poems where they hold each other apart in their places as the stars do.[17]

Frost does not say, in so many words, why, having read poem D one might want to go back to poem A. But it can be inferred that there was something in A that one did not understand then but might become clear now after one had experienced other poems. "I don't like obscurity and obfuscation, but I do like dark sayings I must leave the clearing of to time," Frost said. He could just as easily have said "dark poems."

IV

It cannot be said that Frost's colloquy with Khrushchev, the Russian farmer and man of "dark sayings," had made a palpable difference in the confrontational policies of the United States and the Soviet Union. Frost's not entirely accurate comments to reporters awaiting him as he deplaned in New York were reported as unequivocal statements by Khrushchev about American weakness. "Khrushchev said he feared for us modern liberals. He said we were too liberal to fight. I suppose he thought we'd stand there for the next hundred years saying, 'On the one hand – but on the other hand.'"[18] Frost's New York interview became big news and that angered Kennedy. "Why did he have to say that?" the President asked Udall.[19]

The immediate result of Frost's well-meant but misfiring remarks was that Kennedy cut off all further contact with the poet. He showed no interest in hearing what either his poet-diplomat might have had to say in his own defense or in any messages Khrushchev might have asked Frost to relay to an American president (*I*, 289). Events, too, grossly overshadowed Frost's mission. Even as he was meeting with Khrushchev, the Soviet Union was placing its missiles in Cuba. A decade later, Udall would intimate that Khrushchev's meeting with Frost (and separately with Udall) was part of his audacious plan to turn Cuba into a fortress armed against the United States. Be that as it may, Frost's last gesture to claim a grand public role for poetry and for the poet's power to influence policy had melted away before the hard political facts and unexpected world events.[20]

Frost had traveled to the Soviet Union with a plan. On the eve of his departure he set down the lines of that general plan for the benefit of his biographer and as a contribution, perhaps, to history itself. On the fifteenth of August he briefed Lawrance Thompson:

> The issue before Russia and us is which comes nearer – their democracy or ours – placating everybody. I may tell them what the issue is but won't claim it is nothing to fight about. Let's be great about it, not petty with petty twits. We both have a mighty history. I hope we can show ourselves mighty without being ugly. I get round once in so often to the word magnanimity, don't I? I shall be prophesying not just predicting from statistics – talking of the next hundred years ahead. I may tell them theirs is an imperial democracy like Caesar's Rome, ours a senatorial like the Roman republic. I have been having all sorts of ideas but as I say for dignity I shall depend on the poems few will understand [turning them into "dark sayings"?]. I guess you pretty well know my attitude. I shall praise them for art and science and athletics. I may speak of the severity they've been easing down from towards socialism and our liberality we've been straining up from to the same socialism. And then again I may not. I go as an opportunist on the loose. I'd like a chance to ask the great Khrushchev to grant me one request and then ask him a hard one. (*SL*, 592)

Of peculiar interest to the student of Frost, however, is that the poet, who believed that the thing lost in translation was poetry itself, should have put himself and his poetry in the position of being inevitably lost or – at best – misunderstood. A computer translation would render into Russian the English saw "the spirit is willing but the flesh is weak" as "the whiskey is strong but the cow is dead."[21] There are no indications that anything as dramatically distortive happened to Frost's poems when he "said" them in Moscow and Leningrad or when he spoke with Khrushchev in Gagra, but it was readily apparent that getting his poetic messages across was a hit-or-miss affair at best. Nevertheless, he took chances. He read "Departmental," his tale in couplets of the death of the ant Jerry and of the "special Janizary,/ Whose office it is to bury/ The dead of the commissary," which, among other targets, satirizes bureaucracies and all forms of collectivism – the line "our selfless forager Jerry," Frost said, "sums up all socialism"[22] – and should have been readily understood as such by any literate citizen or leader of the Soviet Union. And seemingly on the spur of the moment (and to the surprise of his American companions) he once read a comic anti-war poem that parodies the nursery rhyme "Hey Diddle Diddle". He had published "Lines Written in Dejection on the Eve of Great Success" in *In the Clearing*, his latest and, as it turned out, his last book. The section of the poem labeled "Postscript" reads:

> But if over the moon I had wanted to go
> And had caught my cow by the tail,
> I'll bet she'd have made a melodious low
> And put her foot in the pail;
> Than which there is no indignity worse.
> A cow did that once to a fellow
> Who rose from the milking stool with a curse
> And cried, "I'll larn you to bellow,"
> He couldn't lay hands on a pitchfork to hit her
> Or give her a stab of the tine,
> So he leapt on her hairy back and bit her
> Clear into her marrow spine.
> No doubt she would have preferred the fork.
> She let out a howl of rage
> That was heard as far away as New York
> And made the papers' front page.
> He answered her back, "Well, who begun it?"
> That's what at the end of a war
> We always say – not who won it,
> Or what it was foughten for.

Only Frost would have run the risk of taking on the Russians with a *comic* anti-war fable that had to run the gauntlet of translation. It did not work. "It meant nothing to his audience, though there was a scattering of polite applause," reported his friend Adams.[23] But perhaps Adams missed something. For, although Frost might not have known why, his choice of a poem parodying the nursery rhyme "Hey Diddle Diddle" would have undoubtedly struck a familiar note for some of his Russian listeners. In fact, it has been noted, "English nursery rhymes *en masse* seem to appeal to the children of Russia." "Colourfully illustrated collections have been published in Moscow," write Iona and Peter Opie, with translations made by eminent poets.[24] Frost was decidedly more successful with "Mending Wall." His Russian audiences already knew the poem (it had been translated in the 1930s) and often requested it. If, as will be recalled, Frost had claimed that "the pleasantest use of a poem" was to see "a fragment of it quoted in an editorial,"[25] one can only surmise the number of times "Mending Wall" had been put to use in political discourse, especially in the protracted controversy over the Communist-built wall that divided Berlin. "Perhaps Frost's most apposite line for the present moment in history is his famous: 'Something there is that doesn't love a wall,'" reads the *New York Times* review of *In the Clearing* five months before Frost went to Russia. "Old-stone savage or new-power-hungry savage," the reviewer concludes, "the good-fences-make-good-neighbors philosophy is riddled again in Berlin."[26] That Frost was reading the poem in the Soviet Union became news when the *Times* printed a page of photographs of the poet in audience among the Russians. Several pictures – under the title of "'Mending Wall' in Moscow" – carried a single caption:

> Some of the gentlest mockery the Soviet Union has endured came recently from the 88-year-old poet, Robert Frost, a cultural-exchange visitor. Among other things, he read from his poem, "Mending Wall," in Moscow: "Before I built a wall I'd ask to know/ What I was walling out./ And to whom I was likely to give offense." The reference to Berlin seemed clear, but Frost would not interpret.[27]

Frost, like everyone else, knew America's official position on the wall, and he was in agreement with his President that the wall should come down. It was, after all, consonant with his dictum that nations must be nations before they could go international. But he was also aware that his poem – indeed, all poems – could be put to different uses, just as jokes told on different occasions to different audiences might aim at different purposes and convey different meanings. It is doubtful, therefore, that Frost read the poem merely because his audiences had asked him to include it in his reading. It seems ingenuous to think, therefore, that he did not read it, as Reeve insisted, "as a commentary on Berlin, which one reporter unfortunately interpreted it to be.'"[28]

For some unstated reason Frost had come to trust this man of power who could turn a shoe into a weapon and a proverb into a tool. It was that trust and a considerable faith in himself that took Frost at the end of his life to Russia. He had no wish to confront the Premier of the Soviet Union before a worldwide audience as President Eisenhower's Vice-President Richard Nixon had ended up doing. He wanted no equivalent of a kitchen debate with Nikita Khrushchev. Rather, he would talk with the Premier – on a very high plane – of national accomplishments such as the flight of the Wright Brothers at Kitty Hawk. He had entitled one of his latest poems "How Hard It Is to Keep from Being King When It's in You and in the Situation," and now, in his eighty-ninth year, he found himself in the rough equivalent of such a situation. Knowing that words are deeds, he now had an opportunity to prove that grand deeds can also be poems.

In fact, even when it became public knowledge, almost immediately after his return from Russia, that things had turned dark for the two super-powers, he remained preoccupied with what he considered to have been his wondrous trip to the Soviet Union and his one-on-one meeting with Khrushchev. At the National Poetry Festival in Washington in October 1962, still hoping for a debriefing meeting with the President, he went over those recent events:

> Everything was so nice, with the great man, too. Just what I wanted him to be; and talked, and went the whole length, everywhere – the greatness of it.
>
> The biggest thing about it was that he wanted – he agreed with me that the great thing was to make the issue great; not to have petty squabbles decide it. The great issue between our two kinds of democracy, we called it. I called it that myself, in courtesy, and he agreed to that. Big – make it magnificent, you know, the great world thought – next hundred years. And whatever came, we didn't name the word "war." We didn't talk about love or peace or any of those silly things. All talk big, but splendid, and the kind of thing that we could rest in, with big trials – trials of athletics and science and all that – and about democracy: who's produced the greater men, the greater leaders, and all that. And the showdowns, I wasn't talking about those, you know, and he wasn't, but we knew what we meant.[29]

And when Norman Thomas, the best-known American Socialist of his time, asked him for clarification or explanation of what he had been reported as having said upon his arrival in New York, he set down carefully his answer:

> I can't see how Khrushchev's talk got turned into what you quote that we weren't mean enough to fight. I came nearer than he to threatening; with my native geniality I assured him that we were no more afraid of him than he was of us. We seemed in perfect agreement that we shouldn't come to blows till we were sure there was a big issue remaining between us, of his kind of democracy versus our kind of democracy, approximating each other as they are, his by easing downward towards socialism through various phases of welfare state-ism. I said the stage or arena is set between us for a rivalry of perhaps a hundred years. Let's hope we can take it out in sports, science, art, business, and politics before ever we have to take it out in the bloody politics of war. It was all magnanimity – Aristotle's great word. I should have expected you to approve. Liberal in a good sense of the word . . . If only a word would stay put in basic English. (*SL*, 595)

Frost dictated his reply to Thomas, but, keeping it, apparently, for revisions, he did not get to mail it.

"Decency, honor, and not too much deceit," he had cautioned diplomats when leaving Brazil in 1954, "are about the best one can aspire to in international relations."[30] But in his one attempt at high international diplomacy, both quixotic and exemplary, this "opportunist on the loose" (as he called himself) had set aside his own advice to diplomats and tried to believe in his country's future.

NOTES

1 "Democracy Losing, Lippmann Asserts," *New York Times*, June 1, 1932, p. 18.

2 *The Writings of Henry David Thoreau*, vol. IV (Boston: Houghton Mifflin, 1906), p. 459.

3 Reported in *Proceedings, National Poetry Festival Held in the Library Of Congress October 22–24, 1962* (Washington: General Reference and Bibliography Division, Reference Department, Library of Congress, 1964), p. 242.

4 Robert Frost, "'For Glory and for Use,'" *Gettysburg Review*, 7 (Winter 1994), 94.

5 Reported in *Congresso Internacional de Escritores e Encontros Intelectuais* (São Paulo: Anhembi, 1957), p. 482. My translation.

6 *Proceedings, National Poetry Festival*, p. 255.

7 A clip of Frost's recitation at John F. Kennedy's Inauguration is available on CD-ROM, *Robert Frost: Poems, Life, Legacy*, compiled by Joe Matazzoni, ed. Donald Sheehy (New York: Henry Holt, 1997).

8 Benjamin Welles, "Khrushchev Bangs His Shoe on Desk," *New York Times*, October 12, 1960, pp. 1, 14. Khrushchev's shoe-pounding nearly forty years ago is still remembered. See "Cold War satellite images are paying off," *Boston Sunday Herald*, July 12, 1998, p. 23, which begins: "If former Soviet Premier Nikita Khrushchev were alive, he'd have to eat the shoe he pounded in fits of socialist passion as he vowed that capitalism would perish."

9 Russell Baker, "Frost Honored on 88th Birthday; Praises His 'Enemy' Khrushchev," *New York Times*, March 27, 1962, p. 39.

10 See, for example, Frederick B. Adams, Jr., *To Russia with Frost* (Boston: The Club of Odd Volumes, 1963); Stewart L. Udall, "'. . . and miles to go before I sleep': Robert Frost's Last Adventure," *New York Times Magazine* (June 11, 1972); and F. D. Reeve, *Robert Frost in Russia* (Boston and Toronto: Little, Brown, 1964).

11 "A Khrushchev Proverb Begins Second Day of Vienna Meeting," *New York Times*, June 5, 1961, p. 12; and "Khrushchev Gets Off Some More Aphorisms," *New York Times* October 18, 1961, p. 18.

12 Reginald L. Cook, *Robert Frost: A Living Voice* (Amherst: University of Massachusetts Press, 1974), p. 82.

13 *Ibid.*, pp. 82–3.

14 *Ibid.*, p. 55.

15 Richard Chevenix Trench, *Notes on the Parables of Our Lord* (New York: D. Appleton, 1855), pp. 13–14.

16 Theodore Morrison, "The Agitated Heart," *Atlantic Monthly*, 220 (July 1967), 78.

17 Robert Frost, "The Prerequisites," in *Selected Prose of Robert Frost*, ed. Hyde

Cox and Edward Connery Lathem (New York: Holt, Rinehart, and Winston, 1966), p. 97.

18 Philip Benjamin, "Robert Frost Returns With Word of Khrushchev," *New York Times*, September 10, 1962, p. 8.

19 Quoted in Udall, "'. . . and miles to go before I sleep,'" p. 30.

20 In August 1954 Frost was sent, along with William Faulkner, to the International Writers Congress in São Paulo, Brazil. Faulkner was more skeptical about such State Department sponsored visits by writers than was Frost. "The artist is still a little like the old court jester. He is supposed to speak his vicious paradoxes with some sense to them," he told an interviewer in 1955, "but he isn't part of whatever the fabric is that makes a nation. It is assumed that anyone who makes a million dollars has a unique gift, though he might have made it off some useless gadget" *(Lion in the Garden: Interviews with William Faulkner,* ed. James B. Meriwether and Michael Millgate [Lincoln and London: University of Nebraska Press, 1980], p. 82).

21 See Lewis Turco, "Comparative Literature," *College English,* 27 (March 1966), 511.

22 Reading at Brown University, December 7, 1955. "All socialism is bad arithmetic," he told Peter J. Stanlis in 1940, "in which two comes before one." (*Robert Frost: The Individual and Society,* [Rockford, Illinois: Rockford College, 1973], p. 56.)

23 Adams, *To Russia with Frost,* p. 26.

24 Iona and Peter Opie, *A Family Book of Nursery Rhymes* (New York: Oxford University Press, 1964), p. 189.

25 *Ibid.*

26 Charles Poore, "Books of the Times," *New York Times,* March 27, 1962, p. 35.

27 "'Mending Wall' in Moscow," *New York Times Magazine,* September 16, 1962, p. 34.

28 Reeve, *Robert Frost in Russia,* pp. 91–92.

29 *Proceedings, National Poetry Festival,* p. 253. Perhaps contributing to Frost's desire to act the diplomat, was the image of Franklin Delano Roosevelt's destiny to exercise great diplomatic power. In language that recalls the language of "The Lovely Shall Be Choosers," Frost recalled: "And He [God] gives him polio, and then he sits on top of the world along with Stalin and Churchill! That row is forever in my mind." (*I,* p. 157)

30 "Robert Frost, 80, Gives A Recipe for Diplomats," *New York Times,* August 11, 1954, p. 27. Some of the material that informs "Robert Frost's International Diplomacy" was presented at the "Robert Frost Colloquium" at St. Lawrence University, Canton, New York, October 19–30, 1993, and reported in the bulletin of the friends of the Owen D. Young Library.

11

GUY ROTELLA

"Synonymous with Kept": Frost and Economics

We live in an age of epistemes as decals: depthless, portable, easy to peel and carry off. Or so we think. Robert Frost did not. But his epistemes were not firmly anchored either. Here is an example. Frost rejects the gentility and aesthetic dandyism of his immediate predecessors (William Vaughn Moody, say, or Oscar Wilde). They, politely or with disdain, luxuriated in art's imposed or elected exemption from the commerce-based estimates of the Gilded Age. They rejected their culture's exaltation of values associated with industrial manufacture and market capitalism, technology and business – the values of utility and commodity – as ultimate standards of worth. Frost shared their doubt that commercial viability and usefulness alone could properly evaluate all things, but he differed from both genteel and art-for-art's-sake assumptions in taking it for granted that his culture's dominant values were real ones, with their own legitimate, if partial, claims on literature and life. Thus Frost's "realism" of subject matter and treatment, his culturally derived or driven recasting of supposedly feminine poetry as a form of manly prowess and competition, and his "commercial" insistence on "the trial by market everything [including poems] must come to" (*CPPP*, 845) seem to exist at a chill, even polar remove from Wilde's heated, anti-utilitarian faith that life imitates art. But the complications twist, then turn. Frost's passionate preference for Jamesian "wishful" thinking, his insistence that knowledge is metaphorical, his subtle but persistent intertextuality, his unmooring of meaning from fixity, and his pleasure in parodic appropriation all have a Wilde, postmodern savor. At the same time, in a century of suspicious writing and reading, Frost's multiple subversions seem somehow "reassuring."[1] It might be put like this: extremes in Frost's work, such as the near (if only apparent) Social Darwinist, businesslike dismissal of feeling in "'Out, Out – ','" on the one hand, and the genteel sparing of beauty from the fiscal pragmatics of haying in "The Tuft of Flowers," on the other, have their meanings only in relation.

Such unresolvable intricacies – the sort exemplified by the rich mixture of conformity and rebellion in Frost's expansively economical economic remark that "Strongly spent is synonymous with kept" – account for an emphasis that unites the diverse accents of the best Frost criticism of the past twenty years. A review of that criticism can prepare for a consideration of some of Frost's intricate attitudes toward things economic. Richard Poirier, Katherine Kearns, and Mark Richardson stress poetry, gender, and prose poetics, respectively, in their work, but they all represent Frost as writing and thinking in terms of binary oppositions which he treats neither as mutually exclusive options nor as the poles of an ironically balanced whole. Instead, Frost treats contraries as relational parties in ever shifting arrangements behind and across borders that link what they separate. Moreover, while Frost treats oppositions as relational and unstable, he also provides a reassuring sense of stability achieved (however momentarily), *and* he additionally indicates that stability itself is provisional in its turn, neither enforced nor enforceable, local and situational, not global.

The now ubiquitous terms "constructivist" and "essentialist" do not appear in Richard Poirier's *Robert Frost: The Work of Knowing* (1977), but they condense an important aspect of his argument there. Poirier is seismographically sensitive to Frost's shaking up of stability, his poetry's alertness to the slippage between sign and signified, to the arbitrariness of language and thought and of literary and cultural structures. But Poirier also marks where Frost stops short of a fully constructivist view. Some nineteenth-century writers, many modernists, and most postmodernists conceive of received religious beliefs, social and political systems, and economic and literary practices as more or less arbitrary human constructions handed down from the past. For them, it usually follows that those constructions (including language, which they see as creating or constraining rather than conveying reality) are inappropriate to contemporary needs and conditions and thus responsible for many cultural woes, especially when their conventions are made systematic and taken to be natural and inevitable. At the same time, precisely because those outworn and culpable practices are conceived of as constructed rather than natural, they are considered amenable to subversion and change, perhaps to progressive subversion and change.

Frost's formative years were in the nineteenth century, and his work has both modern and postmodern attributes. However subversive he was in ways associated with anti-representational and constructivist explanations, Frost trusted language (despite, even because of its being slippery or opaque; we might say he made a linguistic half-turn). And Frost distrusted progressive models, refused to blame contingent social arrangements for fundamental human griefs (although grievances were another matter), and was apt to see certain of his inheritances as natural and unchangeable, perhaps in part because what Poirier calls "his near-mystical acceptance of responsibility for himself" would have been disabled by a fully constructivist position. When Frost's sometimes essentialist view expands to include not only loss and death as permanent and inevitable (there, even a strict constructivist might agree) but also such matters as poverty, war, and inequality, Poirier marks him down as an essentialist who "talks as if history not only partakes of nature but is identical with it."[2] Yet Frost thinks even the inevitable might be – must be – resisted. And whatever recent and contemporary views may stress, the proportions of the essential and the culturally constructed in our condition are as resistant to exact measurement as the mixture of nature and nurture in our selves. As Poirier says, what he judges to be Frost's "limitations of historical vision" are also "the necessary conditions of an ennobling achievement,"[3] an achievement that shows Frost both as "constructively" subverting essentialist thinking and as subject to such thinking. To put it in other terms, Frost could say and mean both this: "When the meaning goes out of anything, as happens, forms crumble" (*CPPP*, 756), and this: "When in doubt there is always form for us to go on with" (*CPPP*, 740), and a good deal in between.

Katherine Kearns' examination of Frost and gender in *Robert Frost and a Poetics of Appetite* (1994) reflects similar complications. She argues that Frost's poetics is aroused by a paradox: *the human* desire for rational behavior is housed in bodies (the human body and the world's) that refuse rational control. Frost erects a "sexualized metaphorical structure" upon that paradox. Within that binary structure, whatever in the self and world is erotically attractive yet likely to lead to formless exhaustion is projected on a "female" other that includes women, nature, poetry, and language, while whatever in the self and world resists attraction and exhaustion is figured as male. Kearns demonstrates that Frost operates within the terms of this conventionally essentialist sexist projection, but she also shows that he does so while remaining thoroughly doubtful about the meaning and value of all of its constituent, apparently hierarchical parts: man and woman, prose and poetry, silence and speech, order and wildness, reason and appetite – ambivalent in ways that subvert essentialism as well as confirm it. Thus Frost's use of irony, his treatment of women characters, the role of eros in his work, his thinking about poetic form, and his embrace and spurning of lyric all involve a relational multiplicity which prevails over any system. For all its appearance of rational, manly candor, Frost's poetry nonetheless shares the dangerous, transformative powers he fearfully identifies as female. Even his defenses are invitations; he insists on polyvalent interpretations and undercuts meaning to keep the reader at bay and draw the reader in.

Mark Richardson's *The Ordeal of Robert Frost* (1997) restores Frost's prose poetics to their place within the literary and cultural debates of his day (in places following leads set out in Poirier's work and in Frank Lentricchia's *Modernist Quartet*). Matters of gender also figure in those debates, and, again, Frost's negotiations of opposed pairs are shown to be irresolvably intricate and remarkably shaded. The general feminization of culture in late-nineteenth and early twentieth-century America exempted poetry, along with religion, children, and women, from the arenas of competition, aggression, and acquisitiveness that concerned it most. Whether it meant to demean and exclude or to idealize and protect, the dominant culture tended to group the poetic, the spiritual, the innocent, and the female together at the culture's margins, thus rendering them all effectively irrelevant to a public center focused on business and manufacture. Male poets born in the Gilded Age and reaching maturity at the turn of the twentieth century confronted a context in which a business-dominated society judged their chosen work not to be worthwhile work at all, and certainly not manly work. Responses were often extreme. Genteel poets welcomed their exclusion from masculine business culture, for instance. They made irrelevance a virtue and saw their refined, elevating poems as a refuge from the "crude," "lowering" materialism around them. Others, Ezra Pound is an example, "manfully" rebelled, reasserting poetry's virile, socially central place and offering modernist experiments as correctives both to the culture-destroying values of business (beauty "Decreed in the marketplace") and to the supposedly effeminate squeamishness about reality of genteel verse ("emotional slither").

Frost's position is more delicate than Pound's and more vigorous than the genteel poets'. More nuanced, it is obedient and rebellious at once, as Richardson shows. Frost both resisted his society's feminization of the poet's work and honored its privileging of commercial competition and conventionally manly virtues when he praised the marketplace, likened the poet's words to battle-cries and military or business ultimatums, and compared the poet's craft to the male athlete's physical prowess. But he also idealized poetry, exempted it from the rules of the marketplace, and considered it feminine. To some readers, such flexible maneuvers signal spiritual drift or a manipulative, self-serving trimming of sails to current conditions. But manipulations, those endless adjustments, maintain a craft's motion. Richardson suggests that Frost's seeming inconsistencies, here and elsewhere, derive from his locating within individuals those opposites which individuals are usually thought to select from, so that the Apollonian or Dionysian choice the genteel poets or Pound could make, Frost could not, or would not – did not, in any case.

Meanwhile, for all his emphasis on multiplicity, provisional maneuver, inconsistency, and subtle gradation, Frost also affirms an essential duplicity underlying whatever cultural construction obtains in this or that time or place. In some sense this duplicity is permanent, but any actual manifestation of it in the momentary realizations of lives, works, and cultural arrangements involves duplicity's components in ever shifting relations. One set of Frost's names for those components is "conformity" and "formity"; another is "alien entanglements" and individual "will." Essentialist and constructivist views might be yet another. As Richardson puts it, in literary terms, the convergence of opposed "disciplines" from without (nature and culture) and within (the individual self) is Frost's . . . "constant symbol of the poet's struggle to socialize his art in an audience and in the literary marketplace and yet preserve its singular integrity and temper."[4] More generally, the engagement of the individual poet's will with received poetic and linguistic forms to see what can be changed and what persists is, in Frost's poems, a type or metaphor of the endless engagement of individual human wills with life and with the received religious, political, and social forms built from and upon it in order to see what in them is conventional, culturally constructed, and amenable to experiment and reconstrual, and what, if anything, is essential and ineluctable. Although they may not please either thoroughgoing essentialists or constructivists, including those who see the self as not at all constructed or as wholly so, such engagements – including "momentary stays" – are irresolvably relational for Frost. They characterize the treatment of economic matters in his life and work, matters which are themselves present there not in isolation but enmeshed with other experiences, subjects, and themes.

Horatio Alger's final book appeared in 1900; it is called *Out for Business, or Robert Frost's Strange Career.*[5] The poet Robert Frost was twenty-six then, and he probably had little call to distinguish himself from Alger's hero, since any observable progress from rags to riches by pluck and luck on his part was well in the offing. The first half of Frost's long life, his "strange career," was marked more by economic decline than improvement; conversely, though, the second half was marked by considerable public acclaim and relative financial success. Perhaps it is not surprising that Frost's attitude toward his economic circumstances – as toward so many other things: inherited poetic forms, for instance – mixes obedient acceptance of those circumstances (seeing them as not only given but natural) with elements of rebellion, critique, and subversion that resist his circumstances and call their "naturalness" into question.

Frost's grandfather had risen from farmer to mill foreman and overseer; his son, Frost's father, graduated from Harvard before marrying a fellow teacher and moving to San Francisco to make a sometimes precarious living in newspaper writing and politics. When, after a series of career disappointments and increasingly unbalanced behavior, his father died of tuberculosis in 1885, Frost was eleven. By the time his mother had paid the funeral expenses and sold the furniture from the family's rented rooms, they had $8.00, and Frost's paternal grandparents were required to send the fare to bring Frost's mother, himself, his younger sister, and his father's body "home" to Massachusetts. The Frost family's version of the classic American journey West for freedom, fame, and profit had failed, and Frost's association of death and displacement with the collapse of his father's hopes for preferment and economic advancement by way of party politics may have contributed to his lifelong distrust of systematic solutions – especially political solutions – to social and economic woes. In the meantime, young Frost had also heard about alternatives or adjustments to capitalism. For almost nine years his father worked for Henry George's *Daily Evening Post*. George in those days was writing and promoting *Progress and Poverty* (1879), his socialist manifesto; Frost's parents were friendly with George (who went out of his way to visit the widow and her children after their move to Massachusetts), and they were sympathetic to his promotion of free enterprise without private monopolies, a kind of economic freedom within restraint Frost might have liked.

The Frost family's declining fortunes were especially precipitous for Frost's mother. Orphaned in Scotland, she was raised in the Ohio home of her uncle, a prosperous, socially prominent banker. Having in some eyes married beneath her, now widowed and poor, alone with two children, her dour in-laws somewhat grudging of financial help, and herself proud against charity, she struggled to make ends meet by teaching school. The work was physically demanding (maintaining discipline was beyond her, a fact that cost her several positions), but it was also work in keeping with her genteel sense of propriety and status. Mrs. Frost's wages were low, and the family lived in a series of cheap rented rooms in Lawrence and Methuen and in Salem, New Hampshire. Soon, Frost was taking odd jobs to help with family finances. In the period between 1886 and his graduation from high school in 1892, Frost worked for brief periods in a shoe factory and a back yard leather-cutting operation, at cutting hay, as a handyman at a seaside resort, as a farmhand, and as bobbin-boy at one woolen mill and a gatekeeper at another. If he enjoyed the varied people he encountered and the new skills he was learning, he often quit his jobs in boredom or frustration. Then and later, his times of regular employment were punctuated by periods of illness and idleness which some characterized as evasive, shiftless, or lazy. The family's persistent, sometimes desperate need for money, Frost's memory of his father's financial efforts and failures, his mother's gentility (including her intense admiration of poetry and books), his own temperamental rejection of his paternal grandparents' real or perceived tendency to equate human value with property and economic position (a rejection that also partially internalized the values it meant to put aside), and a passionate preference for the leisure to read and write, all combined to make Frost deeply ambivalent about work and worth.

As we will see, in poetry, Frost's conflicting feelings and ideas about those (as other) duplicitous matters could meet and be expressed. They would not be resolved. Although such a sentence as "Strongly spent is synonymous with kept" *promises* resolution, seeming to unify idler and worker, spender and saver in an activity so intense (say, making love, or poems) that mere economic laws are suspended, it also reasserts those laws in just the divergent oppositional terms ("spent," "kept") the epigram intends (or pretends) to overcome. As Richardson puts it, resolution or transcendence "constitutes . . . an enduring concern" for Frost, but he "finally entertains this transcendence only as a kind of *unrealizable* ideal."[6]

To return to Frost's life, after his aborted term at Dartmouth, little changed. A number of minor teaching and tutoring jobs alternated with periods of unemployment and job-seeking, a brief turn at newspaper writing, an even briefer stint promoting an elocutionist's recitations of Shakespeare, and work as a lamp trimmer in one more woolen mill. There, Frost had the experience of being locked out and having his pay docked for turning up late; he responded by simply walking away from his job. That event gave rise to "The Lone Striker," a poem typical of Frost's mixed attitudes toward economic matters: he protests against the petty rigidities of capitalism and its punishment of those who can least afford it, but he makes his "social" protest a private matter. Enacted by a capable agent rather than a victim, that protest is a rebellion of avoidance or evasion rather than confrontation, a rebellion that leaves the system that prompted it more or less comfortably intact.

For most of his life, Frost would live on the margins of middle-class versions of career, respectability, and success (and dress the part): he never took a college degree, he changed jobs and houses often and irregularly, he lived by his wits, and until he was well past sixty his finances were nearly always strained. This was an implicit critique of capitalist economics and an active refusal of its rules and values. Yet Frost also admired – and was apt to see as inevitable – an economic system seemingly based on what he considered "natural" competition and struggle, one that rewarded performance and prowess. His own prowess enabled him to make his living at the system's edges, in its nooks and crannies, without suffering its harsher alienations and without surrendering the free time he wanted and needed to do his own supposedly useless creative work. Later in life, when that work had given him reputation and employment, he would sometimes recast his past in laissez-faire terms, implying that his own meritocratic rise from obscurity and poverty proved that the system works, a position that kept his own achievement on view to be admired by keeping the economic circumstance of his victory in place and its rules in play. Those attitudes were also partly determined by the capitalist–communist agon that dominated US economic and political discussion and action from the time of the Russian Revolution in 1917, when Frost was in his early forties, until his death during the Cold War (although Frost could praise Marx for seeing through an old metaphor and installing a new one, he deeply distrusted collectivism of any stripe). Frost's notorious dislike of the New Deal is related to those matters, too, as it is also related to "his near-mystical acceptance of responsibility for himself," to quote Poirier again, and to his Judeo-Christian and psychological (and capitalist) emphasis on the inevitability and necessity of a final judgment, based on merit and "works," and exercised by an ultimate authority, whether construed as God, his absent father, long-term literary reputation, or the free market's final judgment of winners and losers, saved and damned. In Frost's view, too much economic determinism or too much financial assistance would render both individual performance and final judgment nugatory or moot and would empty life and work of meaning.

To come back once more to chronology, Frost's most extended employment in the years after he left Dartmouth was teaching in his mother's school, which he continued to do until 1897, when, borrowing tuition money from his grandfather (he later won a scholarship for the excellence of his work), Frost entered Harvard as a special student, hoping to qualify as a high school teacher of Greek and Latin. In the interval, he had married, and he and Elinor had had their first child. Frost's financial responsibilities had grown; now he wanted to improve his ability to meet them without wholly giving up his hope to have leisure to write, although "leisure" is hardly the word.

Near the end of his second Harvard year, himself ailing, and worried about Elinor's second pregnancy and his mother's illness and increasing need for help with her teaching, Frost resigned from the college and returned to Lawrence. Advised by his doctor to engage in outdoor work (there was fear he had tuberculosis), Frost decided to become a farm-poultryman, raising chickens for eggs and meat. Perhaps this felt like a reversion to the position from which his grandfather had risen, as his failure to graduate from Harvard might have seemed a falling off from his father's attainment. Frost rented a house and barn in Methuen, borrowing money from his grandfather in a formal business arrangement (an interest rate was determined and promissory notes were drawn). Soon, the Frosts' second child was born, and poultry farming was successful enough (and sufficiently troublesome, too: the Methuen landlady complained about slow payment of rent and of chickens invading her kitchen) that his grandfather bought a Derry, New

Hampshire, farm, where the business could expand. Frost's grandfather held the deed and provided a handyman. On his own but greatly dependent, Frost felt these economic arrangements as both a help and a hindrance; for years he had difficulty sorting out his mixed feelings of gratitude, shame, and resentment, and he retained a lifelong ambivalence toward his grandfather's conventional ideas about the virtues of labor, success, and financial stability, as he also did toward matters of personal achievement and outside assistance.

Shortly before the move to Derry, the Frosts' first child, Elliott, died of *cholera infantum*, and Frost and Elinor suffered and somehow endured the desolating marital strains suggested in "Home Burial." Shortly after the move, his mother died in a sanatorium. Frost's grief was sometimes suicidal, but he survived, and then, in 1901, his grandfather died. The will of William Prescott Frost, Sr. granted Frost "free use and occupancy" of the Derry farm for the first ten years after his grandfather's death; then the farm would belong to him. In addition, Frost would receive $500 annually during those first ten years and $800 a year thereafter. This was generous, of course, but also sternly pragmatic; it may have seemed grudging: the will's language insisted that Frost's ten-year free occupancy was "subject however to the duties imposed by law upon life tenants as to taxes, insurance, and repairs." Perhaps Frost's grandfather, although in the long run he was wrong in hard-headedly dismissing his grandson's ability to make a living as a poet, had good reason to impose some safeguards on his sometimes wayward heir. In any event, during the Derry years, Frost's farming was desultory, he was sometimes spendthrift, was often in debt, once borrowed a considerable sum he never repaid, and frequently harried the executor for advances on his annuity. He was also writing splendid poems, although with nearly no success in placing them (five poems were taken in the twelve years from 1895 to 1906), and he tried to make money by writing prose (Frost sold eleven short pieces on the economics – and extra-economic pleasures – of keeping chickens, at ten dollars each – the pieces, not the chickens). By 1906, Frost's financial difficulties caused him to seek regular employment, and he took a teaching job at Pinkerton Academy, where he stayed until 1911 (the family left the farm in 1909). In 1911, his classroom methods having garnered attention, Frost was recruited to teach at the Plymouth Normal School. That same year, and as soon as he legally could, Frost sold the by then twice-mortgaged Derry farm, probably for less than his grandfather had paid for it, although in later years, by some inventive accounting, he idealized the sale as a financial coup.[7]

The Derry years had been a time of loss and recuperation, failure and success, dependence and independence. Frost's work as a farmer had been unremunerative, but it had allowed him the freedom to write, and he had been able to find conventional employment when he needed it, and of a kind in which his imaginative performance won him praise and increased his self-confidence. He had been both improvident and resourceful. Now in his late thirties, he had a large family, a stable position with prospects, and a considerable sheaf of fine if mostly unpublished poems. He was close to achieving the sort of respectability and financial status his grandfather could have admired, and with at least some room in his life for writing. But teaching increasingly threatened to reduce that room to nothing, or to exhaust him to the point where he could not use what room he had. Frost's well-known response was to resign from teaching and leave for England, where he had no prospects whatever. In the period just before departure, he had begun to have greater success in selling his poems to magazines, but the famous events of the British publication of *A Boy's Will* and *North of Boston* by Nutt were nonetheless startling. When the Frosts returned to the US in 1915, he was almost overnight a well-known poet, able to use his grandfather's annuity (which continued to be paid until 1923) to buy a New Hampshire farm, and ready – at the late age of just over forty – to set out on that combination of writing, teaching, and "barding around" that defined the rest of his life.

Frost's timing was good, and lucky. Although he was nearly broke when he returned from England, interest in poetry in America was suddenly strong: magazines and publishers wanted his poems. Public readings were popular, and colleges were about to experiment with hiring artists-in-residence. Frost, overcoming timidity and demonstrating skills of self-promotion, was gradually able to cobble together a living from activities related to his poetry – readings and talks and teaching brought in far more than royalties or magazine payments – while keeping the poetry itself largely free of commercial pressures: he would not write to order or force his rate of production. On the other hand, his cobbled living was just that, and rarely stable. For many years, Frost's teaching positions were temporary and uncertain and his schedule of readings and talks a burden on his writing time, his family, and his health. Several of his children remained dependent on him throughout his life, adding to his financial responsibilities. Although the Depression barely harmed his earnings, and he left a considerable estate at his death in 1963 (with the bulk of its value his manuscripts, his Cambridge house, and the Miami and Ripton, Vermont, prefab and log cabins), he never had significant savings or investments. His homes were spartan and his style of living abstemious. He was open-handedly generous with his children and with certain of his friends, but he could also drive hard bargains, as with his publisher and the colleges who vied for his presence. In any case, even the narrowly economic events of Frost's nearly fifty remaining years are too many and too complex for summary here. My concern has been to suggest some of the biographical sources and contexts of Frost's mixed attitudes toward the economic circumstances in which he found himself. Now I want to discuss a few representative examples of how those mixed attitudes of resistance and acceptance appear in his work.

In the years after court patronage and before the National Endowment for the Arts and university creative writing programs, a major economic issue for most poets was the basic one of how to earn a living. Among Frost's contemporaries, T. S. Eliot worked in banking and publishing, Marianne Moore was an editor and a librarian, H. D. received financial support from Bryher, and Wallace Stevens and William Carlos Williams had careers in insurance law and medicine, respectively. In his twenties and thirties, Frost used a combination of farming, teaching, and his grandfather's liberating and burdensome financial assistance to free enough time from remunerative labor to permit him to do the poet's work. Then, from mid-life on, he got his living from activities connected with writing. Book royalties and magazine appearances brought in some money, but most of Frost's later income came from teaching and from readings and talks, as he exchanged public display of an increasingly honed platform persona for salaries, honoraria, and fees. But well before Frost worked out his successful accommodation with economic necessity, considerations of economic and other vocational conflicts appear in his work, usually quite indirectly and, to say it again, enmeshed with other experiences, subjects, and themes. The early poem "In Neglect" can serve as an example.

The poem's title implies a social position, and "In Neglect" is a condensed social comedy; it lightly mocks both policing adult authorities (the parental "they" who expect the young to prove productive in the world of work) and the idle young lovers who evade those expectations ("we"). In the process, and by treating contraries as relational rather than as mutually exclusive or as amenable to synthesis or resolution, the poem conceives a society whose rules and limits (some of them economic) are both more roomy and more ineluctably real than either profit-demanding adults or work-avoiding young lovers presume them to be.

> They leave us so to the way we took,
>   As two in whom they were proved mistaken,
> That we sit sometimes in the wayside nook,
> With mischievous, vagrant, seraphic look,
>   And *try* if we cannot feel forsaken.   (*CPPP*, 25)

The poem has a biographical context. Family elders on both sides doubted the wisdom of Frost's marriage to Elinor White. Although this promising pair had been co-valedictorians of their high school class, Frost was without prospects; he had dropped out of college and wanted to be a poet, work without pay. He could not expect to meet the masculine responsibilities of keeping a wife and children. No doubt parental disapproval felt to the young couple like neglect or punishment (a shaming), and the poem like revolution or revenge. "In Neglect" does make love's and poetry's case against the dully reasonable demand that Frost get a job and make a living. Ignored by others, the lovers luxuriate in being left to their own devices. They devise a bower of bliss, a sexually charged "nook" where their idle and erotic waywardness makes itself Edenically at home in a place without economics where they can try on roles more various than those society would fix them in. Their disruptive extravagance is a carnival and carnal celebration. It playfully subverts the workaday certitudes of categorical logic ("proved mistaken") and the disappointed adult values the quoted phrase implies, including the practical American expectation that scholarly successes would lead to social and financial ones.

But if its carnival strain disdains and avoids the "responsible" worlds of money and work, "In Neglect" has a chastening counter-strain as well, just as the luxuries and lecheries of carnival signal a farewell to flesh and precede a term of laborious self-denial. For all their energy and seraphic grace, the angelic young lovers are also coy, even stuffy, as if in posturing – playing, theatrically, to an audience (note the italicized "try") – they have already begun to fall toward the "socialized" adult economies they believe they are exempt from. More important in terms of Frost's characteristic inclusiveness in such matters, the neglected lovers are themselves guilty of neglecting the permissive role their "neglectful" elders have played in actually granting to them – by seeming to neglect them – the safe trysting and trying place they imagine they have created for themselves. This, too, has economic resonance. If the terms "proved mistaken" and "neglect" reflect Frost's sense that his grandfather's strings-attached financial aid was both too intrusively helpful and not nearly helpful enough, the exposure of the young lovers' complicitous mix of innocence and knowing manipulation reveals both gratitude and guilt.

To put it in other ways, the poet who writes the poem knows more than does the aspiring poet in it. If familial, social, and financial limits constrict, they also urge stretching; what some lovers, parents, and poets consider as opposed – individuals and society, youth and age, freedom and limitation, lovers and parents, poetic play and unpoetic work, love and money – this poem presents in relation. More generally still, "In Neglect" suggests that, for its own safety, society needs the experienced knowledge that lovers are mistaken when they trust they need not work, will never be forsaken, and can live on love (without money). It equally suggests that, for its very life, society also needs the imaginative, disruptive urge of lovers to resist such labored wisdom. The mixture is inherently unstable, a personal economy that is both resistant to and snug within the wider economy it evades and inhabits. There is something healthy in this paradoxically rebellious acquiescence to societal givens; there is a risk of compromised smugness in it, too, for it takes and holds a position from which no meaningful rebellion against more threatening entrenched oppressions could possibly be mounted.

John Dewey argued that societies derive their particular ways of knowing from the means of production predominant in them, their economies; Dewey called this "occupational psychosis."[8] Psychotic or not, societies – and poets – often borrow economic language to make and examine metaphors of value. Frost was no exception: consider these lines on a once-proud mercantile city now in ruins, "Not even the ingenuities of debt/ Could save it from its losses being met" (*CPPP*, 363). So much for deficit spending as a permanent means of possession. Frost, who said "All metaphor breaks down somewhere. That is the beauty of it" (*CPPP*, 723), frequently uses capitalist figures of ownership both tightly to tie and slackly to loosen connections between possession and self-possession. In "Stopping by Woods on a Snowy Evening," for instance, the relation between the speaker's uneasiness that he might be caught trespassing, on the one hand, and his poised, Thoreauvian sense that he has extra-economic rights to be where he is, on the other, is a small version of the poem's broader meditation on the positive and negative aspects of both obedient and rebellious individual responses to conventional economies of social responsibility or public promise-keeping.

The lighter poem "Trespass" treats similar matters from the owner's point of view (when an interloper stops to ask a property holder for water he makes both trespassing and ownership bearable by restoring the owner's property rights without requiring the owner to enforce them), while in "The Gift Outright" the historical politics of national possession are constructed almost entirely from possessive pronouns and apostrophes denoting ownership, recalling Frost's later notion that "All there is is belonging and belongings" (*CPPP*, 800). Frost's frequent play with the equation and mismatch of possession and self-possession is central in the early poem "Storm Fear," which may convey some of Frost's anxiety about his dependence on his grandfather's financial assistance. During a snowstorm so powerful it erases landmarks and cuts the farm off not only from town but also from some of those parts of itself that communicate and nourish ("Dooryard and road ungraded,/ Till even the comforting barn grows far away"), the speaker says, "my heart owns a doubt/ Whether 'tis in us to arise with day/ And save ourselves unaided" (*CPPP*, 19). The verb "owns" admits to possible weakness, as in "owns up," but it also asserts firm ownership of even the most desolate feelings, a claim that joins with sterner terms of measurement, attention, and inscription ("count," "mark") to reassert the speaker's own self-possessed and self-reliant survivor's poise, or pose.

Similar patterns appear in the much later "Desert Places," with an altered emphasis. There, a loss of self-possession ("I am too absent-spirited to count") involves ownership by others: "The woods around it have it – it is theirs." But the speaker, frightened (and not) by astronomers' "empty spaces between stars," reasserts ownership when he says, "I have it in me so much nearer home/ To scare myself with my own desert places" (*CPPP*, 269). Of course, the claim to possess an internal or other local emptiness large or intense enough to compete with interstellar vacancy carries its own threats to self-possession. Such intricate economies are also at work in "Home Burial," where Frost uses the husband's and wife's relentless employment of singular possessive pronouns to indicate each one's self-absorbed failure to empathize with the other's language for grief, forms of self-possession so disastrously complete that they self-destructively alienate all others.

One result of Frost's partial attachments to local color writing and to realism and naturalism is that the characters in his dramatic and narrative poems are quite firmly placed socially and economically. In those poems, competing ideas about such economic matters as the obligation to charity, the meaning and value of work, and the relationships of labor to gender play important roles. Not surprisingly, considerations of the extent of public and private responsibilities to assist the indigent and unemployed are treated most prominently in Frost's *A Further Range*, his one book of the 1930s, the decade of the Great Depression and Roosevelt's New Deal. But perhaps because the political and economic pressures they seek to address were too near or too great for the cool distance Frost's best and warmest work requires (as Simon Schama wrote in another context, "a dispassionate eye is the condition of a compassionate intelligence"), the serious political poems there, say, "Two Tramps in Mud Time" and "A Roadside Stand," seem smug or sentimental. Lighter or comic treatments, "Not Quite Social," "Provide, Provide," are more successful. But it may be that all these overtly political and economic poems – and especially the economics-drenched so-called "political pastoral" "Build Soil" – say more about Frost's vocational choices, his compromising evasion of both capitalism's rules and consequences, than they do about broader economics or ethics. They often seem besieged and defensive, as if Frost were protecting a narrowed version of the facts and conditions of his own having found both a refuge and a goad in poverty and then proved himself in victory over it. As early as 1920, he was a little glibly (but self-critically, too) praising poverty as "a kind of institution of refuge"

(*CPPP*, 698). In any event, there is more conviction about the opposed but intertwined claims of social obligation and private contentment in the early "Love and a Question" than in the more overtly economic poems of *A Further Range*. In my view, Frost's negotiations with economics are more effective when more concrete and less direct, when economics is not, in a narrow sense, the subject.

Work is an issue in many of Frost's dramatic and narrative poems. In "The Death of the Hired Man," it merges with concerns about charity and social obligation, understood in familial and local terms rather than state or national ones. Fiscal language is prominent at the poem's outset and its conclusion: these phrases cluster near the start: "the market things," "'a little pay,'" "'I can't afford to pay/ Any fixed wages,'" and "'pocket money,'" and these near the close: "'Silas has better claim on us you think/ Than on his brother?,'" "'His brother's rich,/ A somebody-director in the bank',," "'need,'" and "'Worthless though he is'" (*CPPP*, 40–41, 44). Mary, having in the course of the poem subtly prepared Warren to modify his initial reasonable and practical economic resentments of the unreliable and irresponsible Silas, herself assumes and sums up Warren's judgments by calling Silas "worthless" at just the moment when she knows that Warren has been prepared to defend him in extra-economic terms of worth: his artist's skill in building a load of hay, his standing up for the practical values of the community he and Mary and Warren share against the college-educated Harold Wilson's schooled rejection of dowsing and his art-for art's sake claim that "He studied Latin like the violin/ Because he liked it" (*CPPP*, 42), and his (Silas') turning to them rather than to his brother out of a combination of pride and affection that exceeds merely "legitimate" obligations. But if the poem's movingly instructive modulation from abstract economic justice toward fellow feeling and mercy protects Warren, it cannot save Silas: "'Warren?' she questioned./ 'Dead,' was all he answered" (*CPPP*, 45). Frost's poem shows the virtues and limits of a range of justice-based or merciful economic attitudes and systems which are themselves as relational as family and community arrangements; it also shows that beneath or behind those attitudes, systems, and arrangements are griefs upon which they have no purchase.

Similar intricacies are involved in "Blueberries," which considers rights of "property" and the varied proprieties of hoarding and sharing; in "The Code," which explores the relational claims of ownership and labor, worker and boss; and in "The Self-Seeker," which examines the power and weakness of money to recompense for losses past repayment. These poems are all from *North of Boston*, and their treatment of economic among other intricacies differs in kind and quality from those in *A Further Range*; Frost was right to fear the poem thought through in advance or written to reach a fore-gone conclusion.

Several Frost poems concern the connections between gender and econo-mies of work. In "The Hill Wife," too little work deranges a woman; in "A Servant to Servants," too much work does the same, although the woman of the first poem may escape, and the woman of the second compensates for being put upon and exhausted by male demands and privileged presump-tions with her own inventive power, as do others of Frost's female charac-ters, the witch of Coos, for instance. In one of the earliest of Frost's dramatic monologues, "The Housekeeper," all the economic themes I have been dis-cussing come together: matters of vocation, competing valences of owner-ship and self-possession, the relative claims of charity and independence, the worth and value of work, and the relation between labor and gender. "The Housekeeper" (*CPPP*, 82–89) is based on a "true" story, that of John Hall, an acquaintance of Frost in the years when he was raising chickens in Derry. Hall was an expert poultryman, but he kept his birds more for pleasure than for profit, preferring expensive "fancy" breeds he could show to win blue ribbons over prolific layers of eggs he could sell for cash. Hall lived a casual life with his "housekeeper" – actually his common-law wife – and her mother. When Hall's housekeeper left him to marry another man, Frost sus-pected that the rage and grief Hall felt may have caused his death.

Frost's poetic version of Hall's experience emphasizes Frost's own con-cerns in the Derry years, especially his uncertainty about how best to combine socially approved commitments to family, farming, and financial success with his less acceptable preference for poetry, a version of Hall's "weakness" for prize-winning fowl. Autobiography stalks biography here; like the poem's character, John, Frost was a "'bad farmer'" "'brought up by his mother'" and did not "'make much.'" And "The Housekeeper" presents conflicting economic, social, and aesthetic values related to Frost's own sit-uation. Hall's passionate preference for show birds over other niceties (keeping up appearances or profits) may flout conventions harmlessly, even healthily. His enthusiasm converts Estelle and her mother, creating a family bond more intense and intimate than a sanctioned public marriage might. At the same time, though, his preference masks ineptitude and thoughtlessness. Still worse, selfish inattention prevents him from recognizing Estelle's real need for more conventional marital and household arrangements. That unmet need causes family and farm to "smash." Meanwhile, Estelle's desire for a "proper" marriage may be driven more by personal pique than social commitment. However that may be, in spiting John she spites herself and abets destruction, including a real threat to her "unmovable" mother.

From a slightly different angle, the hint that Estelle is pregnant lends added force to her decision to marry, especially since she inhabits a society intensely concerned with regulating economies of sexuality and reproduction. Competing claims define the poem's other pair as well: the visitor speaks for well-intentioned but meddling outside social intervention; the mother, for stoic or desperate resignation in the face of troubles surpassing solution. The resonance of these matters with details of Frost's life and with his mixed views about economies of independence and dependence will be apparent.

Matters of gender in "The Housekeeper" may reflect Frost's unease about the propriety and economic viability of poetry as a man's vocation, anxieties connected to the casting of poetry as effeminate and useless by his mercantile era. John has an artist's care for his materials, but there is something "unmanly" about him, surrounded as he is by hens "'having their plumage done.'" Estelle and her mother fill and hold the purse; he is an impotent hoer. The delicate but suggestive sexualized language of those details, like the question "'What will satisfy her?',", implies a lack of virility in a man who cannot keep accounts or house or "wife." At the same time, such views may be merely social conventions, especially if pregnancy by John prompts Estelle to marry someone else by way of keeping up appearances. In either case, Frost both invokes and questions essentialist views of gender. John's "unmanly" gentleness is risky but also beguiling: "'he's kinder than the run of men'"; "'He's fond of nice things.'" And Estelle's "unwomanly" energy and initiative prove to be both dangerous and creative: her decisive action breaks old bonds and forges new ones; it may also abandon her mother and kill the man she loves. Similarly, Estelle's mother's forcefully poetic speech is attractive and gripping but impotent to alter what it comprehends. To use the term again, Frost does not choose between or resolve the poem's competing economic and other positions but presents them in ever-shifting relation. He had considered calling "The Housekeeper" "Slack Ties," a title recalling his saying a poem should be easy in its harness. Frost may have thought a similar economics works in human lives. This poem's "slackly" unresolved perspectives suggest "easier" forms of life than chafing social bonds permit; its harnessed containments imply that without some ties things smash.

Examples of poems in which Frost's relational treatment of opposed views of economic matters play major or minor roles could easily be multiplied, but I want to conclude with brief discussions of two additional areas in which economic ideas, attitudes, and language appear in Frost's thinking. The first is very general, the second more specific. In a brilliant series of books, Marc Shell has demonstrated the connections between "the money form" and the crisis of representation in philosophy, literature, and art.[9] He argues that the crisis was initiated in ancient times when stamped coinage opened a gap between the intrinsic or natural values of things (a coin's metal) and their nominal or symbolic value (a coin's inscription, denomination, and "backing"). This crisis might be said to underlie all Western philosophical and aesthetic debates about mind and matter, about knowing as discovery or imposition, about being as authentic or invented, about systems as essential or constructed, and about art as true or fraudulent feigning. It has intensified in stages, first as money's symbolic value increasingly diverged from its metal value, then as intrinsically valueless paper backed by reserves of gold or silver replaced actual coins, then again as paper backed by the more abstract full faith and credit of a government replaced gold or silver certificates, and yet again as money grew – and grows – increasingly disembodied and electronic.

Frost did not live to see this most recent intensification of the mind–matter problem, any more than his somewhat postmodern distrust of representation comprehends the extreme expansions of media simulacra and image-based brand-name and celebrity consumer capitalism in the years since his death (although in his own small way he did participate in media and celebrity culture: consider his managing of editors and book reviewers, his making a name for himself through theatrical performances, his canny sales of autographed and rare editions, and his appearances on *Meet the Press* and at the Kennedy inauguration). But if electronic money was beyond Frost's ken, he would have understood it. He witnessed the shift from the gold standard to Keynesian deficit spending; more important, debates about money as substance or substanceless sign were a critical issue of American political life during Frost's formative years. The well-known Thomas Nast cartoon in which an "inflated" doll is offered a cash-like slip of paper bearing the words "This is milk by act of Con[gress]"[10] appeared two years after Frost's birth, and *trompe l'oeil* paintings of paper money by William Harnett, John Haberle, Ferdinand Danton, Jr., and Victor Dubreuil, done in the 1870s, 80s, and 90s, joined Nast cartoons in jokily raising serious questions about paper money's dissolution of materiality in ideation and about the related artificialities of money and art.

Frost was twenty-two when Bryan delivered his "Cross of Gold" speech at the 1896 Democratic national convention and he made his own jokey economic reference to Bryan in an uncollected poem: "There was a young man from Vermont,/ Who voted for Bryan and Want" (*CPPP*, 504). He wrote a semi-comic poem "On the Inflation of the Currency, 1919," in which "The pain of seeing ten cents turned to five" is felt as someone "cutting us in two alive" (*CPPP*, 535). In distinguishing between incurable griefs and curable grievances in his "Introduction to Robinson's *King Jasper*" Frost compares being asked to give up patience in the face of grief to being required to surrender gold (*CPPP*, 743). And his poetry, prose, and talks are saturated with economic language and metaphors. I loosely gather all of this to make the point that Frost's philosophical and aesthetic doubts about perception, conception, and representation in such poems as "Hyla Brook" and "For Once, Then, Something," to mention just two of many, are powerfully connected to the money debates of his own cultural moment, debates which were as much philosophical and aesthetic as they were economic. Those debates were part of and partly responsible for still larger cultural crises of faith and confidence continuous with our own, crises visible in the nineteenth-century, modern, and postmodern fear of and fascination with counterfeiting, copies, fakes, and confidence tricks, and with self-referential art. Frost participated, as, for instance, in "The Mountain," "A Fountain, a Bottle, a Donkey's Ears and Some Books," and the "Preface to *Memoirs of the Notorious Stephen Burroughs.*" Frost was deeply knowing about art's counterfeit, but as to that, as about so many other things, he was also pragmatic, which is part of why his deeply disturbing relational poems are also reassuring. If language is apt to be more opaque than transparent, it might be rendered translucent, made more or less to represent; if money confuses real with symbolic values, and is subject, like us, to waves of inflation and deflation, it can still be kept or spent.

To close, I return to the lovely, impossible epigram I have echoed: "Strongly spent is synonymous with kept." Narrowly taken, the sentence recalls Frost's sometimes attractive or defensive calculations: his being "instinctively thorough" about his "crevice and burrow" (*CPPP*, 257); his saying, "Do you know, I think that a book ought to sell. Nothing is quite honest that is not commercial. Mind you I don't put it that everything commercial is honest"(*SL*, 8–9); his writing, when just over forty, that he knew at twenty a writer is exhausted – spent – at thirty and "took measures accordingly . . . I have myself all in a strong box where I can unfold as a personality at discretion . . . Great effect of strength and mastery!" (*SL*, 29–30) or his stating his preference for a success that butters parsnips over the kind that's "caviare to the crowd" (*CPPP*, 667–68). Broadly taken, the epigram reflects Frost's magnanimity: his saying "What a man will put into effect at any cost of time money or lives is what is sacred and what counts" (*CPPP*, 683); his writing "Belief is better than anything else and it is best when rapt above paying its respects to anybody's doubts whatsoever" (*CPPP*, 702); his asking "For what have we wings if not to seek friends at an elevation?" (*CPPP*, 782); his calling the god of the "great issues" a god of "magnificent waste" (*CPPP*, 868); and his preference for "extravagance" over everything else. Parsimony and extravagance, practical economics and spiritual risk appear together in Frost's down-to-earth remarks on E. A. Robinson's fiscally charged phrase, "'There are no millers any more.'" It is an edict Frost thinks has the widest application.

> It is a sinister jest at the expense of all investors of life or capital. The market shifts and leaves them with a car-barn full of dead trolley cars. At twenty I commit myself to a life of religion. Now, if religion should go out of fashion in twenty-five years, there would I be, forty-five years old, unfitted for anything else and too old to learn anything else. It seems immoral to have to bet on such high things as lives of art, business, or the church. But in effect, we have no alternative. (*CPPP*, 746–47)

When the stoic, elegaic mood of the Robinson piece shifts slightly, this circumstance – Frost's duplicitous sense of the human condition – sends up "superfluity" (*CPPP*, 702), "the wonder of unexpected supply" (*CPPP*, 777), the "great, great, great expense – everybody trying to make [the universe] mean something more than it is" (*CPPP*, 903), and the elating thrill of "risking spirit in substantiation" (*CPPP*, 446). So it is that cautious keeping and vigorous spending oppose and intersect in the economies of Frost's essentially constructivist relational poetry and poetics, where "enthusiasm tamed by metaphor" is crossed by and crosses "the breathless swing . . . between subject matter and form," where when something's held back, it's "held back for pressure."

NOTES

1 Richard Poirier, *Robert Frost: The Work of Knowing* (New York: Oxford University Press, 1977), pp. 4–11.
2 *Ibid.*, p. 233.
3 *Ibid.*, p. 238.
4 Mark Richardson, *The Ordeal of Robert Frost* (Urbana: University of Illinois Press, 1997), p. 2.
5 Jeffrey Meyers, *Robert Frost: A Biography* (Boston: Houghton Mifflin, 1996), p. 59.
6 Richardson, *Ordeal*, p. 10.
7 Lawrance Thompson, *Robert Frost: The Early Years, 1974–1915* (New York: Holt, Rinehart, and Winston, 1966), pp. 367–68, 573–75.
8 Richardson, *Ordeal*, p. 23.
9 Marc Shell, *Art and Money* (Chicago: University of Chicago Press, 1995).
10 *Ibid.*, p. 77.

12

JOHN CUNNINGHAM

Human Presence in Frost's Universe

Frost's poems address the ancient theme of the opposition between absence and presence. Here I will discuss (though not chronologically) ten poems published between 1916 and 1942 in which Frost explores this opposition. They all assume a universe without divine order, absent of purpose, awareness, human comprehension; in them humanity is on its own, the only locus of value, intention, self-consciousness, presence. One does well to be aware of the lure of night and of the deceptive whiteness of snow, to be free of any illusions about them. The heroism available to one is small in scale, and its accomplishments, though real, cannot be grand; it is only the upkeep of human self-consciousness and purpose in a universe otherwise void and absent of meaning, and this scope has shrunk since Frost wrote. These ideas, familiar to the last hundred years, comprise one theme common to the ten poems. One could observe as well that the ethos of the New England countryside has its parallels in the cosmic myths of Yeats, the Christianity of Eliot, and the sequence of ideologies in Auden, though my few pages do not admit of a discussion of these parallels. These ten poems display the poet's attachment to traditional forms and his artistry in using them; blank verse, open couplets, quatrains, sonnet-like poems, one true sonnet, terza rima, and various other lyrical stanzas. They are traditional without being "poetic": as slant rhymes, metrical variations (sometimes bold ones), colloquial diction, clichés, and homely metaphors that very often open onto darkness indicate.

This handful of poems considers the problem of man, with self-consciousness, a sense of value, of right and wrong, of beauty, of harmony, existing as a presence lonely in the universe that seems in them wholly absent of any awareness of man's concerns but rather characterized by mindless forces and unconscious obstacles. The congregation of thoughtless forces clashing with heedless barriers despite a man's almost frantic desire for "someone else additional to him" makes up "The Most of It" (1942). "Spring Pools" (1927) goes further to show nature heedlessly effecting a scene of beauty and harmony and just as heedlessly ready to destroy it. Only the presence of a

human can know of this value, but he is defenseless against a universe ignor-
ant of worth. This absence is generalized in "Nothing Gold Can Stay"
(1923) as the poem shows the inevitable transience of all golden things. "The
Oven Bird" (1916) asks what man with his awareness is "to make" of diminishment; the answer, if the poem gives one, is to learn to expect nothing other
and to "sing" despite such knowledge, to maintain one's humanity, one's
presence with its awareness of value. "Desert Places" (1936), "The Onset"
(1923) and "Stopping by Woods on a Snowy Evening" (1923) reveal the
almost ineluctable temptation to retreat into the nothingness of the natural
world and to give up one's presence and awareness. "Acquainted with the
Night" (1928) and "Design" (1936)[1] cancel any hope of a transcendent
status for value. "The Most of It" shows man's mistake in how the universe
can be "kept"; "An Old Man's Winter's Night" (1916) reveals that only by
maintaining his presence can a man keep a house, a countryside, the outer
world.

"The Most of It" demonstrates clearly the absence of human values in the
universe and yet by inversion teaches of their presence there. Having both
an actor and also an observer of the actor is uncharacteristic of Frost's lyrics;
one is naïve and the other aware. Both are potentially each of us, the every-
man figure split in two, the actor thinking that he keeps the universe and the
other knowing that the actor only "thought" that he did. The first stands on
the stony shore of a lake calling out, often one gathers ("ever" suggests so),
for response and receives only an echo from the facing cliff hidden by trees;
on one occasion a large stag does swim across the lake and lands on the
beach, apparently unaware of the one who cries out. The second offers the
final four words of the poem as his evaluation of the action: "– and that was
all."

"Kept" suggests a *kind of* maintenance, as keeping a shop or a house,
arranging at least some parts of it to accord with one's own desires, to
possess something to which one imputes value. It can also signify oversees,
protects, maintains, controls, perhaps understands, comprehends. It puts
man and his wishes axiologically, if not astronomically, at the center of the
universe. The poem is a short parable of all of us calling for more from the
natural world than it can give, unwilling to be "alone" in it, unwilling to
accept the chasm between oneself and the rest of the cosmos, unwilling not
to have his way ("alone" rhymes with "own"). Egoistically, ill-advisedly,
insistently, he demands more: "He would cry out," stubbornly "would."
Although all the words describing what follows have human connotations –
"answer," "wake," "voice" – ironically they do not, in fact, describe self-
conscious reactions. Perhaps only human beings can love; certainly only they
can know "counter-love," can offer an "original response" characterized by

personal intention, moral values, aesthetic awareness. The universe and human desire are not congruous as the slant rhyme *wants* and *response* suggests.

Not only the universe is against him; the metaphors, meter, and alliteration are also. Imagery of distance and separation point his condition. The lake divides the speaker from the source of the echo and of the buck. The echo derives "from some tree-hidden cliff," and the buck begins "in the cliff's talus" on the "other side" and swims "in the far distant water." In each case, the meter metaphorically states the isolation, two consecutive stressed syllables impeding the iambic movement. The imagery is of unconscious obstacles like the "boulder-broken beach," the talus, the rocks; it is of unself-conscious forces colliding with these opposing barriers, like the sound waves of the cryer's voice bouncing back from the cliff, the buck's "pushing the crumpled water" and "forc[ing] the underbrush" with "horny tread," of "stumbl[ing]," as if blindly, among the rocks. The result is the exploding *b*s above and the irruption of the *p*s of "powerfully appeared . . . pushing . . . crumpled . . . up . . . pouring" near the end and the harsh though feminine rhyme, "crashed" and "splashed." The rocks fall from the cliff just as mindlessly, the boulders strewn mindlessly, and the echo twice mocking because it is not human and because not being human it cannot mock. Imagery, meter, alliteration, and rhyme are metaphoric of human impotence. In the face of these powers and these barriers they figure the illusion of the cryer.

The confusion of antecedents for the pronoun "it" states this illusion of the cryer. He calls out "on life" – boulders, talus, cliff, the unreflective actions of the buck – saying that what "it wants . . . back" is "counter-love." Grammatically "it" refers to unself-conscious "life" that, of course, cannot, in Frost's poetry, know such love or "original response," whereas "it" in fact refers to the one who cries, confusing human values with the natural world quite empty of human purpose and love. Certainly no response comes, "unless it" was the buck, "it" (line 13) that swam, "it" (line 14) that neared, "it" (line 16) that appeared without "proving human," it that is wholly unaware of the human being standing nearby. It is, certainly, an "embodiment" of "the universe," manifestation, incarnation, on this one occasion, but "embodiment" is suspended for five lines before being identified with the stag. This embodiment is emblematic of "the most of it." Frost, as he often does, breathes spirit into this cliché; and by it reveals the mindless confusion in the cryer's thought. "It" is "nothing", "unless" is ironic rather than mitigating. The nihilism pervasive in the speaker's view of the cryer's action allows for no meaning in the universe, no voice, nothing awake, nothing original. That the natural world is a congeries of unreflective forces and obstacles is the burden of the last three quatrains that "answer" the illusive hopes of the cryer stated in the first two quatrains. "And that was all," concludes the observer, but not quite all, only "the most of it"; for the naive cryer does indeed "ke[ep] the universe alone." He only is the locus of values, love, original response in it; only as man maintains his human desires and loves and even naive hopes is the universe "kept." The price, however, is loneliness; otherwise the universe has no keeper, is not kept. The alert, knowing, ironic observer may miss this one fact in his evaluation of the cryer's actions. To understand this sort of keeping, we must work our slow way toward "An Old Man's Winter Night."

The speaker in "Spring Pools" is all too aware of the unknowing phenomena of the natural world but also of the value that, on occasion, they create; yet he knows that, being alien to human concerns, they cannot cherish that value as he can nor know to preserve it. At the short moment between the end of winter and the beginning of spring occurs a situation of harmony, unity, beauty, delicacy, near perfection. Even though they are in the forest – the leaves of which normally close off the light of the sun – these pools can "still" – nevertheless, continue to – "reflect/ The total sky." Earth and heaven seem united, as do the waters and the flowers beside them that they mirror. At least they do so "almost without defect." *Defect* is not an encouraging word, nor does *almost* go without its irony. The two-syllable rhyme with "reflect" introduces an early sense of something not quite right; and the linking of flowers and pools by "chill and shiver" is not hopeful. Because he has witnessed this state before, the speaker knows that the pools, like the flowers, "will . . . soon be gone," not by flowing innocently out of a brook but rather by treacherously moving up by the trees' roots to "bring dark foliage" that will starve the flowers of both water and sunlight. The elements that produced the beauty contribute to its own lessening; unconscious forces seem to work in harmony and then in opposition. *Dark* is moral and ontological as well as descriptive. During the first stanza the speaker manages to control his regret and only implies the opposition between human desire present in him and absent in the natural world.

His restraint disappears in the second stanza. The unwittingly destructive forces passively present become actively threatening in the "pent up buds" that have "it" in them to "darken nature" diminishing it into "summer woods." The slant rhyme is properly jarring. The speaker's own pent up frustration finally breaks out with the spondees of the unthoughtful cliché, "Let them think twice"; but the irony that the trees cannot think even once restores life to the cliché. The rush of the meter in the final lines, figurative of the impending destruction of the near-perfect scene, continues for four lines without punctuation. The waters and the flowers cannot resist the rising meter with its stacked up accents – "To blot out and drink up and sweep away" – that describes the trees' powers to obliterate "these flowery waters and these watery flowers" with their falling meter and surfeit of weak syllables. The poem ends as the speaker subsides into the resignation of the quiet iambs in the last line: "From snow that melted only yesterday."

The universe, in its "absence," unwittingly does produce occasions of beauty and harmony that mortals, with their "presence," find valuable, and they foolishly go on to suppose that value of itself entails the obligation to endure. In Frost it does not. "Nothing Gold Can Stay" begins with one of these episodes and gives over half its lines to charting the diminishment of it. Then it cites two or three more examples and ends with the generalization that is its title. One may suppose that the series of long ōs – gold, hold, only, so, so, so, goes, gold, rather large for an eight-line trimeter poem – represents a continuous moan at universal lessening. The poem opens with a trochee – "Nature's" – warning of nature's dominance, and its last line begins with one – "Nothing" – that by the end is unarguable. The first indication of new life after the death of winter is the pale yellow, golden nascent leaves. Frost uses the noun to describe them, *gold*, not the adjective. For human beings gold is valuable in many ways, beautiful as in jewelry, pure, unchanging, enduring from chemistry, perfect from alchemy, rare and precious from finance. Frost makes it a metaphor for nature's "first green," connecting it and green also by alliteration, and conveys all its connotations to the "early leaf" that he calls "a flower" thereby adding suggestions of loveliness and delicacy to the bud. In this color, nature displays "her hardest hue to hold." The *h* requires more effort to pronounce than some other consonants; therefore, the difficulty in saying this alliterative line runs counter to the ease with which the color passes away. The feminine rhyme "flower" and "hour" suggests the fragility of the flower but also represents our effort to try to preserve it for, perhaps, just two more weak syllables. Flowers are metaphors of mutability, and the speaker knows that the leaf will be a bud for "only . . . an hour." After this delicacy, the syntax moves relentlessly on with "Then . . . / So . . . / So . . . / Nothing." The first stanza begins in the present but looks to the future. With the beginning of the second stanza, the diminishment occurs, "Then leaf subsides to leaf." The delicacy, beauty, rarity of the golden leaf opens out to a larger merely green leaf. Eden, man's beginning, the ancients named the Golden Age; it "sank to grief," downward. What is true of "nature's first green" is projected backward – and forward – as true of the race. It is also true of the cosmos. Dawn, the day's beginning, is bright red gold; but dawn "goes down" to ordinary sunshine. The movement of the sun in the sky has long been a metaphor for the course of each person's life, for its first beginning to its lessened maturity. The movement in each case is paradoxically downward.

One may ask why such a short poem opens so many paradoxes. Green is not gold. One cannot hold a hue. A leaf is not a flower, not even for an hour. The growing leaf increases rather than subsides. The dawn does not go down, but rather the sun comes up. The perfection of Eden should not have in it the wherewithal for sinking. The chemical element that resists bonding with other elements and, thereby, withstands change should not be universally subject to mutability. These paradoxes point toward a disjunction between what the natural world is like, absent of a sense of value or meaning, and the human presence desiring illogically that the valuable should, just because it is valuable, endure. Yet "Nothing Gold Can Stay" is not so dark as "The Most of It" or "Spring Pools." The bud becomes a leaf, not a thorn; golden yellow becomes green and not black, dawn goes down, but night does not come before the poem finishes. Eden sank to grief but not to despair. Moreover bright long $\bar{a}$s and long $\bar{e}$s – nature, green, leaf, leaf, leaf, Eden, grief, day, stay – move counter to the mournful $\bar{o}$s. Diminishment is not so bad as mindless clashing forces or thoughtless obliteration.

In "The Oven Bird" Frost puts and, perhaps, answers the question of what one is "to make of a diminished thing." In his poetry a bird, of course, is incapable of contemplation and reflection. That failing, however, does not prevent its being emblematic of a meditative person: "The bird would cease and be as other birds/ But that he knows in singing not to sing." That he knows and reasons from what he knows to appropriate action makes clear his figurative status. He is "a singer everyone has heard." The poem tells us only that his song is "loud"; a handbook on birds informs us that it is also shrill. The other birds, we may suppose, sang "when pear and cherry bloom went down in showers/ On sunny days a moment overcast"; we may also assume that their song was melodic, tuneful, pleasant to the ear, a song appropriate to a universe of blossoms. They did not attend to the overcast moment and to what the falling blooms signified. The world is now greatly different and their song now inappropriate. We no longer hear it; they "have ceased." The oven bird is prosaic; he says rather than sings: three times, "He says . . ." "He says that leaves are old," that their summer green has long displaced the varied colors of the flowers. "Old" seems an overstatement, but it well marks the great distance here between the two seasons. He uses a matter-of-fact metaphor from percentages – "for flowers/ Mid-Summer is to Spring as one to ten" – yet the process is as certain as the laws of mathematics. And regarding autumn, one to – what? One thousand? "He says . . . / And comes that other fall we name the fall": the autumn does occur, but we give it the appropriate name. It will bring a worse loss, the "fall" of the leaves themselves and will be figurative of the approaching death of winter. When "he says" that the "highway dust" is "over all," we cannot ignore the submerged metaphor of the Biblical Fall that cast the dust of death over the whole universe – "fall" does rhyme with "all" – nor the image of the highway of exile out of Eden into a world of absence, save only for the presence of man. The oven bird is a denizen of this diminished world, "Loud, a mid-summer" and "a mid-wood bird." After a period of quiet left by the silencing of the "other birds," the oven bird "makes the solid tree trunks sound" again, resound, resonate.

"The Oven Bird" is technically not a sonnet, but it behaves as if it thought it were one, having a longer unit of ten lines framed with a couplet at its beginning and another couplet at its finish and a shorter unit that is a quatrain. The longer bit places the scene in the midst of a diminished forest; the setting bristling with details that beg the question "all but frame[d]" by the bird and its song in the second bit and perhaps answered there. The setting is the puzzling "diminished thing" that bird knows and knows not "what to make of." He looks back with regret but without paralysis. What he does make of it is a loud, if not tuneful and beautiful, song offered with the confidence that comes of freedom from the illusion of beauty's permanence that troubles the other birds into silence; moreover, he knows and accepts that worse is to come with "the other fall." Without this awareness and this acquiescence "the bird would cease and be as other birds." His wisdom is paradox: "he knows in singing" his loud, assured song "not to sing" as the other birds, now mute, did not know. "Not to sing" rhymes fittingly with "diminished thing." The speaker tells us that the bird "knows" and "says" – understands, interprets – but we know in Frost that unself-conscious birds cannot do so. The oven bird's actions and its advice are, however, relevant to a human being desirous of understanding his place in a universe where nothing gold can stay; the poem shows the oven bird as emblematic of such a human. The answer, if it is one, is to be rid of foolish illusions about the universe, to be assured in the values that one knows, to sing loudly and confidently: to maintain one's preference, to make the trees echo with one's not-singing.

In "Desert Places" the dead weeds, the stubble, the animals "smothered in their lairs," stars without human life, the vast distance between these stars – all desert places – are not metaphors of literal death but of the death of human presence in a person. Nor are these the only images of death. Freezing snow with its "smooth," undifferentiated whiteness, its emptiness usual in Frost, and night with its darkness and its own blankness convey absence; they offer not the opposites that light and dark ought to but rather both image an absence that is a kind of death. The iambic poem begins unexpectedly with spondees metrically linking these two metaphors: "Snow falling and night falling." The obliteration of presence and meaning, more disastrous than the obliteration in "Spring Pools," comes with unusual rapidity, "fast oh fast," without time even for commas before and after the "oh."

The field is one desert place; the woods are another: "The woods around it have it – it is theirs." The second stanza possesses – encloses – the absence, the "it," of the first, "it" is what the woods achieve with the field. Moreover, the woods "includes" the speaker, too. Or, rather, what the woods and the field signify, "loneliness," encompasses the speaker. With the emphasis on the speaker that begins in the middle of the second stanza, the "desert" receives human attribution, "loneliness"; it includes the man "unawares." "Unawares" is adverbial because the emptiness does not know what it is doing to the human being; it is also adjectival because the speaker finds himself enclosed before he is aware of the danger. He only "looked into [the field] going past"; yet he is already "too absent-spirited" to be an exception to all that the field and the woods represent. His human spirit, his presence, is gone – "unawares." The "its" of line 5 becomes loneliness in lines 9 and 10, an emptiness worse than that of uninhabited stars and of the light-years of vacant space between them. As the snow increases with the advance of winter and as the darkness intensifies with growing night, so the loneliness, once begun, "will be more lonely," not to be stopped by a mere human being. It will become a "blanker whiteness"; the literal has become metaphoric in a trice. It is now "benighted snow": at one with the night but also morally benighted in that the loneliness is without human purpose, presence, and spirit, having "no expression, nothing to express." For the speaker, this desert place is nearer and more "scar[ing]" than all the others; in fact, it is plural, "spaces." The three feminine rhymes, the last one of which leaves the poem seemingly unfinished in its meter, are ironic in sound and intent. The action of the poem is unfinished because as the snow will melt and the night pass into dawn, the loneliness "will be less", the speaker has traveled through it before. Now he must, however, travel through it again; the rhyme scheme is, therefore, *aaxa*.

Indeed it is "always the same"; a comma sets off this metrical unit that begins "The Onset." The descent of absence upon one, an unexpected void, is like the first snowfall of winter "on a fated night." This snow, as white "as may be in dark woods" – white and dark are again paradoxically not opposites – causes the unsuspecting speaker almost to stumble as, startled, he looks "up and round." The open couplets and the absence of end punctuation for five lines, with only two internal commas, allows the syntax to parallel the rush of the falling snow and night. The onset is "fated" only in the sense that the unconscious forces of the natural world have been bringing it to pass since perhaps the beginning of the universe, enigmatic but not fated in any theological sense. The falling of emptiness upon a person seems just as enigmatic, perchance, just as "fated"; as "death [just] descends" upon one. Frost's metaphor is threefold: A (the literal onset of snow and night leads one walking in "dark woods" "almost [to] stumble"); B (death's onset causes one actually to "give up his errand"); C (the onset of the void of spirit causes one almost to fall into the absence of the natural world). In each case is one "overtaken by the end," but only one of the three is amenable to moral discipline. "Errand" is a word with human connotations that snow and night do not have; in Frost's ethics, willingly to "give[] up [one's] errand," however tiresome, is evil. If "hissing" of the first snow on the fallen and dead leaves does not suggest the serpent, then the "disappearing snake" does. At the onset of the final "end" one must indeed give up one's errand, "with nothing done/ To evil, no important triumph won." No person can effect a lasting victory over the void of the universe but each one may attend to one's own errand of the moment. Not to do so is to let the end come too early and to let evil have its triumph too soon. "Evil" in this handful of poems has this precise meaning, abandonment of human presence, descent into absence.

In the second stanza, Frost continues his analogy of the onset of snow and night with the onset of void on the human spirit, "Winter death," a summary of stanza one, has always failed when it has "tried/ The earth"; therefore, all the precedent is "on [the] side" of the speaker. "Triumph won" and "on my side" are, I take it, military metaphors; the second one is also a legal image. As the snow will suffer defeat with the coming of spring and the night will lose to day, so the testing of the speaker will pass, too – at least it always has. He will see the melted snow become "a slender April rill." Yet reminders of "winter death" remain in the spring's renewal of the earth: "withered brake," "dead weeds," a white birch, a white church. A descent of void upon human presence need not wait the coming of winter: the spring birds were silenced by the coming of summer.

The speaker of "Desert Places" needed but to look into the field filling up with snow and night to be ensnared by all that they figure; the person in "Stopping by Woods on a Snowy Evening" is so ill-advised as to stop and "to watch" the "woods fill up" with snow. The opposition between human-ity (the owner of the woods whose "house is in the" village and who will not see the speaker, the absence of "a farmhouse near") and the purposeless natural phenomena (descending snow and night, the woods, the frozen lake) Frost establishes early. Even the horse "must think it queer." Three times the poet uses some form of stop. The setting is becoming blank, undifferentiated whiteness, a desert place on "the darkest evening of the year," literally an overstatement but metaphorically not so to the speaker. For him movement forward ceases; his choice is between the "woods and frozen lake," either offering only death to one who stops. In effect the horse asks "if there is some mistake." To have so stopped could well prove to be such. The "sweep/ of easy wind," free of the thousand mortal shocks that one is heir to, and the "downy flake," like warm bedding, entice the speaker to give up his human errands and to sleep in the void of death. The woods are "dark and deep," not promising words in Frost, deep as the final absence of death, and "lovely" only in the temptation to shuffle off that they offer. With "but I have promises to keep," the speaker and the poem pivot, rejecting the temptation, affirming his promises, a word with human connotations of duty and presence, and accepting the "miles [that he must] go" before he sleeps this night and before he "sleep[s]" finally in death. Repeating the two last lines is congruent with the stacked-up accents at the pivot above as is the alteration of the rhyme from *aaba* to the resolution of *aaaa*. The metaphor of the journey obtains in "The Oven Bird" and in "Desert Places"; the speaker of "Stopping by Woods" finds the human courage to go his miles and to be present.

"Acquainted with the Night" is also a journey of sorts; no way exists within the logic of a stanza that rhymes *aaba* to bring a poem to its close. Frost ended "Stopping by Woods" by adding another *a* and dispensing with the *b*; terza rima offers a like problem. After four tercets, the poet returns to the *a* rhyme and makes a couplet giving a fourteen-line poem that ends in the same line with which it began. The journey is seemingly endless. The tense is present perfect, action having begun in the past, continuing in the present, and probably projecting into the future. If one is lucky, one is never more than "acquainted" with the night, never on familiar terms with it. The poem opens with a generalization: "I have been one acquainted with the night." Then it gives five examples of the generalization,[2] the first three have one line each, the fourth two lines, and a fifth four. Each of the six lines begins with a trochee followed by a spondee ("I have walked out"); the repeated metrical unit marks out the five examples which document the generalization. One might have thought that the four-line fifth illustration was the climax, but Frost drops the parallel construction ("I have . . .") and the recurring meter to offer a sixth. The five take place on earth, but the sixth is "one luminary clock against the sky," the moon, "at an unearthly height." The "night" of the generalization and of the five instances of it give no respite to the journeyer; nor does the sixth. For the "clock . . . / Proclaimed the time was neither wrong nor right." One may not look above, as pilots once looked there for direction, to find human and moral values. Cosmic time moves just as mechanically as the "great buck" in "The Most of It." The Deists were right – Providence does not interfere in the creation – and wrong: for no Providence asserts itself in the poems we have been looking at. One does well in Frost's universe to be acquainted with the night, to know what it is like, but values and meaning are existential in the one who carries out his errands and keeps his promises. They are not transcendental. If this terza rima poem ironically alludes to Dante, I cannot say.

Unlike "The Oven Bird" and "Acquainted with the Night," "Design" is a proper sonnet, with an octave and sestet. The sestet ends, uncharacteristic of the Italian sonnet, with a couplet; Donne allowed himself the same liberty. Donne it was and Herbert, who took the sonnet, used in English for amorous love, and baptized it to use for divine love. This poem ironically teaches the opposite of love or, worse, of no love at all. The title, too, is ironic, pointing as it does the argument from "Design": the universe is so clearly ordered – like, say, a clock – that one can but posit a Designer. Yet the flower, ironically called a "heal-all," normally blue, is ironically in this little design a white mutation; the spider is ironically a white mutation also. Therefore, the moth, unawares, flies into the white web without seeing it as it otherwise might; white ironically forms a "design of darkness." The *a* rhyme ironically links "white" with "right" and "blight"; Frost carries the *a* over into the sestet in its first line and then rhymes it with "night" and "height." The spider seems most innocent, "dimpled . . . fat and white." It is not so from our human standpoint; it is so from nature's, being unaware of value, not free in its choice of action. We have "assorted characters of death and blight/ Mixed ready to begin the morning right." With too much glee – or, perhaps, bitterness – Frost renews the cliché. The word "characters" makes the design into a little drama, but I do not think that a divine playwright shapes their ends. The sestet is largely questions: what choice had the flower in being white? What brought the spider to the height of the flower? What steered the moth there during the night? The answers: 1) "what but design of darkness to appall –": the little design or the little play is the work of some evil omnipotence petulantly to appall us, or, 2) "design [may not] govern in a thing so small": and if it govern not in small things, can it govern in larger ones, is there such an omnipotence at all? The universe has not the wherewithal to value moths, to understand the disjunction between white heal-alls and seemingly treacherous death; only man as he maintains his presence can judge. The irony, here bitter, results from the disjunction between human value and a purposeless universe.

I can now suggest how one "ke[eps] the universe alone," and to do so I turn in conclusion to "An Old Man's Winter Night." The details of the setting beyond those in the title include a farmhouse with some empty rooms, a cellar with barrels, an oil lamp, and a wood fire in the old man's room. The poem introduces a series of oppositions: warmth and cold; light and darkness; waking and sleeping; sounds and silence; life and death; man and nature; presence and emptiness; meaning and nothingness. Each pair is a metaphor of all the other pairs. The sounds of "the outer night" – the roar of trees and the crack of branches – are like the noise of "beating on a box," a sound, I take it, of emptiness; the sounds within are of the old man's "clomping" which "scare[s] the cellar . . . and scare[s] the outer night" and of the jolt as logs in the fire shift, the sounds of presence. We are not told that beating on a box scares the old man. "All out-of-doors looks darkly in at him," threateningly; he, however, cannot return the mindless "gaze." In the empty room where he stands, the moisture has condensed on the freezing window panes; and as he holds his lamp up to the window to look out he receives its light back, reflected from the "separate stars" of the "thin frost" on the glass. This light, for which he is responsible, cannot look into the darkness; human life cannot look into death, into nothingness. Even though he represents human life at its final frontier, aged and forgetful of why he went into the empty room, he, nevertheless, is "concerned with he knew what." His burning lamp, and his concerns, and his fire to which he responds even in his sleep all represent the presence of his humanity. Of course the lamp and the fire and his concerns are burning out; and so, too, is the sun. In this little snuggery of entropy, "one aged man – one man – can't keep a house,/ A farm, a countryside, or if he can,/ It's thus he does it of a winter's night." Surprisingly the old man's keeping moves farther and farther outward: house, farm, countryside. "All out-of-doors" may look "darkly in at him"; but the threat would seem to advance outward, not inward.

On such a winter's night in such a universe, with its noise paradoxically of emptiness, of beating on a box, with its intention seemingly to threaten darkly, with the burning out of the lamp and of the fire and of one's concerns, one may well be tempted to pack it all in when the onset comes, as in Frost come it will. The carrying out of errands and the keeping of promises at such times may seem no other than very stale, flat, weary, and unprofitable, especially when there is no Heaven for one to crawl under, only the earth to crawl upon. Despite a lack of ontological status to assure its value, self-consciousness with its duties is the best one may achieve. To Frost, its achievement seems worth the whistle. To call out for counter-love and original response from the universe is futile, but it seems to have its merits. To recognize the beauty of spring pools. To cherish nature's first green. To notsing, and to do so loudly. These things are heroic acts of presence that face otherwise universal absence. These ten poems attest to Frost's confidence that they matter, and that greatly.

NOTES

1 First published in 1934.
2 They are: "walk[ing] out in rain – and back in rain"; "outwalk[ing] the furthest city light"; "look[ing] down the saddest city lane"; "passing by the watchman on his beat/ And drop[ping] my eyes, unwilling to explain"; standing "still and stop[ping] the sound of feet/ When far away an interrupted cry/ Came over houses from another street, / But not to call me back or say good-bye."

SELECT BIBLIOGRAPHY

I. Works by Frost

The Letters of Robert Frost to Louis Untermeyer. Ed. Louis Untermeyer. New York: Holt, Rinehart, and Winston, 1963.

Prose Jottings of Robert Frost. Ed. Edward Connery Lathem and Hyde Cox. Lunenburg, VT: Northeast Kingdom Publishers, 1982.

Robert Frost: Collected Poems, Prose, and Plays. Ed. Richard Poirier and Mark Richardson. New York: Library of America, 1995.

Selected Letters of Robert Frost. Ed. Lawrance Thompson. New York: Holt, Rinehart and Winston, 1964.

II. Interviews with Frost

Cook, Reginald L. *Robert Frost: A Living Voice.* Amherst: University of Massachusetts Press, 1974.

Francis, Robert. *Frost: A Time to Talk: Conversations and Indiscretions.* Amherst: University of Massachusetts Press, 1972.

Lathem, Edward Connery, ed. *Interviews with Robert Frost.* New York: Holt, Rinehart and Winston, 1966.

Mertins, Louis. *Robert Frost: Life and Talks-Walking.* Norman: University of Oklahoma Press, 1965.

Smythe, Daniel. *Robert Frost Speaks.* New York: Twayne Publishers, 1966.

III. Biographies and memoirs

Anderson, Margaret Bartlett. *Robert Frost and John Bartlett: The Record of a Friendship.* New York: Holt, Rinehart, and Winston, 1963.

Burnshaw, Stanley. *Robert Frost Himself.* New York: G. Braziller, 1986.

Cox, Sidney. *A Swinger of Birches: A Portrait of Robert Frost.* Introduction by Robert Frost. New York: New York University Press, 1957.

Francis, Lesley Lee. *The Frost Family's Adventure in Poetry: Sheer Morning Gladness at the Brim.* Columbia: University of Missouri Press, 1994.

Gould, Jean. *Robert Frost: The Aim Was Song.* New York: Dodd, Mead, and Company, 1964.

Meyers, Jeffrey. *Robert Frost: A Biography.* New York: Houghton Mifflin, 1996.

Muir, Helen. *Frost in Florida: A Memoir.* Miami: Valiant Press, 1995.

Munson, Gorham B. *Robert Frost: A Study in Sensibility and Good Sense*. New York: George H. Doran, 1927.

Newdick, Robert. *Newdick's Season of Frost: An Interrupted Biography of Robert Frost*. Ed. William A. Sutton. Albany: State University of New York Press, 1976.

Pritchard, William, H. *Robert Frost: A Literary Life Reconsidered*. New York: Oxford University Press, 1984.

Reeve, E. D. *Robert Frost in Russia*. Boston: Little, Brown, 1964.

Sergeant, Elizabeth Shepley. *Robert Frost: The Trial by Existence*. New York: Holt, Rinehart and Winston, 1960.

Thompson, Lawrance. *Robert Frost: The Early Years, 1874–1915*. New York: Holt, Rinehart and Winston, 1966.

Robert Frost: The Years of Triumph, 1915–1938. New York: Holt, Rinehart, and Winston, 1970.

Thompson, Lawrance, and R. H. Winnick. *Robert Frost: The Later Years, 1938–1963*. New York: Holt, Rinehart and Winston, 1976.

Walsh, John Evangelist. *Into My Own: The English Years of Robert Frost*. New York: Grove Press, 1988.

IV. Criticism

Bagby, George. *Robert Frost and the Book of Nature*. Knoxville: University of Tennessee Press, 1993.

Barron, Jonathan and Earl Wilcox, eds. *Roads Not Taken: Rereading Robert Frost*. Columbia: University of Missouri Press, 2001.

The Robert Frost Review. Published annually by The Robert Frost Society.

Barry, Elaine, ed. *Robert Frost on Writing*. New Brunswick, NJ: Rutgers University Press, 1973.

Brodsky, Joseph, Seamus Heaney, and Derek Walcott. *Homage to Robert Frost*. New York: Farrar, Straus & Giroux, 1996.

Brower, Reuben. *The Poetry of Robert Frost: Constellations of Intention*. New York: Oxford University Press, 1963.

Budd, Louis and Edwin Cady, eds. *On Frost: The Best of American Literature*. Durham: Duke University Press, 1991.

Cook, Reginald L. *The Dimensions of Robert Frost*. New York: Rinehart, 1958.

Cox, James M., ed. *Robert Frost: A Collection of Critical Essays*. Englewood Cliffs, NJ: Prentice-Hall, 1962.

Cramer, Jeffrey S. *Robert Frost Among His Poems: A Literary Companion to the Poet's Own Biographical Contexts and Associations*. Jefferson, NC: McFarland, 1996.

Faggen, Robert. *Robert Frost and the Challenge of Darwin*. Ann Arbor: University of Michigan Press, 1997.

Frost, Robert. *Centennial Essays*. Compiled by the Committee on the Frost Centennial of the University of Southern Mississippi. Jackson: University of Mississippi Press, 1974–78.

Gerber, Philip L., ed. *Critical Essays on Robert Frost*. Boston: G. K. Hall, 1982.

Jarrell, Randall. *No Other Book: Selected Essays*. Ed. Brad Leithauser. New York: Farrar, Straus & Giroux, 1999. Paperback edn., HarperCollins, 1999.

Jost, Walter. "Civility and Madness in Robert Frost's 'Snow'," *Texas Studies in Literature and Language*, 39 (Spring, 1997), 27–64.

"Ordinary Language Brought to Grief: Robert Frost's 'Home Burial,'" in *Ordinary Language Criticism: Literary Thinking After Cavell After Wittgenstein*. Ed. Walter Jost and Kenneth Dauber. Evanston: Northwestern University Press, 2001.

Kearns, Katherine. *Robert Frost and a Poetics of Appetite*. Cambridge: Cambridge University Press, 1994.

Kemp, John C. *Robert Frost and New England: The Poet as Regionalist*. Princeton: Princeton University Press, 1979.

Kilcup, Karen L. *Robert Frost and Feminine Literary Tradition*. Ann Arbor: The University of Michigan Press, 1998.

Lentricchia, Frank. *Robert Frost: Modern Poetics and the Landscapes of Self*. Durham: Duke University Press, 1975.

Lynen, John F. *The Pastoral Art of Robert Frost*. New Haven, CN: Yale University Press, 1960.

Mauro, Jason. "Frost and James: The Gaps I Mean." *South Carolina Review*. 28 (1998), 2, p. 12.

Monteiro, George. *Robert Frost and the New England Renaissance*. Lexington: University Press of Kentucky, 1988.

Nitchie, George W. *Human Values in the Poetry of Robert Frost*. Durham: Duke University Press, 1960.

Oster, Judith. *Toward Robert Frost: The Reader and the Poet*. Athens: University of Georgia Press, 1991.

Poirier, Richard. *Robert Frost: The Work of Knowing*. New York: Oxford University Press, 1977.

Richardson, Mark ed. *The Ordeal of Robert Frost*. Urbana: University of Illinois Press, 1997.

Rotella, Guy. *Reading and Writing Nature*. Boston: Northeastern University Press, 1991.

Sabin, Margery. "The Fate of the Frost Speaker." *Raritan* 2 (Fall 1982), 128–39.

Sheehy, Donald G. "The Poet as Neurotic: The Official Biography of Robert Frost." *American Literature*, October, 1986, 393–409.

"(Re) Figuring Love: Robert Frost in Crisis, 1938–1942." *New England Quarterly*, June 1990, 179–231.

Tharpe, Jac, ed. *Frost: Centennial Essays*, vols. I & II. Jackson: University Press of Mississippi, 1976.

Thompson, Lawrance. *Fire and Ice: The Art and Thought of Robert Frost*. New York: Russell & Russell, 1942.

Thornton, Richard. *Recognition of Robert Frost: Twenty-fifth Anniversary*. New York: Henry Holt, 1937.

Wagner, Linda W., ed. *Robert Frost: The Critical Reception*. New York: Burt Franklin and Company, 1977.

Wilcox, Earl, ed. *His "Incalculable Influence on Others": Essays on Robert Frost in Our Time*. Victoria: English Literary Studies, 1994.

INDEX

2018x

$19.95

DATE			